SOCIAL NETWORKS AND REGIONAL IDENTITY IN BRONZE AGE ITALY

This book takes an innovative approach to detecting regional groupings in peninsular Italy during the Late Bronze Age, a notoriously murky period of Italian prehistory. Applying social network analysis to the distributions of imports and other distinctive objects, Emma Blake reveals previously unrecognized exchange networks that are in some cases the precursors of the named peoples of the first millennium BC: the Etruscans, the Veneti, and others. In a series of regional case studies, she uses quantitative methods to both reconstruct and analyze the character of these early networks and posits that, through path dependence, the initial structure of the networks played a role in the success or failure of the groups occupying those same regions in later times. This book thus bridges the divide between Italian prehistory and the Classical period and demonstrates that Italy's regionalism began far earlier than previously thought.

Emma Blake is Associate Professor in the School of Anthropology at the University of Arizona. She has published widely on prehistoric Italy, on such topics as monumentality, identity, space and spatiality, social memory, and culture contract. She has conducted fieldwork in Sardinia and codirects the Marsala Hinterland Survey in Sicily.

SOCIAL NETWORKS AND REGIONAL IDENTITY IN BRONZE AGE ITALY

EMMA BLAKE
The University of Arizona

Shaftesbury Road, Cambridge CB2 8EA, United Kingdom

One Liberty Plaza, 20th Floor, New York, NY 10006, USA

477 Williamstown Road, Port Melbourne, VIC 3207, Australia

314–321, 3rd Floor, Plot 3, Splendor Forum, Jasola District Centre, New Delhi – 110025, India

103 Penang Road, #05-06/07, Visioncrest Commercial, Singapore 238467

Cambridge University Press is part of Cambridge University Press & Assessment, a department of the University of Cambridge.

We share the University's mission to contribute to society through the pursuit of education, learning and research at the highest international levels of excellence.

www.cambridge.org
Information on this title: www.cambridge.org/9781107063204

© Emma Blake 2014

This publication is in copyright. Subject to statutory exception and to the provisions of relevant collective licensing agreements, no reproduction of any part may take place without the written permission of Cambridge University Press & Assessment.

First published 2014

A catalogue record for this publication is available from the British Library

Library of Congress Cataloging-in-Publication data
Blake, Emma.
Social networks and regional identity in Bronze Age Italy / Emma Blake.
    pages cm
Includes bibliographical references and index.
ISBN 978-1-107-06320-4 (hardback)
1. Bronze age – Italy.   2. Prehistoric peoples – Italy.   3. Social networks – Italy – History – To 1500.   4. Regionalism – Italy – History – To 1500.   5. Group identity – Italy – History – To 1500.   6. Social archaeology – Italy.   7. Italy – Antiquities.   I. Title.
GN778.22.I8B55   2014
937–dc23   2014004594

ISBN   978-1-107-06320-4   Hardback

Cambridge University Press & Assessment has no responsibility for the persistence or accuracy of URLs for external or third-party internet websites referred to in this publication and does not guarantee that any content on such websites is, or will remain, accurate or appropriate.

For Rob

CONTENTS

Figures		*page* ix
Tables		xi
Acknowledgments		xiii
1	Introduction: The Problem of Italy's Ancient Peoples	1
2	Imports and Specialized Products in Italy in the Recent and Final Bronze Ages	34
3	Group Identity in Prehistory: Theory, Interactions, and Social Networks	66
4	The Recent and Final Bronze Age Peninsular Networks: Assessing Structure and Cohesion	87
5	The Northern Networks from the Terramare to the Veneto	113
6	West-Central Italy: Networks and Neighbors	150
7	Marche, Umbria, and the Apennine Mountain Muddle	182
8	Southern Italy: Networks by Land and by Sea	207
9	Conclusions and Aftermath	240
Appendix		257
Bibliography		295
Index		319

FIGURES

1.1	Major population groups of Italy, third century BC	page 2
1.2	Early Iron Age archaeological "cultures"	13
2.1	Timeline of Recent Bronze Age object types included in the study	35
2.2	Timeline of Final Bronze Age 1–2 object types included in the study	36
4.1	Graph of RBA peninsular network with ties based on shared objects and ≤ 50 km apart, excluding isolates	92
4.2	Map of Italian peninsula showing RBA subgroups	93
4.3	Graph of RBA peninsular network with ties based on shared objects and ≤ 40 km apart, excluding isolates	94
4.4	Graph of RBA peninsular network with ties based on shared objects, with distance measured on a continuous scale	95
4.5	Graph of FBA peninsular network with ties based on shared objects and ≤ 50 km apart, excluding isolates	103
4.6	Map of Italian peninsula showing FBA subgroups	104
5.1	Graph of RBA Terramare network, no hoards, ties based on shared objects	123
5.2	Survival rate and degree centrality of RBA Terramare-Apennine network sites	124
5.3	Map of RBA Terramare-Apennine network with sites that continue into the FBA indicated	125
5.4	Map showing locations of RBA sites in northern Italy included in the study	126
5.5	Graph of RBA sites in northern Italy, hoards included, ties based on objects only	128

Figures

5.6	Graph of large cluster in RBA northern Italy, hoards included, ties based on shared objects only	129
5.7	Map showing locations of FBA sites in northern Italy included in this study	138
5.8	Graph of FBA sites in northern Italy, with ties based on shared objects, hoards included	139
5.9	Map of northern Italy showing FBA sites with factions indicated	143
6.1	Map showing RBA find spots in Etruria and Latium	161
6.2	Graph of RBA network in Etruria, ties based on shared objects	162
6.3	Map showing FBA find spots in Etruria and Latium	163
6.4	Graph of FBA sites in Etruria, ties based on shared objects	166
6.5	Graph showing network of FBA sites in Etruria, Umbria, and Marche	170
6.6	Map of Etruria, Umbria, and Marche showing FBA sites with factions indicated	172
6.7	Graph of FBA sites with Gubbio and Scarceta removed	174
6.8	Graph of RBA sites in Etruria, Umbria, and Marche	174
6.9	Map showing sites in FBA Latium and Etruria, with Rome as a hypothetical node	178
7.1	Graph of RBA network in Umbria and Marche	193
7.2	Map showing RBA find spots in Umbria and Marche	194
7.3	Graph of FBA network in Umbria and Marche, with ties based on shared objects only	198
7.4	Map showing FBA network sites in Umbria and Marche, with Augustan regional boundaries	199
8.1	Map of RBA find spots in southern Italy	223
8.2	Graph of RBA find spots in southern Italy, hoards and ritual deposits included, ties based on shared objects	224
8.3	Graph of RBA south-Italian sites, ties based on shared objects, Aegean pottery excluded	225
8.4	Map showing RBA find spots in southern Italy, with nodes in the non-ceramic network indicated	226
8.5	Map showing FBA find spots in southern Italy	228
8.6	Graph of FBA southern Italy cluster, hoards included, ties based on shared objects	230
8.7	Graph of FBA southern Italy network, Aegean pots excluded, ties based on shared objects	231
8.8	Map showing FBA find spots in southern Italy, with nodes in the non-ceramic network indicated	232
9.1	Map of Italy indicating the Augustan regions	246

TABLES

4.1	Sample sociomatrix	*page* 90
4.2	Measures of cohesion and structure of the major subgroups in the RBA peninsula network	97
4.3	Measures of cohesion and structure of the major subgroups in the FBA peninsula network	105
5.1	Object types circulating in northern Italy in the RBA	127
5.2	Object types circulating in northern Italy in the FBA	138
5.3	Permuted matrix of FBA northern Italy sites, ties based on objects only, hoards included. Divided into two factions	141
5.4	Permuted matrix of FBA northern Italy sites, ties based on objects only, hoards included. Divided into five factions	145
6.1	Object types circulating in Etruria in the RBA	161
6.2	Object types circulating in Etruria in the FBA	165
6.3	Permuted matrix of FBA sites in Etruria, ties based on objects only, hoards included, divided into two factions	167
6.4	Permuted matrix of FBA connected sites in Etruria, Umbria, and Marche, ties based on objects only, hoards included, divided into three factions	171
7.1	Object types circulating in Marche and Umbria in the RBA	192
7.2	Object types circulating in Marche and Umbria in the FBA	196
8.1	Object types circulating in southern Italy in the RBA	222
8.2	Object types circulating in southern Italy in the FBA	229

ACKNOWLEDGMENTS

For a book this long in the making, there are many people and institutions to whom I am indebted for help along the way. Before the book even got started, two formative influences were Ian Hodder and Ian Morris, who each shaped my approach to the archaeological record. At the start of the project, Tufts University granted me a Junior Research Leave to begin working on this book in earnest. I spent the leave at the Stanford Archaeology Center as a Visiting Scholar and received excellent early feedback from colleagues there. I have Lynn Meskell to thank for that time at the Center, and for friendship and mentoring over many years. Comments and questions following talks given at Stanford, the University of Pennsylvania, the University of Arizona, the American Academy in Rome, and Università di Roma–La Sapienza were extremely helpful. I can't thank Carl Knappett enough for introducing me to social network analysis! Carl has also read, heard, and commented on various parts of the book and has provided wonderful insights along the way. Many thanks also to Barbara Mills for reading and commenting on early parts and for numerous conversations about networks. Steve Kuhn's suggestions on statistics were very useful. Joe Galaskiewicz graciously allowed me to audit his graduate seminar on social networks in the School of Sociology at the University of Arizona. I learned a lot in that seminar, and I am very grateful to Joe for giving essential and patient guidance to a network novice that semester and several times since. David Melamed helped me with constructing and analyzing the early iterations of my networks. Suchismita Dash and Donna Feng were outstanding research assistants. My colleagues in the School of Anthropology have been a kind and supportive bunch, showing great interest in my research and providing a happy work environment. I owe special thanks to David Soren and Dani Triadan for sound advice and encouragement always.

I was able to complete the manuscript finally, and improve it enormously, with a Junior Faculty Research Leave from the University of Arizona. I wholeheartedly thank the National Endowment for the Humanities and the American Academy in Rome (AAR), which together funded my postdoctoral Rome Prize at the AAR. Not only did this fellowship allow me to extend my leave from a semester to a full year, but the benefits of being in Rome and at the Academy were extraordinary. I was able to meet the Italian scholars whose work I had been reading and admiring for years. I will be forever indebted to those scholars for their generosity with their time and expertise. Specifically I must mention Marco Bettelli, Anna Maria Bietti Sestieri, Alberto Cazzella, Isabella Damiani, Francesco di Gennaro, Alessandro Guidi, Giulia Recchia, and Alessandro Vanzetti. Also while in Rome, my conversations with Stéphane Bourdin, Kim Bowes, Christopher Celenza, and Christopher Smith pushed my ideas further. In the home stretch, Victoria Moses and Lars Fogelin read through the entire draft and made terrific suggestions; in particular, Lars's comments on the final draft gave me the courage I needed to let go of the manuscript and send it off. Russ Biggs valiantly produced maps and revised graphs in the nick of time.

Most importantly, my family has been there through thick and thin. Robert Schon read and critiqued multiple drafts of chapters and believed in me and in the book unwaveringly. Harry and Charlie have taught me that the book is not everything. My parents and my aunt Peg have been constant sources of support for years. In particular, without my mother's emotional support – not to mention her help with child care – this book would not have been written. I am glad I can finally answer their perennial unspoken question and say, "Yes, the book is done!"

CHAPTER ONE

INTRODUCTION: THE PROBLEM OF ITALY'S ANCIENT PEOPLES

The Roman conquest of Italy was necessarily a piecemeal affair, as the peninsula was divided into myriad autonomous groups whose actions and responses to Roman pressure required specifically tailored strategies on the part of the conquerors. Indeed, it is virtually a truism that it was during the conquest of Italy that Rome learned how to handle disparate groups, a necessary skill when tackling the polyglot world of the Hellenistic east. The groups in Italy do not sum up easily. A handful enjoyed a strong and enduring sense of self-identity, a stable territory, distinctive material culture, and external recognition, such as the Etruscans and the Veneti, but many more constituted groupings of a looser character – sometimes civic, sometimes tribal – whose affiliation and territory were contested even in antiquity (Figure 1.1).

All of these groups ultimately fell to the Romans, of course, and the stronger groups were not necessarily better at resisting the Roman takeover than the weaker ones: one only need compare the Etruscan failure to mount a sustained unified resistance with the temporary success of the unification of tribal groups in the Social War. What is significant, however, is that the better-defined groups were recognized by the Romans and lingered on for a time, in various ways, from reification with the establishment of formal administrative units – the Augustan *regiones* – to the maintenance of "dual" identities for centuries after so-called Romanization.[1] Clearly the ability of regional groups to garner

---

[1] Farney 2007.

1.1. Major population groups of Italy, third century BC (After David 1997: figure 1) (Drawn by R. Biggs)

external recognition had long-term implications. This book proposes a novel explanation for why some regional groups in Italy forged what we can call an ethnic consciousness and others did not. Studies of Italy's regionalism at the time of the Roman conquest have been hampered on the one hand by the biased, limited, and contradictory textual, epigraphic, and archaeological sources and on the other hand by theoretical debates over the labels for these groups. I take a different tack here. Going back to the Recent and Final Bronze Ages, I trace the beginnings of these peoples to regional social networks, an approach that offers new insights into their emergence and subsequent history.

Approaches to Regionalism and Regional Inequality in Early Italy

Who are these population groups, exactly? Bourdin charts two levels of collective identity in early Italy from the textual sources, drawing

Introduction

primarily on Livy and Dionysius of Halicarnassus. Although these authors use the terms differently, Bourdin has teased out enough similarities in their terminology to parse the group labels as follows. The first level groups are political, structured around urban centers, sometimes operationalized in military units, and designated as *populi* in Latin. The *populi* are nested within larger political or cultural units that the textual sources call variously *gens* or *natio* or *nomen* in Latin, which Bourdin equates with ethnic groups.[2] This is a simplification of Bourdin's nuanced discussion, but the point to take away here is that the collective names of early Italy can denote political (civic or tribal), cultural, military, or ethnic groupings and it requires extra analysis to determine what type of entity is being discussed.

The term "ethnicity" is particularly loaded for Anglophone scholars, and indeed is rejected outright by some.[3] Sociologist Anthony Smith's criteria for an ethnic group are a shared name, history, origin myth, distinctive culture, territory, and solidarity.[4] Only a few groups in Italy meet those criteria. With the rise in instrumentalist theories of ethnicity in the wake of Frederic Barth's seminal edited volume,[5] the origin of ethnic groups has lost much favor as a scholarly subject, with the emphasis placed instead on their use-value.[6] We can see this in the current scholarship on early Italy, in which explanations for the evolution of Italy's regional groups treat ethnicization, if the scholars find it a valid concept at all, as a response to outside pressures of various types, first from Greek colonists beginning in the eighth century BC and then from the Roman conquerors. Important studies of the Umbrians and Samnites have taken this perspective.[7] It is only with the spread of writing in Italy from the sixth century BC on that we can use linguistic differences and, ideally, self-definition to confirm the existence of self-defining ethnic groups

---

[2] Bourdin 2012: 176–81.
[3] E.g., Bradley 2000: 19.
[4] Smith 1986: 22–32.
[5] Barth 1969.
[6] Even in the case of the Etruscans, whose origins have been studied more than any of the other ancient peoples of Italy and who offer a rich dataset with which to work, many scholars now frame their work on the emergence of the Etruscans in terms of the rise of social complexity rather than the emergence of cultural distinctiveness. See Vanzetti 2002. Izzet (2007: 114), for example, describes the study of Etruscan origins as "effectively put out to grass some fifty years or so ago."
[7] Dench 1995; Bradley 2000.

among those regional groups. Using those criteria, the ethnic groups of pre-Roman Italy emerge at different times in the first millennium BC. Some, such as the Etruscans, are visible as early as the sixth century BC[8] whereas others, such as the Umbrians, did not appear until the fourth to third centuries BC.[9] Most of these groups never achieved ethnic status and need to be defined in different ways, either in cultural or political terms.[10]

When it comes to the outside influences on these groups, the Greeks – as the spreaders of literacy, high art, complex political systems, new ritual forms, and regional economies – get particular credit for elevating the "cultural quality" and social complexity of Italy and the west.[11] The Romans themselves benefited from, and built on, these earlier cultural encounters: their indirect exposure to Greek culture by way of the Etruscans is well attested. However, the rates of change in Italy following colonial contact were so rapid in some areas, and the hybrid cultural forms that emerged were so varied and unexpected, that accounts beginning with the arrival of the Greeks as the catalysts for regionalism are leaving something out. Thirty years ago, de la Genière ascribed these regional variations to the colonists, not the natives, arguing that with the exceptions of the Iapygians of Apulia and the Elymians of northwest Sicily, the local populations were passive and receptive, and it was up to the Greeks to decide in each case to what degree they would integrate the peoples they encountered.[12] Since she wrote this, the postcolonial turn in social theory has placed native agency at center stage in these interactions.[13] Yet the emphasis on local agency raises new questions. To attribute to the natives themselves the regional variability in colonial experiences, as many now do, begs the question: How did these groups come to be as the Greeks found them? These groups had their own cultural baggage and histories that in large part structured their responses,

---

[8] Bradley 2000: 116.
[9] Bradley 2000: 116.
[10] Herring 2000: 57) suggests the Peucetians and their neighbors in Apulia were tribal groups with cultural identities rather than ethnic groups.
[11] E.g., Forsythe 2005: 32.
[12] "Le non-Grec, qu'il soi Œnôtre, Chône ou Sicule, a subi dans la plupart des cas le sort qui lui était réservé; sa perméabilité à la nouvelle culture s'accorde bien avec la nature pacifique et peu dynamique des milieux de l'Age du Fer . . . " (de la Genière 1978: 275).
[13] E.g., Hodos 2006; Antonaccio 2004.

based on learned behaviors of interaction. Thus, whether adopting a hellenocentric or a postcolonial perspective, scholars beginning the account at the moment of contact must consider the circumstances that led to the native groups responding the way they did.

The impact of Greek colonization is not the only explanation given for the rise of regional groups in Italy. Another line of argument sees regional affiliation as a means of managing resources within a territory. This has been applied to the Etruscans, the idea being that with the expansion of metallurgy in the FBA, the peoples living south of the *Colline Metallifere* – the mineral-rich mountains in northern Tuscany – unified to control the mining industry.[14] Still other approaches frame the emergence of ethnic identities as a by-product of state formation and urbanization over the course of the first millennium BC, a process in which the Greeks played a role but may still be viewed as autochthonous.[15] In all these instrumentalist approaches, ethnicity is understood as a relatively late and imperfectly realized phenomenon, and no group's ethnic status stands up to close inspection. Either the unity of the language is shown to be illusive (Veneti), or the boundaries poorly defined (Picenes), or a collective name is not widespread (Umbrians). Nonetheless, however flawed the label of "ethnic" may be, a condition of regional inequality prevailed. Simply put, the Etruscans and the Peucetii are not equivalent groups, and even if we set aside the term "ethnic," we need to acknowledge that some groups in early Italy were more successful than others. Not all groups can choose at will to forge a tight bond that supersedes other affiliations and garners external recognition; only some can manage it. Therefore, it is necessary to look at the preconditions for their success.

Identifying and tracing the development of Italy's regional groups is far from straightforward. Recent scholars of ancient Italy have noted the challenge of mapping its regions with clear boundaries, and recognized that the regions themselves are, like Anderson's nations, "imagined communities."[16] As the opening chapter to one recent volume on Italy's regional groups observes, "[e]ither the phenomena being described reach beyond [the boundaries], or there is such internal diversity that it is

---

[14] Peroni 1979: 15; Bietti Sestieri 2005: 20.
[15] Herring & Lomas 2000; Cifani 2010.
[16] Isayev 2007: 2.

difficult to argue for the coherence of the area within."[17] This fuzziness at the borders is a condition of social groups, particularly in non-state societies,[18] and it would be foolhardy to insist on rigid territorial distinctions in early Italy. Regardless of the porous boundaries, the phenomenon of regional diversity in Italy at the time of the Roman conquest was real and requires explaining. Even on this point there is little scholarly agreement. Earlier scholarship emphasized widespread diffusion and immigration as the answer to the variety of Italy's ancient ethnic groups whereas the shift in recent decades has been toward accounts of smaller-scale immigration episodes or autochthonous origins. In the case of the former, small groups of settlers from the Danube area, from across the Adriatic, and from the Near East are posited to explain the regional distinctiveness of the Terramare culture in the Po Valley, the Apulian populations, and the Etruscans, respectively.[19] According to this view, so many and varied contacts over a long period of time must have had an impact on regional culture without supplanting the earlier inhabitants outright.[20] In contrast, with theories for a homegrown balkanization, it is the varied topography of Italy and its natural internal boundaries and resources that are meant to account for both the tendencies toward regionalism and for the reason some ethnic groups emerged before others.[21] In these discussions, post-Roman history is erroneously cited as proof of the inherent regionalism of the peninsula. False claims to "continuity" recur perennially in both popular and scholarly literature on Italy. Witness Reich on regionalisms in Italy:

> Finally it is important to remember that regional diversity has always been an Italian characteristic, as the most casual visitor to Italy can recognize. Even today, in spite of the Risorgimento, local loyalties are still stronger than national ties and are based upon genuine regional differences of culture, language and attitude. This diversity is certainly no new phenomenon: a Bolognese industrial worker and a Calabrian shepherd of today are probably no more different than were their Early Iron Age counterparts.[22]

---

[17] Isayev 2007: 2.
[18] See examples in de Heusch 2000.
[19] Cardarelli 2009: 36-7; Pallottino 1991: 47; Magness 2001.
[20] Pallottino 1991: 30; Guasco 2006: 7.
[21] E.g., Salmon 1967.
[22] Reich 1979: 56.

Introduction

But the truth is, Italy's post-Roman regionalism has waxed and waned – or rather, its significance has – enjoying a present-day importance that would be astonishing to nineteenth-century residents of the peninsula.[23] As Lyttelton provocatively put it in an article on the nineteenth- and twentieth-century context, "[t]he real problem posed by Italian regionalism is why there was so little of it."[24] So while environment must certainly play a role in group formation, the danger is in conflating a recurrent tendency toward regionalism with actual continuity.

The Greek Gift of Origins

Italy's regional diversity was evident to Greek colonists in the Archaic period (c. 800–500 BC), who gave many of the peoples of the peninsula names and even histories, as was their wont. As the earliest written accounts of Italy's peoples, the Greek sources are tantalizing. These texts name the peoples and sometimes tell something about the area they occupied, their national character, and origins. But the accounts of the Greek historians are usually no earlier than 500 BC, long after the first period of contact. Works by Antiochus and Philistus of Syracuse and Timaeus of Taormina for example, have not survived, and we only know of them from later references. The most informative Greek sources on the Italian peoples are Herodotus and Thucydides; others have been lost and are only cited by Strabo and Dionysius of Halicarnassus. Despite the absence of firsthand accounts, these textual sources have been so compelling that they remain the fundamental evidence for the cultural history of Archaic and classical Italy. The archaeological evidence has traditionally been fit into this cultural framework. The sources are messy and contradictory, and we are not at all sure whether the Greek and Roman writers are identifying tribal agglomerations, civic identities, or veritable ethnic groups.[25] In their descriptions, the Greeks revealed more about their relationships with those groups than about the groups themselves.[26]

---

[23] See Levy 1996 for a useful overview of this history.
[24] Lyttelton 1996: 33.
[25] Bradley 2000: 117.
[26] Malkin 1998.

The ancient sources chart a complex series of population movements into Italy and within it, beginning with the Oenotrians who came from Arcadia long before the Trojan War.[27] Subsequent mythological waves of immigration to Italy from the east are situated in the period of the Trojan War, and many of these stories chronicle the homeward voyages (*nostoi*) of heroic combatants, both Trojans such as Aeneas and Antenor, and Greeks such as Odysseus and Diomedes.[28] These origin myths, part of a much larger and varied repertoire of myths circulating in colonial territories, sometimes take the form of genealogies, with the Italic peoples made descendants of an eponymous hero. In other cases the myths recount mass migrations. Some of the origin myths are quite fantastical, as is that of the residents of the Aeolian Islands.[29] The myths come down to us from Hesiod in the earliest case, but more commonly, from authors of the fifth century BC and later.[30] The dating of the myths is contentious. Whereas many of the *nostoi* myths have been judged to postdate the canonical Homeric texts,[31] Malkin sees them as products of the early colonial encounters of the eighth century BC, suggesting that, in contrast to the *nostoi*, the mass migration myths emerged "not before the sixth century."[32]

The interpretation of these myths is equally contentious. The traditional view has held that these myths contained nuggets of truth, preserved vestiges of actual events that had mutated over time in the retelling.[33] Other scholars reject them out of hand as colonial importations. Bickerman, for example, argued that the origin myths were not vestigial popular memories, but were instead devised by a few elite scholars.[34] This influential perspective granted the myths virtually no value at all in the study of the Italic peoples, not even for understanding how people constructed their pasts.[35] Still other scholars accord the myths a nuanced value. De la Genière saw these accounts as Greek gifts

---

[27] Pallottino 1991: 41.
[28] Pallottino 1991: 43.
[29] Diodorus Siculus, *Library of History* 5.7.5.
[30] Thucydides 5.2.3.
[31] Bérard 1957: 315, 321.
[32] Malkin 1998: 3.
[33] E.g., Pallottino 1991: 40–5.
[34] Bickerman 1952.
[35] Cornell 1995: 41; Erskine 2005: 128–9.

Introduction

of a past to the indigenous groups they encountered, a past fitting of their present status.[36] De la Genière's approach fits with Jonathan Hall's take on the value of the myths of genealogy told of the Iron Age groups. Hall critiques the historical positivist approach whereby origin myths are "trace elements" of earlier movements of peoples. He writes, "[t]he extreme historicist approach fails to acknowledge the active and constructive nature of myth; by relegating myth to a position in which it is a debased, hazy, and passive reflection of a genuine history, proponents of this school ignore its relative autonomy and vitality."[37] Thus, the rich stories of origins in Italy are better treated in mythopoetic studies as examples of strategies of self-definition than in historical ones. From this perspective, multi-layered and contradictory stories are palimpsests of shifts in those strategies over time.

Anthony Smith has observed that origin myths "emerge into the political daylight at certain junctures; these are usually periods of profound culture clash, and accelerated economic and social change."[38] Although they may constitute a defensive mechanism to these outside threats, they may be seen in a more positive light as well: "these myths also reflect the hopes and possibilities of social development... and the breakdown of traditional economic isolation and subsistence structures."[39] Unlike Hall's Greek myths, there is nothing necessarily vestigial in these Italian myths that would suggest earlier iterations. There is no evidence that the earlier period of cultural contact, with the Mycenaean Greeks in the Recent and Final Bronze Ages, was a similarly transformative time.[40]

Malkin's study of the role of Greek origin myths, in particular the *nostoi*, in mediating encounters between Greeks and Italic peoples (among others) in the Archaic period is relevant here.[41] The Greeks used *nostoi* as accounts of the ethnogenesis of the peoples of Italy, and the stories came to be accepted by some of those groups as true. Like

---

[36] "En plusieurs cas on peut se demander en effet si des centres indigènes n'auraient pas reçu aussi un passé, des origines illustres à la mesure de leur importance ou de leur aspect présents" (de la Genière 1978: 272).
[37] Hall 1997: 86.
[38] Smith 1999: 83.
[39] Smith 1999: 84.
[40] Blake 2008.
[41] Malkin 1998.

Hall, Malkin sets aside questions of the historicity of the myths and instead emphasizes the ways in which the myths functioned to influence the encounters between Greeks and non-Greeks. There is little of the Italic peoples' perspective in Malkin's study, as to be expected in a book focused primarily on textual evidence. But one may ask if the proliferation of conflicting stories in later periods, rather than the redaction into a single version as one might expect, reflects a thread of native input here. Hall argues as much in his brief study of origin myths in Latium and Apulia, detecting traces of indigenous myths influencing the Greek ones.[42] Perhaps some of what seem like Greek myths are, in fact, accounts received from the native groups by the Greeks and then transliterated for Greek audiences. For my purposes, however, what is interesting is the acceptance by Malkin, and de la Genière for that matter, that these non-Greek peoples were already fully formed ethnic groups who lacked a compelling enough origin myth and therefore were willing to absorb the ones the Greeks offered. Malkin draws on Smith's work distinguishing between "fuller" and "empty" *ethnie* (ethnic communities) in support of this.[43] But Smith later distanced himself from this kind of characterization (and implicit value judgment) of *ethnie*, in favor of a distinction between ethnic categories and ethnic communities.[44] Malkin also notes that "more often than not... group definitions are the result of outsiders' articulations that become internalized and accepted."[45] But in the Italic case, Malkin accepts the groups' existence, with the origin myth as modification to an already established identity, whereas it seems more likely that the ethnic communities crystallize only following contact with the colonists.

Malkin notes that the Greek myths were not applied to those groups with whom the Greeks were in close contact, such as the Etruscans, because these groups would have been too well known for such artifice to be believable.[46] Instead, the *nostoi* genealogies belong to peoples that were further away from the Greek settlers and not in frequent contact with them, in what Malkin describes as a process of "peripheral ethnicity." The prime example of this practice is the Greek genealogy for the

---

[42] Hall 2005.
[43] Malkin 1998: 59, citing Smith 1986.
[44] Smith 1999: 105.
[45] Malkin 1998: 55–6.
[46] Malkin 1998: 178–9.

Introduction

Latins. Malkin notes, "[t]hus the Latins, more distant and amorphous, could be given a general name and an eponymous ancestor, Latinus."[47] Hesiod gives Latinus a brother, Agrius or "Savage," whose descendants are therefore the "Wild Ones." As Malkin puts it, this label refers not to an ethnic group, but to a shared lifestyle, possibly of the less Hellenized residents of the mountainous interior of Italy.[48] If it was easier for the Greeks to generalize about more remote groups, Malkin suggests it was likewise easier for those remote groups to accept the Greek genealogies: "Because they did not come under direct control of the various Greek colonies, the extension to them of Greek 'ethnic' myths was apparently not, at least during the first generations of colonization, interpreted as threatening territorial expansion."[49] Thus, the reception and manipulation of the tales in later centuries is of little import to the question at hand. Nor can we use these *nostoi* tales as vestigial Greek memories of Bronze Age visits to the region. As Malkin has observed, the *nostoi* are not "dim reflections" of Bronze Age connections, since Nostos attachments do not overlap with areas where Mycenaean material evidence has surfaced.[50] Although the Greek intentions in deploying these myths are fascinating, the Greeks could not create ethnicities from scratch, or at least not ones that would stick.

Iron Age Regional Systems?

Regardless of the veracity of the Greek accounts, there is no question that by the fourth and third centuries BC, the textual, epigraphic, and material sources converge to delineate a patchwork of distinct population groups covering the peninsula.[51] When did this begin? Prior to the Greek arrival, in the Iron Age (1020/950–800 BC), traces of broad, territorially delimited groupings are already evident in the archaeological

---

[47] Malkin 1998: 179 184, 208. The passage in question is from Hesiod's Theogony (1011f), and most controversially, Odysseus and Circe's progeny, Latinus and Agrius, are described as ruling over the "Tyrsenoi." The Tyrsenoi conventionally are the Etruscans, so, if the text was written down in 700 BC, then the text is confusing as the reverse was true. Malkin takes Hesiod to mean, by Tyrsenoi, Italic peoples in a general sense – not solely Etruscans – but it is still a problematic passage.
[48] Malkin 1998: 186.
[49] Malkin 1998: 179.
[50] Malkin 1998: 207.
[51] Cf. David 1997.

record: diverse material-culture industries and burial practices point to a heterogeneous population. Moreover, there is some correlation between the Iron Age material-culture divisions and the broad linguistic families evident in the next phase. For this reason Anglophone scholars, and until quite recently Italian scholars as well, tend to look to the Iron Age for the origins of the named historical groups.[52] However, the regional groupings visible in the Iron Age – both materially and subsequently, linguistically – cover far vaster territories than those of the named peoples that follow (Figure 1.2).[53]

Within these broad Iron Age archaeological cultures, some smaller scale regional inflections are evident, and the challenge has been to assess the relative importance of these different scales. If one begins with the Iron Age macroregions and traces the apparently inchoate regional units within them to the territorially circumscribed and named peoples of the historical period, the result is an unlikely narrative of progressive atomization from a few large regional groups to many smaller ones.

Because this transition from Iron Age groupings to historical period ones is itself so unclear, virtually no one goes back before the Iron Age – to the Bronze Age – to start the story earlier. In part, this is a function of disciplinary divides: Italian prehistorians have made enormous progress in reconstructing population groups in the Bronze Age, but they do not trace the history beyond the Iron Age to the historical periods, and few classical archaeologists engage with the Bronze Age scholarship. Compounding the problem is the ambiguity of the Bronze Age record. As we shall see, the groupings observed in the Middle, Recent, and Final Bronze Ages in Italy (c. 1700–950 BC[54]) change in each period and do not look much like the historical period groups. In the latter part of the Middle Bronze Age (hereafter, MBA, 1700–1350 BC), the peninsula south of the Po Valley was dominated by one main archaeological culture: the

---

[52] E.g., Bonetto 2009: 25: "La grande omogeneità delle manifestazioni protovillanoviane lascia il posto, fra il 1000 e l'800 a.C., ad una rapida e forte regionalizzazione della cultura materiale, che viene fatta coincidere con il formarsi e l'affacciarsi alla storia dei diversi popoli dell'età del ferro italiana: Etruschi, Latini, Piceni, Umbri, etc." See also Forsythe 2005: 26; Pallottino 1981: 26.

[53] Compare Pallottino 1981: fig. 3 with ibid. fig. 1.

[54] "High" dendro-based dates established by Bettelli (1994) raise the end of the FBA to 1020 BC, but these are not fully accepted.

Introduction

1.2. Early Iron Age archaeological "cultures" (After Cornell 1995: map 1) (Drawn by R. Biggs)

Apennine, which gives its name to the period. The very north of Italy followed a separate trajectory, but most of the peninsula shows considerable uniformity in both ceramics and metals, house styles, settlement size, and social structure (collectively labeled the Apennine culture), although there is some variability regionally in subsistence practices. In the Recent Bronze Age (or Subapennine period, c. 1350–1200 BC, hereafter, RBA) there is greater diversity in the ceramics industry, but this diversity does not seem to be geographically determined except in the Po Valley and north.[55] By the Final Bronze Age (Protovillanovan period, c. 1200–950 BC, hereafter, FBA), some regional patterning is archaeologically visible in both ceramics and metals, particularly in the final phase of the

[55] Damiani 2010.

FBA (FBA 3, 1020–950 BC), but circumstances seem so different in the historical period and in the intervening Iron Age that it has not been possible to trace a direct line of descent.

As a result, a new generation of scholars seems to have given up on the Iron Age as a source for early regionalism. Bartoloni observes that for current Italophone scholars, the eighth century BC constitutes the earliest possible moment of detection of the historical groups because analysis is not possible until writing and institutions are in place.[56] Dench begins her study of the Samnites with the period of Greek colonization. She suggests that the peoples of Italy only come into sharp focus in the third century BC, and that the concern with collective self-definition may have been attributable to circumstance (the Roman conquest) and need not constitute a reification of already extant groups.[57] Cornell describes the "unbridgeable" distance between the literary sources of Italian groups' origins and the archaeological data.[58]

One way around the apparent complexities of the Iron Age is to recognize that the macroregional groupings of that period do not correspond to cultural groups at all, but instead to regional systems – to borrow a term from southwest U.S. archaeology. In many respects, the later prehistoric societies of the southwestern United States offer interesting comparanda. In both cases the population was structured into acephalous tribal or small-scale chiefly groups, within which dispersed communities interacted and thus secured social ties while also engaging in interregional interactions and contacts with other groups further afield. The term "regional system" as applied to the indigenous American southwest refers to groups of sites in non-state societies "having similarities in material culture on a broad geographic scale."[59] Although some disenchantment with the term has set in among southwest archaeologists who see it reifying the dynamic relationships it was meant to highlight,[60] its application to Italy in the Iron Age may offer a fresh approach. Studies of regional systems emphasize unity through interaction rather than cultural norms. Interactions are central to the existence of regional systems, making dispersed small-scale communities demographically viable, for

---

[56] Bartoloni 2009: 63.
[57] Dench 1995.
[58] Cornell 1995: 36–9.
[59] Creamer 2000: 99.
[60] See papers in Hegmon 2000.

Introduction

one thing, through intermarriage. This book emphasizes interactions as the driving force behind regional affiliations. Furthermore, thinking of these Iron Age cultural groups as "regional systems" encompassing smaller units may be a way to reconcile the very different cultural maps of the Bronze Age, Iron Age, and Roman conquest, without suggesting that the changes occurring in the first millennium BC can simply be boiled down to progressive fragmentation. If the Iron Age patterning reveals regional systems, then it provides all the more reason to look earlier in time for the origins of the smaller population groups nested in those systems.

The Linguistic Evidence

The linguistic evidence is not as helpful for illuminating Italy's regional groups as one might expect. The earliest texts written in Italy, upon adoption of the Greek alphabet from the late eighth century BC on, demonstrate the linguistic diversity of the peninsula in the Archaic period. Most of these languages have been identified as belonging to the Indo-European (IE) language family, with Etruscan the notable exception.[61] The IE languages of Italy are grouped together into the Italic language family. Linguists for the most part agree that an intrusion of IE languages at some point prior to the eighth century BC overtook most of the indigenous languages, with a few pre-IE words surviving. Etruria is a special case, about which there is considerable disagreement, but the most straightforward explanation for its anomalous language is that it is a pre-IE language that happened to be preserved in a regional pocket.

Whereas some scholars have argued since the nineteenth century for a unified "proto-Italic" tongue preceding the languages evident by the time these groups become literate, another strand of scholarship insists that there was no earlier unity between, say, the Sabellian and Latino-Faliscan subgroups (other than their both being IE languages), and any similarities occurred later, through interactions.[62] The debate is not resolved, however, and archaeology comes into play here. If one accepts – as most

---

[61] Mallory 1989: 88–9. To the north, Rhaetic also is non-IE. By the time of the Roman conquest, later intrusive languages include Celtic in the Po Valley and Greek, which takes hold in the territories of the southern colonies.

[62] Clackson and Horrocks 2007: 65.

do – that the IE language intrusion is attributable to the arrival of new peoples in Italy, when and how did this occur? Here there is little agreement, as archaeologically the periods of cultural change are not easily explained through migrations. The linguistic diversity within the IE languages of Italy is not much help, as it is not clear if there was one wave of migration of speakers of a single IE language, or if there were multiple, smaller movements of peoples. The Adriatic coastal languages (Venetic, Picene, and Messapic), seem to have been shaped by ongoing contacts with the Illyrians on the opposite shore of the Adriatic, but further details are not possible. Even less can be postulated concerning the spread of IE elsewhere on the mainland. The problem is that the archaeological evidence of the later prehistoric periods does not indicate any moment of major cultural change on the scale one would expect to accompany a massive movement of peoples. The Protovillanovan period of the FBA has been a prime candidate, with the spread of cremation cemeteries from central Europe seen as tied to the introduction of the IE language. But if so, it is puzzling that cremation cemeteries are found in the areas that later became Etruscan, and that supposedly were untouched by the IE language.[63] Mallory sums up the state of our knowledge as follows:

> That Italy was Indo-Europeanized from some time after 3000 BC and prior to 800 BC there is little doubt. That one can also postulate a number of intrusions from outside Italy and still hold to an essential continuity of cultural development in many areas of Italy is also defensible. In a region where both the amount of archaeological evidence and our models for interpreting it still leave very much to be desired, this is perhaps all that we can expect at present.[64]

The Italic language family is divided into four subgroups of languages: Latino-Faliscan, Sabellian, Venetic, and Messapic. Of these, the Sabellian subgroup is the most varied, as it encompasses the Umbrian, South Picene, and Oscan languages, the last with many variants itself.[65] Confusingly, these language groups do not map easily onto the earlier material divisions. The Sabellian subgroup of languages covers portions of territory that were archaeologically "Villanovan" in the Iron Age, and other

---

[63] Mallory 1989: 92–3.
[64] Mallory 1989: 94.
[65] Clackson and Horrocks 2007: 3; 39–49.

portions of territory that was part of the Middle Adriatic cultures. To put it another way, the archaeological culture we call Villanovan covered both Etruscan and Sabellian language groups – one IE and one not. This may support the case for Iron Age regional systems, but makes the job of tracing population groups more difficult. Hall is skeptical of linguistic evidence as an index of ethnicity, noting that while language can be an ethnic marker, it need not be.[66] In the case of Greece, his argument for aggregative self-definition in the Archaic period leads him to posit that at least linguistically, the dialects of Greece represent a convergence from a period when the languages were very different, rather than a divergence from a common ancestral proto-Greek.[67] This contrasts with the case of Italy, in which there is no evidence of a process of language aggregation. Overall, the complex linguistic picture probably reflects an equally complex history. Clackson and Horrocks suggest that there were some early shared roots between the Italic languages, but later convergences must be the explanation for similar innovations across these languages.[68] This scenario does not provide any firm grounds for understanding regionalism in early Italy.

Social Networks and an Interactionist Model of Identity Formation

A new approach to understanding the development of regionalism offers some solutions. Beginning from the theoretical position that interaction leads to shared mentalities and eventually common identity rather than the other way around, this book identifies regional social networks in the RBA and FBA 1–2 that preceded fully articulated regional groups and whose structures, defined through various measures of cohesiveness, were more enduring than their material culture practices or social organization. Further, I argue that the RBA-FBA transition was the key moment of change. From the disparate archaeological evidence discovered around the Italian peninsula, a picture emerges of an area experiencing demographic expansion, increased trade, craft specialization, and

---

[66] Hall 1997: 153.
[67] Hall 1997: 169.
[68] Clackson and Horrocks 2007: 72.

settlement hierarchies. It is also a period of foreign contacts, with the Italian populations trading with Mycenaeans and Cypriots. Although I have argued elsewhere that the foreign contacts had only a limited impact on indigenous culture in Bronze Age Italy,[69] I suggest here that these visits are extremely useful historically in that they allow us to catch a glimpse of some of the short-distance interactions that have been invisible until now. This book is not a comprehensive history of these pre-Roman groups; most groups, particularly the ephemeral ones, emerged later – in the Iron Age and after. However, it does offer an explanatory framework for understanding the rise of regionalism and regional inequality in Italy. Although arguments of *environmental* determinism have little purchase, I will argue for some amount of *historical* determinism in the form of path dependence, showing that the character of the early regional networks had an impact on the ability of those groupings to endure. This is not to say that a region's Bronze Age level of social development is a predictor of its later trajectory. In the RBA, southeast Italy's peoples exhibit the clearest signs of social complexity, but the native populations there never subsequently forged an ethnic consciousness. Instead, I propose that regardless of the level of social complexity, the patterns of intraregional interaction established at the end of the Bronze Age in Italy determined the subsequent histories of those groups. In this book I will argue that social networks are a better way to think about the origins of groups than expressive actions of identity.

How are these regional, social networks made visible? It is generally very difficult to calculate the flows of local interactions in prehistory, as we are largely restricted to exchanges of materials rather than of people and ideas. This problem is compounded when the materials themselves are homogeneous, as is the case in Bronze Age Italy. However, certain objects do stand out, such as Aegean pottery, amber beads, carved ivory and bone, and bronze objects. When seeking material evidence of exchange in the past, the tendency has been to use the point of origin of the object (based on style or more securely, characterization of the material itself) to reconstruct contact between that source and the object's find spot. But from what we think we know of Bronze Age trade, we can

---

[69] Blake 2008.

imagine goods moving around along local routes for short stretches, possibly changing hands frequently, not moving in one directed push. In the ancient small-scale societies that characterized Bronze Age Italy, the co-occurrence of rare objects at neighboring villages was not a thing of chance: it must be the result of mutual awareness and most likely direct contact between them. Therefore, using a social network–analysis methodology, I posit that two sites sharing the same type of object can be said to have a relational tie to each other. Many sites with ties to each other form a web of ties or a *network*. Given the embedded nature of ancient trade, these local exchanges may be understood as the most visible measure of interactions that have otherwise left no archaeological trace. Thus, in areas where material exchanges were occurring, interactions of other kinds were also concentrated.

The results of the application of this approach to the distributions of exotica in the RBA and FBA are a series of independent exchange clusters scattered around the peninsula in each period. These clusters of exchanged goods are the material vestiges of social networks. As with all human groups, the manner in which Italy's peoples communicated and cooperated with each other and with their neighbors had a profound effect on their survival. I argue that the FBA 1–2 patterns of interaction preceded their crystallization into self-identified groups, and that the forms those interactions took – the social networks – later determined the success of the groups. Thus, I posit that the character of the early networks is a predictor of successful identity formation later: those Bronze Age networks that demonstrate cohesion and dense interactions are located where well-defined groups emerge later, as in the case of the Etruscans and the Veneti, whereas the weaker, disconnected networks precede poorly defined groups in the same area, as is the case in Apulia and Basilicata. Clearly, other factors in addition to these early behavioral patterns affected the regions' development. One could argue that resources were distributed unevenly between regions and this determined their prosperity, so, for example, Etruria with its rich mineral deposits and farmland had a leg up on the mountainous and mineral-poor Marche. Likewise, historical events, such as the arrival of Greek colonists, transformed these populations. I nonetheless argue that the behavioral patterns established in the RBA and early part of the FBA shaped how these groups responded to circumstances that befell them later. I propose here that the future character of these regional groups was determined by the kinds of social relationships the Bronze Age residents chose to establish with their neighbors. A caveat: we cannot tell what was happening in areas lacking in exotica, such as Liguria, Lombardy, the Molise, and particularly frustratingly, Latium. If there were social networks in these regions in the RBA or the FBA, they are currently archaeologically invisible. The conclusions from the areas where the evidence is present have broad implications, however: they suggest that group cohesion may be a prerequisite for collective identity formation rather than a defining facet. A predictive, interactionist model of identity formation propels identity studies further. Furthermore, although it is in the FBA 1–2 that we catch sight of the direct antecedents to the named peoples of the historical period, the networks of the RBA are equally interesting for what they reveal about the rise of the FBA groups. The transformations at the end of the RBA take on new importance in this model: in particular, the collapse of the Terramare culture becomes central to the history of regionalism in early Italy.

The present study is limited to the Italian peninsula and does not include Sardinia, Sicily, or the Aeolian Islands, given the islands' evident distinctiveness from the mainland.[70] These islands were not isolated from the mainland in the Bronze Age and some areas such as southeast Sicily were closely tied to the peninsula. Still, their separate histories warrant individual treatments, which are beyond the scope of the present study. Delimiting this study according to the boundaries of the modern Italian nation-state requires some justification. There is nothing to suggest that before the rise of Rome the regions that make up peninsular Italy saw themselves as united in even the loosest manner, nor is there evidence that they would have marked themselves off as distinct from the residents of what is now coastal Croatia or southern France. Italy as a concept has no long history, perhaps emerging, as Dench suggests, in the early third century BC when Rome engaged in both pan-peninsular road construction and tactical displacement of certain groups such as the Picenes. These actions make sense within a new proprietary vision of *Italia* as a whole. By the early second century BC, there is confirmation in Cato's *Origines* Books 2 and 3 in which he seems to be framing

---

[70] Bietti Sestieri 2005: 12.

peninsular Italy as a unit. These sections concern the peoples and lands of Italy, and their *nomoi* (customs). Dench suggests that Cato's choice to talk about these groups (and not others further north, for example), "might, then, be seen as an appraisal of a newly perceived geographical entity made up of peoples closely involved with, or subject to, the Romans."[71] But Rome's new conceptualization emerged in a particular context. As Dench puts it, "interest in conceptualizing common ground, literally and figuratively speaking, is itself suggestive of the peculiar, ethnically interactive conditions of ancient Italy. These are, moreover, the conditions within which Rome 'grew up,' within which she was to formulate her own distinctive ideas of Italy."[72]

In sum, this book revisits that murky period in the late second millennium BC as the formative moment when Italy's regional divisions emerge from the social networks in place. In Italy during the RBA and FBA, although there were indeed contacts with foreign groups, I argue that the more significant interactions occurred at the regional level. These intraregional networks provided the structural preconditions for what followed. The intraregional social networks established at the end of the second millennium BC cemented into the territorial groups of the next millennium. These networks are visible archaeologically in the distributions of certain categories of easily traceable goods including, but not exclusively, overseas imports. The characters of those earlier networks, inferred from the forms those distributions take, were in some cases remarkably long lived, still detectable hundreds of years later in the regional groups that followed. These habitual modes of interaction determined how well or poorly each region was able to respond to the changes the next millennium brought.

Background: From the Apennine Period to the End of the Bronze Age

Any study of Bronze Age regional networks must take into account those political, economic, technological, and cultural factors that would have influenced their formation and character. Although Italy in the

---

[71] Dench 1995: 19.
[72] Dench 2005: 161.

Bronze and Iron Ages underwent fewer large-scale transformations than we observe in the subsequent centuries of the first millennium BC, it was far from static. The starting point for a consideration of Italy in this period is the bifurcation between the territory from the Po Valley north and the rest of the peninsula to the south, obliging two separate histories. Quickly stated, in the Po Valley there was a distinctive population with a uniform material culture, the Terramare group, that began in the MBA, peaked in the RBA, and collapsed at its end, leaving much of that region virtually depopulated in the FBA. Central and southern Italy, although not without many contacts with the north, followed a separate trajectory.

The Middle Bronze Age: General Trends

The MBA in Italy is traditionally divided into three parts: 1, 2, and 3, with MBA 1 and 2 in central and southern Italy corresponding to the Proto-Apennine period and culture, and MBA 3 corresponding to the Apennine period and culture.[73] There are some minor disagreements over the absolute dates of the internal subdivisions, but the basic framework is accepted.[74] As noted earlier, the fundamental division is between the Po Valley and north, and the rest of the peninsula. The Po Valley and pre-Alpine zone in the MBA were home to the pile-dwelling (*palafitte*, in Italian) and Terramare groups, the two closely tied to each other and indeed only differing noticeably in settlement form. The pile-dwelling sites in marshy areas began earlier, in the EBA, and are found mostly in the pre-Alpine zone north of the Po, while the Terramare settlements are characterized by surrounding earthworks of a bank and ditch and are located in the southern Po Plain. Both settlement types are remarkable for their regular layouts, indicating preplanning. There is no evidence of social divisions in these homogeneous settlements. The seemingly sudden appearance of the Terramare on the southern Po plain in Emilia in the MBA probably resulted from colonization of this previously unoccupied area, possibly by some of the pile-dwelling groups to the north, a theory supported by evidence of wooden substructures – pilings – at

---

[73] Bernabò Brea, Cardarelli, and Cremaschi 1997: 25–8.
[74] Compare Bernabò Brea, Cardarelli, and Cremaschi 1997: 25–8 with Peroni 1999: 217–19.

Introduction

the oldest Terramare.[75] Terramare subsistence practices were structured around cereal agriculture with few legumes and livestock raising, primarily for meat, included sheep and goats, swine, and cows, in that order of importance.[76]

In MBA 3 the Italian peninsula south of the Po Valley manifests a broadly common material culture, the Apennine culture, named for the mountain range that traverses the peninsula and where many scholars think the observed commonalities in practices arose through seasonal encounters of transhumant pastoralists bringing their flocks to summer pastures. Populations were small, the economies were near subsistence level, and societies were structured into tribal groups and at most small-scale chiefdoms. Society was organized at the level of the village, with no broader political organization beyond that. There was no evidence of a social hierarchy, although we may expect that some people in practice carried more authority than others. There are no wealthy burials: burials resemble each other and are grouped often into clusters, probably family units. The recurring settlement pattern is one of small agglomerations of huts, whose residents farmed cereals and pulses in some combination and raised livestock: pigs, sheep, goats, and cattle; again in some combination. Horse bones are known in Italy from the Copper Age, but it is not until the MBA that the volume of faunal remains points to a sustained commitment to horse raising.[77]

Although this was nominally the Bronze Age, metals were restricted to weapons and prestige goods. In the north, many hoards containing weapons and axes are known, and metallurgy was practiced with some intensity.[78] In contrast, the metals of the south are often from funerary contexts, suggesting that metals in the south served different

---

[75] Bernabo Brea *et al*. 1997: 27–8; Bernabo Brea and Cremaschi 1997: 190. Others have suggested a Danubian origin for the settlers (Cardarelli 2009: 36–7).

[76] De Grossi Mazzorin and Riedel 1997.

[77] Sherratt 1983: 92–3. Horses had reached temperate Europe sporadically from the Eurasian steppes beginning in the late fifth millennium BC, but were slow to take hold there, and Italy shows a similarly slow adoption. The increased presence of horse remains may coincide with the introduction of the horse-drawn plow and chariot to Europe in the second millennium BC (Sherratt 1983: 97; Clutton Brock 1999: 102). The earliest horse bones are from northern Italy, with many turning up on Terramare sites (Gambari 1998: 248). It takes some time for them to spread south, and donkeys, discussed in Chapter 3, are even slower to arrive (D'Ercole 2002: 327).

[78] Bietti Sestieri 2010: 48.

social roles than in the north. Even though metallurgical production in the MBA was limited, already in that period both local and long-distance circuits are evident, with some objects originating in northern Italy spreading south, presumably via traveling smiths. Central Italy's mineral resources were still underexploited, and the metal objects there show transalpine affinities at this stage.[79] Pottery production was at the household level. Common Apennine forms are bowls and carinated cups, with elevated, often pierced, handles and incised and impressed geometric decorations.[80] Baltic amber had apparently reached the Italian peninsula by the EBA and continued in the MBA, although some of the amber is coming from Sicily.[81] Other exchangeable goods such as salt and sulfur can only be assumed.

The Recent and Final Bronze Ages: Peroni's List

Italian scholars divide the Italian Late Bronze Age into an early part, the *età del bronzo recente* or Recent Bronze Age (RBA), and a later part, the *età del bronzo finale* or Final Bronze Age (FBA). When relevant, scholars subdivide the RBA and FBA further, into RBA 1 and 2 and FBA 1, 2, and 3. The RBA in central and southern Italy is characterized by a homogeneous material-culture facies, the Subapennine, with much continuity with the preceding period. The pottery, still of household production, continues the Apennine tradition of elevated molded handles, but the pots are now almost completely undecorated.[82] For the FBA, the term "Protovillanovan" is used in the north as well as the rest of Italy, although at the regional scale, local labels are more commonly used. Thus, FBA 2 in Latium is generally called Latial I. In European chronology, FBA 1–2 corresponds to Hallstatt A (1200–1020 BC) and FBA 3 is contemporary with Hallstatt B1 (1020–950 BC). Conflicts between the traditional chronology and the dendrochronological and C14 dates make the correlation of the scheme to actual years tendentious.[83] Although progress

---

[79] Bietti Sestieri 2010: 43.
[80] Bietti Sestieri 2010: 129.
[81] Negroni Catacchio et al. 2006: 1465.
[82] Bietti Sestieri 2010: 130.
[83] The dates have been shifted back a century or so in the past ten years, thanks to Marco Bettelli's work on the early phases of Latium (Bettelli 1994, reaffirmed by Bietti Sestieri

in research is not dependent on a resolution of the absolute dating issues, the cultural labels attached to the chronological periods are more problematic. Terms such as "Apennine" and "Protovillanovan" imply unified cultural groups when in fact, all we have are common material products, and such misnomers may be impediments to a clear understanding of these periods.

The RBA and FBA are difficult to synthesize succinctly. Forty years ago, the Italian archaeologist Renato Peroni listed seven transformations to Italy from the RBA through the EIA that, as he saw it, laid the groundwork for the emergence of state-level societies by the eighth century BC.[84] He noted: population growth; agricultural intensification (including the expanded use of the horse, plow, and sickle, the cultivation of marginal areas, and terracing); the proliferation of metal goods pointing to both technical improvements and an increase in the volume of bronze working; larger and more stable, long-lived settlements; growing social complexity, from simple chiefdoms to complex ones (although social differences are muted and clear class divisions do not emerge before the FBA); an "increase in the size and range of the markets" encompassing temperate Europe, the Aegean, and Italy; and finally, new ways of accumulating wealth, primarily in the form of metals, but in other craft products as well.[85] Subsequent research has shown that many of the transformations Peroni identified were not widespread, but instead limited to particular regions, and they occurred at very different rates or not at all in some areas. Indeed, Peroni's main source, from which he extrapolated to the entire peninsula, was south Etruria. He also considered the RBA to be the fundamental moment of change, the "qualitative leap forward,"[86] whereas in most regions, the FBA seems to be the more significant period.[87] The EIA is in many ways a culmination of trends evident in the FBA, such as the localization of craft industries, and most significantly, increasing social complexity in the form of site hierarchies, elite burials, concentrations of wealth, and protourbanism. Peroni's list

---

[2010]). These dates are derived in many cases from comparisons with the Hallstatt culture, whose dates have also been revised.

[84] Peroni 1969 and 1979.
[85] Peroni 1979: 14.
[86] Peroni 1979: 20.
[87] Bietti Sestieri 2010: 171–4.

captures this complex transition from prehistory to protohistory, and despite the different rates of change, most regions had experienced these transformations sooner or later by the end of the Iron Age.

Tracing Regionalism in the MBA, RBA, and FBA

In his 1979 publication, Peroni only alluded to regionalism briefly, seeing it as a later phenomenon. He did note that the intensified metals industry engendered feelings of territoriality for the first time, in the FBA.[88] Since Peroni's publication however, a series of careful studies of the local ceramic data have revealed, in the MBA and FBA at least, evidence for regionalism. Although not well known outside of Italy, this research definitively problematizes the traditional picture of a uniform peninsular culture in the MBA, RBA, and FBA. What these studies do not do is build up any clear alternative picture.

The MBA Apennine ceramics are a useful starting point. They are homogeneous enough, broadly speaking, to warrant the application of a single term for the pots found throughout the Italian peninsula. Yet in an important study, Macchiarola delineated seven regional groups within the Apennine facies, based on the distribution of ceramic types within the broad repertoire. In some cases the ceramic forms are exclusive to particular regions, while in others they may span more than one region, but the relative densities vary regionally. Macchiarola's regions do not map neatly onto either the networks of the RBA and FBA or the named groups of the historical period. For example, the west-central Italy group (*gruppo medio tirrenico*) encompasses what are later south Etruria, Latium Vetus, and portions of Umbrian territory. Similarly, her south Tyrrhenian group (*gruppo tirrenico meridionale*) covering part of modern-day Basilicata, the southern portion of Campania and the Aeolian Islands, does not map onto any later regional grouping.[89] However, one factor is nonetheless telling: the author notes that few ceramic types have a wide diffusion; in other words, although all these regional types are closely enough related to constitute a single Apennine facies, no one type spreads very far. Some adjacent groups share a few pottery

---

[88] Peroni 1979: 15.
[89] Macchiarola 1995: Tav. 12; p. 443.

types, but the co-occurrence drops off beyond that. As Macchiarola puts it, "[t]he circulation of ceramics, but also probably of models and ideas, thus seems to privilege internal circuits within each group; more rarely involving two contiguous groups, while widespread distribution seems to have undergone a contraction [compared to the preceding phase of the MBA]."[90] Interestingly, when there are shared ceramic types between regions, the strongest ties are east-west, across the Apennines.[91] Macchiarola observes that the west-central Italy group and the middle Adriatic group, roughly at the same latitude and even overlapping in the Apennines, have more ceramic types in common than either does with other regional groups north or south of it. The same holds true for the Ofanto group on the Adriatic to the south, and the north Campanian group on the Tyrrhenian Sea. Again, both groups are at approximately the same latitude.[92] This pattern lends indirect support to the idea of mountain mobility and possibly transhumance facilitating the sharing of objects. These region-specific patterns in pottery types in the MBA could easily be reframed as networks rather than groups, thus avoiding the implied identity claims, and providing a useful model for thinking about these connections.

The regionalism picture changes radically in the RBA, which is unexpected given how many continuities are otherwise evident archaeologically between the MBA and RBA. Damiani in her detailed work on Subapennine ceramics described various elevated handle forms and delineated forty-two type families of open tableware forms. Her results demonstrate that these types were more easily organized chronologically than geographically.[93] To identify geographic distinctions in the types' distribution, Damiani divided the peninsula into six broad territories: the Po River area; Romagna; mid-Tyrrhenian; mid-Adriatic; south Ionic-Adriatic; and south Tyrrhenian.[94] She then looked for variations in the

---

[90] "La circolazione dei manufatti ceramici, ma probabilmente anche quella di modelli e idee, sembra quindi privilegiare circuiti interni a ciascun gruppo, piu raremente coinvolge due gruppi contigui, mentre la distribuzione su ampia scala sembra subire una contrazione" (Macchiarola 1995: 457).
[91] Bietti Sestieri 2010: 128.
[92] Macchiarola 1995: 457.
[93] Damiani 2010: Table 6.
[94] Damiani 2010: 448.

distributions of the handles and tableware families. Damiani's objective was to identify the patterns of diffusion and circulation, not cultural groups, so in this respect her approach is quite close to the network model applied in this book. The results of her study are rather complex. The spatial extent of distribution varies enormously depending on the artifact type. The handle types and tableware families range from narrow to wide distributions, and significantly, are more likely to be found in more than one region than to be exclusive to one.[95] Among the tableware families, Damiani describes just six of the forty-two as circumscribed to a particular area, and even some of those have a sporadic presence in other regions.[96] The handles are also widely distributed. Of the bird-shaped handles, 25 percent of the types within that broad classification are found in three or more regions, and 15 percent each in one, two, four, and five regions. For the horned handles, the majority of types, more than 65 percent, are found in five or six regions.[97] This may be read as an indication of the intensity of circulation of even pottery objects in the RBA, but for our purposes, the conclusion to take is that no regional groups are detectable from the Subapennine pottery of this period. Damiani's study does not concern the regionally defined Terramare ceramic styles. Although Damiani included the Po Valley in her study, she was only focusing on the Subapennine ceramics found there.

North of the Subapennine zone one may identify two unambiguous RBA regional groupings in Italy. In addition to the aforementioned Terramare culture, the Canegrate culture of the pre-Alpine territory of western Lombardy and eastern Piedmont, home later to the Celtic Insubres, is archaeologically visible in the RBA. Although in principle I am hesitant to use migration to explain newly emergent regional groups, the Canegrate culture seems a clear-cut case of a group of newcomers from across the Alps who brought with them the then-novel burial practice of cremation, as well as their own decorated pottery.[98]

By the FBA, regional groupings are more archaeologically visible. Indeed, in contrast to the Anglo-American trend of pushing ethnic origins later in Italy, Italian prehistorians have been seeking the traces of

---

[95] Damiani 2010: fig. 88.
[96] Damiani 2010: 451.
[97] Damiani 2010: fig. 88.
[98] De Marinis 2000a.

Introduction

regional groupings in the FBA, particularly in its final phase, FBA 3. Although the material culture of the period is broadly labeled "Protovillanovan," some relatively well-defined regional facies are evident within that general grouping, based on both ceramics and the metals. Indeed, one of the major transformations of the FBA is the new regionally inflected metal industries that align for the first time with regional ceramic facies.[99] Although this process is most clear in Etruria, much of the rest of the peninsula to a lesser degree echoes this expansion in the consumption and production of metals, and an improvement in quality as well. This is true in Apulia,[100] the eastern Veneto,[101] and Marche,[102] although the mountainous interior of the central Adriatic, for one, was bypassed by these trends.[103] As a result, some scholars reject the blanket cultural term "Protovillanovan" altogether, in favor of localized cultural labels.[104] Scholarly recognition of this regionalism is relatively new. As Bietti Sestieri has noted, "research in the past few years has demonstrated that many of the processes of regional formation of the Italic peoples mentioned in the ancient texts, which were generally thought to begin in the EIA, were already under way in the FBA."[105] She attributes this emergent regionalism in part to the greater archaeological visibility of the period compared to the preceding ones, and also to new structural factors, namely the population increase in the FBA that would have stimulated regional group formation.[106] However, Bietti Sestieri goes on to observe that the regional groupings emerging in the FBA and at the start of the IA varied enormously in size, in some cases narrowly corresponding to later regional territories and in others, such as the Villanovan and fossa-grave groups, covering large portions of the peninsula.[107]

---

[99] Bietti Sestieri 2010: 172–3.
[100] Bietti Sestieri 1988: 35.
[101] Bianchin Citton 2003: 121.
[102] Bergonzi 2005: 703.
[103] Barker (1995) showed that in the Biferno Valley, the RBA and FBA are characterized by limited bronze working and the continued use of lithic tools.
[104] E.g., De Marinis (1999: 511–12) favors "Protoveneto" over Protovillanovan for the Veneto in the FBA.
[105] "le ricerche degli ultimi anni hanno mostrato che molti dei processi regionali di formazione dei popoli italici noti dai testi storici, il cui inzio veniva fatto tradizionalmente coincidere con la I età del ferro, sono già attivi nell' età del bronzo finale" (Bietti Sestieri 2010: 171).
[106] Bietti Sestieri 2010: 171.
[107] Bietti Sestieri 2010: 173.

Among the narrowly defined regional groups, two in central Italy have been especially well studied. In central Italy in FBA 1, two local facies of the Protovillanovan ceramic repertoire are visible, separated by the Fiora River. The Chiusi-Cetona facies covers Marche, Umbria, and the Etruscan interior.[108] The Tolfa-Allumiere facies covers southern Etruria, and is temporally divided between an earlier Tolfa period and later Allumiere period, although those distinctions are not relevant for the purposes of this study.[109] In FBA 2 there is for the first time a distinction in material culture between southern Etruria and Latium, and with this distinction comes a new Latium-specific chronological ordering, beginning with Latial period I. Much of the material culture between the two regions stays the same in this period, truth be told, but there are some differences in the distributions of cinerary urn-lid types, and in the size of the cemeteries, and in the practice of including weapons in the graves, which is common in Latium in this period but unheard of in Etruria.[110] To the north, in eastern Lombardy and the Veneto, a regional facies of the Protovillanovan group emerges, with a pottery repertoire and some specific metal types that resemble the Tolfa-Allumiere material.[111] In Emilia-Romagna, there is no real Protovillanovan facies because as described earlier, the region was depopulated. In the southwest, in Calabria and eastern Sicily toward the end of the FBA, a local metalworking industry sustained by Calabrian ores serves to distinguish this region from others.[112] Campania at the end of the FBA, on the other hand, displays the cultural heterogeneity that characterizes it in the IA, with multiple burial practices and a mix of material culture elements, suggesting an exceptional polychromatic cultural landscape.[113] In southern Italy, in contrast, when Matt-Painted Geometric pottery emerged in the eleventh century BC, it showed no regional variation across the south, and it is only from the later ninth century and early eighth century that regional types become apparent.[114]

---

[108] Zanini 1996; Bietti Sestieri 2010: 226.
[109] Bietti Sestieri and De Santis 2004.
[110] Bietti Sestieri and De Santis 2004: 171–2.
[111] De Marinis 1999: 511–12.
[112] Bietti Sestieri 2010: 173.
[113] Cerchiai 2010: 13–20.
[114] Herring 2000: 55.

Introduction

Whereas all the previous studies have focused on pottery primarily, one early study stands out for its use of the metal data. In 1980, a group of prehistorians led by Peroni made what they considered at the time to be an interesting experiment, which they saw as a foundation for subsequent work by others.[115] They observed that running parallel to the prevailing emphasis (in 1980) on the cultural unity of the peninsular FBA, there were studies identifying regional groupings that presaged the full-fledged cultural groups of the historical period: thus, scholars were independently speaking of Protoveneti, Protoatestini, and so on. In an explicit emphasis on this local angle, Peroni and the others attempted to identify local facies from the distributions of bronze artifact types in the FBA. They first identified smaller groupings that they called "isoide," based on coterminous clusters of one or more object types. For example, Isoide 7 consists of the distributions of a dress-pin type and a fibula type, which combined cover a territory of northern Italy that includes part of western Lombardy, with a southern boundary at the Po. They then overlaid those isoide onto larger area maps and where there was "a certain number of types" of objects, they would identify them as territorial units, and when those units were of a certain size and density of objects, they labeled them facies.[116] They noted that within the facies there were smaller clusters they called *gruppi* (groups). Although most of their groups do not appear to correspond to any cultural groupings or even ceramic groupings of which we know, several in west-central Italy map nicely onto the local networks I identify in this research. This is to be expected as my dataset includes some of the same objects as theirs. The authors did not attempt to link these facies to later cultural groups, and their interpretation of the facies was not fully articulated in the publication.[117] From what they wrote, it seemed that rather than exchange networks, the facies and their *gruppi* were more like distribution ranges of objects. Nonetheless, this work was a prescient early attempt to detect regional groups using means other than simply local

---

[115] Peroni *et al.* 1980: 86.

[116] Unfortunately, no further detail was given on the criteria for recognizing isoide, territorial units, or facies. Peroni *et al.* 1980: 12.

[117] For the most part, the facies' boundaries are simply determined by empty spaces on the map. Peroni *et al.* 1980: 85.

ceramics. Surprisingly, the challenge of this early study was not taken up by subsequent scholars.

Thus, given on the one hand the lack of dissemination of these regional studies in the Anglophone scholarly community, and the sense on the other hand that the local ceramics evidence has been taken as far as it can go (until clay sourcing becomes more widespread) in the hunt for cultural groups, the time is ripe for a new approach, methodologically and theoretically, to the problem of Italy's early regional groups. With this in mind, we can proceed with identifying the Bronze Age networks and tracing them to their conclusion. Chapter 2 presents the imports and specialized products circulating in Italy in the RBA and FBA, tracing their individual histories and weaving them into a bigger picture of foreign contacts and long-distance exchange in this period. This chapter also introduces the particular object types to be used in the analysis that follows. In Chapter 3, I pull back from the Italian evidence to discuss in some detail the broad theoretical debates in archaeology surrounding collective identities and their formation, and introduce social network analysis as a valuable tool for community detection in archaeology. I draw on the concept of path dependence to argue that in looking at the historical circumstances of regions and their networks of interactions one can predict the subsequent success of particular groups. Covering the peninsula as a whole, in Chapter 4 I use the distributions of imported objects in the RBA and FBA 1–2 to construct chronologically sequential networks that I argue correspond to real networks of interaction in the peninsula in these two periods. I stop with FBA 1–2 because by FBA 3 the regional groups are in some cases already visible from the locally produced material culture, and we are already clearly on our way to the territorially defined groups of the Iron Age.[118] I demonstrate that within these networks there are several dense self-contained clusters of interaction. I compare the structures of these clusters using a range of measures of cohesion, including density of ties, centrality of ties, and network diameter. In several important cases, these clusters map onto the territories of the named population groups of the mid–late first millennium BC. To test the theory of the importance of these early social

---

[118] Indeed, the FBA3–EIA transition is poorly defined archaeologically and many objects span both periods.

networks in determining group success later, in Chapters 5 through 8 I consider four geographic areas over time: the Po Valley and the Veneto (Chapter 5); the mid-Tyrrhenian area (Chapter 6); Marche and the north central Apennines (Chapter 7); and southeast Italy (Chapter 8). In each of these case studies I begin with a historical and geographic overview of the region. I then examine the character of the Bronze Age networks, the history of the later population groups, and compare the early networks and later peoples. The study of the Po Valley and the fall of the Terramare culture take on particular importance as it will be argued that the Terramare culture's dissolution made possible the rise of some of Italy's most long-lived regional groups. The final chapter of the book looks ahead to the fate of Italy's regional groups following the Roman conquest, framing their disappearance in network terms rather than simply in the erosion of regional group identity. In other words, the Romanization of Italy entailed the dismantling of the ancient networks and the mapping of new ties between sites around the peninsula. I identify the last vestiges of these early groups and speculate on the rise of the post-Roman groups – not phoenix-like from the ashes of the old, but rather as fresh beginnings owing far more to Rome than to the peoples who occupied Italy before it.

CHAPTER TWO

IMPORTS AND SPECIALIZED PRODUCTS IN ITALY IN THE RECENT AND FINAL BRONZE AGES

The traditional approach to exotica in Bronze Age Italy is to see them, sensibly enough, as evidence of foreign contacts. Scholars have extrapolated from the material evidence the nature and extent of the influence of these contacts, the parties involved, and developments in those interactions over time – all conclusions subject to intense debate. In this chapter I try a different approach. The material evidence for foreign contacts that I introduce here is what I will be using in subsequent chapters to construct *local* networks of exchange and interaction in Italy. From the broad range of craft materials that circulated I have selected those object types that are sufficiently represented (coming from three or more find spots) and discreetly dated (to either the RBA or FBA 1–2, but not both). The result is forty RBA object types and twenty-six FBA object types (Figures 2.1 and 2.2).

My research rests on some premises about how these exotica reached Italy and circulated there, and the significance of those visits. I explain them here.

Long-Distance Exchanges in the RBA and FBA: The Bigger Picture

This study covers the RBA and the first parts of the FBA because it is in these two periods that a significant increase in the distinctive goods discussed in this chapter occurs. This phenomenon of the proliferation of imported goods and local specialized craft production occurs to

Imports and Specialized Products in Italy

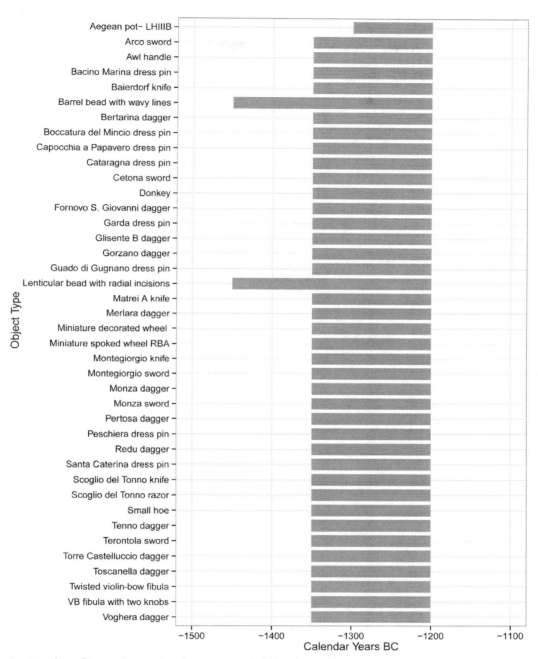

2.1. Timeline of Recent Bronze Age object types included in the study

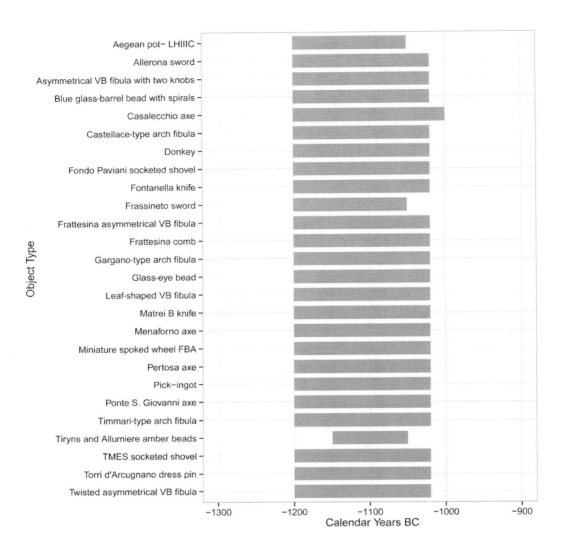

2.2. Timeline of Final Bronze Age 1–2 object types included in the study

varying degrees throughout the Mediterranean. By the FBA, this intensive circulation leads to a convergence of metal types across a broad area of Italy, Greece, and east and central Europe that Harding has described as a veritable "koinè."[1] Harding sees Europe as the motor, with most of the object types originating there. These objects include tools, weapons, and dress ornaments. Common object types are swords, dress pins, fibulae, knives, daggers, razors, and axes. Although some of the objects may have been solely decorative, the new tools and weapons go

[1] Harding 1984: 11.

beyond aesthetics to involve real technological innovations. The flange-hilted swords, for example – long and sturdy and designed for cutting and thrusting – must have transformed warfare in the regions that adopted them, and increased the need for body armor to protect against slashes.[2] The European metal forms had numerous local variants, and although the origins of many object types remain unknown, it is clear from the rapid copying that regionalism and the localized absorption of styles prevailed over a demand for foreign exotica. In this way the forms were "naturalized," as Sherratt has put it, rather than being imitated with the aim of passing them off as foreign objects.[3] The process is quite different from the Italian copies of Mycenaean pots, which so closely emulated the originals that a semblance of foreignness must have been a goal of their makers.

Whereas in the RBA a north-south polarization is evident along the peninsula – with metals clustered primarily in the Po Valley and the Aegean-style pots in the south – in the FBA, circulation patterns change: the northern Adriatic takes on an expanded role in trade, following the collapse of the Terramare culture, and central Italy becomes an important place for the production and circulation of bronze objects. In southeast Italy, Late Helladic IIIC (c. 1200–1050 BC, hereafter LH IIIC) pots from Achaea have been found at Punta Meliso and Roca Vecchia, suggesting a continuation of long-distance trade with the Aegean, although locally made versions by this period are more common than imports.[4]

Of further interest are the means by which these goods and technologies spread across such long distances in the first place. Belardelli and Bettelli note a correlation between the distribution of the pottery known as Handmade Burnished Ware (HBW) and finds of certain bronze objects that are of probable Italian origin, such as violin-bow fibulae, in Greece.[5] HBW is an intriguing class of pottery whose intrusive presence at Mycenaean palatial sites in levels just before and just after collapse has led some scholars to see it as the material signature of the migrating peoples who may have been implicated in the destructions.[6] Although Belardelli

[2] Harding 1984: 155–65.
[3] Sherratt 2000: 85.
[4] Cultraro sees the importation of these pots to Italy coinciding with the circulation of bronze, glass, and amber – all part of this FBA metallurgical koinè. Cultraro 2006: 1549.
[5] Bellardelli and Bettelli 2007.
[6] Bankoff 1996.

and Bettelli's aim is to demonstrate the probable Italian origins of some of the HBWs, and thus the movement of Italian settlers to Greece, the association between the two categories of artifacts – that is, the bronzes and the ceramics – complicates the picture of the migrations rather than simplifying it. The HBW is typically described as a low-value ceramic repertoire for domestic consumption, the product of a marginalized group. The presence of relatively valuable bronze imports – if brought, as suggested, by the same immigrants who made the pottery – requires a reconsideration of the social status of the newcomers. Second, the hypothesized association requires that south Italian migrants settling in Greece made a conscious point of preserving their own pottery traditions in lieu of adopting the potter's wheel that by then prevailed in Mycenaean Greece, and to which they had already been exposed back home in Italy. If true, this scenario would only serve to highlight how limited the absorption of Mycenaean material culture had been in Italy, a conclusion that runs counter to the argument for close association.

In an alternative theory, Sherratt suggests that itinerant metallurgists were responsible for the spread of these bronze objects, and makes no mention of actual migrations of people permanently resettling in the east.[7] Certainly the local variations of the object types suggest a groundedness and regionalism despite the obvious evidence of interactions, and do not require movements of peoples. As the hypothesized FBA koinè is contemporary with the increase in the spread of Cypriot goods to the west, Sherratt suggests Cypriot traders may have been partly responsible for the dissemination of these forms. She notes that the finds in the Aegean and eastern Mediterranean are largely from coastal sites, implying seaborne movements. She sees in LH IIIB the appearance of small Cypriot-manned boats such as the Cape Gelidonya wreck carrying mixed cargoes to the west, operating independently of the palaces.[8] From the LH IIIB on, Sherratt argues for "increasingly direct Cypriot exploitation of long distance routes from the east to the Central Mediterranean and the Adriatic."[9] She argues that the fact that amber and European bronzes are circulating in the twelfth and eleventh centuries BC, at exactly the

---

[7] Sherratt 2000: 85.
[8] Sherratt 2001: 234.
[9] Sherratt 2001: 235.

same time as the distribution of Cypriot bronzes, is not a coincidence, but rather they are all traces of the same phenomenon of FBA Cypriot ventures to the west. Her argument is that in this period, Cypriot traders opened up metals to sub-elite groups in a system of distribution that ran counter to the Bronze Age palaces, effectively undermining palatial hegemony over the metals trade. She suggests that early ironworking on Cyprus was part of the same phenomenon, with iron serving as an alternative metal that reached sub-elite markets.[10] Sherratt puts the driving force behind these changes in the hands of people from the east, but what of the new materials on offer from the Europeans? While the Cypriots may have been responsible for the eastern leg of the movements, there is no evidence they were involved in any of the transalpine transmissions that must have taken place, and the rich body of material originating in central and eastern Europe that does make its way to the Aegean or the East can have had little to do with the Cypriots. Further, the Italian peninsula is in fact somewhat bypassed by the Cypriots, having yielded scant Cypriot objects and no oxhide ingots, thought by many to be made on Cyprus.[11] The Cypriot overthrow of the old structures of metal exchanges may have been one of the by-products of this koinè, but it cannot be taken as its cause.

Giardino interprets the evidence differently from Harding and Sherratt, giving the Aegean credit for jump-starting this "intensive circulation" of metal objects in the RBA and FBA.[12] Despite the fact that this circulation of metal objects and types occurs just as that of Mycenaean imports to Italy declines and then ceases, Giardino argues that this koinè was established by the Mycenaeans, "to provide the powerful states of the Near East with a regular supply of metals from the west."[13] Giardino merges the two events by proposing two metal koinès,

---

[10] Sherratt 2000: 87–8.

[11] Lo Schiavo 2006. Cypriot tripod fragments have been found in hoards from Contigliano (Rieti) and Piediluco (Holloway 1981: 78). The tripod fragments are dated to the twelfth or eleventh century BC, but the Contigliano hoard is dated to the late tenth or ninth century BC. If the pieces were two centuries old, their origin was probably long forgotten, and one cannot posit direct contact with Cypriots to explain their presence. On the mainland, a Cypriot Rude Style sherd has been identified at Eboli, in Campania (Vagnetti and Lo Schiavo 1989: 219).

[12] Giardino 2000: 99.

[13] Giardino 2000: 97.

with the earlier one of the RBA going into decline with the collapse in the east, affecting mainland Italy and Sicily in the process. His evidence consists of some newly fortified sites in Calabria, a destruction level in the Lipari acropolis, and a "weak echo" of troubled times in the later, classical texts such as Diodorus Siculus.[14] Giardino attributes the widely distributed metal forms of the RBA to a second koinè emerging in the tenth century BC, after a lull, centered on the western Mediterranean and away from the Aegean. Giardino describes a major increase in metal exchanges in the western Mediterranean starting around 1000 BC, linking Sicily, Sardinia, Italy, and the Iberian Peninsula.[15] He includes the western spread of iron technology as a by-product of this second koinè.[16] The break he posits between the first and second episodes of interaction is not easily observable archaeologically (it is the period when the cosmopolitan site of Frattesina, discussed in Chapter 5, reaches its apex, after all), and it seems more likely that the shift in emphasis he notes, with the Aegean and the east dropping out of the interactions and Iberia and the west entering into them, occurs in the second phase of the same long period of interaction between the central Mediterranean and other areas. On the Aegean side of things, scholars have argued that in the tenth century BC, copper and tin were in very short supply, with iron being the primary metal.[17] However, chemical analyses of Late Bronze Age (LBA) and Dark Age copper alloys in Greece show no significant drop in tin content over this period, which would be expected in the case of a bronze shortage; there is no deterioration in the quality of bronze products.[18] Morris has argued that while there may have been less bronze available, it was not gone completely, and that changing preferences were partially responsible for the growing popularity of iron.[19]

Any explanation must draw on the evidence of the site of Frattesina, in the Veneto. Frattesina flourished from the twelfth to early ninth century BC and demonstrates that the goods circulating over long distances were

---

[14] Giardino 2000: 102.
[15] Giardino 1995: 339–41.
[16] Giardino 2000: 103–4.
[17] Snodgrass 1980.
[18] Kayafa 2006.
[19] Morris 2000: 208–16.

not just metals. Excavations there have yielded evidence of other crafts, with workshops for glass, antler, bone, and ivory. Imported materials found at the site include elephant ivory, amber, ostrich eggs, and Mycenaean pottery. Frattesina peaks in the eleventh and tenth centuries BC. It is thought to have succeeded "in part thanks to outside – Aegean – influence, and the most accredited scenario links the Aegean presence to metal prospection and the amber trade."[20] The actual number of Mycenaean pottery sherds at Frattesina amounts to two, both from LH IIIC.[21] For northern Italy as a whole, Mycenaean sherds have been found at ten sites, amounting to a handful of sherds in total.[22] This is not much on which to base an Aegean presence. Borgna suggests instead that the Cypriots were responsible, echoing Sherratt's theory that the entire metals koinè could be in large part attributable to them.[23] Pearce rightly suggests that the success of Frattesina need not be explained in terms of the east Mediterranean at all, although clearly some of the imports indicate connections with that region.[24] Perhaps more interesting in the FBA are the growing links between northeast Italy and Tuscany, which take the form of shared, finished metal types and a new preference for Tuscan copper sources over those from the previously favored south Alpine Trentino district. Pearce attributes this shift in preference, which is remarkable given that the Alpine sources were in fact closer to the Veneto, to the opportunity of getting Tuscan tin at the same time, which was not available in the Alpine region.[25]

Beside the question of supply we may also consider the reception of these foreign objects and how the handling of the pottery differs from that of the other materials. In Adriatic Apulia, Radina and Recchia observed that Mycenaean pots are found in settlements while amber and glass beads are found in graves. As Radina and Recchia acknowledge, the absence of beads from domestic contexts is to be expected, as they easily retain their value whereas a broken pot may not, so the beads are far less likely to be lost or discarded in settlements. On the other hand,

---

[20] Pearce 2000: 110.
[21] Vianello 2005: 125; Pearce 2000: 110.
[22] Salzani *et al.* 2006.
[23] Borgna 1992; Sherratt 2000.
[24] Pearce 2000: 113.
[25] Pearce 2000: 111.

the absence of Mycenaean pots from the Apulian graves is noteworthy. Radina and Recchia suggest that whereas the beads could be fitted into local ritual practice, the Mycenaean and Italo-Mycenaean pots could not.[26] The more one examines this phenomenon of the intensification in the production and circulation of craft products, the more it seems too complex to be attributed to a single set of actors, and in any case, it played out differently in different regions. For the purposes of this study, what is significant is that it occurred and that the objects used in my construction of the regional networks fit into a much broader phenomenon. Let us look at each category of material and the object types included in this study in turn.

Aegean Style Pottery, Imported and Local

Finds of Aegean pottery in Italy span some 500 years, and their character and distribution change over time.[27] Scholars have increasingly highlighted the multivariate nature of the phenomenon of Aegean contact with Italy and its long time depth, charting the shifting distributions of imports and their variety.[28] We do not know for sure if the Mycenaeans brought all their material to Italy themselves, as Cypriot traders could just as easily have done so, but the fairly convincing evidence that some Mycenaean potters, at least, settled on Italian soil and made pots for some sustained period is strong indirect support for the traders being often or mostly Mycenaean.[29]

Aegean-Italic contacts are generally organized into three phases, based on the dating of the Aegean ceramics found in Italy.[30] There are

---

[26] Radina and Recchia 2006: 1558–60.
[27] The Aegean chronology, organized conventionally into stages of the Middle and Late Helladic periods (MH and LH), is based on Manning and Weninger (1992).
[28] Although Mycenaean material constitutes the overwhelming majority of the visible imports, there is a very small number of possible Minoan imports (Pålsson Hallager 1985).
[29] See Gillis 1988 for a useful discussion of diverse trade forms and traders in the LBA Mediterranean. See Sherratt, 2001: 222 note 17, for the point that Cypriot traders were trading Mycenaean pots in the eastern Mediterranean. For the case for Mycenaean potters in southern Italy, see Buxeda i Garrigós et al., 2003.
[30] Vagnetti 1993. The imprecision in dating the often small Mycenaean sherds has led Vianello (2005: 43) to recommend a broader division into two phases, LH I-LH IIIA1 and LH IIIA2–LH IIIC.

apparently a few Middle Helladic (MH) III (seventeenth century BC) Aegean sherds from the indigenous site of Monte Grande in southern Sicily, but these were found in a later (LH I) context and the dating of those sherds is not universally accepted.[31] By 1600 to 1445 BC or so (LH I–II), Mycenaean imports are securely present at a handful of sites, notably the aforementioned Monte Grande, the Aeolian Islands, the island of Vivara off the Tyrrhenian coast of southern Italy, and Capo Piccolo in Calabria.[32]

In the next phase, the numbers of imports to Italy increase enormously. The period from the second half of the fifteenth through the thirteenth century BC (LH IIIA–IIIB) marks the peak of Mycenaean imports in Italy, contemporary with the apex of the Mycenaean civilization in the Aegean. During this time the overall numbers of Mycenaean potsherds in Italy increase, and they are found in new sites as well. It is to this period that some of the sites yielding the most numbers of sherds – notably Scoglio del Tonno, the necropoleis of southeast Sicily, and the Milazzese period villages on the Aeolian Islands – belong.[33] A few sherds are known from west-central Italy in this period, and the north.[34] In LH IIIB, production of local copies of Mycenaean pottery begins. Three main sites for the so-called Italo-Mycenaean wares are along the Ionian coast of southern Italy – Termitito (in Basilicata),[35] Broglio di Trebisacce (Calabria),[36] and Scoglio del Tonno (Apulia)[37] – but Italo-Mycenaean wares are found in smaller numbers at many sites in southern Italy.

In LH IIIC1, at the end of the thirteenth century BC and in the early twelfth century BC following the collapse of the palatial centers in the east, Mycenaean-style ceramics are still widely distributed in southern Italy, but the actual imports have been largely replaced by locally made copies. Whether this was to fill the demand because the imports had dried up, or because exiled Mycenaean potters were on hand to produce them,

---

[31] For the early dates for the material from Monte Grande, see Castellana 2000; Leighton (2005: 277) is not convinced.
[32] Lattanzi *et al.* 1987.
[33] Vagnetti 1993: 146–7.
[34] Bietti Sestieri 1988: 27–8. In the north, LH IIIB pottery has turned up at two places (Bianchin Citton 2003).
[35] De Sìena 1986.
[36] Peroni and Vanzetti 1998.
[37] Taylour 1958.

or for other reasons, remains unresolved.[38] In addition, six sites in the Veneto and Po regions of Northern Italy have yielded some Mycenaean sherds from this late phase.[39] Marazzi sees these northern finds as evidence of a route along which Baltic amber would travel through central Europe, down the Adriatic to the Aegean, with some Aegean goods following the reverse route in exchange.[40] However, only three of the ten sherds in the north that were tested archaeometrically were shown to be from Greece, the rest originating in southern Italy.[41] By LH IIIC2, late in the twelfth century BC, a severe contraction in Mycenaean imports is evident: Mycenaean ceramic finds are limited to sites in Apulia, Broglio di Trebisacce in Calabria, and Nuraghe Antigori on Sardinia.[42] Based on the metal finds, there is a case to be made for continued contact between Greece and Italy through the eleventh and tenth centuries.[43] As these metal forms are of European origin and there are very few finished objects actually exchanged, they are not proof of continued interactions between Italy and the Aegean. In any case, there are no further incontrovertibly Aegean ceramic materials found in the west for several centuries, until the eighth century BC.

In this study I use the Aegean-style ceramics from two periods in my RBA and FBA datasets: LH IIIB and LH IIIC, respectively. There are nineteen secure find spots of Aegean pottery in the RBA and thirty-four in the FBA. Many of the Aegean-style sherds found in Italy are too fragmentary and nondescript to be securely dated to one or the other of these periods, so those examples have been excluded from my dataset. I do not group according to any other criteria than chronology; that is to say, I do not distinguish according to vessel form or decoration or origin. In practical terms, with a relatively scant dataset, subdivisions would obscure any broader patterning. On theoretical grounds, furthermore, there is little reason for that degree of detail. The mixed assemblages at sites and the variegated nature of the cargos of Bronze Age trading vessels

---

[38] Differentiating between LH IIIB and LH IIIC sherds is difficult, so the exact numbers of sherds attributed to this phase must be treated with caution (Vagnetti 1993: 151).
[39] Bianchin Citton 2003. Unfortunately, these were all surface finds with the exception of one of the two sherds from Frattesina (Rahmstorf 2005: 669).
[40] Marazzi 2003: 109.
[41] Jones *et al.* 2002: 221–61.
[42] Mederos Martín 1999: 240–1.
[43] Eder and Jung 2005.

together suggest that on the supply side, the ceramics that circulated were not restricted by any of these criteria.[44] Having an Aegean-style pot of any form, variety, or origin would have been significant in its own right.

Amber

Amber reaches Italy starting in the EBA and is found throughout the peninsula. The two zones with the highest concentrations are Sardinia and northeast Italy.[45] Scholars assume amber was an exotic item and a status symbol to Bronze Age peoples, although some amber comes from local Italian contexts and its value is not clearly determined.[46] In later periods, amber was thought to have healing properties and to be sacred, but we do not know if it was similarly perceived in the Bronze Age. Apart from some exceptional figurative pieces and cylinder seals, most amber in RBA and FBA Italy takes the form of beads, pendants, and "buttons."[47] More than sixty amber beads have been found in FBA graves in Italy.[48] Amber beads have turned up on many sites in Italy, and there is no apparent significant correlation between sites with Mycenaean pottery and those with amber beads, with only a few sites containing both.[49] Negroni Catacchio and others suggest from the evidence that prior to the Iron Age, amber circulated as finished objects rather than as unworked material to be processed at many sites.[50]

Negroni Catacchio has, in a series of publications, developed a typology of the amber beads.[51] Most shapes, such as discoidal beads, are too generic to be of any chronological use as they span the entire Bronze Age.[52] The so-called Tiryns and Allumiere beads, on the other hand, with their relatively tight chronology, are particularly useful and so have received the most scholarly attention. The Tiryns and Allumiere beads are recorded at eleven and five of the find spots used in this study,

---

[44] Blake 2008: 16–22.
[45] Negroni Catacchio *et al.* 2006: 1465.
[46] Cultraro 2007.
[47] Negroni Catacchio *et al.* 2006.
[48] Toti 1987: 81.
[49] Vianello 2005: 90.
[50] Negroni Catacchio *et al.* 2006: 1461.
[51] See Negroni Catacchio *et al.* 2006 for a recent summary of these forms.
[52] Negroni Catacchio *et al.* 2006: 1453.

respectively. The Tiryns beads are subcylindrical with a ridge around the central part. The Allumiere beads are cylindrical with grooves encircling them. Their shapes can range from squat to narrow, and this lack of formal standardization may be the result of localized workshop production. The two types are often found together.[53] The find contexts for the Tiryns and Allumiere beads in Greece strongly point to a date of LH IIIC, with the earliest examples belonging to the early part of this period and the latest to Final LH IIIC, with their production and circulation ceasing in the Submycenaean period.[54]

It is still debated where the beads were produced. As no Tiryns and Allumiere beads are found near the Baltic, it seems unlikely that they were worked and distributed from there. With Greece at the center of the distribution map of these objects, it is probable that they were made there and then fanned out to the west and east.[55] This raises the debate over the Mycenaean role in the circulation of amber in the western Mediterranean. The history of Baltic amber in Sicily is illuminating here. Baltic amber was introduced to Sicily in the MBA, and Cultraro for one attributes its arrival to Mycenaean traders.[56] He notes that "the distribution patterns of manufactured items of amber exactly coincide with those of glass paste ornaments," assuming apparently that the latter objects are Mycenaean as well.[57] If Mycenaeans brought the amber, it is surprising that southern Italy, with its imported Mycenaean pottery, should yield so few amber objects. The same pattern, as we shall see, holds true for glass items. Instead, the other area of Italy that has produced quantities of both is northern Italy, but without many Mycenaean ceramics. Likewise, southern France has both amber and glass beads, but has yet to yield a single sherd of Mycenaean pottery.[58] Sardinia, the other major find spot of amber, does have Mycenaean sherds, but not in the numbers of southern Italy. It is difficult to avoid the conclusion that the Mycenaeans had little to do with the movements of amber in Italy.

---

[53] Negroni Catacchio *et al.* 2006: 1459–60. In the west, Sardinia has among the highest concentrations of the Tiryns and Allumiere beads.
[54] Cultraro 2006: 1543–4.
[55] Negroni Catacchio *et al.* 2006: 1461–3.
[56] In earlier periods, local Sicilian amber sources had been exploited (Cultraro 2007: 387).
[57] Cultraro 2007: 387.
[58] Harding 1984: figs. 17 and 24.

Renfrew suggests we avoid speaking of an amber "trade" as if that were the goal, and instead see amber's distribution as a by-product of travel.[59] In this case, we may ask who were the travelers, if not the Mycenaeans? There is much work to be done on this thorny question, but for the purposes of this study, the focus is on the distributions of the Tiryns and Allumiere beads within peninsular Italy, regardless of their place of origin.

Ivory and Antler

The first imports of ivory to Italy are recorded in the MBA, in the sixteenth–fourteenth centuries BC, as finished products. One such imported piece is a small carved duck head from Roca Vecchia in Apulia, which may have been the knob on a pyxis lid. It was made of hippopotamus tooth, and the excavator is not certain if it was carved in the Aegean or further east, but in any case it was certainly imported as a finished piece.[60] Two carved pieces of elephant ivory, one with a horned protome and one a boar-shaped "belt hook," come from an MBA tomb at Trinitapoli, also in Apulia.[61] Aside from a few objects from Sicily and some knife handles, there are virtually no attestations of ivory in Italy in the RBA.[62] By the FBA, there is some evidence for ivory working on Italian soil, but the trade in ivory seems to have been unsystematic, with a range of raw materials (hippopotamus tooth, both Asian and African elephant tusk) arriving in both finished and unworked forms. Frattesina and Torre Mordillo show clear evidence of ivory working on site from the waste pieces found there.[63]

Almost all of the ivory objects found in Italy are unica, with the exception of some of the combs. In addition to ivory, the combs were also made of antler, bone, and bronze. Based on their form, it seems likely that their function was to tighten the weft while weaving, although many of the fancier combs were probably not ever meant to be used.[64] The combs

---

[59] Renfrew 1993: 12.
[60] Guglielmino 2005: 40–1.
[61] Tunzi Sisto 2005. The excavator thinks these were, in fact, locally made.
[62] Bettelli *et al.* 2006: 907–8.
[63] Arancio *et al.* 1995.
[64] Provenzano 1997: 534.

were decorated with incised geometric patterns or circles, and varied widely in form, making them difficult to organize into a classification scheme. Bignozzi's typology of seventy-six MBA antler/bone examples yielded nineteen types.[65] By the FBA, most combs are found in funerary contexts, but presumably the ones that were for daily use were made of a more perishable material, namely wood, and have not survived. Instead, what have come down to us in the archaeological record are pieces with a probable symbolic rather than functional significance.[66] Among the FBA examples, the combs known as the Frattesina type are a coherent group and constitute one of the classes of objects used in my study, turning up at five of the find spots.[67] The Frattesina-type combs have a flat handle of semicircular shape with a pierced extension at the top, and are decorated with small incised circles, either with or without concentric circles inside each. There is considerable variation in the exact shapes, in the number and placement of the circles, and in the length of the teeth. The examples from Frattesina itself, as well as the one from Torre Mordillo, are made of elephant ivory, whereas those from other sites are as yet untested but may be made of other materials. Formally the Frattesina-type comb is coherent despite this variability in material.

In the FBA, as the combs suggest, ivory working becomes closely tied to that of bone and antler: the materials seem to have been used interchangeably for the same objects, and it is probable that the same craftspeople were working with both materials.[68] Nonetheless, there are certain objects that were almost always made with antler. The northeastern portion of the Italian peninsula seems to have been home to a vibrant antler-working industry. Frattesina in particular has yielded plentiful evidence of deer antler working at the site; in addition to finished products, there were also thousands of raw and partly finished pieces and discards on the site.[69] I selected four distinctive antler object types on which there is enough information to group them

---

[65] Bignozzi 1988.
[66] Bettelli and Damiani 2005: 17–26.
[67] Bettelli *et al.* 2006. Whereas most examples of this type fall securely into the FBA, the one from the Terramara of Santa Rosa di Poviglio is from an RBA context and has been left out of my dataset.
[68] Bettelli *et al.* 2006: 908.
[69] Bellato and Bellintani 1975.

chronologically into either the RBA or the FBA. The awl handles with shaped heads (*manici di lesina con testa sagomata*),[70] the miniature decorated wheels,[71] and *zappette* (small hoes) date to the RBA.[72] The miniature spoked wheels span the RBA and FBA,[73] and I have dated them according to their find context. The wheels may have been the heads of bronze dress pins; they are extremely common on Terramare settlements, as are dress pins, discussed later.[74] The awl handles have a narrower chronological range than the wheels, although the two objects are found together at many sites. The handles' distribution is clustered largely in the "Terramare" region, but with a sizeable grouping along the northern Adriatic coast. The hoes and the small spoked wheels cluster in northeast Italy, with none found along the Tyrrhenian coast and a light scattering in the south.[75] These objects clearly constitute a local industry rather than an exotic import, but the standardized forms suggest a fairly limited number of production centers. The Terramare settlements excelled at worked antler and the decorated awl handles almost certainly originated there.[76] Regardless of their exact origin, the patterns of their circulation make these objects useful markers of regional interaction.

Glassy Materials

Glassy materials in Bronze Age Italy include glass itself, glassy faience, and faience. The term "faience" in the ancient world refers to a material made of ground quartz with a silica glaze creating a surface vitrification that does not penetrate to the interior, which retains its gritty crystalline structure. Glassy faience is the term used for material in which glass is present in equivalent amounts to crystalline inclusions, and there is no sharp distinction between surface vitrification and interior matrix; the color penetrates to the core and the whole is an undifferentiated

---

[70] Thirty-four find spots. Pasquini 2005: 987.
[71] Five find spots. Raposso and Ruggiero 1995.
[72] Twelve find spots. Pasquini 2005: 986. Provenzano 1997: fig. 296.5–7; fig. 295.12 and 13.
[73] Twenty-three RBA find spots, six FBA find spots. Pasquini 2005: 989–90.
[74] The miniature wheels are also known to exist in bronze, but without a complete catalog of them, I have left the bronze examples out of this study.
[75] Pasquini 2005: fig. 1.
[76] Provenzano 1997.

vitreous mass.[77] Faience beads are first known in northern Italy from the EBA, produced locally but using technology probably originating in the Danube region. The composition of these early beads resembles Slovakian production.[78] Glassy faience appears in Italy in the early part of the MBA, when it is found in both central Italy and the north, limited to a conical button form and with a composition of LMHK (Low Magnesium High Potassium) type, which is not known in the Aegean and is considered "European."[79] Even though the distribution range now includes central Italy, the total number of the buttons remains small, just a couple dozen.[80] This low number leads Bellintani and others to suggest that glass working was a craft that existed only as an offshoot of metallurgy, probably involving the same people.[81]

True glass beads make their first appearance in Italy in MBA 1–2, almost exclusively in the south, where their composition and associations with Aegean ceramic imports suggest an Aegean origin.[82] Thus, in MBA 1–2, there is a distinction between the central and northern portions of the peninsula, with its local production of glassy faience beads, and the south, where imported glass beads are prevalent. In MBA 3, in the south and on the islands, there is an expansion in number, variety, and distribution range of both glass and faience beads, with a slight dropping off in the subsequent RBA. In central and northern Italy, the numbers are smaller, but there is still an increase from the preceding periods. In the north, the beads are found in small groups at individual sites. The bulk of all the faience and glassy faience beads from the RBA period are Aegean in typology and composition, and were either imports – or in some cases, local imitations using the High Magnesium Glass composition, brown or blue (HMBG) in the Terramare and southern Veneto.[83] For example, two faience openwork beads from northern Italy are of a type found in large numbers in Greece and the eastern Mediterranean from the thirteenth century BC.[84] Beads of LMHK composition, which had prevailed in the MBA, were not produced in this period. The social

---

[77] Noble 1969: 435.
[78] Bellintani *et al.* 2006: 1496–8.
[79] Bellintani and Residori 2003: 492.
[80] Bellintani and Residori 2003: 486.
[81] Bellintani *et al.* 2006: 1501.
[82] Bellintani *et al.* 2006: 1501–3.
[83] Bellintani *et al.* 2006: 1518.
[84] Rahmstorf 2005.

Imports and Specialized Products in Italy

value of these beads seems to vary regionally in Italy. In Sicily and Apulia, large assemblages of dozens or even hundreds of beads are known from domestic and funerary contexts. In the north, the numbers are much smaller, and in at least one case seem to have been shared within a group: at the necropolis of Franzine Nuovo, nineteen beads were spread across various graves, with no grave containing more than four beads.[85] Bellintani and others see the arrival of imported glass beads in Apulia as linked to the market for Baltic amber, with the coastal groups in Apulia acting as intermediaries.[86] Two types of RBA glass beads are included in the current study: glass barrel beads with wavy lines and faience or glassy faience lenticular beads with radial incisions. In Italy, they come from five and four find spots respectively, all from northern Italy. There are comparanda of both types from the Aegean, but specific production centers are not known.[87]

The picture changes in the transition to the FBA in the north, where all the faience and glassy faience beads disappear, and the quantity of glass beads in Italy grows exponentially. Some 2,500 beads are known from Italy, the majority from the site of Frattesina, which was a production center.[88] Indeed, it is the only known production center of true glass in Europe in the Bronze Age.[89] These are high-quality glass beads of blue color primarily, of LMHK composition again. The two distinct types of glass beads to emerge in the FBA are the blue-barrel beads with white spirals and the glass-eye beads, both of which are included in this study. There are seven find spots of the former and four find spots of the latter. Besides being found in Italy, they are prominent north of the Alps, in Switzerland.[90] We would seem to be observing a shift from Aegean sources in the RBA to local production in the FBA.

Bronzes

The metal industry in Italy in the RBA and FBA shows ties to the rest of Europe and to the Aegean. The key objects of the bronze industry

---

[85] Bellintani *et al.* 2006: 1506.
[86] Bellintani *et al.* 2006: 1511–12.
[87] Bellintani and Residori 2003: 488.
[88] Bellintani and Residori 2003: 490.
[89] Angelini *et al.* 2004.
[90] Bellintani *et al.* 2006: 1513.

are swords, daggers, razors, axes, fibulae, dress pins, and knives. Several of these evolve stylistically in an unbroken fashion from the RBA to the FBA. Bronze objects show a radically different distribution pattern from the Mycenaean pottery. Few bronze pieces are found in the south, where the bulk of the Mycenaean ceramic material lies. Bronze objects are generally found inland whereas the Mycenaean ceramics are discovered in coastal areas. That they are not present at the same sites (the bronzes are found at cult sites, hoards, and cemeteries more frequently than at habitations, while for the pots, habitations and cemeteries are the most common find contexts) may be understandable because of very different use and discard practices, but one would expect some geographic overlap at least. These differences in distribution patterns are surprising given the presence of some of these bronzes in Aegean contexts. If the Aegean pots and Italian bronzes were two sides of the same exchange systems, then we might expect to find the remnants of both concentrated – or at least present – at the major sites, but this is hardly the case. This is further evidence that the exchange system was not a simple bilateral one. Typologies for the bronze object types have been developed over many decades, using dated parallels in Greece and Europe to date objects from hoards and grave assemblages in Italy. The main Italian FBA hoards include the Surbo group, Gualdo Tadino, Piano di Tallone, Mottola, and Coste del Marano hoards. Most of these hoards are thought to belong to founders because they are composed of broken pieces, bars, and ingots.[91]

In the RBA and FBA, northern Italy stands out for the quantity and diversity of the bronze objects found there, first in the Terramare and pile dwelling sites, and then, in the FBA, in the Veneto. South of the Po River, bronze finds are fairly limited before the Iron Age, although the numbers observed in the RBA and FBA represent a marked increase from the MBA. From each category of bronze object, there are several types whose distributions in the peninsula may usefully be treated as data for this study, based on quantity of find spots and secure dating. The work of Bianco Peroni and others in the relevant volumes of the *Prähistorische Bronzefunde* has been essential in the construction of the dataset.[92] The object types I have selected do not constitute a comprehensive list of all the objects

---

[91] Bietti Sestieri 1973: 385.
[92] E.g., Bianco Peroni 1976; 1979; 1994; von Eles Masi 1986; Lo Schiavo 2010.

circulating or even all the find spots of each type, but rather, these particular types benefit from both well-published find spots and sufficient numbers to be of use. The metal industry's character changes between the RBA and the FBA. In the RBA, also known as the Peschiera horizon after the northern site of Peschiera del Garda with its extensive bronze finds, production is centered in the north. Bronze objects cluster in the north and there are virtually no hoards in the south.[93] In the FBA, the Protovillanovan period, with the fall of the Terramare culture, production shifts more toward west-central Italy and the south. Bietti Sestieri sees "regional spheres of bronze production" in the FBA in Italy,[94] but the broadly similar forms across the peninsula point to interregional ties as well.

Knife

Six closely related knife types are included in this study, of which four are dated to the RBA, and the rest to the FBA 1–2. Based on their find contexts, knives seem to have been used at times as tools and at other times, as weapons.[95] The early ones may have been used for thrusting, such as a dagger, as much as for cutting, given the sharpened tip. Some are found as votive offerings on mountains or in rivers, which is typical of the handling of weapons. But large numbers also come from settlements, so they probably had a practical function as a tool, not just a weapon. Further, the knives turn up on some occasions, particularly in the south and a bit later but also in the RBA, in female graves and male graves without weapons, which further indicates a different function than weaponry. In the north the links with male graves containing other weapons are more consistent, but they nonetheless seem to have had multiple functions.[96]

Most knives are found in northern Italy in this period. Of the RBA types, the Baierdorf variety is known from four find spots,[97] Matrei A from seven,[98] and Montegiorgio from four.[99] The only RBA knife

---

[93] Bietti Sestieri 1973: 385.
[94] Bietti Sestieri 1973: 410.
[95] Bianco Peroni 1976: 97.
[96] Bianco Peroni 1976: 97–101.
[97] Bianco Peroni 1976: 13–14.
[98] Bianco Peroni 1976: 16–19.
[99] Bianco Peroni 1976: 12–13.

thought to originate in southern Italy is the Scoglio del Tonno type, found at four secure sites, three of which (including the type site) have also yielded Aegean pottery.[100] The FBA types are Fontanella (seven find spots)[101] and Matrei B (five find spots).[102] All the knives are flange-hilted, with holes of varying size and number along the center of the tang. The hilts end in open rings (Baierdorf; Matrei B, usually; Montegiorgio) or prongs (Scoglio del Tonno, Matrei A). The Montegiorgio type has a blade with an almost straight-cutting edge and a convex back. The other knife types are all carp's-tongue varieties, with the blade narrowing into a thin point.[103]

Daggers

Twelve dagger types are included in this study, all dating to the RBA. Some, such as the Bertarina dagger, may be dated more precisely to RBA 1 whereas the Torre Castelluccia dagger seems to belong to RBA 2.[104] However, for the most part, these chronological subdivisions are difficult to establish; therefore, throughout this study I use RBA more generally. The blades are all leaf-shaped with the exception of the Merlara dagger, whose blade is slightly concave below the hilt. They are distinguishable from each other by the treatment of the handle, either flange-hilted (Bertarina,[105] Gorzano,[106] Merlara,[107] Pertosa,[108] Tenno,[109] Toscanella[110]), with an ogival tang (Fornovo S. Giovanni,[111] Glisente Type B,[112] Monza,[113] Torre Castelluccia[114]), or a triangular

---

[100] Bianco Peroni 1976: 14–15.
[101] Bianco Peroni 1976: 19–20; De Marinis 1999: 532.
[102] Bianco Peroni 1976: 16–19.
[103] Bianco Peroni 1976: 14–15.
[104] Damiani 2010: 395–6.
[105] Twenty-three find spots. Bianco Peroni 1994: 157–61.
[106] Five find spots. Bianco Peroni 1994: 152–3.
[107] Fifteen find spots. Bianco Peroni 1994: 154–6.
[108] Fifteen find spots. Bianco Peroni 1994: 149–52.
[109] Five find spots. Bianco Peroni 1994: 156–7.
[110] Twenty find spots. Bianco Peroni 1994: 164–6.
[111] Bianco Peroni 1994: 120–1. Six find spots.
[112] Six find spots. Bianco Peroni 1994: 138–40.
[113] Four find spots. Bianco Peroni 1994: 132.
[114] Forty-three find spots. Bianco Peroni 1994: 122–30; Percossi *et al.* 2005: fig. 3.13; Sabbatini and Silvestrini 2005: fig. 4.3.

Imports and Specialized Products in Italy

tang (Redu[115]). Exceptional in this group is the Voghera dagger, with an openwork handle ending in a ring.[116] The flange-hilted varieties belong to the broader group commonly known as "Peschiera daggers." The most prevalent of the dagger types is the Torre Castelluccia dagger, found at forty sites. It is characterized by an ogival tang with a single hole through it and a lanceolate-shaped blade. This type's dense clustering in the north suggests a production center in that region, even if several examples made their way further south down the peninsula.[117] The fifteen known find spots of the Pertosa dagger span the Italian peninsula, and the fact that the majority come from the center and south of the peninsula has led Bianco Peroni to suggest a production center in that region.[118]

Razors

The only razor included in this study is the Scoglio del Tonno razor, characterized by a blade with a concave edge and a large aperture in the center.[119] It has been found at ten secure find spots and dates to the RBA. Aside from the type site, it has been found exclusively in the north, as indeed are most of the razors of all varieties in this period.[120] They were presumably made in the north, therefore.

Fibulae

Nine types of fibula are included in the study, of which two are from the RBA and seven are from the FBA. The twisted violin-bow fibula of the RBA, found at fifteen find spots, is one of the earliest of the violin bow fibulae. This fibula takes the characteristic form of its class, with the bow running parallel to the pin in the manner of a safety pin, or

---

[115] Seventeen find spots. Bianco Peroni 1994: 143–5.
[116] Eight find spots. Bianco Peroni 1994: 170–1.
[117] Bianco Peroni 1994: 122–4. This type is subdivided into three varieties: A, B, and C, but the differences are minor and not chronological, so I have grouped them together here. Variety A has a more marked shoulder than B and C, and is the one with find contexts outside the Po Valley.
[118] Bianco Peroni 1994: 152.
[119] The more famous Pertosa-type razor was excluded because it spans the RBA and early FBA (Bianco Peroni 1979: 12–14).
[120] Bianco Peroni 1979: 9–11.

more precisely, resembling the object that gives it its name. On the twisted violin-bow variety, the bow wire is twisted to varying degrees of tightness. It has a flattened pin rest and a spring composed of one revolution of the wire to provide the tension. It is found primarily in northern Italy at Terramare sites, but a few are located further south. In addition to the examples from Italy, several are known from sites in Greece, including Mycenae, Korakou, and Sparta.[121] Also from the RBA is the violin bow fibula with two knobs, found at four sites in central and southern Italy, in addition to examples from Lipari.[122] Of the varieties of violin bow fibulae dating to the FBA, their appearance can be gathered from their names: the asymmetrical violin-bow fibula with two knobs,[123] the Frattesina-type asymmetrical violin-bow fibula,[124] the leaf-shaped violin-bow fibula,[125] and the twisted asymmetrical violin-bow fibula.[126] In the case of the fibulae with knobs, the bow wire thickens to form a knob at each end, one just before the pin rest and one just before the spring. On the leaf-shaped fibulae, the bow wire is flattened and widened into a leaf shape, and the flattened surface is decorated either with bosses or geometric incisions. Three of the fibulae in the study are arch fibulae, in which the bow forms a semicircle above the pin. The Castellace arch fibula, from seven find spots, has a bow that is slightly squashed in the central part, sometimes oval or square in section, and decorated with incised lines as the arch descends toward the spring and the pin rest.[127] The Gargano- and Timmari-type arch fibulae are very large, with the Timmari type in particular ranging from 13–23 cm in length. The types are very similar and Bietti Sestieri combines them into a single category of arch fibulae.[128] Both types are decorated with incised lines such as

---

[121] Von Eles Masi 1986: 2–4; Lo Schiavo 2010: 85–6.

[122] Lo Schiavo 2010: 87.

[123] Six find spots. These can be with or without incised decoration on the bow. Von Eles Masi 1986: 11–12; Lo Schiavo 2010: 89–90.

[124] Five find spots, primarily in the northeast. Von Eles Masi 1986: 5.

[125] Five find spots, all in central and southern Italy; incised and impressed decoration on the flattened bow. Lo Schiavo 2010: 91.

[126] Seven find spots. This type combines von Eles Masi's two types: the fibula ad arco di violino asimmetrico ritorto tipo Boccatura del Mincio and the fibula ad arco di violino asimmetrico alto ritorto tipo Frattesina, as the two differ very little. On the Frattesina variety, the arch is slightly higher than that of the Boccatura del Mincio type. Von Eles Masi 1986: 5–7.

[127] Lo Schiavo 2010: 99–101.

[128] Bietti Sestieri 1998: 24.

Imports and Specialized Products in Italy

zigzags or herringbone patterns, with the Timmari type, in particular, fully covered in such designs. On both types, in the place where knobs are located on some varieties of violin-bow fibulae, there are groups of two or three raised rings, usually closely spaced. The find spots of the three arch types are all in the southern part of the peninsula.[129]

Swords

Seven sword types are in this study, five from the RBA and two from the FBA.[130] Of the RBA types, the Cetona and Montegiorgio types are variants of the Naue II flange-hilted sword, a cutting sword widely distributed through Europe and the Mediterranean. The Cetona type has four holes in the hilt and two or three on each shoulder of the blade. The eight peninsular find spots include deposits in water, in a mortuary assemblage in a cave, and on a mountain peak. These swords are distributed inland down the Apennines as far as Abruzzo.[131] The Montegiorgio sword blade is much narrower than its semicircular shoulders, and the hilt has either one or no hole, except along the shoulders themselves, where several holes are found. The nine examples from secure contexts have been found in ritual contexts, including two securely in watery deposits, one in a funerary context, and one on a mountain. Bianco Peroni suspects that others from the Veneto region whose provenance is not known were probably found in watery contexts as well, although their find information has been lost. The type spread throughout peninsular Italy.[132]

Another class of RBA swords is the tanged swords. Of these, the Arco,[133] Monza,[134] and Terontola[135] types are included in this study. The Monza sword's blade is long and thin with narrow shoulders. The tang flares out briefly above the shoulders and then narrows, ending in a point. These are found exclusively in the subalpine northwest zone. The Arco and Terontola swords' tangs both thicken at their terminals, and

---

[129] Gargano: four find spots. Timmari: five find spots. Lo Schiavo 2010: 101–3.

[130] The well-known Pertosa sword is not included here as it covers too broad a chronological range, spanning the end of the MBA and the RBA (Bianco Peroni 1970: 23–7).

[131] Bianco Peroni 1970: 63–5.

[132] Bianco Peroni 1970: 57–61.

[133] Five find spots. Bianco Peroni 1970: 33–4; Pellegrini 1993: 79.

[134] Five find spots. Bianco Peroni 1970: 30–3.

[135] Seven find spots. Bianco Peroni 1970: 35–7.

the blades are short and wide. The main difference between the two types is that the Arco sword's shoulders have two holes and the Terontola type does not. Both types are mostly found in the north.

The two FBA sword types in this study, Allerona[136] and Frassineto,[137] are both flange hilted. The Allerona sword is an Italian variant of the Letten type from central Europe.[138] Its distinctive feature is a rectangular extension at the end of the hilt, between the two prongs. There are one or two holes on each shoulder and one or two more on the main part of the hilt. Like the Cetona sword, the four known examples come from the central Apennines. The Frassineto type's blade is relatively short, and the prongs at the hilt terminal are generally well defined. The shoulders have two or three holes, as does the hilt itself. This smaller and more lightweight sword must have been much easier to wield in combat, and constitutes an innovation. Three of its four find contexts are watery deposits.[139]

These swords in their distribution do not conform to the regional clusters of the other artifacts considered here. Rather, they are scattered, separated by considerable distances. This, together with the often apparently ritual nature of their deposition, suggests a very different disposal pattern than observed with the other objects. To put this in concrete terms, more than 35 percent of sword find spots are secure ritual deposits, while ritual deposits make up less than 10 percent of all the find spots in the study. Rarely do the swords turn up in graves, and never on settlements. This variability suggests a counterpoint to the regionalism of many of the other objects' distributions. The swords seem to have been transported long distances and then deposited in what may have been pan-regional cult sites. Such cult sites may have aided communication between disparate groups.

Dress Pins

Bronze dress pins, consisting of one long (c. 7–20 cm) rod with no pin rest and a distinctive head, are among the most common personal ornaments found in Italy from the RBA and FBA. They are thought to have been

---

[136] Five find spots. Bianco Peroni 1970: 67–71; de Marinis 1999: 532.
[137] Bianco Peroni 1970: 64–7.
[138] Bianco Peroni 1970: 71.
[139] Bianco Peroni 1970: 64–7.

Imports and Specialized Products in Italy

affixed to clothing in various ways or, less commonly, used as hair pins. As a class of object they do not seem to have been reserved exclusively for either men's or women's clothing, although some cemeteries show apparent gender differentiation in their distribution.[140] Nine dress-pin types are included in this study, eight from the RBA and one dating to the FBA. Of the RBA types, the Bacino Marina,[141] Garda,[142] Peschiera[143] and Santa Caterina[144] types all present variations on a decorative theme of folding the wire in the upper part of the rod and spiraling it to form the terminal, and belong to a class that Carancini in his typology has labeled *spilloni a spirale*. These types are most common in the north, very often from settlements, but some examples do find their way to central and southern Italy. The Guado di Gugnano[145] and Boccatura del Mincio[146] types both have enlarged biconical heads, but differ in that the Boccatura del Mincio rod is perforated just below the head, and the Guado di Gugnano type is perforated farther down the rod at a point where the rod thickens, with incised decorations in that zone. The Guado di Gugnano type is also much bigger. The Cataragna type resembles the Boccatura del Mincio closely in its small size and perforation just below the head, but the head is globular instead of biconical. It is found almost exclusively in the north, with twenty-six examples from Peschiera del Garda alone.[147] The Capocchia a Papavero dress pins are small, with a straight plain rod and a head in the shape of a poppy, with some incised decoration on it. They are also only found in the north, from five find spots.[148] The only FBA type included in this study, the Torri d'Arcugnano type, is found in the northern and central parts of the peninsula. It has a biconical head of varying size and sometimes some incised lines encircling the upper part of the rod, but is otherwise quite plain.[149]

---

[140] Carancini 1975: 379–81.
[141] Nine find spots. Carancini 1975: 126–8.
[142] Five find spots. Carancini 1975: 129–30.
[143] Eight find spots. Carancini 1975: 130–33.
[144] Nine find spots. Carancini 1975: 122–6.
[145] Eleven find spots. Carancini 1975: 172–3.
[146] Five find spots. Carancini 1975: 176–8.
[147] Eight find spots. Carancini 1975: 179–80. Moscosi di Cingoli is the only find spot outside of the far north (Sabbatini and Silvestrini 2005: fig. 4:9 and 13).
[148] Carancini 1975: 236–7.
[149] Fifteen find spots. Carancini 1975: 226–7.

Axes

The absence of a comprehensive catalog of the Bronze Age Italian axes has prevented the inclusion of many of these objects in this study.[150] Nonetheless, we will work with what we have. Four axe types are included in the study, all from the FBA. The Pertosa,[151] Ponte San Giovanni,[152] and Casalecchio[153] types are all winged axes, differing in the shape of the wings and the concavity of the blade. The Menaforno axe is a shaft-hole type found at five sites, all in the central Apennines.[154] The Pertosa type is found all over the peninsula, but with a predominance in the central zone, and the Ponte San Giovanni and Casalecchio types are similarly dispersed. The function of axes is determined by their orientation on the handle. Those attached parallel to the handle may have been weapons, whereas those attached perpendicularly to the handle could have been weapons also, but may have been for chopping wood instead.[155] In the absence of preserved wooden handles, the shape of the axe head and the location of its shaft hole, if present, can allow inferences about its original position. Finds' contexts of axes provide further information: those found in graves, often in male graves with objects that are clearly weapons, were probably weapons. Thus, one of the find spots of the Menaforno type is a grave containing two knives and an Allerona sword, which by association suggests the axe was used as a weapon. All the other examples were found in hoards, rendering their function indeterminate.

Socketed Shovels

Socketed shovels are a feature of Italian hoards of the FBA. The shovels group into two main types, the Fondo Paviani type[156] and the "Tra Manciano e Samprugnano" (TMES) type,[157] both of which are included

---

[150] The second volume of Carancini's catalog of axes in Italy is eagerly awaited. The first volume, although entitled *Le asce nell'Italia continentale II* because it covers the later axes, appeared in 1984 and Volume I has not appeared yet.
[151] Sixteen find spots. Bietti Sestieri 1973: 399.
[152] Seven find spots. Bietti Sestieri 1973: 399.
[153] Five find spots. Bietti Sestieri 1973: 399.
[154] Carancini 1984: 199–200.
[155] Carancini 1984: 236.
[156] Four find spots; Bellintani and Stefan 2008: 11.
[157] Nine find spots; Bellintani and Stefan 2008: 11–12.

Imports and Specialized Products in Italy

in this study. The former is thought to be slightly earlier than the latter, although they are found at some of the same sites. The two types differ in the relative width of the shoulders: the Fondo Paviani type is narrow shouldered and the TMES type is wide shouldered. Both may have been produced at Frattesina. The TMES type is often found in hoards with pick ingots, discussed later in this chapter. The function of these socketed shovels is uncertain. The wear on the blade strongly suggests they were not simply ingots, but did have a purpose as a tool. Some have suggested they were used as chisels, or scrapers, or some generic cutting tool, or as agricultural implements. Because they are often found in hoards with metallurgical tools, one theory is they are somehow used in metallurgy.[158]

Pick Ingots

One bronze object type included in this study, the pick ingot, falls outside the standard group of finished objects. This ingot (*pane a piccone* in Italian) is present in a number of hoards dating to the FBA, and has been found in seven secure find spots. The pick ingots are in the shape of pick-axe heads, but differ from the actual tools by the rough surface on one side because they were made in an open mold, and a rough percussive edge not sharpened for working. Sometimes the central shaft hole is missing. When a hole was present, if it was not intended for a handle – as would be the case for an actual pick – it may have helped in the extraction of the ingot from the mold. The pick ingots span the entire FBA, according to Pellegrini.[159] They are found in France, Switzerland, and the Balkans, and the variations in mineral make up, with the percentages of tin deviating widely, point to multiple production centers.[160] Pellegrini thinks the form originated in the Alpine region and then spread out, probably by means of trade routes down the Adriatic and eventually on to Greece.[161] The Italian examples' find spots are in the northern and central parts of the peninsula.

---

[158] Bellintani and Stefan 2008: 5.
[159] Pellegrini 1989: 590–1.
[160] Pearce 2000: 113.
[161] Pellegrini 1989: 593.

Donkeys

Finally, the early introduction of the donkey may be understood as a technological innovation of sorts whose distribution can be mapped in the manner of any other object. Donkey bones are known from one site in the RBA and eight sites in the peninsula in the FBA. Donkeys are excellent pack animals, and as such would have facilitated overland exchanges between regions of Italy; indeed, Brodie has argued for the Aegean that donkeys made possible long-distance overland bulk transport for the first time.[162] Although the extent of the donkey's early exploitation in Italy is unknown, it certainly had the potential to make a major impact.

The wild ass had probably first been domesticated by the fourth millennium BC in Egypt and western Asia, spreading to the Aegean by the third millennium BC.[163] The earliest context for domesticated donkey in Italy is in RBA strata at Coppa Nevigata, in Apulia, where molars were retrieved.[164] Subsequently, several FBA sites including Luni sul Mignone in central Italy and Frattesina in the north have yielded donkey remains.[165] De Grossi Mazzorin attributes the donkey's introduction to contacts with the eastern Mediterranean, noting the absence of early donkey remains from northern Italy – with the exception of Frattesina, famous for its eastern Mediterranean contacts. As Renfrew has noted, the introduction of a new technology or product can happen long before it is actually adopted, and it is the latter moment, rather than the introduction itself, that is of greater significance.[166] With scant traces of the donkey in the RBA and FBA in Italy, the donkey's impact had yet to be felt in these periods, so is better treated as an exotic artifact than a change in practices. This distribution of early donkey remains is limited, but does suggest a pattern of south-to-north spread, with the earliest reaching southern Italy before spreading north. This contrasts with the arrival of the horse, which spread from north to south.[167] In fact, the largest cluster of sites yielding donkey remains is in west-central Italy,

---

[162] Brodie 2008.
[163] Sherratt 1983: 96; Clutton Brock 1992: 65.
[164] Bokonyi and Siracusa 1987: 207.
[165] De Grossi Mazzorin 1998: 174. Cf. Tagliacozzo 1994: 620–1.
[166] Renfrew 1978: 90.
[167] De Grossi Mazzorin 1998: 174.

an area with relatively little evidence of East Mediterranean contacts in this period. More studies of faunal remains from Italian sites of the RBA and FBA will hopefully clarify the picture, but in the meantime, the donkey find spots may be incorporated into the peninsular networks here.

Reconstructing Patterns of Interaction from Traceable Objects

Interactions between sites involve some combination of the movements of goods, peoples, and ideas. Of these three, the movement of goods receives the most attention from archaeologists, but on occasion, communication may have been the perceived goal, more so than profit derived from commerce.[168] Luckily for archaeologists, at least some exchange of material objects is the norm in interactions between groups that lack the shared structure offered by say, monetary systems.[169] Therefore, it is not unreasonable to expect a material residue of interactions between regions, and this is what archaeologists count on. As Upham notes, "The appearance of nonlocal commodities and their incorporation into local material assemblages is probably only the most visible (and maybe least important!) aspect of [the linkage of groups]."[170] An absence of a single recognizable import from Region A to Region B and vice versa does not preclude the possibility of interaction between A and B altogether, but it makes it extremely difficult to argue for such contacts. Of course, the presence of an import is not *sufficient* to prove direct interaction between Regions A and B, but such an import is virtually necessary.

In regions where, as mentioned earlier, interactions are to be expected, the mere presence and absence of imported objects is of limited interest. Instead, scholars wish to characterize those interactions, whether in terms of their nature, their scale (that is, degree of intensity), and their impact or significance. In prehistoric contexts there is no way to determine the particular combination of the material and immaterial bundled into each interaction. These bundles may fall anywhere between the two extremes Renfrew describes – "exchange of goods without a

---

[168] Renfrew 1993.
[169] Renfrew 1975: 6–7.
[170] Upham 1992: 150.

wide range of accompanying information, and exchange of information without goods"[171] – although as mentioned earlier, we can usually expect some materials to change hands in ancient societies. Further, the myriad problems in archaeological recovery mean that what is found cannot be treated with confidence as a direct measure of what was originally imported.[172] Therefore, the quantity of material objects that were retrieved signals one unknown portion of the total interaction, and as prehistoric archaeologists can only get at the interactions that leave behind material traces, we may underestimate the extent of other, more ephemeral encounters – or miss them altogether.

Given the problems inherent in relying solely on identifiable imports, is it possible to use other evidence for interactions instead? Attempts have been made to quantify interaction intensity in other ways besides imports. Plog's study of the frequencies of shared design elements in neighboring Olmec communities' pottery is one such example;[173] Kristiansen and Larsson's study of Bronze Age Europe is another example, with immediate relevance to the current study. In it, the authors attempt to move beyond the limitations of the material evidence to argue that in the Bronze Age, ideas, technologies, and raw materials flowed between northern Europe and the Aegean and the East Mediterranean rather than finished goods.[174] Therefore, the evidence for Kristiansen and Larsson's deeply connected Bronze Age world is not the expected imports, of which there are very few. They emphasize ideas and raw materials changing hands rather than a high volume of finished products being moved. Indeed, they critique Harding's downplaying of the Mycenaean influence on Europe,[175] saying he gives too much attention to finding identifiable imports when loose local imitations inspired by the foreign objects are more indicative of profound influences.[176] Similarly, Cazzella has used resemblances in design elements on various objects in the Aegean and central Mediterranean to argue for contacts between those areas from the third millennium BC, in spite of an absence

---

[171] Renfrew 1975: 6.
[172] Renfrew 1975: 40–1.
[173] Plog 1976.
[174] Kristiansen and Larsson 2005.
[175] Harding 1984.
[176] Kristiansen and Larsson 2005: 16–9.

of identifiable imports in that period.[177] Although the purposeful copying of foreign objects and their appropriation into a local culture are undeniably important, it seems improbable that this could happen in the absence of actual imports as models. Kristiansen and Larsson employ the sequence "transmission, transformation, and institutionalization" to model the mechanisms of diffusion, but without evidence of direct transmissions, the model remains contentious.[178] The shared symbols that Kristiansen and Larsson identify are those of the elites, as they themselves observe,[179] so there is no way to know to what extent these symbols resonated with the majority of the population. We must therefore continue to rely on the imports themselves to gauge the nature, intensity, and impact of interactions, bearing in mind all the while the limitations of the empirical evidence. What is different in my study is that, based on the premise that Bronze Age trade – even when involving goods from long distances – was inherently local in its structure; the interactions being revealed are primarily at the regional level, not the interregional one. The theoretical position underpinning this approach will be examined in Chapter 3.

---

[177] Cazzella 1999.
[178] Kristiansen and Larsson 2005: 27; see Nordquist and Whittaker 2007 and Kristiansen and Larsson 2007.
[179] Kristiansen and Larsson 2005: 126.

CHAPTER THREE

GROUP IDENTITY IN PREHISTORY: THEORY, INTERACTIONS, AND SOCIAL NETWORKS

> Se, come riteniamo, nella distribuzione e circolazione dei beni,... è da riconoscere uno dei meccanismi fondamentali della formazione di aggregazioni culturali, nel cambio ci si dovrebbe andare a guadagnare.[1]

In her study of the Samnites, Emma Dench emphasizes what could be called the use-value of ethnic groups. She rejects explanations for ethnic behavior based on origins, seeing the groups as tactical constructions. Her approach to ethnicity is an instrumentalist one in which ethnic groups do not constitute innate phenomena, but rather are artificial creations that serve practical purposes.[2] This approach is demonstrably more accurate than primordialist accounts that naturalize particular group origins, but from a comparative perspective, instrumentalism alone does not explain why some groups succeed at stable identity construction and some do not. A piece of the puzzle is missing, and that piece is interaction. I argue that habits of interactions preceding the formation of self-aware territorial groups constitute a core around which the groups can form. These habitual interactions first occur before the groups' self-definitions have crystallized, and the nature of those networks of interactions will structure the character of the ethnic groups

---

[1] Peroni *et al.* 1980: 12 (my translation): "If the distribution and circulation of goods is recognized as one of the fundamental mechanisms for the formation of cultural groups, we should be looking at exchange."
[2] Dench 1995.

that follow. In what amounts to path dependence – that is, the process by which preexisting behavioral patterns will shape subsequent actions – the peoples are constrained from total reinvention by the networks already in place. In other words, without a strong preexisting network, it will be very difficult to form a cohesive group. In this chapter I examine the relationship between regionalism and social networks more carefully, and consider the applicability of the methods of social network analysis to problems of identifying and assessing prehistoric groups materially. Because ethnicity is such a tinderbox of a concept, and entails too categorical a distinction between groups that are, in practice, spread along a continuous scale of cohesion anyway, I will be circumspect in my use of the term in early Italy. The analysis of the groups is more usefully framed in terms of the degree of success in maintaining their territorial integrity and in garnering external recognition. Neutral terms, it is hoped, will prevent the analysis from being sidetracked into tangential wrangling over names. Nonetheless, it is true that ethnicity's conceptual power has engaged some scholars such that the best theoretical discussions of collective identity and archaeology have focused on ethnic groups. For that reason I will treat ethnicity explicitly in the next section, as a means of examining the archaeological correlates of collective identities more generally.

Problems with Ethnicity in Archaeology

Archaeologists have a tough time with ethnicity, and there are few scholars who would suggest we can access ethnicity through archaeological remains alone. Jonathan Hall takes a pessimistic view of the possibility of detecting ethnicity from the archaeological record.[3] Drawing on ethnographic examples, he emphasizes that an isomorphic relationship between bounded material-culture assemblages and ethnic groups is far from a given, and that the mobilization of material culture in strategies of ethnic expression may stop and start over time. This makes it difficult for archaeologists to know if changes in material-culture patterning denote changes in social boundaries or are simply changed expressions of otherwise established groups. Some identity emblems

---

[3] Hall 1997.

and shared practices may be adopted beyond the group, and it is not always clear which emblems and practices are group specific. Further, the artifacts themselves are complex entities. Gosselain's ethnographic work on sub-Saharan pottery technologies has shown that each pot is the product of the choices made at each stage of the *chaîne opératoire*: "technical traditions may incorporate elements of multiple origins, as some are transmitted between people who belong to the same social group, whereas others are borrowed from people belonging to other groups. This articulation constitutes the core of any cultural construct and explains why such constructs are, like identity, heterogeneous and profoundly dynamic phenomena."[4] This renders the job of linking pots to people even more complicated. Hall in his book on ethnicity winds up by stating that "[t]he obvious conclusion to be drawn – unpalatable perhaps to some – is that the entire enterprise [of identifying ethnic groups] has little chances of success in situations where the only evidence to hand is archaeological."[5] From Hall's perspective, the emergence of differentiated material culture in the regions where we know later there were ethnic groups need not constitute the moment of ethnogenesis. Instead, the changed material culture may signify some other behavioral shift, one that is occurring within a group that has long since been ethnically defined, or has not developed an ethnic consciousness.

Other approaches have emphasized common practices rather than objects as indices of early ethnicities. Kamp and Yoffee suggested that we approach ethnicity through particular behaviors instead of material-culture distributions.[6] Similarly, for Jones, ethnicity emerges from shared dispositions and practices (Bourdieu's *habitus*) that give authenticity and credibility to the tactical stress placed on ethnic belonging.[7] Her framework is meant to bridge the primordialist/instrumentalist divide and open up a way for archaeologists to use material culture to approach ethnicity. Morgan also advocates identifying norms of conduct.[8] Practices and norms may get us closer to group identity than objects can, but they are also difficult to spot and interpret archaeologically. This leaves archaeologists working without textual evidence in a

---

[4] Gosselain 2000: 209.
[5] Hall 1997: 142.
[6] Kamp and Yoffee 1980: 226.
[7] Jones 1997: 128.
[8] Morgan 2001.

bit of a bind. As Whittaker has baldly stated, "Archaeology cannot dig up ethnicity and it is time the debate shifted to the domain of social history."[9] If we accept that self-ascription is a necessary criterion for ethnicity, one that differentiates it from looser forms of cultural or regional groupings, then we can only find ethnic groups in historical periods when their names become known.

The decision to look no earlier than the Archaic period for Italy's ethnic groups may be justified on more than simple empirical grounds. For some scholars, ethnicity is no more than a product of state control. From this perspective, as de Heusch notes for African ethnic groups, "[t]he *ethnie* X or Y would merely designate an administrative fiction, that is to say an arbitrary and static mode of division designed by colonial bureaucracy for political purposes to check populations in perpetual formation."[10] If the groups in question eventually internalized that externally imposed ethnic identity, it could be understood as an epiphenomenon of the condition of colonial exploitation. Whittaker argues as much for the hundreds of indigenous tribes of North Africa in the Roman period. Smith's work offers some nuance to this categorical rejection of ethnicity as a valid concept. He distinguishes between ethnic communities and ethnic categories, noting that the latter can exist without the former, and the two together emerge only in conditions of outside stimulus. I quote the relevant passage at length:

> [The ethnic community] is itself a development out of the global phenomenon of the ethnic category. We start from a world divided into ethnic categories, that is, cultural units of population with some sense of kinship or ancestry, some common dialects and deities, but little collective self-awareness, few shared memories, and no common name or territory or solidarity. Only travelers, missionaries and scholars may note their close affinity, and perhaps by their activities help to weld them together, as did the missionary pastors of Bremen who reduced the Ewe dialects to a common Anlo script, or the native missionaries among the Yoruba tribes whose cultural work helped to unify them in the mid-nineteenth century (Welch 1966; Peel 1989). From these categories certain processes of ethno-genesis give rise to fully formed ethnic communities, or what the French term *ethnies*, which we may define as named human populations with shared ancestry myths, historical

---

[9] Whittaker 2009: 202.
[10] Heusch 2000: 99.

memories and common cultural traits, associated with a homeland and having a sense of solidarity, at least among the elites.[11]

This notion of a two-stage process – one that, rather than Jones's recursive mutual influence from practice to identity and back, begins with a loose set of shared actions and only then moves to self-conscious identification under particular political conditions – has more rigor in its clear testability. From this perspective, the peoples that we first recognize in Italy in the mid-first millennium BC with their languages, origin myths, cultures, and territories, probably emerged, in some cases quite rapidly, upon contact with the Greeks and prior to their arrival were simply the regional groups that Smith would call ethnic categories. Whether one calls the historical period groups "ethnic" or not, Smith's process is valuable in that it provides a theoretical framework for tracking a group from prehistory to history. This long time depth is important. Morgan urges us "to re-examine past assumptions about the complex of relations from which individual communities were constituted."[12] Even if one takes the instrumentalist view of ethnicity of Barth, Patterson, and others,[13] an ethnicity cannot be fabricated out of nothing; it is a new iteration of an earlier, weaker grouping, often locality based. The question becomes, then, what kinds of regional groups succeed at becoming ethnic groups?

Moreover, knowing the end result – a named group – and then looking earlier allows us to introduce a predictive element and seek the factors that made some groups emerge at different moments from others. As noted in Chapter 1, the Bronze and Iron Ages have so far provided, at best, limited traces of regionally inflected material culture, itself not easily translatable to actual groups. At first glance, Smith's two-stage process would seem to underline the importance of the Greek colonists even further and reduce the region's earlier history to a nebulous stasis. But in fact, even if the historical peoples are in many cases unrecognizable in the earlier periods, as we shall see there are changes afoot in the Bronze Age nonetheless. The Final Bronze Age is when the first examples of Smith's ethnic categories emerge, in the spatial forms that would in

---

[11] Smith 1999: 105.
[12] Morgan 2009: 25.
[13] Barth 1969; Patterson 1975.

some cases last a thousand years. We therefore must begin the stories of the named peoples earlier if their later history is to be fully understood.

An Interactionist Theory of Group Identity

The challenge, then, is to detect those early regional groupings and determine their character. A prerequisite of a regional group – indeed, of most social groups – is communication between members. Rather than seeking material emblems of a regional identity, or traces of shared practices, what about seeking material traces of that communication? Communication between group members is a form of interaction. We may expect that members of a group will interact more often with other members of their group than with people external to their group. In fact, there is plenty of research in social psychology confirming this, and this is the principle on which community structure and community detection are based.[14] Interactions between members of a group may take any number of forms, from face-to-face visits to exchanges of gifts to business transactions to acts of domination and violence, but the important thing is that they occur. Each interaction constitutes a tie between two members of a group. The collected interactions or relations between members of the group form a structure or network tying people together.

Most, indeed almost all, interactions in the distant past are lost to us. But some interactions may leave traces in the archaeological record. Those interactions involving the circulation of artifacts may be traceable. In fact, many of the material-object distributions that we interpret in terms of expressions of affinity or social status or economy may be reconceived as evidence of interactions. From a single artifact at a site, it may be difficult to determine a link to another site. However, if two sites have examples of the same type of object, in some cases it may be possible to use this as evidence of communication between the two sites. How so? In Bronze Age Italy, where long-distance trade was limited, nonlocal objects would have circulated along local exchange routes. One may expect the co-presence of identical rare objects at nearby sites

---

[14] Girvan and Newman 2002. Cf. Webb 1982 as an example of the benefits to the group derived from positive interaction.

to be far from coincidental. Obtaining a distinctive object would have been a source of interest, and the presence at both sites suggests enough communication for the knowledge of the object's presence to travel. In other words, someone at each site would have known that the other had obtained the same object, and this may have influenced the decision to obtain one as well. The exact circumstances of the co-occurrence of objects are impossible to reconstruct, but likely scenarios include a single trader moving from site to site with a set of goods obtained farther afield, or people from site A giving a matching object to people from site B and keeping one for themselves. There are myriad other possibilities for how two objects of the same type should end up near each other. Rather than being exchanged, the objects may have been subject to display, or may have served as symbols mediating relations between individuals and groups, or even individuals and other material objects. In any case, given how small scale the movements of goods were and how rare and distinctive these objects must have been, in all cases we can postulate some mutual knowledge and thus some level of interaction. Regardless of the mechanism by which the goods moved around in a particular area – one person going from settlement to settlement, or redistribution mechanisms, or formalized exchanges between settlements – the co-presence of matching objects must have entailed mutual awareness and most likely direct contact. These intrusive objects, even if not always of high value, were novel enough that their dissemination in a small-scale society such as this would not have gone overlooked. There is some precedent for this assumption: Coward, in her study of interactions between sites in the Epipaleolithic and Early Neolithic Near East, used the co-occurrence of material culture in sites with contemporary stratigraphic contexts as "a material reflection of some sort of social relationship (in its widest sense) between those sites."[15] We can infer similarly here.

Given the embedded nature of ancient trade, these local exchanges may be understood as the most visible measure of interactions of all kinds that have left no archaeological trace. On a macroscale, adding up all the paired sites results in a network of interactions. We can posit that in areas where material exchanges were concentrated, interactions of other kinds were also concentrated. Again following the principle of

[15] Coward 2010: 464.

in-group behavior, concentrated interactions occur within groups, so we can detect groups in these interaction clusters. Of course, people will interact with others from different groups in all sorts of ways, and to varying degrees. Indeed, these out-group contacts are essential, not just because groups are rarely entirely self-sufficient, but in order to avert intergroup conflict.[16] Nevertheless, one would expect fewer material objects in common between groups than within them. Thus, one method for spotting regional groupings in the archaeological record is to look at the clustered distributions of distinctive categories of material culture.

The theory that the distributions of distinctive objects are material traces of past interactions – in this case, intense regional interactions – is premised upon a particular understanding of Bronze Age trade. By the looks of it, trade, although on the rise from the MBA on, was nonetheless limited in Italy in the RBA and FBA. Before the donkey took hold as a standard pack animal, overland travel would have been slow and laborious; as a trader or smith, there would have been little impetus to traverse the entire peninsula when one could off-load one's wares in just one area. We can see this in the progressive decline in bronze objects originating in the north as one heads south down the peninsula.[17] For goods coming by sea, given the linguistic and cultural hurdles to traveling around the peninsula, one must expect that maritime traders would stick to the coastal areas. The fall-off in quantities of imports toward the southern interior despite the existence of several "emporia" sites along the southern coasts with large numbers of imports would seem to confirm this picture.[18] Further north, goods do reach the interior, but as we shall see in the following chapter, by the FBA at least the exotica are found in clusters. In 1981, Negroni Catacchio suggested that interactions and exchanges in the FBA may have occurred in the context of feasts where groups from neighboring villages would congregate.[19] Out of these gatherings a sense of regional identity emerged. She sought the origins of political complexity in these gatherings, noting that the intercommunity festivals would require coordination beyond the village

---

[16] Nelson 1989.
[17] See distribution maps in Bianco Peroni 1970.
[18] Vagnetti 1999b: Map B. In fact, even the locally made Italo-Mycenaean wares do not penetrate the interior (Levi, Sonnino, and Jones 2006: 1095–7).
[19] Negroni Catacchio 1981: 144–5.

level. I am not convinced of that, but her point about these hypothesized festivals as the mechanism for the exchange of exotica between nearby communities is compelling, if unprovable.

This picture of limited and highly localized trading patterns in the Bronze Age is not peculiar to Italy. A good analogy may be the Aegean in the Early Bronze Age, when exchange was ramping up but had not reached the scale and complexity that it would in the Late Bronze Age. Thus, Dickinson in his description of Aegean trade in the Early Bronze Age notes that "exchange... still seems rather haphazard, disorganised and small-scale, probably linking individual communities rather than whole regions."[20] This is not to say that goods did not travel long distances in Greece, but rather that proximity was a critical feature of most of the exchanges. Dickinson argues in the Aegean case for "the existence of local networks linking the central mainland to remoter parts."[21] The same could be said for Italy. If no long-distance traders, whether by land or by sea, were covering all of the peninsula's interior, then when goods are found at sites near each other we can hypothesize that they arrived there by local hands. Usually nonlocal objects are used by scholars to make claims about interregional interactions,[22] but given this picture of Bronze Age trade, I propose that they can illuminate local interactions as well. Edensor's vivid description of medieval rural life conveys something of the radical localness of Bronze Age Italy:

> In medieval times, walking was usually bounded by an individual's 'day's walk circle', an area within which most everyday activities and adventures were confined.... To venture beyond these confines was likely to be dangerous, grueling and viewed as potentially criminal... Moreover, there was a dearth of through tracks, due to the locally constituted boundaries of society and space. Bodies moving through space... by virtue of their remove from the usual tightly bound social networks, were outside the pale, an exclusion that was all too evidently inscribed on their bodies through poverty, nakedness, insanity and starvation.[23]

The life of Bronze Age long-distance traders or traveling smiths may not have been as bleak as suggested here, especially when bringing nice

---

[20] Dickinson 1994: 240.
[21] Dickinson 1994: 242.
[22] E.g., Mizoguchi 2009.
[23] Edensor 2000: 83.

Group Identity in Prehistory

objects or special skills with them, but they must certainly have been viewed as out of the ordinary, in spite of Kristiansen and Larsson's arguments to the contrary.[24] Furthermore, there was some mobility at the group scale, with resettling of small groups in various parts of the peninsula: the Canegrate culture of the RBA seems to be an example of this.[25] One could cite other, more tenuous examples, too, such as that of a few Mycenaeans residing in the southern port towns,[26] or the Terramare people arriving from the Danube area,[27] or the small-scale resettling and seasonal transhumance in the Apennines.[28] In the first millennium BC, the movements of groups rather than individuals are even clearer, from some Etruscans settling in Campania,[29] to Celts migrating into northern Italy,[30] to the movements of former mountain groups into the coastal plains, such as the Lucanians into Basilicata and the Volscians into Latium.[31] Greek colonization may be included in this list. But in the Bronze Age, the material record does not reveal many such events, probably because there were yet to be the population pressures that are a primary trigger for such movements.

What kinds of groups are we talking about in the Bronze Age? These were certainly not ethnic groups, for all the aforementioned reasons. As discussed in Chapter 1, populations were most likely organized into segmentary or middle-range societies in this period, covering in some cases fixed territories. The topic of whether regional identities emerged during the period in question, or existed already and simply became visible then because of the new evidence of intrusive materials, will be explored in the following chapters. As for what happens after the Bronze Age, if one perceives ethnicity as a particularly intense and cohesive form of regional grouping, and one accepts the premise that interaction is essential to groups, then one may hypothesize that the kinds of interactions occurring within the regional groups that were successful at self-definition in the historical period would differ from those of their counterparts who were not.

---

[24] Kristiansen and Larsson 2005.
[25] De Marinis 2000b.
[26] Buxeda *et al.* 2003: 281.
[27] Cardarelli 2009: 36–7.
[28] But see Bispham 2007: 181. See also Chapter 7 in this volume.
[29] Cuozzo 2007: 229–32.
[30] Häussler 2007.
[31] Guasco 2006: 100–1; Smith 1999: 474.

The evidence for networks of interaction in regions that later form the territories of named groups has broader implications than the Italian case alone, demonstrating a correlation not between collective identity and active material-culture expression, but rather between identity and community connectedness. This last criterion, one that Anthony Smith gives for ethnicity,[32] may be considered a "weak" marker when compared to, say, a common name, territory, and language. But if one examines the structure of that connectedness, rather than its presence or absence, then one may begin to assess the strength of a particular group. Moreover, there is the problem of archaeological visibility: these earlier traces of territorially delimited community solidarity may be the only evidence we are going to find of the group's beginnings. But the structural approach goes beyond simple expediency in that it is not just the only evidence we have, it is the best evidence. If we accept that group identity is actively constructed through social interaction, then interactions and social networks are of central importance in its formation.[33]

Path Dependence

At issue here is path dependence. In its loosest form, path dependence is the notion that "what happened at an earlier point in time will affect the possible outcomes of a sequence of events occurring at a later point in time."[34] As this loose definition amounts to the old adage that "history matters," some scholars advocate a narrower definition that offers greater analytical payback.[35] Margaret Levi suggests that "[p]ath dependence has to mean, if it is to mean anything, that once a country or region has started down a track, the costs of reversal are very high. There will be other choice points, but the entrenchments of certain institutional arrangements obstruct an easy reversal of the initial choice."[36] Path dependence in various iterations is increasingly used in the social sciences.[37] In economics, path dependence is often reformulated in terms of increasing

---

[32] Smith 1986: 29–30.
[33] Jenkins 1996: 16–24.
[34] Sewell 1996: 262–3; cf. Putnam 1993: 179.
[35] Page 2006: 87.
[36] Levi 1997: 28.
[37] Martin and Sunley 2006: 398.

returns, although Page critiques this oversimplification, arguing that what may look like "increasing returns" dominating decision making are, in fact, negative externalities limiting alternative options.[38] Mahoney distinguishes between self-reinforcing sequences – whereby if one way of doing things is going well then the group is likely to continue doing things in that manner – and reactive sequences that entail a chronological string of events leading from an initial event to the end result, all causally linked.[39] The former type of sequence would seem to fit well with the regional networks of early Italy. If we think of these networks as institutional, then what we are talking about is what Martin and Sunley call "institutional hysteresis,"[40] "the tendency for formal and informal institutions, social arrangements and cultural forms to be self-reproducing over time, in part through the very systems of socio-economic action they engender and serve to support and stabilize."[41] The most well-known proponent of this notion is Douglass North, whose work has focused on the influence of history on institutions.[42] As informal institutions, networks – once established – may continue in much the same way over long periods of time, not simply because of inertia, but because there are reliable payoffs to be had from those relationships. Changing the dynamic by severing old ties and establishing new ones is risky, and the costs of changing course grow over time.

As the concept of path dependence has grown in popularity in the social sciences, some have advocated a more rigorous application of the term, parsing it into distinct phenomena.[43] Writing about path dependence's use in evolutionary economic geography, Martin and Sunley, for example, unpack the term "region" into its constituent parts – institutions, people, place-based technologies, and so on – and question how, at the micro level, one sees path dependence at work. They question whether all components of a regional system (in their case, a regional economy) manifest this path dependence.[44] Since this microscale analysis that they

---

[38] Page 2006: 90.
[39] Pierson 2000: 252; Mahoney 2000: 508–9.
[40] Setterfield 1993.
[41] Martin and Sunley 2006: 400.
[42] North 1990.
[43] E.g., Page 2006.
[44] Martin and Sunley 2006: 410.

advocate is difficult to do for contemporary regions we can infer it is well nigh impossible for the Bronze Age data. The long time span and limited evidence with which I am working in the distant past prevent more than a generalized application of the concept. Path dependence is nonetheless useful for thinking about developments at the regional level, and the manner in which these groups evolve collectively. Indeed, the concept may be applied in a very real sense to a regional landscape in which old routes between villages will facilitate interactions whereas the effort in forging new roads may be devalued in the short term.

So when we think about regional path dependence, there are some nuances that we miss out on with our scant dataset. What can be done is to use path dependence discursively, to understand why Bronze Age networks may have survived in regions long after their utility. One of the classic examples of this is the QWERTY keyboard case famously illustrated by David.[45] The keyboard almost all of us use today, with the letters arranged to read QWERTYUIOP on the top alphabetical row, was one of several developed in the 1860s for typewriters. For various short-term reasons, the typewriters using this particular configuration of keys came to dominate the market early on. The keyboard was replicated and perpetuated because of market forces, even though there are more efficient alternatives, and is now so rooted in the culture and in people's motor memory that it would be very difficult to change now. Although this is a case of "technological lock-in," not institutional structure, it powerfully demonstrates how habits of behavior, once established, become increasingly difficult to break even when they are bad habits. This point is very important when assessing the condition of the groups at the moment of the Roman conquest. The recent trend of pushing ethnicity formation very late indeed, as a response to Roman aggression, overlooks the incredible difficulties of changing course so far along. Clearly, the threat of annihilation (whether physical, cultural, or both) seems like a good motivator to unify, but old relationships, perpetuated previously with some measure of positive results, may have been hard to change.[46] This notion of "path dependence" has particular value for Italy, although it is not to say that there was a character to each regional group in the

---

[45] David 1985.
[46] Ruane and Todd (2004: 225) make a similar point about the self-reinforcing nature of "solidaristic linkages."

sense of a personality. Dench effectively dismantled Salmon's take on the Samnite character, depicted as strong and rugged like the mountainous land from which they came.[47] Rather, "character" is to be understood here as the structured patterns of communication within a region.

Social Network Analysis

The methodological approach best suited for studying the interactions between or within groups is social network analysis (SNA). Emerging in the early part of the twentieth century, social network analysis now constitutes an important subset of social science research, and has been applied fruitfully in many fields.[48] Social network analysis concerns the nature of the relations, or ties, between social units, or nodes. These nodes can be individuals or groups of any kind: people, corporations, towns, nation-states, families, and so on. The ties between nodes form a structured social environment whose character determines the functioning of the group in question.[49] For example, weakly constructed networks with few connections between nodes will impede communication between units. Another example of a weak network would be one with too many "cutpoints" – nodes that constitute the only connection between other nodes. The group will be vulnerable to dissolution if one of these cutpoints is removed. In contrast, networks with abundant ties between nodes and numerous alternative pathways along which to travel will be able to withstand shocks to the system, such as the destruction of a single unit, thus encouraging group survival. This emphasis on relations may be contrasted with identity studies emphasizing the attributes of an individual as the most important determinants of action. Thus, a key tenet of social network analysis is that "structural relations are often more important for understanding observed behaviors than are such attributes as age, gender, values, and ideology."[50] Another tenet of network analysis is that "structural relations should be viewed as dynamic processes."[51] This has important implications for understanding change over time, and distinguishes networks from the

---

[47] Dench 1995; Salmon 1967.
[48] Freeman (2004) offers a nice history.
[49] Wasserman and Faust 1994: 9.
[50] Knoke and Yang 2008: 4.
[51] Knoke and Yang 2008: 6.

"structures" that are contrasted with dynamic "agents" in Giddens's "structuration." Nevertheless, the organization of past networks has an impact on the options available for subsequent ones.

For archaeologists, social networks have enormous explanatory value, although to reveal past networks from the material record – a very different dataset from that of most network studies – can be a challenge. Researchers in other fields using network analysis typically draw on either interviews or archival material for their evidence; of concern is whether the evidence is accurate and valid. Reconstructing these relations from the archaeological record alone poses an additional challenge, and necessarily limits what can be said. First of all, most of the interactions occurring in the distant past are archaeologically invisible. The material record that does exist offers only an indirect reflection of past interactions, not a record of the interactions themselves. We have to be confident that the simplified abstractions that are the networks we construct are some valid measure of the interactions that occurred in the past. Brughmans describes this as "the most difficult hurdle for archaeological network analysts to overcome... the interpretative jump from identifying patterns in static network structures using SNA to explaining them in terms of past social processes."[52] Further, archaeologists are generally trying to combine geometric (spatial) interactions with topological (relational) ones, often a delicate task.[53] Thus, the range of what archaeologists can do with social network analysis is somewhat circumscribed.

Several recent works have addressed the problems and potentials of SNA in archaeology. Brughmans's informative review of network analytics in archaeology highlights the disciplinary amnesia regarding earlier graph theoretic methods in archaeology.[54] He notes the many precursors to formal network analyses from the 1960s on in archaeology, which have been forgotten in the current wave of network studies. He critiques the narrow application of SNA by archaeologists, arguing that this rich and well-developed methodology has more to offer than archaeologists seem to realize. In particular, he points to the relatively untapped potential

---

[52] Brughmans 2012: 19.
[53] Knappett 2011: 42–3.
[54] Brughmans 2012.

of complex network modeling in archaeological studies. In the case of the current study – and I would argue many archaeological studies – the application of complex modeling would risk drawing the results too far from the empirical data and more straightforward techniques are appropriate. Although his critiques are valid, a narrowness of method is to be expected in this early stage and it will only be with the maturing of these approaches in archaeology that we can expect to see more diverse methods applied. At the moment it remains novel simply to engage in a formal network analysis of archaeological data.

Knappett's *An Archaeology of Interaction: Network perspectives on material culture and society* charts the potentials for a fusion of SNA and theories of materiality so that the relations between objects and people can be more formally analyzed using network analytical methods.[55] Although his third chapter serves as a useful primer to SNA for archaeologists, Knappett's application of network methods "to tackle the sociomaterial world" breaks new ground. The result is a truly novel contribution to network literature, not just to archaeology. This concern with the sociomaterial world is reflected in other recent works by archaeologists. Chapman, focusing on the later prehistory of the Balkans, posited that the circulation of objects may have functioned as a form of "enchainment."[56] Most recently, Hodder's exploration of how objects and humans are "entangled" uses the notion of networks discursively but not formally, although his figure 9.2 is essentially a network graph complete with nodes and directed ties.[57] This theoretical vein running through current archaeological theory, essentially building on Thing Theory and Actor-Network Theory, while intriguing, is tangential to my project in this book. I am more concerned here with the mechanisms and the architecture of interactions between people.

More relevant, then, is the body of literature concerning the novel application of established network methods to archaeological or historical datasets. Archaeologists and ancient historians are increasingly using social networks as explanatory tools perhaps, as Brughmans implies, because the advent of user-friendly network analytic software programs

---

[55] Knappett 2011.
[56] Chapman 2000.
[57] Hodder 2012: Fig. 9.2.

such as UCINET and PAGEK has made it possible for anybody beyond the utterly innumerate to do it.[58] As Brughmans's article describes, social network analysis is a growth area in archaeology. Archaeologists working in the southwestern United States drew on network concepts – if not formal analysis – relatively early,[59] and arguably the most ambitious archaeological project using network analysis concerns southwest archaeology. Mills and Clark's Southwest Social Networks Project is compiling a massive database of artifacts (4.3 million ceramics, as well as other materials, from 700 sites) in the precontact southwestern United States to reconstruct and analyze networks as they evolve at 50-year intervals from 1200 to 1550 AD.[60] Elsewhere, Mizoguchi's study of the role of the topological (rather than geographic) position of polities in the establishment of hierarchies in Japan provides a new explanation for the process of state formation there.[61] Studies of node centrality such as this are a good option for archaeologists, perhaps because intuitively we are used to thinking about locational advantage in circumstances of uneven development. A new edited volume includes numerous archaeological applications of network analysis.[62]

Scholars working in the Mediterranean, both archaeologists and ancient historians, have been slower to adopt these techniques, although that is changing fast. Broodbank's *An Island Archaeology of the Early Cyclades* is a landmark work in the emphasis placed on quantifying relationships and interactions between islands, replacing "the unitary island" as the ideal unit of analysis with a focus on the ties between islands.[63] Applying many of the methods and language of social network analysis without labeling them as such, Broodbank uses proximal point analysis to demonstrate the explanatory value of these interisland relations for reconstructing the development of the Cycladic societies in the Neolithic and Bronze Ages. Recently Knappett has teamed with physicists to push Broodbank's work further, constructing a complex

---

[58] Brughmans 2012: 18.
[59] E.g., Braun and Plog 1982; Rautman 1993.
[60] Mills *et al.* 2013.
[61] Mizoguchi 2009.
[62] Knappett 2013.
[63] Broodbank 2000.

network model, complete with simulations, for the Bronze Age Aegean.[64] In addition, a recent volume by ancient historians, *Greek and Roman networks in the Mediterranean*, opens with a virtual manifesto for the application of social network analysis to the ancient world.[65] The editors, in writing the introduction, demonstrate considerable knowledge of the theory and method of social network analysis and its potential; however, the majority of the contributors to the volume consistently use the notion of networks metaphorically – that is, as a good conceptual idea rather than as a formal method for quantifying and characterizing the relationships between entities. Rutherford's chapter, in which he maps religious delegations (*theoriai*) to festivals in ancient Greece, is the one exception. Using epigraphic evidence, Rutherford constructs network graphs and matrices to demonstrate the links that the *theoriai* create between the cities and sanctuaries from which they come and go.[66] Rutherford concludes somewhat deflatingly that although social network analysis can offer some "valuable insights," there are certain drawbacks to its use in the ancient world. One is that our data may be too fragmentary to be applied successfully. This is certainly valid, and will be an issue to address for my data as well. Rutherford's second concern – that the method is not refined enough to allow for distinguishing details such as different types of ties between cities – can be allayed, as at least one method has been developed for characterizing the attributes of the ties in the same manner as the nodes.[67] Overall, the volume may be understood as a valuable "warm-up" to the business of applying social network analysis to ancient Mediterranean data.

Also within the realm of ancient history, Graham applied social network analysis to the data from the fourth century AD Antonine itineraries – textual accounts of routes around the empire described in terms of distances between towns.[68] Graham's goal was to elucidate differences in conceptions of space in various regions of the empire. Ruffini's network analysis of Byzantine Egypt using textual evidence

---

[64] Knappett *et al.* 2011.
[65] Malkin, Constantakopoulou, and Panagopoulou 2009.
[66] Rutherford 2009.
[67] Evans *et al.* 2009.
[68] Graham 2006.

from sixth century AD papyri of the nome of Oxyrhynchos and the village of Aphrodito is also notable.[69] Ruffini is able to reconstruct the contrasting networks of the two contexts under study, revealing a very centralized hierarchical network of powerful elites at Oxrhynchos and a localized nonhierarchical network at the village level at Aphrodito. The differences are not simply scalar: the author argues that the network structure of the nome in which Aphrodito was located must have been very different from Oxyrhynchos.[70] Most recently, Irad Malkin takes a network perspective to explain how, by the end of the Archaic period, a Greek identity could crystallize just as the population itself was at its most dispersed geographically. Although he does not quantify his network data, Malkin's use of networks as explanatory, rather than formal, is valuable.[71] Closer to home, Fulminante uses various centrality indices to predict urbanization patterns in Latium Vetus from the FBA through the Archaic period.[72] Rossenberg's 2012 dissertation also employs formal network analyses on central Italian data for the Early Bronze Age.[73] Clearly there is a groundswell of interest and application of these methods.

Discussion

As we have seen, archaeological approaches to regional groups have been frustrated by the lack of concrete expressive actions preserved in the material record. If we think of an ethnic group as a particular type of social network rather than as a group constructed around a set of shared attributes, then we may make some progress because there is the possibility of detecting, even indirectly, intra-group interactions from the archaeological record. Peeples, working in the American southwest, has similarly reframed networks in terms of relational identities.[74] In Peeples's study, these relational identities are distinct from active expressions of identity or categorical identity. It is in the moments of

---

[69] Ruffini 2008.
[70] Ruffini 2008: 147.
[71] Malkin 2011.
[72] Fulminante 2012.
[73] Rossenberg 2012.
[74] Peeples 2011.

the two identities' convergence that collective action can occur. This is a compelling way to think about groups and how change takes place. In Bronze Age Italy, we can use network analysis to clarify the nature of interactions around the peninsula and model their impact on regional histories. The properties of the networks in the future regions – such as the connectedness of a group, the centrality of individual nodes, and the density of ties between nodes – can to a certain extent determine the group's success. As noted already, in the RBA and FBA, regional differences in local material culture remain difficult to spot or, if visible, difficult to interpret. But the distributions of nonlocal, intrusive objects tell a different story. Instead, the uniformity of local material-culture practices masks clear regional divisions among the peoples of the peninsula. These regional divisions manifest themselves in dense relations between settlements a short distance apart from each other, and limited interactions outside of those clusters. These interactions are visible in the distributions of intrusive objects across the peninsula. Mycenaean pottery, amber beads of Tiryns and Allumiere type, selected bronze objects and glass beads, and even donkey remains stand out in the material record.[75]

Using one body of material evidence to study prehistoric communities is akin to the fable of the blind men erroneously describing an elephant based on the single portion of the animal's anatomy that each touched. Yet if communities are relational, and composed of networks of people linked together by shared practices, we may expect that whatever materials circulate through those networks will, in their distributions, leave some trace, however incomplete, of the interactions between nodes in those networks. This is the premise I am working from in using intrusive materials to identify regional communities in RBA and FBA Italy. Therefore, working from the find spots themselves and drawing on social network theory, I use the uneven distribution of selected artifacts as evidence of ties between indigenous sites. This is based on the contention that if there were regional groupings, then their members would communicate more internally than with other regional groups and that the communication would, on occasion, involve the circulation

---

[75] Vianello 2005; his gazetteer of Italian sites with Aegean material includes the quantities; the reader may seek the totals there.

of goods that had come into the group from outside. To sum up, we can expect that variations in the densities of interactions between sites will correspond to regional groups; clusters of dense interactions will presumably occur within regional groups and fissures in the network will occur between regional groups. In the next chapter, I outline my methodology in detail and present the peninsula-wide results.

CHAPTER FOUR

THE RECENT AND FINAL BRONZE AGE PENINSULAR NETWORKS: ASSESSING STRUCTURE AND COHESION

Introduction

Using the object types described in Chapter 2 and the theoretical framework outlined in Chapter 3, I focus on detecting and characterizing regional groupings in peninsular Italy in the RBA and FBA using social network analysis. This is an exercise in community detection, seeking subgroups within the broad peninsula-wide network. Out of the complex material record of the Italian peninsula in the RBA and FBA, the networks offering the best chance of revealing regional groupings must include parameters for both the geographical proximity of sites and the objects they share. As noted in Chapter 2, the objects included in the study are not generally the locally made items of everyday use, but relatively rare and distinctive pieces. As a result, the dataset is rather small. In some parts of the peninsula there are few such objects, probably too few to detect any networks. One might also contend that the exchange of these relatively rare items must have been an infrequent activity, so that we are observing the traces of exceptional interactions rather than quotidian ones. However, these are precisely the kinds of highly valued objects that we can imagine forming part of significant and deliberate exchanges, whose patterns we must consider if we are to understand social dynamics in this period. Networks are artificial constructions that one hopes are an accurate approximation of reality. To make them convincing, the methodological choices behind their construction need to be transparent, as this chapter demonstrates. This means that it will be rather dry in parts, and for those readers interested in the results more than the process, I recommend examining the figures and skipping ahead to the discussion section toward the end of the chapter.

Constructing the Networks

The dataset is constructed as follows. I compiled a list of the find spots of the reliably dated and well-studied objects from the RBA and FBA described in Chapter 2 (Figures 2.1 and 2.2). These come from 182 RBA sites and 132 FBA sites (Appendix).[1] As many sites span both periods, the actual total number of sites is 272. Of these, forty-two sites are found on both lists. Each of the sites is a node, to use the SNA terminology. The nodes fall into five functional types: burials, settlements, hoards, ritual deposits, and casual or unknown find contexts.[2] Two similar objects at a settlement and a ritual site, for example, may have served to link the two places together in spite of very different site activities. This is the rationale for conflating different find contexts under the single term "node." Nonetheless, although I have recorded all the find spots for each object, in my peninsular analyses I work with a reduced matrix from which I have removed nodes that were hoards, ritual deposits, or casual or unknown find contexts. As I attempt to elucidate regional identities, I am concerned that objects from these find spots do not represent regional activities, but rather long-distance ones.[3] The networks discussed in this chapter, therefore, consist of 162 nodes in the RBA matrix and 107 in the FBA matrix. Because two sites cannot be linked if they are not contemporary, find spots that are clear cases of secondary deposition, in which Bronze Age objects are found in later contexts, were excluded.[4] For each find spot I recorded its geographic coordinates as precisely as possible, although in many cases the locations were approximate, taken

---

[1] The find spot list was compiled using published data and is as up-to-date as possible, although there will certainly be unpublished or very recent find spots I have missed.
[2] Peroni et al. 1980: 9–10.
[3] In the regional case studies in Chapters 5 through 8, I add those excluded sites back in.
[4] Clear examples of secondary deposition include the Tiryns and Allumiere beads from Populonia and Osteria dell'Osa, respectively (Negroni Catacchio et al. 2006: 1464–6); a Torri d'Arcugnano dress pin from the Iron Age settlement of Monte Venere (Zanini 1996: 132); and the Bertarina dagger from a sixth century BC grave in Calabria (Bianco Peroni 1994: 159).

from the center of the nearest modern settlement if no other information was provided.

With the aforementioned data, I constructed two sequential networks: one for the RBA and one for the FBA. The most basic network one could construct with this data would be one composed of two sites (nodes) with a simple co-occurrence of an artifact type resulting in a tie. Although such a network has the virtue of being conceptually intuitive, it glosses over the realities of Bronze Age trade as discussed in Chapter 3. Because there are relatively few objects and ties compared to sites, the artifact types take on undue importance. In other words, leaving geography out altogether obscures exactly the local exchanges we are trying to reveal and puts the focus back on the objects themselves. Therefore, a slightly more complex set of criteria – one taking distance into account – is needed. Thus, the network used here is the sum of all the sites (nodes) with at least one of the selected artifacts, with ties defined as the links between nodes that share at least one object type and are also a short distance apart. I define "short distance apart" as 50 km, or a two-day walk or manageable day's sail in the case of coastal sites best linked by water.[5] Although some sites are closer to each other than 50 km, beyond 50 km would mean more than two days of travel, which would likely reduce the frequency of movement between two points. Therefore, 50 km seems like a reasonable working threshold of proximity.

Starting with the RBA dataset, I calculated the distances in kilometers between all the RBA find spots, creating a mileage matrix in a Microsoft Excel spreadsheet in which the rows and columns were the find spots of all the object types, and each cell contained the distance between the two sites whose row and column intersected at that cell. I then incorporated the object information into the matrix, replacing the distance measure with a "0" in the cells if the two sites did not share any object types, and leaving the distance measure in place if they did.[6] I imported that spreadsheet into UCINET, one of the standard social network analysis

---

[5] Dobson (2005: 8) estimates an average of 15 miles (c. 24 km) a day for overland travel in Anglo-Saxon period Northumbria, compared with 81 miles (c. 130 km) a day for sea travel if sailing and 41 miles (c. 66 km) a day if rowing.

[6] In this kind of matrix, cells along the diagonal – that is, the cell where, for example, Row 4 and Column 4 intersect – are always "0" as a find spot cannot be a distance from, or share objects with, itself.

Table 4.1. *Sample matrix. Both column and row titles are find spots (nodes)*

	Agliastroso	Alpe di Santa Giulia	Arceto	Bismantova
Agliastroso	0	0	0	0
Alpe di Santa Giulia	0	0	1	1
Arceto	0	1	0	1
Bismantova	0	1	1	0

software programs, and binarized those distances so that sites that were 50 km or less apart from each other and shared at least one object type would have a direct tie (expressed in the matrix as "1") and those more than 50 km apart, even though they shared an object type, would lack a tie (expressed in the matrix as "0") (Table 4.1).

As discussed in Chapter 3, two nearby sites sharing the same object type can reasonably be thought to be tied together – that is, to have a relationship. For example, the sites of Moscosi and Cisterna di Tolentino both yielded examples of Glisente B daggers and twisted violin-bow fibulae, and they are 21 km apart. Therefore, the two cells where they intersect each contain a "1" to represent that tie. The result is a symmetric, binary, one-mode adjacency network. In that label lie several key choices on my part of which the reader must be aware. The network is symmetric because the posited ties are undirected: Moscosi and Cisterna di Tolentino are equally joined to each other by the same object type, rather than Moscosi being connected to Cisterna di Tolentino without Cisterna di Tolentino being connected to Moscosi. If we knew that someone in Moscosi had given the dagger to someone in Cisterna di Tolentino as a gift then we could make the ties directed, with the connections going from Moscosi to Cisterna di Tolentino, but not the other way. However, this is rarely possible given the nature of prehistoric evidence. Even if we could determine the directionality of these goods, we could not tell if the exchange was, in fact, mutual because something was given in return. Because of these uncertainties, ties simply represent the undirected co-occurrence of these objects.

Second, it is a binary matrix because ties are either present or they are absent, as indicated by a "1" or "0," rather than being valued. This, too, was a choice. Some sites share more than one object type (Moscosi and

Cisterna di Tolentino with their fibulae and daggers, for example). One could calculate strength of ties based on the numbers of different object types co-occurring at two sites, giving a tie of "3" for three objects shared, for example. However, the inconsistencies in the excavation histories of the find spots militate against this method. Some sites have been excavated thoroughly and we may be confident that what the reports contain is the total of what could be found at the site. Other sites have been only partially excavated, and some find spots were the locations of mere casual finds. Indeed, the variations in site function complicate straightforward quantitative comparisons. Likewise, I did not include the quantities of each object type at each site in these calculations, as the focus is not on the sites themselves but the ties between them. For all these reasons, it would be inappropriate to hold up each site to the same level of quantitative precision. Finally, this is a one-mode adjacency network because all the nodes belong to the same type (find spots).

The RBA Peninsular Network

I will begin with the RBA network and analyze its structure using various measures. The standard measure of connectivity in network analysis is density: the ratio of actual ties between nodes to all possible ties. For example, in a hypothetical network of six nodes there is a maximum of fifteen possible undirected ties. If there are only six actual ties, then the density of the network is .4 or 40 percent. In the RBA network as I designed it, the number of possible ties must reflect the fact that many sites are more than 50 km apart and so could never be tied. Density calculations thus required an extra step: the calculation of ties between sites based solely on their being 50km or less apart, regardless of objects shared. There were 2,218 possible ties based on proximity alone, compared to 894 actual ties based on both proximity and shared objects. Dividing 894 actual ties by 2,218 possible ties, the density of the RBA peninsular network is 40.3 percent. This is far higher than the density of the simplest network, in which ties are based on co-occurring object types but not distance; when we take distance out as a restriction, the number of actual ties goes up to 4,600, but density goes down to

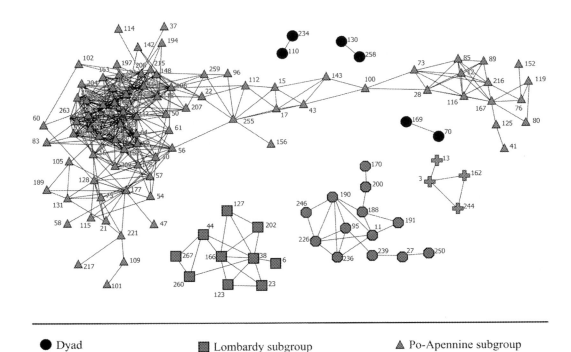

- ● Dyad
- ■ Lombardy subgroup
- ▲ Po-Apennine subgroup
- ✚ Trentino subgroup
- ◉ Southern subgroup

4.1. Graph of RBA peninsular network with ties based on shared objects and ≤ 50 km apart, excluding isolates

17.9 percent. This demonstrates that proximity did indeed play a significant role in object sharing.

Looking at the network in graph form reveals further details about its structure (Figure 4.1). The network is unconnected, meaning that not all sites are reachable from all other sites. There are forty-four isolates – that is, sites with no ties to any other site – out of 162 sites total, as well as self-contained clusters of sites or subgroups. In network terms, a subgroup is a subset of nodes within a network.[7] Every site in each subgroup is reachable by every other site in the subgroup, but is not connected to any sites outside its subgroup. The smallest subgroups are dyads, or pairs of sites that are only connected to each other. There are four dyads here. The three larger subgroups are of particular interest.[8] One notices

---

[7] Wasserman and Faust 1994: 19.
[8] Indeed, the fact that the subgroups are sizeable and self-contained enables them to be labeled "networks" in their own right. To distinguish them from the peninsular

The Recent and Final Bronze Age Peninsular Networks

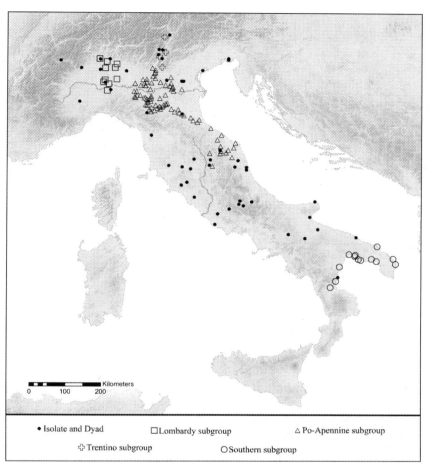

4.2. Map of Italian peninsula showing RBA subgroups (Drawn by R. Biggs)

immediately a massive network containing eighty-three sites. The second largest has just thirteen sites, the third has ten, and the fourth, just four sites. This graph is not a map and is not arranged topographically, but we can ground the subgroups geographically and see their distribution (Figure 4.2). Most of the sites in the big subgroup are in the Po Valley, but it extends east to the Veneto and then south into what are now Marche and Umbria. The second-largest subgroup is located in what is

network, they will continue to be called subgroups here, but when examined independently in subsequent chapters, they will be relabeled as networks.

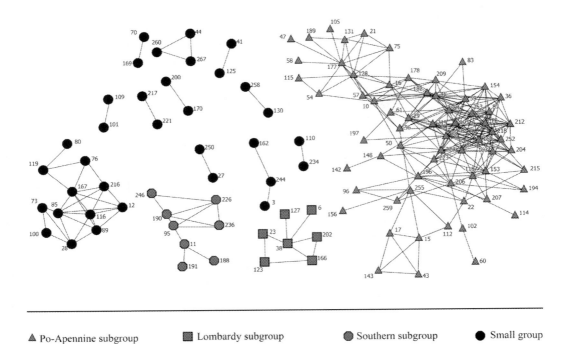

▲ Po-Apennine subgroup   ■ Lombardy subgroup   ⬣ Southern subgroup   ● Small group

4.3. Graph of RBA peninsular network with ties based on shared objects and ≤ 40 km apart, excluding isolates

now Apulia and the Gulf of Taranto and will be labeled "Southern." The third subgroup is located in Lombardy.[9]

Before proceeding, let us revisit the 50 km parameter. To test its validity I set the proximity cutoff at 40 km as well, and include those results here so that readers can compare for themselves the two graphs (Figure 4.3). The subgroups are the same, minus a few sites, because of the narrower criteria. Thus, by limiting the criteria for a tie even further to include sites no more than 40 km apart as opposed to no more than 50 km apart, there will be fewer ties between sites. The number of isolates in this network is forty-eight, up from forty-four. The Po-Apennines subgroup has broken into two groups, the smaller labeled 'small subgroup' here.

I also experimented with treating distance as a valued measurement on a continuous scale rather than setting a limit on proximity. Thus, I

---

[9] The fourth, with just four sites, is located in Trentino-Alto Adige. It will not be analyzed here.

The Recent and Final Bronze Age Peninsular Networks

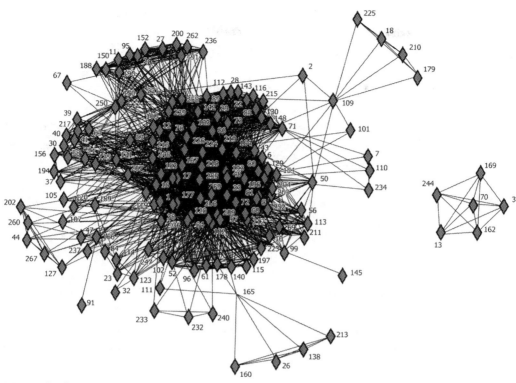

4.4. Graph of RBA peninsular network with ties based on shared objects, with distance measured on a continuous scale

took the inverse of the actual distance in kilometers so that the closer the sites were to each other geographically, the greater the strength of the link between sites with the shared objects (Figure 4.4). The results were uninformative, with the network structure determined by artifacts rather than geography. This clustering may be explained by the fact that the peninsular network is so sparsely connected that any tie, no matter how distant the nodes are, takes on great numeric importance, thus obscuring the geographic distinctions and emphasizing the artifact distributions instead. This graph does permit us to see which individual sites were important, as those are the ones on the edge of clusters with many ties emanating from them, such as Timmari (243) and Frattesina (109). Although this method may be useful from the perspective of long-distance exchange networks and exposes important sites by their position in overlapping artifact distributions, it does not illuminate the regional networks that are the focus here. There is a considerable body of sociological research demonstrating that physical proximity encourages social relationships and that shared attitudes and norms emerge from such relationships. The proximity itself is a causal force in the development of group unity, which in turn influences individual decision making, the adoption of innovations, perceptions of risk, and so on.[10] Moreover, in light of the limited technologies of mobility in Bronze Age Italy, beyond a certain distance we cannot be at all sure that sites had any contact with, or awareness of, each other. Therefore, building proximity into the network parameters is essential.

To return to the subgroups, Wasserman and Faust list four general properties of cohesive subgroups:[11]

1. The mutuality of ties (requires direct ties between all members)
2. The closeness or reachability of subgroup members (all members must be reachable even if not directly tied)
3. The frequency of ties among members (each node must have many ties to others in the subgroup)
4. The relative frequency of ties among subgroup members compared to nonmembers (must be relatively cohesive compared to the remainder of the network).

Property 1, in which a subgroup is defined in social-network terms as a "clique," is an extremely narrow definition of cohesion, one that is rarely met empirically. Indeed, among the subgroups observed here, none achieve direct ties between all nodes. The second property, the reachability of all nodes in a subgroup to each other, is met by all the RBA subgroups and indeed serves to define them as subgroups. Further, the extent of this reachability can be compared. As will be discussed in this section, the average distance between two nodes in a subgroup and the distance between the two nodes that are the furthest apart in the subgroup are worth noting as an indicator of how easily communication may occur within the subgroup. The third property is both restrictive and vague: "many" is a relative concept, but certainly means more than the single tie of many of these nodes in the subgroups. As for property 4, the comparison of the frequency (or density) of ties among members

---

[10] See Burt 1987 for a review of the early literature on this research.
[11] Wasserman and Faust 1994: 251–2.

Table 4.2. *Measures of cohesion and structure of the major subgroups in the RBA peninsula network*

Subgroup	Density*	Weighted Clustering Coefficient	Avg Geodesic Distance	Diameter	Max Flow	Cutpoint Ratio	Degree Range	Network Centralization
Po-Apennines [n=83]	.4855	.571	3.701	11	27	.108	41	29.16%
Southern [n=13]	.8333	.517	2.705	7	4	.10	6	28.79%
Lombardy [n=10]	.6429	.508	1.711	3	6	.13	7.93	61.11%

of a subgroup with those among the members of the whole network is also achieved, as in all cases the subgroups are far denser than the peninsular network. However, as we have already noted, interpreting density measures becomes complex when two criteria are folded into the definition of ties. Therefore, the subgroups here demonstrate properties 2 and 4 of cohesive subgroups.

The next step is to look more closely at the structure of the subgroups themselves. Comparing the subgroups demonstrates the differences in their structures, differences that, as we shall see, can have an impact on the success of the subgroup and the options available to its members. Table 4.2. presents various measures of cohesion and structure with which to compare the three largest subgroups in the RBA network.

Density of ties is one of the key indices of cohesion. As discussed earlier, the greater the number of ties between nodes in a network, the greater the possibilities for communication and social relationships. In this case, "possible ties" is defined as the number of ties between sites based on distance alone, 50 km or less apart. One can expect that – in general – the larger the network, the less dense the ties and this pattern holds to a certain extent here, where the Po-Apennines subgroup is the least dense of the three. To overcome the size bias, calculating the clustering coefficient is useful. This "egocentric" measure – calculating the density of the "neighborhood" of each site – is adjusted to give more weight to the larger neighborhoods. This correction for size means that, for example, the Po-Apennines subgroup, although showing the least density, has a weighted clustering coefficient of .571, which is the highest of the three subgroups. What that means is that within the subgroup, the nodes around one node will tend to be densely connected to each other, not just to the original node. When the density is low but the clustering coefficient is high, this suggests internal clusters of densely connected sites, but the clusters are not well connected with each other. In the case of the Po-Apennines group, the disparity between the density and the clustering coefficient suggests some internal cleavages, and we can observe these on the graph, with one large dense cluster and a smaller one at the end of the subgroup's "tail," separated by nodes with few ties. We will come back to the historical significance of this network structure later in this chapter.

The Southern subgroup's density is belied by its graph, where relatively few ties are evident. This is owing to the particular circumstances of this subgroup, both in the RBA and as we shall see, in the FBA. The sites are almost all coastal and all contain Aegean-style pottery, which constitutes the basis of the ties observed here. However, many of the sites are farther apart than 50 km, and so the total number of possible ties based on proximity is fairly low. With a low divider, the result is a density that is unexpectedly high. I will discuss the reasons for this pattern at the end of the section. Several of the sites form a cluster within the subgroup that may be distinguished from peripheral sites such as Otranto and Torre Mordillo. As for the Lombardy subgroup, because both the density and clustering coefficient measures are high, these together suggest a cohesive group with no internal cleavages. We can observe this from the graph as well.

Measures of connectivity provide a sense of how information and objects would move around a network. The geodesic distance is the number of ties in the shortest possible path between two nodes.[12] Two nodes that are adjacent or have a direct tie to each other have a geodesic distance of one. But even without a direct tie they may still be reachable to each other through other nodes. If Node A has a direct tie to Node B, but not to Node C – but B and C have a tie – then A and C are reachable via B, and they have a geodesic distance of two. There can be multiple paths linking nodes, but we assume that the shortest possible path is the preferred one. The "diameter" of a network is the largest geodesic distance in the network. The diameter of the network, then, indicates the distance between the two nodes that are the furthest apart, and thus measures how spread out the network is. The average geodesic distance between nodes in a network is also informative, giving a general sense of how easily information can move. The more compact

---

[12] Knoke and Yang 2008: 60–2.

a network is, in other words, the shorter the average distance between nodes, the quicker information can travel, and the more connected it is. Network size will affect average geodesic distance, so predictably the Po-Apennines subgroup is the least compact and Lombardy the most. However, the southern and Lombardy subgroups are not so different in size and yet the latter is far more connected than the former. We can note, then, that of the three subgroups, the Southern subgroup scores lowest on connectivity.

We can also consider not just the shortest paths linking nodes in a network, but the number of possible paths of any length connecting two nodes as well. The total number of pathways between two nodes is called a *flow*.[13] Flows can indicate the strength or weakness of a network: the higher the flows, the less chance of communication between nodes breaking down. Of course, in a small network there are fewer possible pathways and the flow values will be lower. In the RBA network, Po-to-Apennines unsurprisingly has the highest maximum flow at twenty-seven. However, the Southern group – larger than the Lombardy one – has a lower maximum flow, suggesting greater vulnerability. And indeed, as evident in the graph, the Southern subgroup has four "cutpoints" or nodes that, once removed, would sever connections or disconnect the group.[14] The Lombardy subgroup, alternatively, has just one cutpoint whereas the Po-Apennines subgroup, with its attenuated southeastern portion, has nine. The larger the site, the more likely it is that there will be cutpoints, so it is more helpful to view these numbers as percentages. Dividing the number of cutpoints by the total number of nodes, we can compare the three subgroups' vulnerability to fragmentation. More than 30 percent of the Southern subgroup's nodes are cutpoints, compared to just 10 percent of the Lombardy subgroup's and 11 percent of the Po-Apennines's. Cutpoints are typically used to assess the vulnerability of the connectivity of two nodes in a network, but here I am treating them as indicators of the strength of the subgroups as a whole. This is because, for the purposes of this study, we are less interested in the long-term survival of individual ties, as the sites themselves do not in many cases last beyond one period. Instead, the focus is on the character

---

[13] Hanneman and Riddle 2005: Ch. 7.
[14] Wasserman and Faust 1994: 112–4.

of the network overall. From that perspective the cutpoint percentages suggest that the Southern subgroup was particularly vulnerable to disconnection.

The maximum flow measure and a related one, the number of geodesic paths between nodes, can be used to assess the relative strength of individual nodes. As I noted earlier, we are not really concerned with individual nodes per se, but these measures can reveal information about the entire network. Those sites with the most options for reaching other sites can be said to be more connected. Of interest here is the overall variability in the connectivity of nodes within a subgroup. Looking at an individual node's ties in a network helps to characterize the network structure as a whole. The range in numbers of ties – that is, comparing the least connected node to the most connected node – can highlight the variability in roles and social positions of particular nodes. As Wasserman and Faust put it, "the degree of a node is a measure of the 'activity' of the actor it represents."[15] We can use this data for what it tells about the network as a whole and the extent to which sites occupy similar positions and display similar levels of "activity." The ties of individual nodes in a symmetric network such as this are called "degrees." The number of possible degrees depends on the size of the network, so the range in nodal degrees is made comparable across networks by expressing the degree as a proportion of total ties rather than as a raw number. The narrower the range, the more homogeneous the network's nodes can be said to be. The Southern and Lombardy subgroups show a similar degree range demonstrating fairly high variability in nodal degrees, with the maximum number of degrees six or eight times higher than the minimum. The Po-Apennines group is in a class apart, with an enormous range in degrees, and a maximum that is fully forty-one times higher than the minimum. This speaks to the heterogeneous structure of this subgroup, with sites such as Montagnolo and Capitan Loreto tied to only one other node, and Campegine tied to thirty-three others. Overall, the impression of all three subgroups is that although there may have been only limited site hierarchies in this period, some sites in each subgroup were more actively involved in interaction networks. The patterning we observe could be explained in any number of ways, though – for example,

---

[15] Wasserman and Faust 1994: 100.

the "active" sites could have been better located geographically, or they were excavated more extensively so yielded more objects, or their function (e.g., cemetery or cult site), may have encouraged greater deposition of such objects. For these reasons we cannot read too much into this pattern beyond noting it.

We can reframe nodal degrees, and therefore nodal activity, in terms of node centrality and apply it to the network as a whole. Network centralization measures the variability in node centrality in a network. In other words, while degree range is the difference between the degrees of the node with the most ties and the node with the least ties in the network, degree centrality notes the difference between the number of direct ties of the most central or active node with the numbers of ties of all the others.[16] In the Freeman Graph centralization measure, a score of 1 is a network with total centrality (one node is connected to all others, while all other nodes are only connected to that one central node) and 0 is a totally decentralized network with no single node having more ties to other nodes than any other. The more decentralized the network, the fewer positional advantages any single node can enjoy over others.[17] Both the Po-Apennines and Southern subgroups have fairly low centralization scores, suggesting that these networks were not dominated by any single, powerful site. The Lombardy subgroup, on the other hand, is quite centralized with Canegrate, a cemetery with numerous grave goods, playing a pivotal role in connecting sites to each other (although the sites can, in most cases, reach each other along other paths).

Summing up the RBA peninsular network, then, it is disconnected and the subgroups within it are really freestanding networks in their own right. There is one enormous network spanning northern and northeastern Italy with a tail extending into the Apennines, a smaller cohesive and fairly centralized network to the north and west in what is now Lombardy, and far to the southeast, another network structured around the circulation of Aegean pottery in modern-day Apulia and

---

[16] Wasserman and Faust 1994: 176. There are several other commonly used centrality measures, including closeness centrality and betweenness centrality, which are useful if the focus is on particular site roles in a network.
[17] Knoke and Yang 2008: 64–5.

Basilicata. Across the rest of the peninsula, isolated sites and pairs of sites are the norm. If there were other regional networks in place they are invisible using the method here. Framing the networks historically, the Po-Apennines is the network of the Terramare culture, showing its economic reach into Marche and the Apennines. The Lombardy network corresponds to the group known as the Canegrate culture, thought to have migrated into the territory from the north and west, bringing with them the burial practice of cremation. By the Iron Age, the group had lost its distinctiveness and fused with others into the Golasecca culture.[18] The southern Italian network differs from the other two in its coastal character, and it is difficult not to interpret it as a product of long-distance (in particular, Aegean) contacts rather than local ones. The three RBA subgroups do not map in any clear way onto the territories of the named groups of the first millennium BC. The two northern subgroups are mostly in territories that were later resettled by Celtic groups (in Lombardy, the Insubres and in the Po Valley, the Boii and Lingones). In the south, the RBA subgroup traverses the territories of several groups, depending on how one draws the later territorial boundaries: the main ones being the Daunians, Peucetians, Messapians, and Oenotrians. Thus, in the RBA, although the networks can be grounded to recognizable groupings, these do not survive into the first millennium BC in any clear cut way. Through much of the peninsula in the RBA there is no trace of regional networks of interaction at all. This corroborates Damiani's study of local pottery production in the RBA south of the Po Valley, in which she concluded that differences in forms and styles were not apparently regionally inflected.[19]

The FBA Peninsular Network

When we move forward in time to examine the peninsular network of the FBA, the picture changes enormously. Some of the RBA sites remain in use in the FBA: of the 107 FBA sites in this network, 40 of them were also in the RBA network. But there are many RBA sites that either do not survive to the FBA or cease to participate in the network in an

---

[18] De Marinis 2000a.
[19] Damiani 2010.

The Recent and Final Bronze Age Peninsular Networks

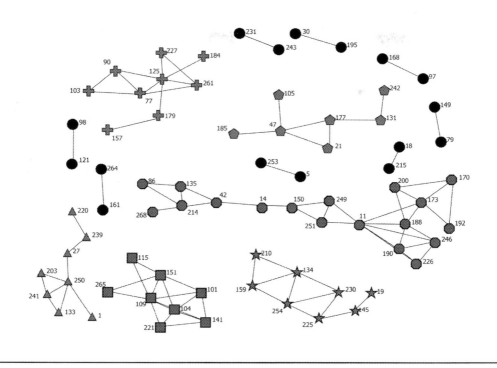

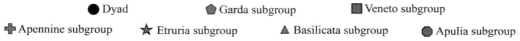

4.5. Graph of FBA peninsular network with ties based on shared objects and ≤ 50 km apart, excluding isolates

archaeologically visible manner, and many new sites emerge. As with the RBA network, we can calculate the density of this network by first calculating the number of ties based on proximity alone (two sites within 50 km would have a tie), and using that as the divider to calculate density. There were 477 ties based on proximity only, and of those, 185 ties based on shared objects as well. That calculates to a density of 38.8 percent. As in the RBA network, this ratio is more than double the density of the hypothetical simple network, in which ties are based on shared object types but not distance: there, density is at 17.4 percent (1,976 ties). Although these densities are in line with those of the RBA, the graph generated from the FBA matrix looks radically different (Figure 4.5).

As in the RBA, the peninsula-wide network is disconnected, with many isolated sites (33 out of 107) and eight dyads. But now, more than half of the sites are spread fairly evenly across six large subgroups, with no single

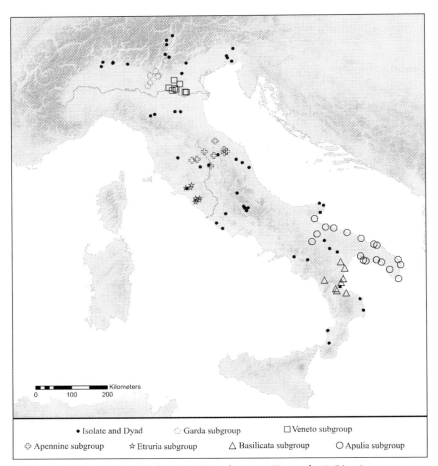

4.6. Map of Italian peninsula showing FBA subgroups (Drawn by R. Biggs)

subgroup dominating. When the network is grounded geographically, the picture becomes clearer (Figure 4.6).

The largest subgroup contains eighteen sites and is centered in Apulia, and includes seven of the original sites from the RBA Southern subgroup. Three more of that former subgroup's nodes are now included in a smaller subgroup of eight sites, Basilicata. This demonstrates beautifully the impact of the removal of a cutpoint: these three sites along the arch of the boot had been connected to the Apulian sites in the RBA Southern subgroup by the site of Cozzo Marziotta.[20] With that

---

[20] There is not a lot of information about that site because it was only partially excavated and little of it remains, but there is no evidence of an FBA period occupation (Gorgoglione 1986: 23).

Table 4.3. *Measures of cohesion and structure of the major subgroups in the FBA peninsula network*

Subgroup	Density*	Weighted Clustering Coefficient	Avg Geodesic Distance	Diameter	Max Flow	Cutpoint Ratio	Degree Range	Network Centralization
Apulia [n=18]	1.00	.523	3.588	8	4	.278	6.89	24.26%
Apennine [n=9]	.632	.400	1.944	4	3	.222	5.95	53.57%
Etruria [n=8]	.46	.522	2.107	5	3	.25	4.04	23.8%
Veneto [n=8]	.593	.621	1.429	2	5	0	4.60	57.14%
Basilicata [n=8]	.53	.353	2.143	4	3	.375	4.96	52.3%
Garda [n=7]	.41	.273	2.048	4	2	.57	4.03	46.67%

site's disappearance, the original RBA Southern subgroup split in two.[21] The Apennine subgroup contains nine sites and two more subgroups contain eight sites each, and are centered in the future Etruria and the Veneto. The last subgroup to mention, with seven sites, is up in the area around Lake Garda. The overall picture is of a disconnected peninsular network composed of roughly equivalent self-contained subgroups, with no group clearly dominating.

Applying the same measures of cohesion to the FBA subgroups that I did to the RBA subgroups yields some interesting results (Table 4.3).

First of all, density: this measure reveals not simply levels of cohesion, but differences in the nature of the subgroups themselves. In the Apulia subgroup, every site has yielded Aegean pottery so that distance between sites is the only restricting factor. Therefore, when distance is accounted for, the result is a density of 100 percent. But this does not make the Apulia subgroup a clique in network terms, which requires direct ties between all sites, so the density measure in this case simply does not apply. It belies the actual geographic constraints of this subgroup on the ground: the sites are almost all coastal and extend in a long string around the heel of Italy's boot. As we shall see, other measures of this subgroup's cohesion are low. As for the other subgroups' densities, the numbers are also somewhat misleading. The Veneto has the highest number of actual ties, but as the sites are generally quite close to each other, it also has the highest number of possible ties, resulting in a density of just under .60. The other subgroups range from .632 density in the case of the Apennine subgroup to a low of .41 for the Garda subgroup.

---

[21] Of course, there may have been another as yet undiscovered site linking these two FBA subgroups, or it may be that outside of the abstraction of this network these sites were in contact. However, within the terms of the method employed here, there was no connection between the two sites.

The weighted clustering coefficients vary more widely than the RBA subgroups' did, with a high of .621 for the Veneto subgroup – here reinforcing the cohesion suggested by the high density score – and a low of .273 for the Garda subgroup, which exhibits few clustering tendencies. Basilicata is also quite low, at .353, and I will later argue that these subgroups may be the product of external rather than local factors, and are the kind of patterns one would expect with a "ports-of-trade" model in place, as described by Renfrew.[22] The Apulia, Etruria, and Apennine subgroups show middling clustering – that is, some tendencies toward neighborhoods forming around particular nodes. These patterns will be explored more closely in the relevant chapters.

As other measures of cohesion, average geodesic distance and network diameter are informative. The Veneto subgroup has the lowest average geodesic distance (1.43 ties on average linking any two nodes in this subgroup) and the smallest diameter (two). By both measures, this is the most cohesive subgroup. The Apulia subgroup is the least compact, with the highest average geodesic distance and a diameter of eight. These numbers quantify what is already observable from the graph of this distended network. Between these two outliers are the other four major subgroups, all falling within a narrow range of middling compactness.

As for flow, again the Veneto subgroup scores the highest, with a maximum flow of five, reinforcing the cohesive characterization the other measures have provided so far: not only are distances short between sites in that network and there are many direct ties, but the redundancy of ties is further evidence of the strength of this network. The Garda subgroup has no more than two paths linking its sites, making it more vulnerable to disconnection. The maximum flows of the other subgroups cover a narrow range between three and four. When we look at the percentage of nodes of each subgroup that are cutpoints, the value of the maximum flows becomes even clearer. The Veneto subgroup has no cutpoints at all: the removal of any site would not disconnect the subgroup. In stark contrast, more than half of the Garda subgroup's nodes are cutpoints, rendering it very vulnerable to disconnection. Three of the Basilicata subgroup's eight nodes are cutpoints, which makes this subgroup quite vulnerable also. The other subgroups' cutpoint ratios are

[22] Renfrew 1975: 41–4.

tightly grouped between 22–28 percent, suggesting an equivalent level of slight vulnerability to disconnection.

The FBA subgroups' degree ranges, measuring the span of differences in nodal activity within each subgroup, vary from a low of 4.04 for Etruria to a high of nearly seven for the Apulia subgroup. This is, in fact, a fairly narrow bracket, and suggests that there were not such great differences between site activity levels in any of these subgroups. Thus, while the subgroup structures differ in many respects, they share a modest disparity between most active and least active nodes. Centralization scores for each subgroup range from a low of 23.8 percent for Etruria to 57.14 percent for the Veneto subgroup. There seems to be a bifurcation between, on the one hand, the subgroups with fairly high centralization scores – with Veneto, Apennines, and Basilicata all over 50 percent and Garda (close to 50 percent) – and, on the other hand, those with low centralization scores, in particular Etruria and Apulia. In the Veneto, Basilicata, and Apennine subgroups, therefore, there is the potential for one node to occupy a dominant position: in the Veneto, Frattesina is the only node to have a direct tie to every other node, and in the Apennines and Basilicata, Gubbio and Torre Mordillo respectively have direct ties to all but two nodes. The Veneto and Apennine subgroups are well connected on the whole, which is why these group centralization scores are not higher. Indeed, for the entire FBA network, Frattesina and Gubbio are the most prominent sites, but the structures of their particular subgroups limit these two sites' prominence. The Basilicata subgroup is a different case: there Torre Mordillo's power may have more to do with its role as cutpoint in what is a structurally vulnerable network. Without that site, the network would break into two triad strings and an isolate.

To sum up, from the RBA to the FBA, huge changes to the structure of the peninsular network are evident. The FBA sees a rise in the numbers of autonomous subgroups or networks. This may mean that these smaller networks formed for the first time, or it may mean that in the FBA there was greater access to the kinds of objects that reveal these circulatory pathways. There is no longer a numerically dominant subgroup, nor one that spans a large portion of the peninsula. Instead, we observe circumscribed groups occupying self-contained territories, in three distinct bands across the peninsula. In some cases there may be some continuity with the RBA. The FBA Apulia and Basilicata networks seem to be two reconfigured pieces of the formerly whole RBA Southern subgroup. Four sites in the FBA Garda network were part of the RBA Po-Apennines subgroup, as were three sites in the FBA Veneto network, suggesting that with the collapse of the core of the Terramare culture, these peripheral portions of its network managed to survive on their own. The Apennine network of the FBA is the most interesting example of this, where there is just one site that was also in the RBA Po-Apennines network (Gubbio), but all the FBA sites are in roughly the same area as the RBA sites that made up the southern end of the Po-Apennines network. This new regionalism in the FBA network mirrors the evidence for regionalism in the local ceramics, particularly the Protovillanovan facies. In the case of the Etruria and Apennine subgroups, they fit neatly into the zone of the Tolfa-Allumiere and Chiusi-Cetona pottery facies, respectively.[23] Likewise, the Veneto and Garda networks both cover the territory where the local ceramic repertoire of the FBA is distinctive enough to be assigned the label "Protovillanoviano padano."[24]

Discussion

This chapter has demonstrated that during the RBA and FBA on the Italian peninsula, circulations of highly specialized objects exhibited strong clustering tendencies. Both the RBA and FBA networks suggest that the peninsula was in no way unified, but was instead divided into smaller subgroups with varying degrees of internal cohesion. Moreover, between the RBA and FBA networks there are clear discontinuities. While the FBA network presents a more widespread phenomenon of self-contained regions, the RBA network reveals a very powerful Terramare culture and its economic reach and probable social ties further south. The Lombardy network, although near the Po Valley network, remains a separate entity, and a tightly cohesive one at that. This is as one might expect from the Canegrate culture, a group thought to have formed from the migration of Celtic groups into the region, who must have maintained a fairly inward-focused enclave in this period. As for the southern network in the RBA, its inherent weakness was made evident by its disconnection

---

[23] Zanini 1996; Bietti Sestieri and De Santis 2004.
[24] De Marinis 1999: 511–2.

in the FBA. I will argue in more detail in Chapter 8 that this network and its FBA descendents were the artificial products of foreign trade. In addition to these three networks, the Apennine cluster in the tail of the Po-Apennines network is so distinctive that it warrants separate treatment, and will be examined more closely in Chapter 7. The RBA network thus reveals clearly several extant regional groups of that period, but these groups cannot be taken as direct precursors of the historical groups of the first millennium BC.

Therefore, the key moment of change – when we can first detect traces of a recognizable regionalism in Italy in the form of a proclivity to circulate goods within a circumscribed area and not beyond it – is the FBA 1–2. It is in the FBA network that we can see the antecedents of the Etruscans, Veneti, the Apulian groups, and the north-central Apennine peoples. One may compare the map of these subgroups (Figure 4.6) with a map of the peoples of Italy at the time of the Roman conquest (Figure 1.1). It must be emphasized that with such a limited body of evidence, we are at best catching glimpses of social groups and that some areas – such as Northwest Italy or Calabria – may have had their own regional networks that remain invisible without sufficient objects to reveal them. The numerous isolated sites and pairs in the network await reinterpretation with the discovery of more finds. Nonetheless, in some areas such as west-central Italy, the absence of any clear network in the RBA, despite several find spots in the area, suggests that we are not overlooking the network; it simply was not there until the FBA.

Although the comparison of the later regional territories with the Bronze Age networks is compelling, one might wonder to what extent this geographic correlation between the Bronze Age clusters and the later groups is merely a function of proximity or attributable to the distributions of settlements more generally. In other words, we would expect that sites that are near each other in the Bronze Age would be more likely to be located on land that is in the same regional territory at a later date. This begs the question: Are Bronze Age sites that share objects with each other more likely to belong to the same regional territory later, independent of distance? In other words, is the sharing of objects a good predictor of later regional affiliation, independent of distance?

We can test this statistically using multiple regression analysis, with regional affiliation as the dependent variable we are attempting to predict, and ties based on shared objects and ties based on proximity (in this case, less than or equal to 50 km apart) as the independent variables. To do this, I created two matrices out of what was formerly just one, with one matrix of ties based on proximity and a second matrix of ties based on shared objects. The third matrix, the dependent variable, is composed of ties based on the site's location in a named group's territory, or what I am calling simply "regional affiliation."[25] In that last matrix, all sites in what is the future Etruria, for example, will share a tie, recorded as a "1." The method is necessarily anachronistic as the Bronze Age sites in most cases do not survive into the historical period when these regional affiliations come into view. But even though the sites themselves do not continue, the habitual patterns of interaction among people living in that same area may. To be clear, we are testing if the Bronze Age evidence serves as a predictor of these later conditions. As the dependent variable is binary – two sites either share a regional affiliation or they do not – it is customary to use logistic regression in this situation rather than linear regression, as there are statistical problems with the predicted values when using simple linear regression.

When I ran the regression on the FBA matrices, the results confirmed that both independent variables influenced ethnic affiliation significantly. For obvious reasons, proximity is hugely significant because the group territories are to some extent spatially delimited and find spots within those territories will necessarily be near each other. Therefore, it is no surprise that the unstandardized coefficient for proximity is, in this case, as high as 78 percent. This means that two sites that are near each other have a 78 percent probability of later regional affiliation. However, where it gets interesting is that the other independent variable – the co-occurrence of FBA objects – significantly influences regional affiliation as well. The unstandardized coefficient is just under 7 percent, meaning that if two sites shared an object in the Bronze Age then they increase

---

[25] In the find spot database, I recorded which regional group's territory each find spot fell into at the time of the Roman conquest, drawing on Wittke *et al.* 2009, Bradley *et al.* 2007: Maps 1–3, and Pallottino 1981: Fig. 1. Identifying regional groups was easier to do in some cases than others, as many groups by their very nature had imprecise territories and their borders are unknown. These group names are included in the Appendix.

the likelihood of regional affiliation by 7 percent. This does not seem like much, but it is statistically significant (p-value < .001) allowing us to reject the null hypothesis of no association between the sharing of objects in the Bronze Age and later regional affiliation. Still, one may ask, why is the influence of exchange so limited? This regression covers the entire peninsula, where there are many sites in regions showing no continuity into the first millennium BC, and no strong subsequent regional identities. That there is any pattern, therefore, is noteworthy. In the RBA, the pattern does not hold; unsurprising given the absence of any direct continuity with the first millennium BC groups.

What changed in or around 1200 BC? The Terramare culture collapsed catastrophically at the end of the RBA, as described in Chapter 1. This is usually treated as a regional scale event, but I will argue from the network data that this collapse had consequences far south of the Po Valley. Comparing the RBA and FBA network maps (Figures 4.2 and 4.6) it appears that the disintegration of this network opened up a vacuum that either led to the creation of new regional networks or made existing ones more visible by allowing a broader movement of goods into the rest of the peninsula. I will explore both possibilities in Chapter 5.

This chapter covered the entire peninsula and revealed the broad patterns. For individual regional histories, more detail is needed. The clearest examples of network antecedents to the groups that follow occur in Etruria and the Veneto, where the FBA subgroups fit neatly within the territories of later peoples (Etruscans and Veneti, respectively). These regional "success stories" will be explored in more detail in Chapters 5 and 6. In other regions the pattern is more complicated. In the mountainous parts of what is now Marche, Umbria, and eastern Tuscany, the FBA Apennine subgroup crosscuts at least three later regions, an anomaly that may be the outcome of population movements in the intervening centuries; Chapter 7 will attempt to clarify the picture there further. In the south, the loosely constructed subgroups of the RBA and FBA cross subsequent purported regional borders, suggesting an ongoing condition of weak affiliations. Competing land and sea networks further complicate the picture there. Applying the notion of path dependence outlined in Chapter 3, these inherent weaknesses in the networks may have affected the emergence of the named groups in Apulia, as will be explored in Chapter 8.

As this chapter makes clear, networks are powerful historical tools, illuminating interactions independently of the local material culture assemblages. Nonetheless, the complex subsequent histories of these regions cannot be simplistically predetermined by the earlier subgroups detected there. Demographic movements from beyond the peninsula had a major impact on the populations of the peninsula. Likewise, environmental resources and pressures played a role in determining the success of particular regions. Nonetheless, from this complex and lengthy history we can draw some links over time that point to a form of path dependence: *when circumstances were fortuitous*, certain regional networks that demonstrated cohesion in the FBA show endurance over time whereas those lacking early cohesion do not.

CHAPTER FIVE

THE NORTHERN NETWORKS FROM THE TERRAMARE TO THE VENETO

Introduction

We have already observed that northern Italy in the Recent and Final Bronze Ages stands out markedly from the rest of the peninsula, following a separate history and cultural trajectory. The peninsular study in Chapter 4 revealed two clear RBA networks in the north when the rest of the peninsula was virtually devoid of them, and new networks emerge in the FBA as well. The RBA networks in the north offer the strongest supporting evidence that the networks in this book do correspond to real social networks in the Bronze Age. This is because the northern examples map neatly onto recognized Bronze Age groups whose internal material homogeneity independently corroborates the posited ties. The Po-Apennines subgroup – a network in its own right[1] – spans both sides of the Po River, covering the central plain. It comprises parts of the modern political regions of Emilia-Romagna, Lombardy, and the Veneto, and this network is clearly dominant in terms of area covered during the RBA. To the west, the Lombardy network covers a more circumscribed area. In the FBA, the Veneto network is visible in the northern Po Delta and southern Veneto. The geographic area of the Veneto network overlaps with the territory of the earlier Terramare network and indeed, some of

---

[1] Now that we are looking closely at particular regions rather than the peninsula as a whole, the subgroups are more appropriately thought of as networks, and are labeled as such in Chapters 5–8.

the same sites turn up as nodes in both networks, but the time periods are distinct. Also in the FBA in the north, there is a network of sites around Lake Garda. We can look first at the history of the region and then revisit the network data in light of this background.

Northern Italy is transected laterally by the Po River and its vast flood plains, which extend to the base of the Apennines in the south and to the pre-Alpine zone in the north. The Po is the longest river in the Italian peninsula, some 220 miles, and being navigable, has always been of central economic importance. It flows eastward from Alpine Piedmont and toward its mouth, in what is now the Veneto, spans out into a delta of tributaries before reaching the Adriatic. The river's wide plain offers rich agricultural land, but is subject to flooding – a factor that affected the settlements in the region in ancient times. In the Bronze Age the Po had more branches and was less controlled than now, and managing it appears to have been a central task of the ancient occupants of the region.[2] North of the Po in the pre-Alpine zones, populations clustered near the major trans-Alpine passes by Aosta and the lake region, and so, unsurprisingly, cultural influences from across the Alps are strong in northwest Italy.[3] As early as the RBA, the distinctive Canegrate culture displays cultural markers suggesting a transalpine origin, and scholars have speculated that the Terramare culture itself originated north of the Alps in the Danubian area, based on similarities in material culture between the two areas in the MBA.[4] To the northeast, the Caput Adriae or head of the Adriatic connected central Europe to the Mediterranean and the Aegean beyond. These geographical features thus had a determining impact on the populations in those areas. De Marinis, writing of the MBA, observed, "è oltremodo significativo osservare come la parte occidentale e quella centro-orientale dell'Italia settentrionale siano tra loro quasi incomunicabili e gravitino decisamente da una parte verso nord-ovest e dall'altra verso nord-est."[5] The first part of his point is well taken for the RBA and FBA as well, although we shall

---

[2] Bietti Sestieri 1997: 757.
[3] Häussler 2007: 45; 49.
[4] Most recently, Cardarelli 2009: 36–7.
[5] De Marinis 2006: 1311. "It is extremely important to note that the western and east-central parts of northern Italy have almost no communication with each other, with the former gravitating to the northwest and the latter towards the northeast."

see that the gravitational pull shifts in those later periods. Nonetheless, the internal divisions in the region mean that in my coverage I will be focusing selectively on those areas where the network data may provide some new information.

The Terramare and Others in the MBA and RBA

Unlike the rest of the peninsula, the Po River valley was home to a clearly articulated regional group in the MBA and RBA, known now as the Terramare culture. The Terramare culture is visible from its distinct settlement forms, craft objects, and advanced metallurgical production. The Terramare settlements are found primarily in the plain south of the Po, and are characterized by the presence of earthworks surrounding the habitation area. For a long time scholars distinguished these bank-and-ditch enclosures from the agglomerations of huts built on piles located north of the Po from eastern Lombardy to the eastern part of the Po plain. These pile dwellings were situated in waterlogged areas, and gave their name to the *palafitte* (Italian for pile dwelling) culture. Major *palafitte* sites include Peschiera, Bor di Pacengo, and Isolone del Mincio. Increasingly, authors present the differences in settlement forms between the Terramare and *palafitte* sites as functional alternatives to the threat of flooding rather than proof of two separate cultural groups. The Terramare and *palafitte* sites share much in the way of material culture, and it is common now to speak of the Terramare-palafitte culture as a unity.

The Terramare culture is named for the characteristic deposits of rich black earth at its village sites. This fertile soil was highly prized by farmers in recent times, the so-called terra marna from which the culture's name derives. The Terramare appear in the second part of the MBA (in the sixteenth century BC) quite dramatically, across the central portion of the southern flank of the Po River's plain. Excavated Terramare sites include Montale and Santa Rosa di Poviglio. There is growth in both the size and number of villages in the Po plain in this period, suggesting a population increase of some magnitude.[6] On the Emilian plain just south of the Po River, there is an increase from sixteen settlements

---

[6] Barbieri and Manzelli 2006: 13–15.

at the start of the MBA to eighty-five by the period's end.[7] These new settlements are very different from what came before and also different from nearby sites. In Emilia-Romagna, the distinction between the Apennine culture in the southern part of Romagna and the Terramare culture in the northern Emilia zone is quite clear. The growth is so sharp and the settlement forms so novel in that area that some scholars argue that people moved into the area from elsewhere, possibly from north of the Po where pile dwellings had been in use since the EBA.[8] There, the Polada culture, centered around Lake Garda, seems to evolve into the *palafitte* culture without evidence of any break.[9] To explain the sharp demographic upturn, other scholars suggest a migration from even further afield, notably Hungary.[10] Although there are some shared material-culture styles between the Terramare and Danubian sites, the connections are as yet unconfirmed and migrations are notoriously difficult to prove archaeologically.

The Terramare villages were generally arranged over a compact surface area surrounded by banks and ditches, presumably to prevent flooding of the huts.[11] The huts, of wood, were often constructed on piles for the same reason,[12] although at some settlements the huts were constructed directly on the ground. This contrasts with Apennine settlements, which lacked surrounding earthworks and whose huts were always built at ground level.[13] Perhaps most remarkably, reconstructions of the huts derived from preserved postholes show that each hut was arranged along the same axis as its neighbor, creating a very orderly layout. This careful planning is unusual for this time, especially as there is no evidence that it was done under the aegis of an authority. Rather, the homogeneity of the settlements in size and layout, and the lack of distinctions in personal wealth within the settlements and in the burials, suggest relatively egalitarian communities.[14] Indeed, the Terramare villages seem to have been a minimally hierarchical society, at least in the MBA.[15]

---

[7] Barbieri and Manzelli 2006: 93.
[8] Bernabò Brea *et al.* 1997: 28; Bietti Sestieri 2000: 758.
[9] Bonetto 2009: 24.
[10] Cardarelli 2009: 36–7.
[11] Although see Pearce 1998: 744.
[12] Barbieri and Manzelli 2006: 92–6.
[13] Bernabò Brea *et al.* 1997: 25.
[14] Barfield 1994: 140.
[15] Barbieri and Manzelli 2006: 92–6.

In the RBA, Terramare social structure seems to have gotten more complex. The earthworks surrounding some of the Terramare become positively monumental, suggesting a need for defense rather than just flood prevention. Moreover, some people are settling off the plain, on hilltops.[16] The added defenses and the new elevated sites together point to some new security concerns. In Emilia-Romagna in the RBA, some sites are abandoned and a few sites become much bigger, suggesting the emergence of site hierarchies with a few larger sites dominating other smaller ones.[17] The early Terramare villages rarely exceeded 2 ha in area, but in the RBA they are 16 ha (e.g., Fondo Paviani); 22.5 ha (Case del Lago); and even 60 ha (Case Cocconi).[18] However, the apparent distinctions in status between settlements are not visible archaeologically at the intrasettlement level, so we must hesitate before positing the emergence of elites. Terramare burials are extremely modest, consisting of urned cremations with uniformly few grave goods.[19] Influences from the Apennine culture become more evident the further south one goes in the Terramare region, but north of the Po the contacts are minor, suggesting a difference in levels of interaction.[20]

Terramare metallurgy advanced progressively. From the MBA on there was a broader range of metal objects than there had been in previous periods, with bronze being used for weapons and tools and not just personal ornaments as was the case in the EBA.[21] The metallurgical industry reaches new heights in the RBA.[22] Many of the expanded villages of the MBA and RBA show evidence of on-site metalworking, particularly north of the Po at sites such as Bor di Pacengo and Cisano.[23] The expansion is significant enough that at their height the Terramare-*palafitte* peoples had the most technologically advanced metals industry in Italy. The metals in their raw form seem to have come from further north, from the Carpathians and the eastern Alps, rather than from the Etruscan ores. This underexploitation of Etruscan metal sources in the MBA cannot be

[16] Barbieri and Manzelli 2006: 103.
[17] Barbieri and Manzelli 2006: 96.
[18] Pearce 1998: 743.
[19] Barbieri and Manzelli 2006: 96–7.
[20] Bernabò Brea *et al.* 1997: 28.
[21] Barbieri and Manzelli 2006: 13–15.
[22] Bernabò Brea *et al.* 1997: 28.
[23] Bietti Sestieri 2000: 759.

attributed to a lack of contacts between the Terramare and Etruria: connections with Etruria are evident in the spread of shared ceramic forms and antler products.[24] Instead, it would seem that mining of Tuscany's *Colline Metallifere* was still on a limited scale, serving only the surrounding area in this period.

In the RBA, along with the expanded metallurgy, craftworking intensified in other media also – including wood and bone carving – to the extent that Barbieri and Manzelli characterize these industries in the north as "semi-specialized."[25] Pottery production, in contrast, continued to be handmade, probably at the household level. The pottery evolves considerably between the MBA and RBA, but common early forms are hemispherical bowls and cups with raised, molded handles with axe-shaped extensions. Changes to these industries are evident in the RBA, when Subapennine pottery from the peninsula south of the Po spreads all over, even up to the Terramare-dominated Po plain. Further, in the RBA more trade in metals is posited, a feature of the "metallurgical koinè" described in Chapter 2 that carries along in its wake other goods as well, such as amber and glass beads.[26]

At the end of the RBA, just when the Terramare culture seems to be at its height, it collapses. The widespread abandonment of sites from around 1200 BC points to a sharp population drop and social dissolution that would not be reversed until the Iron Age.[27] Much of the area was depopulated, particularly south of the Po. North of the Po the crisis seems to have been less extreme. In the Valli Grandi Veronesi, the banked settlements continue into the FBA.[28] Bietti Sestieri suggests that the sites may have been abandoned in that area also but were reoccupied quickly, with settlements resuming again in the FBA.[29] What caused the collapse? Scholars now favor a multicausal explanation, involving the population outgrowing what the soil could support, combined with a worsening climate. Although the causes are debated, the outcome is clear: the near total abandonment of the area.[30] Supporting the environmental

---

[24] Bietti Sestieri 2003: 57–8.
[25] Barbieri and Manzelli 2006: 98.
[26] Barbieri and Manzelli 2006: 96; 103.
[27] Barfield 1994: 139; Barbieri and Manzelli 2006: 105–6.
[28] Bernabò Brea, Cardarelli, and Cremaschi 1997: 29.
[29] Bietti Sestieri 2000: 759.
[30] Cremaschi *et al.* 2006.

explanation is the fact that the crisis was not culture specific, touching even the southern margins of the Po plain whose residents in material-culture terms were Subapennine rather than Terramare.[31]

In addition to the Terramare peoples in the RBA, northern Italy bears traces of another archaeologically distinctive culture, the so-called Canegrate culture, named for the typesite in the town of that name in Lombardy. The Canegrate people occupied the Prealps and Alpine zones in western Lombardy, northern Piedmont, and the Swiss Canton Ticino. The main source of information on this group comes from their cremation cemeteries, and little is known about the settlements. Nonetheless, from the cemeteries it can be gathered that there were few, if any, real social divisions other than some interesting gender distinctions in burial practices.[32] The Canegrate fineware pots, at least those pieces from funerary contexts, are distinctive in appearance, with many biconical urns of various sizes and carinated bowls, typically decorated with geometric patterns of incised grooves and circles on the upper half. The decorative grooving is a feature of some Terramare and palafitticolo ceramics in their latest phases, but for the most part the Terramare and Canegrate ceramic repertoires are quite distinct. Bronzes from Canegrate were analyzed and found to have a different chemical composition from the bronzes at Terramare sites.[33] De Marinis concludes from this, "Si tratta di due mondi scarsamente communicanti."[34] The impression is that the Canegrate peoples' ties seem to have been to the west and north, southeast to France and Switzerland, and even farther afield into central Europe. Prior to the Canegrate culture, there had been an earlier population in the region, the so-called Scamozzina culture, but there is little trace of continuity in ceramic styles between the earlier and later groups. As a result, the evidence suggests that the Canegrate peoples originated north of the Alps and came to settle in the area. They may have been of Celtic origin in light of the later language of the area, but this remains very speculative.[35]

---

[31] Bietti Sestieri 2000: 759.
[32] De Marinis 2000b: 117.
[33] De Marinis 2000b: 98–99.
[34] De Marinis 2000b: 117. "These are two worlds, barely communicating." But see Cupitò 2011 for evidence of some connections.
[35] De Marinis (2000b: 117–19) himself reports this standard view with some reservations, however, suggesting that the ties to the north may be the result of contacts flowing north rather than south.

The Canegrate apparently lose their distinctiveness in the FBA, merging with other groups to form, in the Iron Age, the Golasecca culture. The Golasecca culture occupied the northwest edge of the former Terramare territory, in eastern Piedmont and west Lombardy, in the ninth to fourth centuries BC. In the intervening FBA, the so-called Protogolasecca culture is evident – characterized by small communities with a warrior ethos, but as yet few traces of social hierarchies. The FBA is thought to have been the formative period for the Golasecca groups that followed.[36] Golasecca is a purely archaeological term and the peoples of the Golasecca culture are not referred to as "Golaseccan" but instead seem to be a Celtic group, possibly the ancestors of the Lepontii who occupied the area in the second century BC. Certainly the language of the region, once it is written down in the seventh and sixth centuries BC, is Celtic.[37] Häussler sees the Golasecca group extending as far back as the twelfth century BC, citing the influx of Urnfield cultural traits from north of the Alps at that early date.[38] However, if we take the Canegrate group to be intrusive and one of the progenitors of the Golasecca group, then the transalpine cultural influences may have begun even sooner. In the seventh and sixth centuries BC, the Golasecca settlements show strong Etruscan influences. This influence is most obvious in the adoption of the Etruscan alphabet, but Etruscans are also posited as the driving force behind Golaseccan urbanizing efforts and in expanded trade in the region.[39] The changes are quite remarkable. In addition to the aforementioned adoption of writing, the peoples of the Golasecca culture had large planned settlements and a well-defined aristocratic class, apparently underpinned by the wealth gained from participation in extensive trade networks to southern France, north across the Alps, and into Italy. Although the traditional story has accredited the Etruscans with these transformations, a more nuanced account notes the differences in Golaseccan forms of urbanism compared to Etruscan, with the former's lack of monumental architecture, and the modifications to the Etruscan alphabet in adapting it to Lepontic. Although the Etruscan

---

[36] De Marinis 2000a: 124.
[37] Häussler 2007: 48–9.
[38] Häussler 2007: 49.
[39] Häussler 2007: 49–52.

presence may have been a catalyst for Golaseccan cultural changes, it did not determine the forms these changes took.[40] The so-called Golasecca phenomenon collapsed in the fourth century BC, apparently caused by the influx of new waves of Celtic settlers. Although their arrival was significant to the ancient authors writing from their cultural vantage point of Roman-ness, it may not have been as important on the ground. The "Celtic" qualifier distracts from assessing the impact of these settlers, as does the term "invasion." Once the Celtic invasion and its size are called into question, as scholars have been doing, a reassessment of its impact becomes necessary. Haussler suggests that Golasecca culture may already have been unstable in order to collapse so quickly.[41] The extent to which the new arrivals were "invaders" is debated, and the precise traditional date of 388 BC for the Celtic invasion almost certainly boils down what was in fact a more complex and lengthy process. New material culture (Hallstatt and subsequently La Tène styles) made its way into the region well before the fourth century BC, and most tellingly, so did funerary rituals, as early as the fifth century BC. Therefore, a gradual process of emigration seems more likely.[42] Nonetheless, whether violent and rapid or gradual and peaceful, the new peoples mark the end of the Golasecca settlements. At the time of the Roman conquest, the peoples of northern Italy are identified by local tribal names, such as the Insubres, Boii, and others. Even if there were some vestiges of the earlier Golasecca culture as Häussler suggests,[43] in the region south of the Po where the Golasecca culture had never taken hold, Celtic culture seems to have dominated. From the second century BC on, a rebuilding of the region is evident, with new urban centers, coinage (that may, in fact, have begun even earlier), and the renewed spread of writing (both in Latin and Lepontic) are evident. As Haussler notes, the Roman conquest itself occurred after these developments were already underway, and so it is too simplistic to summarize these multifaceted processes as "Romanization."[44] Further, this complex post-Bronze Age history rules out a priori any network persistence: path dependence is unlikely in the

---

[40] Häussler 2007: 49–52.
[41] Häussler 2007: 53.
[42] Häussler 2007: 53.
[43] Häussler 2007: 55.
[44] Häussler 2007: 56–66.

face of such demographic upheaval. With that in mind, let us take a look at the networks.

The RBA Networks

The above history raises several questions that a network analysis is well suited to answer. To what extent are these known cultural groups – the Terramare and Canegrate cultures – visible, and do their networks resemble their archaeological cultures? Was there anything about the internal structure of the Terramare network that may have contributed to its collapse? How far did the Terramare's economic reach extend in the peninsula? We can explore those questions here.

As observed in Chapter 4, a network covering the area of the Terramare group and extending beyond it is evident in the RBA. This network has an interesting configuration as it consists of a core group of nodes with multiple ties linking them, and then a tail-like extension that in geographic terms runs south and east, hugging the lowlands along the northern edge of the Apennines to the Adriatic coast, and then inland into the Apennines in what is later Umbrian territory. The first question is, to what extent is this network's peculiar configuration a function of the co-presence of objects, and to what extent does distance come into play? In other words, would the sites in the tail be as densely tied to the other Terramare sites if distance were not a limiting factor? We can check this by removing distance as a criterion for a tie, and constructing a new version of the Terramare network in which ties are established based on the co-presence of objects only. The 50 km cut off was important when working at the peninsular scale for the reasons outlined in Chapter 4, when the goal was community detection. Now, however, working with a smaller group of sites and with the aim of understanding network structure rather than detecting it, that distance parameter is not necessary. By looking at the co-presence of objects solely, we can get a general sense of how goods were moving around. The results, shown in Figure 5.1, are interesting.

The density of this reconfigured network is 37 percent, which is relatively dense, and it has a high clustering coefficient (CC) (.807, weighted CC of .682). The sites of the tail are, for the most part, inserted

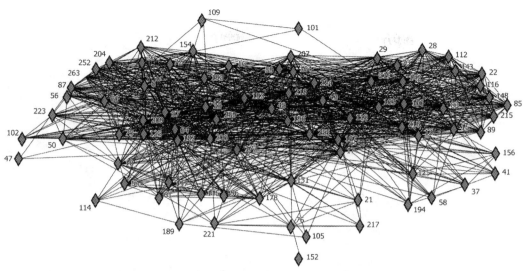

5.1. Graph of RBA Terramare network (Po-Apennines subgroup), no hoards, ties based on shared objects only. N=83.

into the core without any evidence of a geographic distinction: clearly, it was distance that created that attenuated tail, not the scarcity of objects.

Around this dense core group there is a "halo" of less-connected nodes that appear topologically peripheral if not geographically so. These are the sites with the lowest degree scores (number of ties to other sites) in the network; in other words, these sites were not central players in the Terramare network, although they did participate in it. It is among this peripheral faction that the greatest rates of survival into the FBA are to be found. Thirteen sites in the Terramare network continue in the FBA – out of eighty-three total – making a survival rate of 15.7 percent overall. But among the least connected sites in the network, the survival rate is much higher (Figure 5.2).

Of those sites with the twenty lowest-degree centrality scores, seven survive into the FBA – a survival rate of 35 percent, more than twice the average. Among the twenty-one most connected sites in the network, only one survives into the FBA, at a rate of 4.8 percent. The chart demonstrates an inverse relationship between connectedness and survival. Of course, this is in part geographic: the degree of activity in this network is geographically inflected to the extent that the core sites are also near

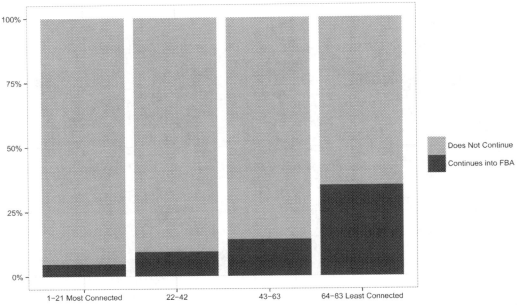

5.2. Chart of RBA Terramare-Apennine network comparing rate of survival into FBA of sites with their degree centrality scores. N=83.

each other and the peripheral sites are, for the most part, geographically peripheral as well (Figure 5.3).

In short, the core Terramare sites are in the area of collapse and those outside the core area were more likely to survive. But what is worth noting is the tail: this is technically outside of the Terramare area geographically, but virtually none of the surviving sites in the FBA are from the tail of the network. This suggests that rather than being a simple "extension," these sites along the Adriatic coast and Apennines were tied extremely closely to the core Terramare sites, and therefore could not withstand its collapse. This is more apparent in the network graph than on the map. Thus, physical distance from the Terramare zone was not the determining factor in a site's survival. What mattered was the degree of integration in the network: the more weakly a site was tied to the Terramare network, the better its chances of survival. The nodes in the halo, such as Frattesina and Fabbrica dei Soci, withstood the Terramare collapse more often than the other nodes. If less dependence on the Terramare network in the form of fewer ties helped to ensure survival, then we could infer that the scale of the collapse was attributable in part to the very integration that had made the network so strong in the first place.

The Northern Networks from the Terramare to the Veneto

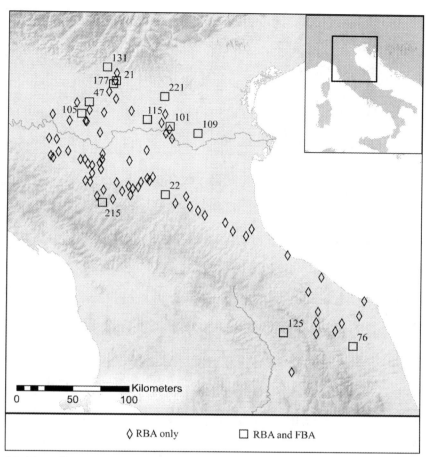

5.3. Map of RBA Terramare-Apennine network with sites that continue into the FBA indicated. N=83 (Drawn by R. Biggs)

Whatever the external causes of the Terramare collapse might have been, the snowball effect was social, not environmental.

Let's look at the north overall now. This means that somewhat counterintuitively we will break up the Terramare network along geographic lines, excluding much of the southern tail, and add in all the other sites in northern Italy that are not part of the Terramare network, including isolates and the sites in the Canegrate network.[45] Now I can also add in the hoards and ritual deposits that were excluded from the peninsular study of Chapter 4 because their relationship to local networks was

---

[45] We will return to the tail in Chapter 7.

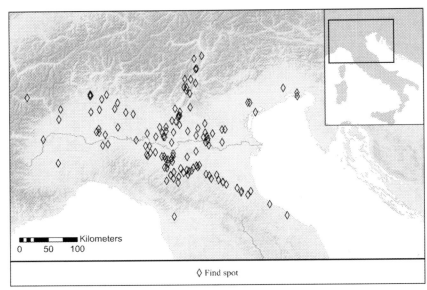

5.4. Map showing locations of RBA sites in northern Italy included in the study. N=126 (Drawn by R. Biggs)

unclear. These sites can be included now because the task of exploratory community detection is over and hoards and ritual deposits contribute to the picture of activity at the intraregional level. There are a total of 126 sites in northern Italy in the RBA with objects that are part of the network set (Figure 5.4). Of these sites, thirteen are cemeteries, seventeen are hoards and ritual deposits, sixty-five are settlements, and thirty-one are unknown or sporadic finds. There are thirty-seven object types from this study circulating in the region, found at as few as two sites and at as many as thirty-one sites (Table 5.1).

We can examine the relationships between sites by taking the distance parameter out of the RBA northern Italy group since we are focusing on a circumscribed area and can imagine that goods would move around fairly easily. Figure 5.5 shows the network of sites in graph form. The first thing to observe is that there are no isolates: examples of all the objects are found at more than one location in the region. The only dyad is in the Veneto. The four-site cluster in the later territory of Rhaetia, observable in the peninsular RBA network as well, is, as noted earlier, structured entirely by the co-presence of one object type: the Matrei A knife.

Table 5.1. *Object types circulating in northern Italy in the RBA*

Object types present in northern Italy in the RBA	Number of find spots
Torre Castelluccia dagger	31
Bertarina dagger	21
Awl handle	21
Miniature spoked wheel	19
Toscanella dagger	19
Redu dagger	16
Merlara dagger	14
Guado di Gugnano dress pin	10
Bacino Marina dress pin	8
S. Caterina dress pin	8
Scoglio del Tonno razor	8
Twisted violin-bow fibula	8
Voghera dagger	8
Small hoe	8
Peschiera dress pin	7
Cataragna dress pin	6
Terontola sword	6
Barrel bead with wavy lines	5
Capocchia a papovero dress pin	5
Fornovo S. Giovanni dagger	5
Matrei A knife	5
Monza sword	5
Pertosa dagger	5
Arco sword	4
Baierdorf knife	4
Cetona sword	4
Gorzano dagger	4
Lenticular bead with radial incisions	4
Montegiorgio sword	4
Tenno dagger	4
Boccatura del Mincio dress pin	3
Garda dress pin	3
Montegiorgio knife	3
Monza dagger	3
Glisente B dagger	2
LH IIIB Aegean-style pottery	2
Miniature decorated wheel	2

We can look more closely at the largest cluster in this northern network, consisting of 117 nodes. Most of these nodes are Terramare sites. It has a density of .2109, meaning that about 20 percent of all possible ties are actually in place. This is not especially dense, but given the number

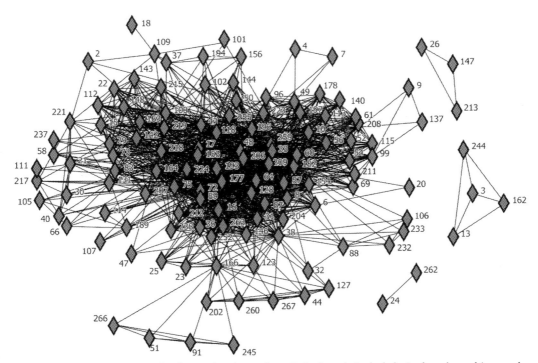

5.5. Graph of RBA sites in northern Italy, hoards included, ties based on objects only. N=126.

of nodes in the cluster, it is not unexpected. The weighted clustering coefficient is .623, which is high enough to suggest that there is some internal clustering occurring (unweighted, the CC is even higher, at .836). Interestingly, the Canegrate cluster identified in the peninsula analysis in Chapter 4 has dissolved into the main Terramare cluster, although the Canegrate sites are mainly on the margins. This marginality is evident in graph form, with the node sizes adjusted to reflect degree centrality scores (Figure 5.6).

Apart from the sites of Canegrate (node 38 on graph) and Appiano Gentile (node 6), the former Canegrate network sites have low centrality scores compared to the Terramare sites. The object types underpinning the fusion of these two networks include the Guado di Gugnano and Capocchia a Papavero dress pins, and the Torre Castelluccia, Redu and Glisente B daggers. Without the distance limits in place, it becomes clear that the Canegrate people participated to a certain extent in the Terramare exchange networks. Even if they were not involved in the densest exchanges, the network picture suggests more contacts between the

The Northern Networks from the Terramare to the Veneto

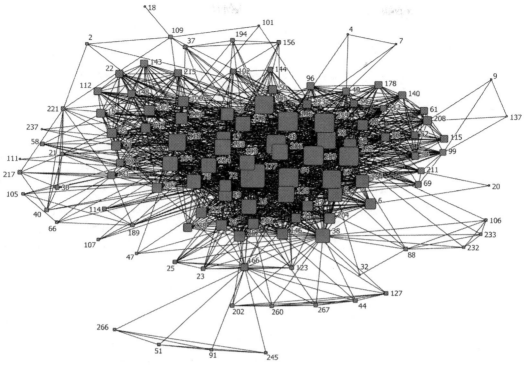

5.6. Graph of large cluster from Fig. 5.5 (RBA northern Italy), hoards included, ties based on shared objects only. Node sizes adjusted to reflect degree centrality scores. N=117.

two groups than is traditionally argued.[46] In light of these interactions, perhaps the Terramare collapse should be taken into account when analyzing the disappearance of the Canegrate network in the FBA. Whether the network's disappearance meant the destruction of the group or a decline in its commercial fortunes, there may be more circumstances in play than the standard account of the group's slow cultural morphing into the Protogolasecca culture.

The FBA in the Veneto

Historical Context

"Lo sviluppo di un aspetto regionale specifico avviene con un certo ritardo rispetto ad altre regioni italiane, in un momento avanzato della

---

[46] E.g., De Marinis 2000b: 100; 117. See also Cupitò 2011 for other evidence of interaction.

prima età del ferro, quando compare la facies paleoveneta, conosciuta in particolare nei centri di Este e Padova."[47]

In the period of the Terramare collapse, those peoples living in the eastern margins of the Terramare culture, which later forms part of the Veneto, seem to have fared better than those in the central plain. As noted earlier, these survivors exhibited less integration in the RBA: many of these were the "halo" sites. In fact, the impact of the crisis is inconsistent in the Veneto. At its western edges, the shock in the Veneto was as severe as in Emilia. But in the territory of Verona, some sites continued. In the Garda region at the RBA–FBA transition there is a reorganization of population rather than a complete collapse, with some new sites appearing. Many of the new sites in the FBA1–2 such as Casalmoro, Calcinato, and Mariconda, are short-lived, disappearing in FBA3, whereas Frattesina and Montagnana survive and new sites appear.[48] Leonardi describes the process as "una serie concatenata di volontarie 'implosioni' di tipo sinecistico."[49] In the eastern plain of the Veneto, the area is alive with new centers, primarily along rivers.[50] This region flourished in the FBA with a high number of settlements, many of which were involved in a robust craft industry, metallurgy, and trade.[51] The diffusion of the Protovillanovan material culture in the region is evident.[52] Foreign goods increase considerably.

Exceptional among the sites of the Po delta is Frattesina, a trading and craft center that seems to have played a critical role in the FBA metals koinè, as noted in Chapter 2.[53] Located on the right bank of an ancient branch of the Po, the Po di Adria,[54] Frattesina is primarily an FBA site, although some objects dated to the RBA suggest some activity

---

[47] Bietti Sestieri 2000: 764. "The development of a distinctive regional aspect occurs with a certain delay compared to other Italian regions, in an advanced phase of the EIA, when the Paleovenetic facies appears, known particularly from the sites of Este and Padua."
[48] De Marinis 1999; Leonardi 2010: 29–30.
[49] Leonardi 2010: 30, "a concatenated series of voluntary synoecistic 'implosions'." How voluntary these implosions were may be debatable.
[50] Bonetto 2009: 269.
[51] Bianchin Citton 2003: 121.
[52] Bonetto 2009: 24.
[53] Bianchin Citton 2003: 121.
[54] The Po di Adria branched off from the Po around Bergantino/Castelmassa and then ran between the Po to the south and the Adige to the north.

on a minor scale late in that period.[55] It is not known if the site grew immediately following the collapse of the Terramare culture or if it arose in a more gradual process.[56] However it began, Frattesina was in full swing by the middle of the FBA, when a flourishing and diverse craft industry is evident at the site. Antler and bone, bronze (as well as lead and gold), glass, ivory, amber, ostrich eggs, and Aegean-style pottery were imported and, in some cases, worked at the site. The site is estimated to have been about 20 ha in size during this peak period, and was the nexus of activity in the region around the Po-Tartaro-Adige Rivers.[57] We do not know a lot about the internal organization of Frattesina except to say that the habitations seem quite homogeneous in size, and that the craft working took place in these domestic areas rather than in a separate zone of the site. Frattesina continued for several centuries. Bietti Sestieri attributes Frattesina's remarkable efflorescence and skilled craft working to influence from Etruria: she sees the craftspeople demonstrating techniques learned in Etruria and suggests that the settlement was founded by Etruria to serve as an outpost from which "Protoetruscans" could manage their long-distance trading networks. This would explain Frattesina's Protovillanovan material culture, with the entire region lacking, as she sees it, regional distinctiveness.[58] The culture in the period is commonly referred to in the Italian scholarly literature as *Protovillanoviano padano*. Indeed, Bietti Sestieri recognizes in the material culture of the Veneto not just a Protovillanovan accent, but more precisely a direct link to the Chiusi-Cetona facies of central Etruria and Umbria, discussed in more detail in Chapter 6. In the Veneto in the FBA, there is a common pottery repertoire and some region-specific metal types, all of which loosely resemble the Chiusi-Cetona material of the same period.[59] An actual Etruscan origin for Frattesina is an intriguing hypothesis, if as yet unproven.[60] Bietti Sestieri suggests that with the collapse of

---

[55] Bellintani 1992: 259–60.
[56] Arenoso Callipo and Bellintani 1994: 13–4; 18; Bonetto 2009: 369.
[57] Arenoso Callipo and Bellintani 1994: 14.
[58] Bietti Sestieri 1997: 764.
[59] Bietti Sestieri 2010: 195.
[60] Also speculative is the proposition that Cypriots and/or Phoenicians were the ones bringing these exotic goods to Frattesina, and even working there (Cassola Guida 1999: 64; Mastrocinque 1999: 232).

the Terramare-*palafitte* group, two poles of activity emerged: one centered on Frattesina and the other centered on Etruria with its metal sources.[61] We will see what the network evidence reveals with regard to this.

Although Frattesina is remarkable, it was not the only settlement in northern Italy in the FBA with traces of craft production and long-distance trade: other settlements demonstrate impressive long-distance contacts, such as Mariconda di Melara, Fondo Paviani, and Montagnana-Borgo S. Zeno.[62] Of these, Montagnana is particularly noteworthy. Founded in the twelfth–eleventh centuries BC, it was eventually bigger than Frattesina itself, reaching 65 ha in the tenth and ninth centuries BC.[63] Foreign contacts at the site are perhaps attested by an Aegean sherd and an ivory comb, which admittedly does not sound like much, but bear in mind there are only a handful of Aegean sherds or ivory objects known in the north. From the tenth century BC on, Etruscan metals were being imported to the site.[64] Thus, in the Veneto, the FBA is a period of great growth, in sharp contrast to the areas to the west. The subsequent history of the Veneto is similarly divergent, and indeed, after the RBA we cannot treat northern Italy as a unit again. In the Veneto in the Iron Age, nucleated settlements emerge that will later become urban centers: Este, Padua, Treviso, Vicenza, Altino, and Oderzo.[65] Archaeologically the Iron Age group in the Veneto is known as the Atestine culture, but this is purely based on the material culture, distinguished from the Golasecca culture to the west, as described earlier.

Sometime in the Early Iron Age (EIA) the decline and final abandonment of Frattesina and other sites along this stretch of the Po di Adria occurred, possibly because this river was no longer popular for water traffic. Arenoso Callipo and Bellintani suggest this may have been because a wetter climate in the EIA made the waterway less predictable.[66] This crisis at the end of the EIA1 leads to a sharp break and following that

---

[61] Bietti Sestieri 2003: 59.
[62] Bietti Sestieri 1997: 765.
[63] Bianchin Citton 2003: 127.
[64] Bianchin Citton 2003: 127.
[65] Bonetto 2009: 24.
[66] Arenoso Callipo and Bellintani 1994: 16.

break, the Paleoveneti culture emerges, which demonstrates a distinct local production independent of central Italy.[67] The Etruscans – or more accurately for this period, the peoples of what becomes Etruria – seem to shift their focus to Bologna and Verucchio, sites that replace Frattesina in similar roles of combined craft production and trade centers.[68] Even more locally, Frattesina ceded her power to sites such as Este and Padua, and the Tartaro and Adige Rivers apparently take over as arteries of movement.[69]

The Veneti, occupying a portion of putative Atestine territory, come into view by 750 BC and are thought to evolve from that group. The western boundary of the Veneti traditionally was Lake Garda and the Mincio River, the southern border was less certain, following either the Tartaro River, the Po or the Adria, or some combination of stretches of these rivers. To the east Venetic territory encompassed the Adriatic coastline as far as the Tagliamento River in the Northeast, and pushing northward toward the Alps, although the northern boundary of the Veneti is also poorly defined. The Veneti were mentioned by many ancient writers but with little trustworthy information.[70] To what extent did the peoples of the northern and southern Veneto belong to the same group, and see themselves as joined? There is a distinction in development between the north and the south. In the southern Veneto there is evidence of urbanizing tendencies as early as the eighth century BC at Este and Padua, which become full-fledged city-states by the sixth century BC, whereas the northern Veneto does not urbanize until Roman colonization.[71] The north-south divide in settlement patterning is understandable geographically, as the southern Veneto consists of fertile plains while the north is mountainous and may not have been able to support dense population centers. Instead, sanctuaries in the north seem to have linked

---

[67] Bietti Sestieri 2010: 198–9. Here the term Paleoveneti refers to the group preceding the named people of the historical period, who appear a few centuries later. Some scholars use Paleoveneti for the ancient Veneti more generally, as a means of distinguishing them from the modern populations of the Veneto (Capuis 1993: 8).

[68] Bietti Sestieri 1997: 765–6. But see Bonetto (2009: 25), arguing against regional groups before the EIA.

[69] Bonetto 2009: 271.

[70] Lomas 2007: 22.

[71] Capuis 1993: 114–21; Lomas 2007: 23.

populations dispersed into small villages in a manner posited for the Apennines as well.[72]

The issue is made more complex by the presence of other groups in the area: Rhaeti (and perhaps Celts) in the Vicentine Prealps; Etruscans in the Po Valley; and Etruscans and Greeks in important trading settlements like Adria.[73] Although the ancient authors saw the Veneti as an ethnic group, the archaeological evidence is more ambiguous. There are cultural links and similarities with the Celts, and the Venetic city-states may have made political (civic) identities more salient than ethnic ones. From the sixth century BC, when writing was adopted in the region, hundreds of inscriptions in Venetic are found in both the northern and southern Veneto, suggesting linguistic unity. However, the alphabet in the Venetic script, drawn from the Etruscan alphabet, displays considerable regional variation, tempering the picture of unity somewhat.[74] A fifth-third century BC inscribed stone in Venetic mentions the term "venetkens," which according to Lomas, "may be the first attested ethnic for the Veneti as a group."[75]

Aspects of Venetic society, or rather Venetic elite society, echo Etruscan elite society in the same period (sixth–fourth centuries BC). The Veneti are known archaeologically from their large cremation cemeteries and from the votive deposits at sanctuaries. Among the mobile material culture, the bronze situlas stand out, although these cannot be taken as an exclusive ethnic marker of the Veneti: their distribution, in fact, extends far beyond Venetic territory into central Europe, not to mention northern Etruria and Bologna.[76] Nonetheless, the rich iconography of these vessels, as well as bronze plaques and carved tombstones, make for compelling study. The recurring themes in the imagery suggest a fairly prominent role for women, a concern with horses (also reported by the textual accounts), and the standard elite package of warfare, feasting, and games.[77] Venetic sanctuaries have been the main source for information about the Venetic language and religion. The sanctuaries

---

[72] Lomas 2007: 29.
[73] Bonetto 2009: 25.
[74] Pandolfini and Prosdocimi 1990: 245; 250-7.
[75] Lomas 2007: 37.
[76] Bonetto 2009: 25; Capuis 1993: 153-4.
[77] Lomas 2007: 32.

lacked monumental architecture, at least of any permanent material, but are identified by their altars and are extremely rich in votive deposits. Offerings included numerous statuettes and bronze plaques, often with cult dedications inscribed on them.[78] Located outside the cities, the sanctuaries may have marked the boundaries between urban and rural zones.[79]

The case for a Venetic ethnic identity is about as strong as can be found short of the Etruscan case. As Capuis puts it: "Anche se, al pari di altre popolazioni preromane, manca una produzione letteraria originale sufficiente a definirli 'cultura storica', è indubbio... che i Veneti costituiscono una delle compagini etnico-culturali meglio definite dell'Italia preromana."[80] The perception by the ancient writers (including Livy, himself a native of Padua) of a coherent group called the Veneti – combined with the shared language, the self-descriptor, common religion, and fixed territory – does indeed suggest a unified group that endured in the region until the Roman conquest. Meanwhile, the Cenomani, a Celtic group, began arriving in trickles in the sixth century BC and started pouring in seriously in the fourth century BC, settling primarily in the western Veneto.[81] Archaeologically, these arrivals are evident in the fourth century BC in the Veronese plain, where sites are abandoned and the western boundary of Venetic territory retreats to the Adige River from the Mincio. A Celtic ethnic element there is very clear materially from the second century BC, but must have been in place before then.[82]

The Roman takeover of the region seems to have been relatively untraumatic, with much voluntary assimilation by the Veneti of Roman culture even prior to their becoming Roman citizens in 49 BC.[83] In the ancient literary tradition, the Veneti were attributed Trojan ancestry just like the Romans. This invented history seems to have encouraged (or justified) cooperation between Romans and Veneti, and all in all,

---

[78] Mastrocinque 1987.
[79] Bonetto 2009: 276.
[80] Capuis 1993: 8. Translation: "Although, like other pre-Roman populations, there is no original literary production sufficient to define it as a 'historical culture,' there is no doubt... that the Veneti are one of the best defined ethnic-cultural units of pre-Roman Italy."
[81] Bonetto 2009: 26.
[82] Malnati *et al.* 1999: 368–9.
[83] Lomas 2007: 38–9.

relations between Rome and the Veneti were amicable. Sometime between 18 and 12 BC the Veneti became part of Region X (later called Venetia et Histria).[84] Region X covered the northeastern portion of Italy from the Po River and the northern half of the Po Delta in the south, along the Adriatic coast over to the Raša River in Croatia, known in antiquity as the Arsia River, which was then the border with Illyricum in ancient times, and extended west as far as the Adda River. Thus, the ancient region combined the modern regions of the Veneto, the eastern part of Lombardy, Trentino-Alto Adige, Friuli-Venezia Giulia, as well as territory outside of modern Italy (the "Histrian" part of the region). The Augustan region in its western zones included Celtic peoples by the time of the Roman conquest, but these are not acknowledged in the later naming of the region. The Veneti's enthusiasm for Roman culture is evident archaeologically in the changes in cult practices, funerary rituals, and new city planning. The second and first centuries BC saw adoption of Roman practices at both the public and private levels. Latin came to replace Venetic in all inscriptions in the first century BC. The sanctuaries either fell out of use or were "Romanized" with temples and dedications to Roman gods. By the first century AD there is little evidence of any Venetic culture surviving. The region's flourishing economically under the empire must have encouraged this openness to Roman culture.[85] Ironically, it could be argued that the very cohesion of the Veneti made it possible for them collectively and individually to buy into Roman life when it was beneficial economically: here group unity was used to mobilize the population as a force for change, not as a basis for resistance.

The FBA Networks

What does the network data contribute to the historical picture of this well-defined group? As noted in Chapter 4, there is a cohesive network in the Veneto starting in the FBA, at the time when the local material culture is labeled *Protovillanoviano padano*. What is interesting, however, is that the Protovillanoviano padano range covers eastern Lombardy

---

[84] Bonetto 2009: 34.
[85] Lomas 2007: 39–40.

The Northern Networks from the Terramare to the Veneto

and the Veneto – a broader area than that covered by the FBA network. The Veneto network maps better to the Iron Age Veneti than does this Protovillanovan group. As noted earlier and in Chapter 4, the dissolution of the Terramare network left behind two smaller networks on what were formerly the northern and eastern margins of the Terramare core, as well as a regional cluster, now disconnected, where the Adriatic and Apennine "tail" of the RBA Terramare network extended. As this central-Italian FBA network will be discussed in Chapter 7, here we can focus on northern Italy proper. Let us begin by looking more closely at the two visible FBA networks: one labeled "Garda" because it was centered around Lake Garda in eastern Lombardy and western Veneto, and one in the Veneto proper. As we saw in Chapter 4, Garda is not a particularly cohesive network, with a high cutpoint ratio and a large diameter making for an ineffective circulation of goods. The Veneto network, however, is a model of a cohesive network, with a redundancy of paths permitting the easy circulation of goods.

We can look at these two networks more closely by removing the distance parameter and adding in the hoards and ritual deposits as nodes. There are forty-three sites, of which – along with the four hoards and four ritual deposits – nine are cemeteries, eighteen are settlements, and eight are find spots of sporadic nature or unknown function. As the map (Figure 5.7) indicates, the forty-three sites are scattered in several geographical groupings: a few sites just south of Lake Maggiore; a string of sites in the Adige Valley down to Lake Garda and just south of it, following this popular pass through the mountains; a large cluster in the southwest Veneto; a scattering of sites in Liguria and on the southern edge of the Po Valley; and a small cluster of sites in the Friuli region at the head of the Adriatic.

The object types circulating in northern Italy in FBA 1–2 are twenty-one in number, found at anywhere from one to nine find spots (Table 5.2).

Whereas many of the sites have just one or two objects, Frattesina stands out with its nine FBA object types. With no distance cut off, the resulting network is much larger than the first FBA one: there are now just three isolates and one dyad, and the other thirty-eight sites are joined together (Figure 5.8).

This new large network demonstrates internal clustering and low density, with a density rate of just 14.1 percent. There are two cutpoints in

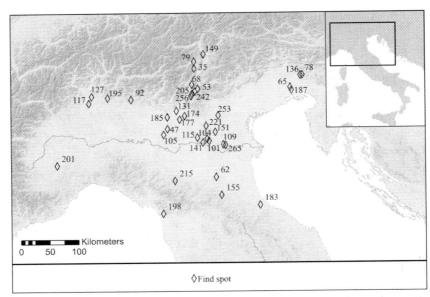

5.7. Map showing locations of FBA sites in northern Italy included in this study. N=43. (Drawn by R. Biggs)

Table 5.2. *Object types circulating in northern Italy in the FBA*

Object types present in northern Italy in the FBA	Number of findspots
Torri d'Arcugnano dress pin	9
Tiryns bead	7
TMES socketed shovel	6
Blue glass barrel bead with spiral	5
Matrei B knife	5
Pick ingot	5
Twisted asymmetrical VB fibula	5
Fondo Paviani socketed shovel	4
Fontanella knife	4
Frattesina asymmetrical VB fibula	4
Glass-eye bead	4
LH IIIC Aegean pots	4
Allerona sword	3
Allumiere bead	3
Asymmetrical VB fibula with two knobs	3
Miniature spoked wheel	3
Ponte S. Giovanni axe	3
Frattesina comb	2
Donkey	1
Frassineto sword	1
Pertosa axe	1

The Northern Networks from the Terramare to the Veneto

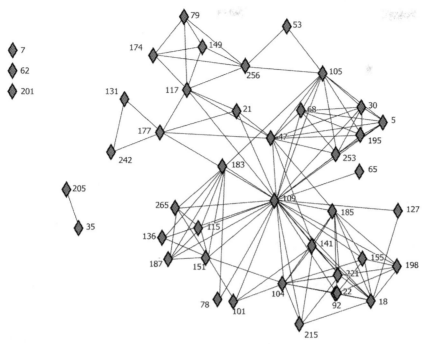

5.8. Graph of FBA sites in northern Italy, with ties based on shared objects only, hoards included. N=43.

the network, but their impact alone is rather small – simply disconnecting one or two sites each.[86] However, there is a cutset of three sites that, if removed, would split the network apart.[87] This, along with the low density, suggests a rather vulnerable and unstable network. Further, there is little evidence that the network's internal structure is geographically inflected, with the exception of the sites belonging in the Veneto cluster described in Chapter 4: these do stay together. In sum, this grouping should be understood as an artificial construct rather than a direct reflection of regional interactions of the period. It is nonetheless useful for revealing such features as ties between clusters. From this perspective, direct ties between far-flung sites such as Ca Morta and Angarano point to the widespread circulation of some of the FBA objects in this area, rather than exposing any real affinities between sites across such

---

[86] The two cutpoints are Frattesina (node 109) and Peschiera del Garda (177).
[87] The three sites in the cutset are Casalmoro (47), Frattesina (109), and Poggio Berni (183).

long distances. The network is decidedly centralized, with a centrality score of 60.16 percent, quite close to that of the original distance-defined Veneto network and higher than that of the Garda network (see Table 4.3). Among the nodes of this large network, Frattesina stands out for its advantageous placement at the center of things. This is immediately evident from the graph, and we can quantify this impression by calculating what is called the "betweenness" centrality score of the sites in the network. This calculates the number of times a particular node is positioned on the geodesic (shortest) path linking various pairs of nodes in the network. A normalized score makes it a ratio of the actual betweenness score to the total possible betweenness scores. The premise behind this score is, if information must pass through Frattesina to get from one site to another, then Frattesina is in a position of power as mediator. According to Knoke and Yang, "The more often that actor i is located on the geodesic path between numerous dyads, the higher actor i's potential to control network interactions."[88] Frattesina has a normalized betweenness centrality score of 49.926, which is high given that fully twenty-nine of the forty-three sites in this network have a score of 0. The next most-central site according to its betweenness score is Golasecca with a centrality score of 11.769, which is surprising given that the site is far from central geographically. It is followed fairly closely by Peschiera del Garda and Casalmoro. Betweenness centrality scores are very low beyond that group, unsurprising given this low density network. However, we can assess centrality another way by using nodal degree scores – that is, the number of ties a site has. Here again, Frattesina dominates – with a normalized degree centrality score[89] of 71.429 – followed distantly by Casalmoro with a score of 28.571. By multiple measures, Frattesina dominates this northern network.

Faction analysis of this artificial network reveals an interesting internal cleavage (Table 5.3). Faction analysis works by permuting the nodes of the matrix into blocks, or factions, whose members have relatively more ties with each other and relatively fewer ties outside the faction.

---

[88] Knoke and Yang 2008: 67–8.
[89] Normalized nodal degree scores are calculated by taking the ratio of actual ties a site (node) has with other sites to the maximum possible ties a site could have.

Table 5.3. *Permuted matrix of FBA northern Italy sites, ties based on objects only, boards included. Divided into two factions.*

Ideally, there should be higher densities within factions than outside of them, or in matrix terms, along the diagonal rather than off the diagonal. In the ideal type, the cells in the blocks along the diagonal should be all 1s and the cells in the outer blocks should be 0s. Note that in setting up this algorithm, one does not input which nodes should belong to which faction; one simply selects how many factions the network should be divided into. Thus, when conducting the analysis, one may try out various numbers of factions into which the network should be permuted to see which is the best fit. In the case of the FBA northern network, we can keep things simple by partitioning it into two factions. The result is that the factions' density scores are higher than the average for the network over all, which was admittedly very low, whereas the off-diagonal densities are less than the overall average. The proportion correct is .623, meaning that 62.3 percent of the time, sites on the diagonal have a tie whereas sites off the diagonal do not. Here the off-diagonal (extra-factional) densities are both .03, while the diagonal densities range from .21 to .30. It would seem, therefore, that there are two subgroups within this network.

What is noteworthy is the selection of sites for the factions. Remember: the factions are generated automatically according to what combination of nodes produces the densest grouping. Faction 1 contains the Garda network sites and sites to the immediate north and south (Figure 5.9). Faction 2 includes all the sites of the original Veneto network, only one of the sites of the original Garda network (Ponte S. Marco), and all the sites to the far northeast and the south. These factions are imperfect records of actual relations, but they hint at some apparent geographically inflected distinctions (recall that there is no geographic data built into the network we are currently working with, or into the faction analysis). That the Veneto network is in the same faction as all the sites to the south of it while none of those sites to the immediate west and north are in that faction – other than Ponte S. Marco – is worth considering more closely.[90] This pattern is particularly surprising as the western sites are much nearer in physical distance to the original Veneto group than

---

[90] Two sites farther west – Isolino di Varese and Costa Cavallina – are included in this faction, although they point to long-distance movements of goods.

The Northern Networks from the Terramare to the Veneto

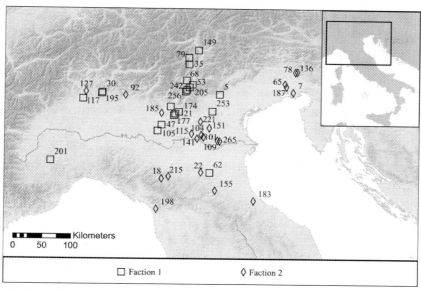

5.9. Map of northern Italy showing FBA sites with factions indicated. (Drawn by R. Biggs)

are the sites to the south. It would seem that already in FBA 1–2 there was a firm western boundary to the regional group, probably at the Mincio River south of Lake Garda, across which there were only limited exchanges occurring. The Mincio is the hypothesized western boundary of the Veneti in the historical period, so it is remarkable that this border might have been demarcated so early. As for the southern sites in the faction, the pattern of ties is so consistent that these deserve a closer look. Four of the six sites in the south that belong to the Veneto faction have Tiryns beads, a fifth has two varieties of glass beads, and the Poggio Berni hoard has bronze tools and a pick ingot. The Tiryns beads were circulating in a markedly circumscribed fashion. Two further find spots of Tiryns beads are in Etruria, which contributes to the picture in the scholarly literature of close relations between the Veneto and Etruria in this period. The site of San Michele di Valestra at the southern edge of the Po Plain looks like a stepping stone to Umbria from the Veneto, as it is a find spot for blue glass-barrel beads with spirals, an object type also present at Gubbio. Nonetheless, it must be emphasized that the visible ties between these two regions are thin, and we should not overstate the interactions.

We can see if the pattern holds when we divide the matrix into more factions: let us try five (Table 5.4). The proportion correct is higher than with two factions: .884. Faction densities range from .05 (a faction composed of the isolates and dyad) to .79, although if we disregard that first faction, the range for the others is .44–.79. So far, so good. However, things get very complicated when we look more closely at the factions. With the permuted matrix, we see that the Veneto cluster is split between two factions (Factions 3 and 5) and expanded to include the southern sites and the northeastern ones while the Garda cluster is split between two factions (Factions 2 and 4), with only some of the sites in the immediate vicinity of the lake finding themselves in the same faction. Beyond all these extra subdivisions, we can nonetheless see the same cleavage: Factions 3 and 5 contain the Veneto cluster and points south and northeast; Factions 2 and 4 contain the Garda cluster and points immediately north and south of it. The one exception each time is Ponte S. Marco, which has objects such as a Tiryns bead that associate it more strongly with the Veneto cluster. Further, the sites to the far west show no consistency in their associations with the two larger groupings, falling fairly evenly between them.

To sum up, it would seem that goods circulating within the Garda network in the FBA were part of an even broader circuit that involved the Val d'Adige alpine pass, Lake Garda, and slightly further south. This may mean that the Garda network should be understood less as a local phenomenon and more as a segment of a longer-distance transalpine route. Although it is beyond the scope of the present study, it would be interesting to expand the network analysis north to see if the Garda network proves to be an extension of something larger. In contrast, the Veneto network had more to do with its immediate southern neighbors than it did with the Garda network and the other sites to the north and west, although it had some ties to the Friuli region at the northern tip of the Adriatic. If, as is argued, the Veneto was part of long-distance trade routes linking Europe to the Aegean in the FBA, this analysis suggests that the goods were probably not moving down the Val d'Adige. The sites to the immediate south with which the Veneto network shows ties make a natural bridge toward central Italy. The role of the Adriatic itself in these circuits is another story,

Table 5.4. *Permuted matrix of FBA northern Italy sites, ties based on objects only, boards included. Divided into five factions.*

one which these terrestrial short-distance networks are not equipped to answer.

Discussion

To conclude, the network data in northern Italy in the RBA and FBA largely mirror the historical picture revealed by archaeological work in the region, but with some notable differences. In the RBA, we can detect a vast network corresponding to the Terramare culture and a smaller dense network in western Lombardy that maps onto the Canegrate culture. Although the two networks appear distinct in the peninsular map, when we remove the distance parameter and join sites by shared objects alone, the Canegrate sites display connections with the Terramare sites, even if most of the sites remain marginal to the core Terramare group. In the RBA the Terramare network's reach extends southeast down the peninsula as far as the central Apennines and the eastern edge of the future Etruria. With the Terramare culture's collapse, we can see that there were repercussions in Marche and Umbria, with the dissolution of many of those sites, or at least a decline in their access to distinctive objects. However, closer to the Terramare territory proper, but on its margins, those sites with only limited ties in the Terramare network weathered the collapse far better, with far higher survival rates. Thus, even if the triggers for the collapse were environmental, the magnitude of the collapse was in part a function of interdependence (much as we witness globally today).

By the FBA, with both the Terramare and Canegrate networks gone, two much-smaller networks among a scattering of dyads and isolates are evident: one around Lake Garda, and one in the southwest Veneto, with the site of Frattesina at its center. The latter is a cohesive network whose integrity remains even following the reconfiguration of the network to remove distance as a parameter. Of interest is the evidence of ties to the immediate south, and few ties to the west. This fits with the picture we have from other evidence that Frattesina and its neighbors interacted closely with Marche and the Apennines. The extent to which those interactions can be extended to include Etruria will be explored in Chapter 6. The network data also suggest that the western boundary of Venetic territory was already delineated in this early period, further proof of an early start to this group. Capuis described the Veneti as second only to the Etruscans among the peoples of pre-Roman Italy for their territorial influence and economic dynamism.[91] We seem to be observing as far back as the FBA in the Veneto both an established territorial definition and an economic reach extending beyond that territory. Indeed, this reach may be one of the legacies of the Terramare culture.

Aftermath: The Roman Period

The northern networks of the Bronze Age were on territories that in the Roman period were organized administratively under Augustus into several regions: Region VIII, X, and XI. As will be discussed further in Chapter 9, the Augustan regions give insight into the status of the pre-Roman population groupings and territories at the end of the first millennium BC. Pliny the Elder's descriptions of the populations of each region cannot be taken as given, but even the errors are useful for showing the Roman attitudes toward these areas, and what by this late period was common knowledge and what was not. The Celts of northern Italy constitute an interesting case. Until recently it was universally accepted that they were an invasive late arrival into northern Italy in the fourth century, whose foreignness precluded them from discussions of regional ethnicity formation.[92] Williams and others have problematized this received narrative, noting that there is some evidence that Celtic peoples had settled in the region earlier than previously supposed: by the sixth century BC rather than the fourth. Moreover, already in the Iron Age, the Golasecca culture of the region was Celtic.[93] One scholar has even suggested that the northern Italian Celts may have coalesced as a group only *after* their sixth century BC settlement in the region, where the bonds derived from a shared language triggered the emergence of a Celtic identity.[94] Although intriguing, this theory, as Williams points out, is not usually how we understand ethnicity formation to occur.[95]

---

[91] Capuis 1993: 8.
[92] See Williams 1997 for an overview of these perspectives.
[93] Williams 1997: 75.
[94] Prosdicimi 1987.
[95] Williams 1997: 75–6.

Even though group identity certainly can strengthen and reify from foreign exposure, we would expect the character of the group to be more place specific rather than a new affirmation of a pan-European affiliation not easily sustained.

The subsequent picture of two of the Celtic groups, the Boii and Senones in the fourth and third centuries BC, conveys something of how complex the processes were. These two groups, occupying the modern-day provinces of Emilia and coastal Marche respectively, were among the peoples who arrived as part of the Celtic invasion. Although the La Tène weapons and fibulae and the burial rites in their cemeteries speak to this origin, the additional presence of numerous Etruscan items in the graves makes easy ethnic identifications difficult. From the finds at the cemetery of Monte Bibele, where Celtic grave goods seem to replace Etruscan ones only gradually, Williams rejects the notions of "Celtic" as a discrete ethnic grouping in Italy and instead proposes a mélange of ethnicities in the Po Valley only imperfectly expressed through archaeological markers.[96] This mélange would help to explain why Region VIII, for example, lacks an ethnonym and instead came to be named for the major Roman road running through it, the Via Aemilia.[97]

After this complex later history, it is no wonder that there are no surviving traces of the earlier Canegrate or Terramare cultures by the time of the Roman conquest: the Celtic groups' material culture and way of life owed nothing to the earlier Terramare-*palafitte* groups, and probably very little to the Canegrate group. All ties to the Bronze Age past had been effectively severed. Several scholars have called attention to the tendency to dismiss the Celts as "foreign" and exclude them from models of regional identity formation in Italy, and their objections are valid.[98] Nonetheless, from our perspective, the combination of demographic collapse at the end of the RBA and the influx of new settlers six centuries later can only mean the disappearance of the earlier networks. Nor does the Garda network, unstable and built on external connections rather than internal cohesion, survive into the historical

---

[96] Williams 1997: 76–8.
[97] Thomsen 1947: 113.
[98] E.g., Prosdocimi 1987 and Williams 1997.

period, although the Val d'Adige pass has never ceased to be used. The Veneto group does endure, however, even managing to withstand Celtic influences, to emerge as one of the most stable and well-defined regional groups before the Romans. Its beginnings lie in the Bronze Age.

CHAPTER SIX

WEST-CENTRAL ITALY: NETWORKS AND NEIGHBORS

Introduction

In Chapter 4, I precipitately labeled the network identified in west central Italy "Etruria" because of its location. This admitted anachronism draws attention to a key research question of this area: What are the circumstances behind the rise of the Etruscans, Latins, and ultimately Rome itself? This question has made west-central Italy the most studied area of Italy in the Bronze Age and arguably in all periods. Along with investigations into the rise in social complexity and the path to statehood in the region, scholars have sought the origins of the region's cultural distinctiveness. To what extent was Etruria's rise influenced by its relations with groups in the north and east of the peninsula? The Veneto and the Po Valley by the Iron Age manifest many similarities in material culture with Etruria, all forming part of the broader "Villanovan" label. When and how did these cultural similarities come about? Another central question concerns the nature and extent of the ties between Etruria and Latium. Etruscan influence on Latial society and, most notably, on the urbanization of Rome, is well attested in the Archaic period, but the linguistic differences and each region's strong self-identification in the first millennium BC make it clear that by then the Latins and Etruscans were distinct.[1] If one goes back in time far enough, Etruria and Latium look very similar to each other and to their neighbors. When did they separate culturally? With these questions in mind, this chapter will

[1] Cornell 1995: 151–72.

situate the network data for this region within its historical and geographic contexts, and look more closely at the structure of the network and what it reveals.

Historical and Geographic Background

The phenomenal rise of Etruscan society beginning in the eighth century BC and peaking from 700 to 470 BC – the Orientalizing and Archaic periods – is a story frequently told. The urbanization of the Iron Age plateau communities, their increasing control over surrounding territories, and a new articulation of elite identity all occur over the course of these centuries.[2] The wealth of the Etruscan elites, their intensive and fruitful interactions with Greeks and Phoenicians, their engineering technology, their complex religious beliefs and nimble adoption of writing for their own ends, and their artistic achievements and commercial acumen are without equal in the central and western Mediterranean in these periods. Although organized into autonomous city-states, the cultural uniformity overlying regional variations makes it clear that they were a coherent and self-defining group. The historic territory of the Etruscans is delimited by the Arno River to the north and the Tiber River to the south and east, two of the three major navigable rivers in the peninsula.[3] The territory benefits from fertile soils in its alluvial plains and a number of rivers in addition to the major boundary-making Arno and Tiber: in fact, it is also the portion of Italy in which the Apennines are at their narrowest, allowing for a much wider belt of agricultural land from the coast than from other areas outside of the Po Valley. Etruria is also home to some of the richest mineral deposits in the Mediterranean, particularly in the northwest of the region where the Colline Metallifere or "Ore Mountains" had sources of copper, lead, silver, and even tin. On the island of Elba, iron was plentiful and in the southern part of Etruria, the Monti della Tolfa were also good sources of copper, iron, and lead, among other minerals. In addition, the hills adjacent to the Fiora Valley have deposits of limonite, pirite, and lead.[4] Although

---

[2] Riva 2010: 6.
[3] The Po is the third navigable river.
[4] Zifferero 1991.

the development was not uniform around this territory as the resources were not evenly distributed, its natural advantages were clearly decisive in shaping Etruscan success.

To the south, ancient Latium[5] was bounded by the Tiber to the northwest, the sea to the west, the Anio River (a tributary of the Tiber) to the north, the Apennines to the east, and extended as far south along the coast as Cape Circeo at the end of the Pontine Marshes.[6] The southern and eastern boundaries of Latin territory were not hard and fast, from what the ancient sources report, and the mountain-dwelling Volscians may have settled in southern Latium in the fifth century BC until the territory was reclaimed by the Latins.[7] Bietti Sestieri points out, "Lazio is considerably poorer than Etruria in practically every kind of natural resource."[8] However, it does contain a relatively fertile farmland, if not as rich as Campania to the south.[9]

In the case of the Etruscans, the material evidence has been helpful in determining that wherever the Etruscans may have come from originally, their forebears were in the region certainly by the RBA. The importance of that period for subsequent developments is well treated in Barker and Rasmussen's 1998 book *The Etruscans*, where the authors emphasize population growth and agricultural intensification as the necessary preconditions for the eventual rise in social complexity in the region. However, the devil is in the details. Some scholars argue that urbanization was the result of the intentions of the already complex FBA societies, while others see social complexity being engendered by the rise of the protourban centers.[10] None of the changes were rapid, however. The Iron Age and Archaic period-material records of the Etruscans show undeniable continuities with the preceding Protovillanovan and Villanovan material cultures, in spite of massive social transformations. Although the retrojection of the Republican Roman gens back to prehistoric periods is, as discussed earlier, problematic,[11] one can nonetheless note that

---

[5] That is, Latium Vetus, as opposed to the modern administrative region of Lazio, which extends north of the Tiber and covers most of what in antiquity was south Etruria.
[6] Cary and Scullard 1989: 31.
[7] These historical movements are possibly visible in the intrusive burials in Satricum in this period; for a thoughtful treatment, see Smith 1999: 474–5.
[8] Bietti Sestieri 1992: 26.
[9] Smith 2007: 162.
[10] See Riva 2010: 11–3 for a useful overview of this debate.
[11] Smith 2006.

the gradually emerging social hierarchies can be traced in a continuous line over the course of the Iron Age.[12]

Etruria in the RBA shows traces of an emergent site hierarchy, with some larger population centers such as Luni sul Mignone and Sorgenti della Nova replacing the scattering of smaller settlements of the preceding period. Although these larger sites presage subsequent changes, almost none survive the Bronze Age. At the end of the Bronze Age and start of the Iron Age, populations settle in large groups on the steep-sided plateaus that will become the urban centers of the following phase.[13] This massive resettlement is accompanied eventually by the abandonment of the earlier sites, but not immediately: there is some evidence of the coexistence of old and new centers for a time.[14] Regardless of this time lag, the settlement shift was clearly momentous: of the ninety-seven FBA villages Pacciarelli identifies, only eleven continue into the EIA.[15] Population pressures may have caused the resettlement onto more spacious plateaus, although Guidi sees the nucleation as a political act, with the leaders of individual villages – already formed into a federation – taking the next step of uniting spatially.[16] Northern Etruria goes through a similar protourban phase, but the sites are smaller and spaced farther apart. Pacciarelli argues that the northern and inland centers had less control of their surrounding territories,[17] but Riva does not accept this explanation, arguing instead that the new protourban centers in the north were all strategically located to access resources, be they mineral, marine, or agricultural.[18] Further, Riva insightfully notes that urbanization at a particular site never occurred in isolation from other sites going through the same process: these urban sites grew up "as a network of settlements that were accessible to one another and the wider world."[19] She contrasts this situation with Samnium and Picenum, two regions lacking a cluster of protourban settlements that could advance together toward city status.[20]

[12] Riva 2010: 6–7.
[13] Riva 2010: 5.
[14] Riva 2010: 14.
[15] Pacciarelli 2000: 107–8; fig. 60.
[16] Guidi 1993: 455.
[17] Pacciarelli 1994: 236.
[18] Riva 2010: 19–20.
[19] Riva 2010: 22.
[20] Riva 2010: 22, note 74.

Hand in hand with these settlement changes was agricultural intensification: in west-central Italy, the RBA – and especially the FBA – constitute a turning point in the scale of agricultural production. Whereas the EBA and MBA had seen the "progressive infilling of the landscape," the RBA marked "the watershed in subsistence and technology": "Faunal and floral assemblages over the next 400 years point to a diversification and intensification of production on unprecedented levels, and signal an important departure from previous agricultural development in the peninsula."[21] Along with more land being put under cultivation, there were changes to animal rearing as well. From all the sites for which the evidence exists in southern Etruria, there is an increase in the percentage of ovicaprines in the RBA and FBA, and a decrease in cattle, with percentages of pigs remaining generally unchanged.[22] Changes to religious practices in the RBA and FBA in west-central Italy would seem to underline the agricultural intensification, particularly "the appearance of votive offerings, including food, especially cereals, in pits and ditches within settlement sites."[23] These offerings suggest a society for whom food production had taken on a greater role than ever before – perhaps with a corresponding decline in hunting – and by the FBA, a larger population.

Although there is a general increase in the use and circulation of metal in Italy in the FBA, Etruria stands out with the highest densities of metal objects. Likewise, it is in Etruria that there is the first evidence of a regional metalworking style at a time when metals from Latium, for example, maintained a pan-Italian style. This is almost certainly attributable to the focused exploitation of Etruria's own rich metal sources and consequent internalized metals industry.[24]

The case for a more complex social organization is most convincing in south Etruria. There, in the FBA, the appearance of some larger settlements (max. 20 ha) in elevated positions and defended, along with other sites of just 1–2 ha, would seem a textbook example of a two-tiered hierarchy of settlements.[25] By the EIA the large defended settlements are two orders of magnitude larger than those of the previous period.

---

[21] Barker and Stoddart 1994: 150–1.
[22] De Grossi Mazzorin 1998: 172–3.
[23] Whitehouse 1995: 86.
[24] Bietti Sestieri 1992: 30; 36; 62.
[25] Bietti Sestieri 2010: 233.

The average size of defended settlements in south Etruria in the FBA was 4.5 ha; in the EIA the big settlements average 110 ha in size.[26] Religious transformations in the RBA and FBA in west-central Italy may also signal changes in social structure. Cult sites in caves, which had prevailed previously, fall out of use, replaced by votive offerings within settlement sites and at springs and other natural water sources. Finally, at the end of the period in the tenth century BC, the first known open-air cult site on the peninsula appears, near the Laghetto del Monsignore spring at Campoverde.[27] Whitehouse links the changing religious practices to increasing social complexity taking the form of complex chiefdoms in Etruria and Latium. She posits an emergent elite using religion as a tool to control broader swathes of territory than was necessary in earlier periods when more localized religious practices and political units prevailed.[28] Other than the settlement size differences and these religious practices, however, elites are hard to spot in west-central Italy: before the EIA, the burials show no conclusive evidence of distinctions in wealth, nor is there evidence of elites from the internal organization of settlements.[29]

Peroni gave these changes a causal sequence that is fairly straightforward: the new intensification of agricultural activities engendered population growth and larger, more stable settlements, and the need for more complex political structures. In the RBA, these agricultural communities "used their economic reserves to acquire bronze utensils and arms," and eventually with the rise of aristocratic classes in the FBA, local markets emerged to facilitate their obtention not just of metals, but of finished craft products as well.[30] He sees the Mycenaean demand for metals stimulating mining in the Carpathians and the eastern Alps, leading also to expanded finished metal production.[31] This expanded metallurgical activity includes the mining itself, metallurgical production by specialized craftspeople, and the circulation of finished products within Italy. An alternative explanation developed by Bietti Sestieri in several publications proposes that with the rise in metallurgical activity,

---

[26] Di Gennaro 1986: 143.
[27] Guidi 1980: 149; Whitehouse 1995: 86.
[28] Whitehouse 1995: 86–7.
[29] Barker and Stoddart 1994: 159–62.
[30] Peroni 1979: 15.
[31] Peroni 1979: 21.

regions needed to control the routes along which the metals circulated and those regions with metal sources needed to protect them. These new imperatives led to a sense of territorial boundedness that eventually resulted in ethnic identities.[32] Although this debate concerns the peninsula as a whole, it is in south Etruria where the debate is played out.

By the Iron Age, material traces of the Villanovan culture covered a broad although discontinuous swath from what would later be Etruria north and east up to the Po Valley, the Adriatic coast, and down to Campania. It seems possible that this meta-region was at least, in part, the outcome of migrations first from the northeast into central Italy and then from central Italy into Campania in the EIA, in what may have been unrelated movements; what is not well understood is the extent that this Villanovan group constituted an internally recognizable cultural unit. The term "Villanovan" is not an ethnic designation, but rather a suite of material-culture traits including cremation burials and some social differentiation.[33] The traditional explanation put forward by Mansuelli to explain Villanovan material around Bologna was the movement of people from Etruria north. Bietti Sestieri proposes instead that Frattesina's population moved south – to Bologna and Verucchio – and maintained earlier ties to Etruria, creating a connected group.[34] As we saw in Chapter 5, the network evidence cannot settle this debate; however, we will keep this theory in mind when looking at the networks of west-central Italy in this section.

Against this backdrop, Latium and Etruria start to diverge developmentally. From 900 BC, Etruria's settlements begin to nucleate into urban centers whereas Latium's settlements do not do this for several more centuries. Instead, in Latium from 900 BC, protourban settlements from 50–100 ha in size can be found, spaced fairly regularly, so probably controlling a 100–150 km² territory.[35] When urbanization does occur in Latium, Rome is just one among several such centers. Archaic Satricum,

---

[32] Bietti Sestieri 1997: 378; 2000: 761; 2005: 20. The expansion of metallurgy in the RBA was "uno dei fattori piu importanti della crescita del livello di definizione territoriale, stimolata dalla necessità di controllo delle vie di approvvigionamento e di scambio e, nelle regioni produttrici come l'Etruria, delle aree di estrazione" (Bietti Sestieri 2005: 20).

[33] Haynes 2000: 15.

[34] Bietti Sestieri 2010: 210.

[35] Bettelli 1997: 218, drawing on Pacciarelli's research.

for example, displays an urbanizing impulse at the same time Rome does: it had paved roads and public buildings and also underwent a period of expansion. A similar story can be told for Gabii. Indeed, Smith situates the urbanization of Rome within the regional context of the "rise of an urban society" in Latium and further suggests that Rome's position of dominance in Latium was not secured until at least 338 BC.[36] Carandini has also argued that Rome in this period was not much bigger than other protourban centers such as Gabii and Ardea, although acknowledging that the earliest settlement at Rome does predate the others, going back to the MBA.[37] Bettelli, however, distinguishes Rome from the other cities by its larger size and distance from them, suggesting that its hinterland was vaster as well.[38] All agree nonetheless that it is in the Archaic period when Latium urbanizes, with the nucleated settlements of the Iron Age evolving into urban centers with planned layouts, civic religious structures, and specialist workshops. Nijboer frames the urbanization of central Italy in economic terms, emphasizing the emergence of extra-household craft industries and the ensuing need for wider contacts to expand demand.[39] This economic setting may be contrasted with a still small-scale economy in the Bronze Age, one in which the seeming isolation of parts of central Italy make sense: there was little impetus to reach much beyond one's region.

Rome's urbanization is the most famous example of this process, and also the most contentious. Pallottino long argued that Rome's urbanization came about under Etruscan control, during the rule of the Tarquins – the Etruscan dynasty of kings whom we know from textual sources.[40] Cornell sees Rome's urbanizing efforts of the late seventh and sixth centuries BC as homegrown, owing little to Etruscan influence; he pushes the Tarquins later, to the second half of the sixth century, only after Rome is already a city.[41] Rasmussen sees an Etruscan influence beginning earlier and being stronger. He reinstates earlier dates for the

---

[36] Smith 2007: 169.
[37] Carandini 1997: 481–2.
[38] Bettelli 1997: 218.
[39] Nijboer 2004.
[40] Pallottino 1993: 205–17. He does not, in fact, contend that this process began from scratch with the Etruscans, just that they pushed forward processes that were already under way.
[41] Cornell 1995: 122–41.

Tarquins, but does not go so far as to call Archaic Rome Etruscan or even "Etruscanized."[42] The debate hinges on the extent to which ethnicity mattered. Cornell says it did not, suggesting that whatever urbanizing efforts the Tarquin kings may have engaged in, they did so as individual kings of Rome, not because they were somehow representatives of Etruscan culture.[43] This fits with Smith's contention that Rome's urbanization was part of a broader trend across Latium, involving the settlements of Gabii, Lavinium, and Satricum, among others.[44] That urbanization was occurring on a regional scale in Latium would seem to contradict the picture of Rome becoming a city from Etruscan intervention alone.

Latium's slowness in urbanizing compared to Etruria has been attributed to the former region's poor mineral resources. However, the languages are so different that one may expect a divergence in activity earlier. What do the Bronze Age networks indicate? Here we are primarily concerned with the origins not of social differentiation, but of regional identities and therefore, it is of considerable interest if we can detect behavior suggesting affiliations or cleavages. Archaeologically, in the RBA and FBA, it has proven difficult to distinguish the regions of Latium and Etruria. The two regions' material culture looks the same in the Subapennine and Protovillanovan phases, and both display a demographic growth from 1300 BC on.[45] Further, both areas were isolated from southern Italy: in the RBA and FBA, the Tyrrhenian coast seems to have been rarely navigated north of Campania, leaving Latium and Etruria removed from the Aegean contacts occurring further south. Aegean-type pottery, whether made in Italy or Greece, evidently did not move much up the Tyrrhenian coast, as there are very few sherds in west-central Italy at all: Barker and Stoddart describe it as "virtually bypassed by Mycenaean imports."[46]

---

[42] Rasmussen 1997.
[43] Cornell 1995: 165. Along with Pallottino, Rasmussen (1997) sees an important role for Etruscans in the process.
[44] Smith 2007: 169.
[45] Smith 2007: 162–3.
[46] Barker and Stoddart 1994: 153. This contrasts with the Adriatic. See Cazzella and Recchia 2009 for comparison of these divergent regional histories. Even the site of Vivara in Campania, a coastal settlement with considerable Aegean imports, shows no strong ties with Etruria (Marazzi and Mocchegiani Carpano 1998). Despite the evidence of metallurgy at this short-lived trading post, there is no confirmed link with

West-Central Italy: Networks and Neighbors

If the entire region remained fairly removed from south-Italian business, it is their contacts with the north that distinguish the future Etruria and Latium from the MBA through the FBA, with Etruria showing connections with the Po Plain, the Veneto, and Marche, while Latium does not. Bietti Sestieri reconstructs the historical process as follows: the closer ties emerging in the FBA between the north and Etruria were an outcome of the collapse of the Terramare complex and the likely movement of some of those peoples from the Po Plain into northern Etruria, bringing technologies with them. The result is a fairly homogeneous material-culture grouping, the Protovillanovan culture, that encompassed present-day Tuscany, Umbria, Marche, the area around Bologna, and the Veneto. In addition to similar ceramics in this area, the distributions of bronze objects, particularly in hoards, suggest movement of goods along this northeast-directed corridor.[47] At the southwesternmost point of this corridor, metal finds from the Fiora and Albegna valleys in Tuscany showed links with northern Italy in the RBA and FBA.[48] Likewise, chemical analyses indicate the presence of metals from Tuscan ores in northeast Italy in the FBA, possibly, as Pearce suggests, because Tuscany had a source for cassiterite (tin oxide), while the closer Alpine sources did not.[49] Distributions of pick ingots in the FBA also show links between the two regions. These objects seem to have been produced with both Tuscan and Alpine ores, possibly with Frattesina playing a key role in their distribution.[50] South Etruria appears somewhat peripheral in this period.[51] Latium was not entirely excluded from these exchanges. Baltic amber reached Latium as well as Etruria, most notably, probably overland from northeast Italy.[52] On the whole, however, northern objects in Latium are rare, and the core relationship was apparently between Etruria and the north.

the Tuscan ores (contra Pare 2000: 24). Indeed, in Vivara's heyday (seventeenth to fifteenth centuries BC) there is no evidence of extensive exploitation of the Tuscan metal sources for export, although there is compelling evidence that the copper ores were being used locally in northern Etruria as far back as the Copper Age (Barker and Rasmussen 1998: 48–50).

[47] Bietti Sestieri 2010: 230.
[48] Pellegrini 1995: 512–17.
[49] Pearce 2000: 113.
[50] Pearce 2000: 112–13; Pellegrini 1995: 517.
[51] Bietti Sestieri 2005: 17–9.
[52] Negroni Catacchio et al. 2006.

The Etruria Network

Having reviewed the background and circumstances of Etruria's surge forward in the first millennium BC, we can now turn to the network evidence in the region. As we saw in Chapter 4, there is no trace of a network in west-central Italy in the RBA, but a clear one emerges in the FBA. In the comparative analyses that followed in that chapter, the FBA Etruria network exhibited middling cohesion and connectivity, never outscoring the Veneto in particular on any of the measures of cohesion. To examine this network more closely, as I did in Chapter 5, I reconfigure it slightly. First of all, I relax the "tie" criteria by eliminating the proximity cut off – that is, that the sites must be within 50 km of each other to have a tie. At the regional scale the distances are fairly circumscribed anyway, so the 50 km parameter is not necessary. This permits us to see how goods were moving around and in this way, we can account for the sites that may not be recognized yet. The second change to be made to the network is the addition of the hoards and ritual deposits, formerly excluded and now potentially useful for what they may reveal about activity regionally. The focus for the moment is on south Etruria, not Etruria as a whole. Those find spots located in what will later be northeast Etruria show closer connections to sites to the east of them, in Umbria and Marche, rather than to south Etruria. We will reintroduce those sites later in this chapter, and the Apennine network will be treated in Chapter 7.

In the RBA, there are four find spots in south Etruria, three closely spaced in the Fiora Valley and one in the area of Tolfa Mountains further south (Figure 6.1).[53]

Although these numbers do not represent all the sites in the region – just the ones with the objects being tracked – the low number of sites is a reflection of the general paucity of sites in this period. In the Tolfa Mountains region, only eleven RBA sites have been recorded, compared to fifteen in the MBA, suggesting a slight contraction in population in this period.[54] The objects circulating in the region in the RBA number three types, and of those, only the miniature decorated wheels are found at two find spots, while the other two objects are found at just one find spot each in the area (Table 6.1).

---

[53] The four sites consist of three settlements and one hoard.
[54] Toti 1987: 20–1.

West-Central Italy: Networks and Neighbors

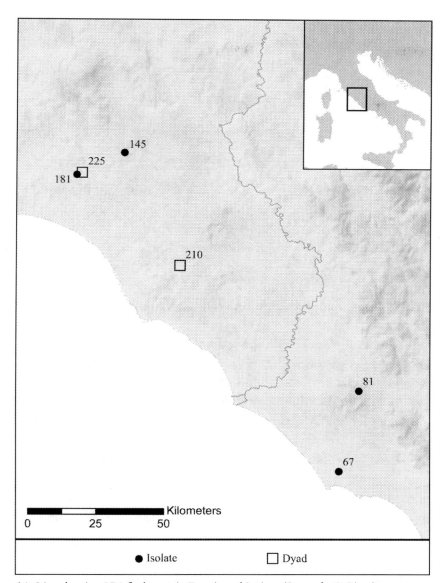

6.1. Map showing RBA find spots in Etruria and Latium (Drawn by R. Biggs)

Table 6.1. *Object types circulating in Etruria in the RBA*

Object types present in Etruria in the RBA	Number of find spots
Miniature decorated wheel	2
Arco sword	1
Matrei A knife	1

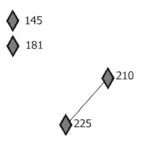

6.2. Graph of RBA network in Etruria, ties based on shared objects

Thus, very few object types are actually recorded in the area in this period. South Etruria is undoubtedly the most thoroughly studied portion of the peninsula, which means that the data are as trustworthy as one is likely to find anywhere. Nonetheless, in the peninsular network we saw that there were no ties among the three sites there. When we look at the updated network in graph form, with the addition of the Piano di Tallone hoard, there is one dyad only and Mezzano and Piano di Tallone are isolates (Figure 6.2).[55]

It would seem that in this period nothing is reaching the region in large enough quantities to move around, and it is not possible to make a case for a network. The Canegrate and Arco swords from Lake Mezzano came from the north, but this does not prove that contacts between the north and Etruria were as intense as Pellegrini, for one, suggests.[56] The vast Terramare network's reach did not extend this far and certainly in the RBA the ties between Etruria and the north were limited.

In the FBA, the four RBA find spots are still in use (or, in the case of the Piano di Tallone hoard, finally deposited) but there are ten new find spots as well (Figure 6.3). This increase in find spots parallels an overall increase in sites in the area, with thirty recorded, suggesting a demographic expansion.[57] Growth is further demonstrated by the larger size of some of the sites, in particular Monte Rovello, with an estimated 100–300 people, and Elceto, a settlement with an estimated

---

[55] The Piano di Tallone hoard is somewhat problematic as an RBA find spot because its contents span such a long period, so clearly it was not deposited until much later. Found in 1906, it was apparently a founder's hoard as it contained ingots and broken pieces, primarily (Pellegrini 1992: 341–4). We cannot say whether the Matrei A knife ever circulated in this area in the RBA, or was brought in after. In any case, it is an isolate in the RBA so it does not tell us much.

[56] Pellegrini 1995: 512.

[57] Toti 1987: 21.

West-Central Italy: Networks and Neighbors

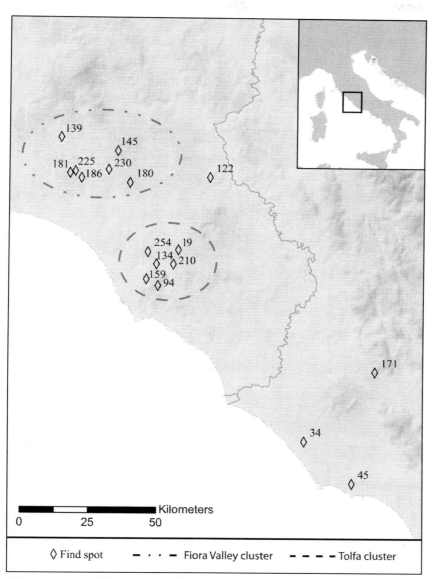

6.3. Map showing FBA find spots in Etruria and Latium (Drawn by R. Biggs)

population of 800.[58] The geographic bifurcation hinted at in the RBA is made clearer in the FBA, with two fairly evenly matched clusters: one in the Fiora River Valley and one in the Tolfa region. The local material culture of the FBA also delineates these two groups, a point I will return

[58] Toti 1987: 20, 22.

to shortly.[59] As noted earlier, the Tolfa cluster's location is a mineral-rich area.[60] It straddles portions of the later territories of the Etruscan cities of Cerveteri and Tarquinia, but is recognized as an important FBA region as well.[61] Although there is no direct proof that the minerals were being exploited in this period, it seems likely as many minerals are even now, after millennia of extraction, readily available to collect from the surface.[62] To the north, the Fiora Valley – in the future territory of the Etruscan city of Vulci – was densely settled in the FBA.[63] As in the Tolfa region, a slight dip in the number of sites in the RBA (down to six, from ten in the MBA) is followed by a clear increase in the FBA, with twenty-six FBA sites recorded.[64] With the exception of the site of Sorgenti della Nova, which hangs on until the eighth century BC, all of these FBA sites would be abandoned in the EIA, when the center of gravity shifts south to the rising city of Vulci.[65]

Of the fourteen find spots in central and southern Etruria in the FBA, seven are settlements, one is a cemetery, one is a settlement and a cemetery, and five are hoards.[66] By the FBA in Etruria, the formerly scattered dots rearrange themselves into the constellation of a coherent network, with just two isolates out of the fourteen sites. The ties between sites are established by the circulation of ten object types in the area (Table 6.2), of which the donkey and the Pertosa axe are most widespread, turning up at four sites each.

Four other object types are found at three sites each, and the rest of the object types are known from just one site in the region. The sites with the most object types, Scarceta and Monte Rovello, have four each. Luni sul Mignone has three object types; Piano di Tallone, Mezzano, Torrionaccio and the Manciano-Samprugnano hoard have two object types each; and the rest just one. Surprisingly absent from the Tolfa cluster is Elceto

---

[59] Bietti Sestieri 1998: 23.
[60] Cristofani 1986: table IX.
[61] Toti 1987.
[62] Toti 1987: 42.
[63] Negroni Catacchio 1981: 52.
[64] Negroni Catacchio 1981: table 16.
[65] Negroni Catacchio 1981: 156.
[66] It should be noted, however, that Mezzano, which was a lakeshore settlement and is counted as a settlement here, yielded a sword and an axe that are more likely to be the traces of a ritual deposit at the lake than material from the settlement (Baffetti *et al.* 1993).

Table 6.2. *Object types circulating in Etruria in the FBA*

Object types present in Etruria in the FBA	Number of find spots
Donkey remains	4
Pertosa axe	4
Casalecchio axe	3
LH IIIC Aegean-style pottery	3
Leaf-shaped VB fibula	3
Torri d'Arcugnano dress pin	3
Allumiere bead	1
Frattesina asymmetrical VB fibula	1
Pick ingot	1
TMES socketed shovel	1

as a find spot. It is the largest FBA settlement and considered to occupy a dominant position geographically as well.[67] Although it has much amber, no Tiryns or Allumiere beads are among the assemblage, nor any of the other object types included in this study. Likewise, the interesting walled settlement of Crostoletto di Lamone in the Fiora Valley is also absent from this study, for lack of relevant object types.[68]

So much for the building blocks of the network; we can turn to its structure, however, recalling that ties are now based exclusively on shared objects, not proximity (Figure 6.4). The first observation is that this is not a particularly dense network, meaning there are not that many actual ties between sites.[69] The second feature of the network is that it is bifurcated, with one site, Scarceta, linking two subgroups together. When we compare this network graph to the map, we see that this bifurcation largely mirrors the geographically distinct clusters discussed earlier (see Figure 6.3). This bifurcation is the direct result of subregional trends in object circulations. So, for example, the LH IIIC pottery is exclusively in the southern cluster as are the Torre d'Arcugnano dress pins.[70] Even those objects that are found in both clusters demonstrate a stronger presence in one than the other, such as donkey bones (south) and Pertosa

---

[67] Toti 1987: 40.

[68] Whereas the settlement was occupied from the MBA, the walls, made of dry masonry, date only to the RBA; Negroni Catacchio (1981: 119) suggests their construction may have been in response to some sort of crisis.

[69] Its density is .242 (44 ties).

[70] Another site in the Tolfa area, Fosso Vaccina, has yielded LH IIIC sherds but I learned of it too late to include in this study (Barbaro *et al.* 2012).

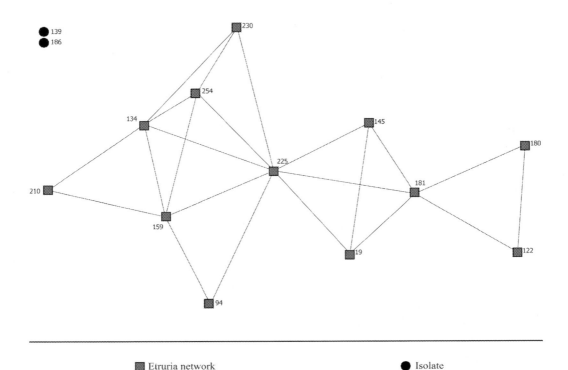

6.4. Graph of FBA sites in Etruria, ties based on shared objects

axe (north). Looking at this network graph – given that distance does not factor into the ties at all, only the co-presence of objects – it is quite remarkable that the network divides fairly neatly into two subgroups according to those geographic distinctions.

We can test this hypothesized clustering another way, using faction analysis, as we did in Chapter 5. Here we compare the observed pattern to an ideal type, in which the network is divided into two components that are fully connected internally (density of 100%), but with no connections between them. When I stipulate two factions, the result is two blocks of nodes that match fairly closely with the geographic divisions evident in the map, albeit with significant differences from the ideal type in that these are sparser blocks than the ideal 100 percent density. Still, in both blocks the density is higher than that observed overall: .62 for Group 1 and .29 for Group 2 (along the diagonal) (Table 6.3). Group 1 contains mostly Tolfa sites and Group 2 mostly Fiora sites, although two of the Fiora Cluster sites end up in Group 1 and one Tolfa site ends up in

West-Central Italy: Networks and Neighbors

Table 6.3. *Permuted matrix of FBA sites in Etruria, ties based on objects only, hoards included, divided into two factions*

	134	94	230	159	225	210	254	122	19	181	186	139	145	180
134			1	1	1	1	1							
94				1	1									
230	1				1		1							
159	1	1			1	1	1							
225	1	1	1	1			1			1	1		1	
210	1			1										
254	1		1	1	1									
122										1				1
19					1					1			1	
181					1			1	1				1	1
186														
139														
145					1				1	1				
180								1		1				

Group 2. Nonetheless, twelve out of fourteen sites were placed in the correct geographic groups without recourse to any spatial information, just shared objects. This supports the premise stated earlier that the circulation of objects in this period was highly geographically delimited: the same types of objects are more often found near each other, regardless of their place of origin. The 50 km parameter may be a crude measure as the distances separating the two subgroups here are even shorter: the shortest possible tie between the two clusters is Pianizza-Torrionaccio, a distance of just 27 km. It would seem that the evidence for the local circulation of goods is even more compelling at the subregional level than it is at the peninsular level.

The site serving as the primary link between the two clusters is Scarceta. One network measure that captures the importance of positioning in determining site roles is the betweenness centrality index. As noted in Chapter 5, that position brings power because the node in the middle mediates the relations between the two outer nodes. In the case of this network, Scarceta has a normalized betweenness score of .415. A maximum normalized betweenness score, in a so-called star network in which Scarceta was the only site with direct ties to any others, is 1.0.[71] In such

---

[71] The score is normalized by expressing it as a percentage of the maximum possible betweenness scores for that site (Knoke and Yang 2008: 68).

a case, the other sites would be completely dependent on Scarceta to mediate all contacts. As Scarceta's betweenness score is well below that maximum, it is far from exhibiting hegemonic control. Nonetheless, the second most-centralized site in the network, Piano di Tallone, scored half that many points. Further, nine of the sites in the network have no betweenness score at all, so Scarceta is clearly important here. What is so special about this site? Partly Scarceta stands out for its retrieval processes rather than its depositional ones: Scarceta has been well excavated for many years and has yielded a lot of objects – more than sites that have not been excavated so extensively. Nonetheless, the site itself has some interesting features that suggest it was of importance in the past. Zanini has described Scarceta as the most important site in the Fiora Valley from the MBA to the early FBA.[72] This collection of huts, which began in the MBA, has some key features distinguishing it from other contemporary villages by the FBA. For one thing, there is a large oval structure containing traces of metalworking (casting molds) as well as domestic refuse. Its size and metalworking make it stand out from the other huts on the site. This sort of differentiation in living space within sites is something not seen generally until the Iron Age in the region, although Luni sul Mignone and Monte Rovello also contained large buildings. Finds of slag from smelting point to metallurgical activity elsewhere on the site and other specialized craft products come from the FBA levels as well.[73] The traces of metalworking are not unique in the area: the nearby settlement of Pitigliano has also yielded a casting mold of a winged axe of probable RBA date.[74] Since Pitigliano has been only partially excavated, we cannot say much more about the activities there, unlike Scarceta.[75] This is clearly the moment when the latter site reached its apex and seems to have taken on a central role in the short-distance circulation of goods.

So far there is a fairly clear picture of a bifurcated network in central and southern Etruria with two internal clusters that correspond rather

---

[72] Zanini 1999: 309.
[73] Poggiani Keller 1993.
[74] Pellegrini 1985: 47–8.
[75] Pacciarelli 2000: 103. Pacciarelli (2000: 103) further suggests that comparatively high numbers of cattle bones at both sites may be further evidence of the high status of both sites.

West-Central Italy: Networks and Neighbors

well to geographic clustering on the map. This simple story is made more complex when we take account of the local ceramics. The local ceramic production of the sites in the Fiora cluster, which is inland, is generally noted as part of the Chiusi-Cetona facies that extends east through Umbria and Marche.[76] As noted in Chapter 1, the Chiusi-Cetona facies was an archaeological complex in the Etruscan interior and Umbria. First identified by Zanini through the local ceramic typology, it was contemporary with the Tolfa-Allumiere facies to the south and maintained ties to the Adriatic and Po regions.[77] Furthermore, matching metal object types from the Fiora cluster and from sites in the northeast point to exchanges.[78] Fugazzola Delpino posits the existence of a terrestrial route across the Apennines linking the Veneto to South Etruria as far back as the Apennine period, but becoming increasingly visible by the FBA.[79] Cocchi Genick, too, has argued that in the MBA the Grotta Nuova facies of central Italy had ties to the Po area, and that by the end of the RBA, the Terramare facies had penetrated the Tyrrhenian area fully.[80]

In spatial terms the links in the FBA are not clear. There is a considerable distance between the Apennine sites and the Fiora cluster: the two nearest sites are around 65 km apart,[81] and the peninsula network revealed no ties between the two areas as a result. However, we can explore the possibility of ties by adding the Chiusi-Cetona facies sites to the Etruria network and removing distance as a parameter. The resulting network is dramatically different (Figure 6.5). This new network has one large connected subgroup with three internal clusters that correspond to the three geographic areas (Fiora, Tolfa, and Apennines of Umbria and Marche) with considerable ties between them and a few sites "out of place" – that is, appearing in different clusters in the network from their geographic "home" (see map, Figure 6.3).

---

[76] Bietti Sestieri 1998: 23.
[77] Zanini 1996.
[78] The Manciano-Samprugnano hoard contained pick ingots whose distribution is primarily north and east, as well as dress pins with matches at Pianello di Genga (Pellegrini 1995: 514–17).
[79] Fugazzola Delpino 1992: 296.
[80] Cocchi Genick 2006: 1114–17.
[81] This is very approximate as the location of one of the sites, the Manciano-Samprugnano hoard, is known only very generally.

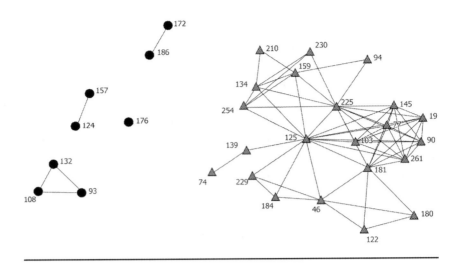

▲ Etruria-Marche-Umbria network   ● Isolate and small group

6.5. Graph showing network of FBA sites in Etruria, Umbria, and Marche

While we can observe these clusters visually, we can also reveal them using factions. When we permute the matrix of the connected subgroup, this time in order to compare it to an ideal type of three factions (since that is the possibility being considered here), something interesting comes to light (Table 6.4). The first observation to make is that dividing the subgroup into three factions is a valid approach, as the resulting densities of the factions are high and there are limited ties between factions. The first faction contains all the sites of the Tolfa cluster, with only one outlier – Sorgenti della Nova from the Fiora cluster – included (Figure 6.6). Factions 2 and 3 are a mix of Chiusi-Cetona and Fiora sites with only Blera from the Tolfa cluster included. Without a geographic boundary to distinguish it, the Fiora cluster is completely absorbed into the larger Chiusi-Cetona facies. It would seem that the Tolfa cluster really was distinct from the Chiusi-Cetona facies, but that the Fiora cluster constitutes an extension of it, at least in terms of the goods circulating if not in geographic terms. The sparse connections between the Chiusi-Cetona sites and the Tolfa group – later home to Cerveteri and Tarquinia, among the most powerful Etruscan cities – suggest that the rise of south Etruria was not the direct result of influence from the east and north. The local ceramic evidence supports the picture provided by the networks and

West-Central Italy: Networks and Neighbors

Table 6.4. *Permuted matrix of FBA sites in Etruria, Umbria, and Marche, ties based on objects only, hoards included, divided into three factions*

	94	159	134	230	210	254	225	90	77	103	19	261	181	125	145	74	122	180	229	46	184	139
94						1																
159	1		1		1	1	1							1								
134		1		1	1	1	1							1								
230		1			1	1																
210		1	1																			
254		1	1	1			1							1								
225	1	1	1	1		1		1	1	1	1	1	1	1	1							
90							1		1	1	1	1	1	1	1							
77							1	1		1	1	1	1	1	1							
103							1	1	1		1	1	1	1	1							
19							1	1	1	1		1	1	1	1							
261							1	1	1	1	1		1	1	1							
181							1	1	1	1	1	1		1	1		1	1		1		
125		1	1			1	1	1	1	1	1	1	1		1				1	1	1	1
145							1	1	1	1	1	1	1	1								
74																						1
122													1					1		1		
180													1				1			1		
229														1						1	1	
46													1	1			1	1	1		1	
184														1					1	1		
139														1		1						

faction analysis. Zanini observed that the pots of the Chiusi-Cetona facies exhibit more ties with the north than the ceramics of the Tolfa Allumiere facies do, citing one distinctive type of globular pot with an outturned rim and cordoned meanders that is found in northern Etruria, Marche, and the Veneto.[82]

Moreover, the networks of the FBA in central Italy reveal some important insights into the Villanovan group of the Iron Age. In the FBA, the sites in Etruria, Umbria, and Marche form a network covering part of the future Villanovan area, and in Chapter 5 we saw that the Veneto network showed ties to Marche as well. Combining these patterns, it would seem that the FBA network presages the Villanovan group of the Iron Age. However, the distinctive internal clustering in Tolfa highlights subregional groupings that were in place before the Iron Age, and

---

[82] Zanini 1999: 309–11.

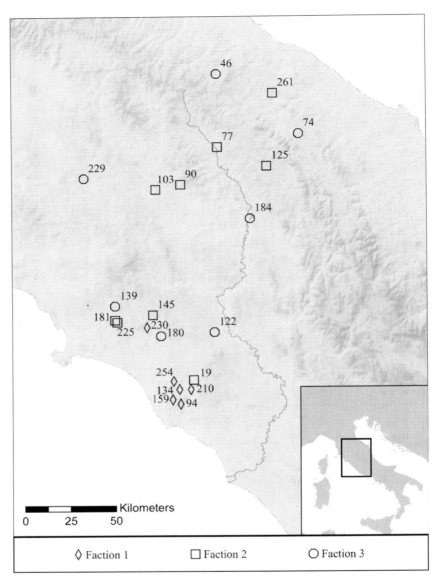

6.6. Map of Etruria, Umbria, and Marche showing FBA sites with factions indicated (Drawn by R. Biggs)

become visible again after the Villanovan period. If this early cluster in south Etruria both precedes the Villanovan period and postdates it, I would contend that the Villanovans were not a coherent group that later fragmented. Instead, as I argued in Chapter 1, the network data suggest a collection of smaller groupings whose interactions in a regional system led to certain commonalities of behavior that were archaeologically visible, obscuring the local distinctiveness for a period of time.

In this network displayed in Figure 6.5, we observe again a key role for Scarceta (node 225), which joins together all three clusters, but particularly for Gubbio-Monte Ingino (Gubbio-MI, n. 125), which is even better positioned. The settlement of Monte Ingino occupies a strategic position on a high point (900 m above sea level) overlooking the Gubbio Valley. It has RBA levels but, like Scarceta, manifests an intensification of activity in the FBA.[83] Although part of its prominence in the network here may be owing to its exceptional excavation history, the excavators selected it precisely because it was an important site. When we calculate the betweenness centrality scores for this network, Gubbio-MI scores highest, with a normalized betweenness score of .23697 or 23.7 percent, although this is actually not that high, given that it is out of 1.0. This low score is because this is a low-density network; therefore, the power of any individual site over others is necessarily limited. In this expanded network Scarceta slips in importance to second place in centrality measures, with a normalized betweenness centrality score of 10.92 percent. Again this is low, but to put it in perspective, of the thirty-one sites in this network, twenty-three have a betweenness score of "0," so even a low score is worth noting. In this new network, Scarceta is no longer a cutpoint but remains an important player, and if Gubbio-MI is removed, then Scarceta does become a critical cutpoint. In other words, if both sites are removed, then the network breaks apart (Figure 6.7). In sum, this expanded FBA network is not particularly cohesive.

Now that this reconfigured network has revealed expanded relationships in the FBA, what if we look back to the RBA? We can construct a similar matrix for the RBA, one including both the Apennine sites and the few in Etruria, in which ties are based on shared object types alone (Figure 6.8). The result is a very disconnected collection of sites indeed, with two dyads, a triad, and the rest isolates. There are no ties between the Apennine sites and the ones in Etruria. In the RBA, the sites that were so important in the FBA are already in place, but are not yet playing important roles: Scarceta is only linked to one site, San Giovanale in the Tolfa region of Etruria, which may point to an early

---

[83] Malone and Stoddart 1994a: 106–10.

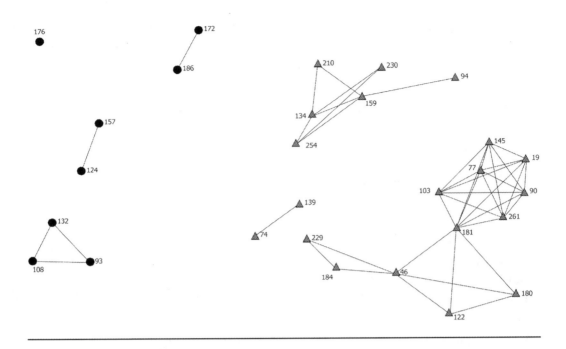

▲ Etruria-Marche-Umbria network　　　● Isolate and small group

6.7. Graph of FBA sites with Gubbio and Scarceta removed

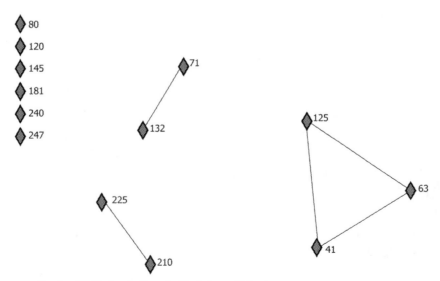

6.8. Graph of RBA sites in Etruria, Umbria, and Marche

connection between the two later clusters; however, without more data, that remains highly speculative. Gubbio-MI is part of the triad, which is composed of only other Apennine sites. The network observed in the FBA does not extend back to the RBA, and there is next to nothing in these RBA graphs that prefigures the networks of the FBA.[84] The fact that in this disconnected RBA world, Scarceta and Gubbio-MI should be among the only sites with ties seems significant. With the subsequent FBA network in mind, we may consider the dyad containing Scarceta and the triad containing Gubbio-MI as signs of those sites' nascent importance, but otherwise, the RBA network is no predictor of what follows. As we saw in Chapter 5, the RBA sites in the Apennines formed the tail of the vast Terramare-Apennine network. The goods circulating in that network did not reach south Etruria. The interactions between Etruria and the north would seem to begin in earnest only in FBA 1–2.

Etruria and Latium

So far the focus has been exclusively on Etruria and its relations to the Apennines, but another question posed at the start of this chapter concerned the earliest traces of a distinction between Latium and Etruria. Material differences between Etruria and Latium are visible only from the second half of the FBA. In the first part of the FBA, nothing materially distinguishes Latium from Etruria: both regions display the Tolfa facies of Protovillanovan culture. In the second part of the FBA – that is, the eleventh to early tenth centuries BC – we see the first local culture, labeled Latial I, emerge.[85] From the peninsula-network data presented in Chapter 4 there are no ties between Etruria and Latium, and between sites in Latium themselves, in either the RBA or the FBA. Part of the problem is the dearth of find spots in Latium, where luxury objects seem to have reached only sporadically. In the RBA, the sites in South Etruria

---

[84] To be clear, goods moved locally before the FBA. From the Neolithic period through the FBA, Tuscany, for example, had been in the habit of importing volcanic material as a temper in clay, bringing it in from 15–20 km and sometimes from as far as 50 km away. It is not clear if the finished pots were imported, or just the volcanic raw material (Levi 2004: 236). Rather, there is no *network* in place in the RBA.

[85] Bietti Sestieri 2010: 270–1.

and Latium Vetus are separated by distance, but independent of that, the shared objects are not there. Latium's two RBA find spots, Cavallo Morto and Colle della Mola, have each yielded object types for which there is no match at the south Etruria sites: at Cavallo Morto,[86] a cemetery, a violin-bow fibula with two knobs, and at Colle della Mola, a settlement, a Torre Castelluccia dagger.

In the FBA, however, the data look quite different. There are three new find spots in Latium Vetus in the FBA, and although they have no ties to each other, they each have yielded an example of an object type also found in South Etruria. At Campo del Fico, a cemetery, an Allumiere bead is matched by examples at Monte Rovello's cemetery of Poggio La Pozza-Allumiere. At the settlement of Casale Nuovo, LH IIIC pottery finds matches at three sites in Etruria, as discussed earlier.[87] At Palestrina, a sporadic find of a Pertosa axe is matched at four sites in Etruria. What do we make of this? Certainly the fact that in Latium Vetus and in Etruria there is LH IIIC pottery is probably not coincidental: by that I mean that these finds are all traces of the same set of circumstances, probably an individual trading these goods through the area. The distance between the southernmost find spot in Etruria and the find spot in Latium means that these sites do not appear to be tied, at least according to the criteria used in this book. But given the incomplete nature of the material record, we could easily be missing intervening sites. In fact, all it would take is one find spot to link the two. A likely candidate is Rome itself, or more accurately, in this period, the villages on the site of the future city. Rome is approximately 50 km away from both San Giovenale and Casale Nuovo. LH IIIC pottery from Rome, if found, would link the two regions. What of the other two cases of shared object types? Campo del Fico and Monte Rovello are about 80 km apart; the nearest find spot of Pertosa axes in Etruria, Blera, is 83 km from Palestrina. Moreover, there is the problem of crossing the Tiber to contend with, given only a few fordable spots.[88] The nearest easy crossing place on

---

[86] Cavallo Morto is quite noteworthy for being the earliest cremation cemetery in central Italy, according to Angle *et al.* (2004: 128).

[87] Casale Nuovo has yielded fifteen or so Aegean-type sherds. One, the painted handle of a stirrup jar, was produced in Italy. The other sherds are plainwares, mostly of Aegean origin, but at least three are from southern Italy (Angle 2003: 116–17).

[88] Kuusisto and Tuppi 2009: 7.

West-Central Italy: Networks and Neighbors

the Tiber in all three cases is the natural ford at the bend in the river just south of the Tiber island, in Rome.[89] In terms of distance, for all three pairs, Rome would be a good intervening node, although perhaps with another site as well to the north of the Tiber: both Monte Rovello and Blera are about 56 km from Rome. From Rome to Campo del Fico, the distance is approximately 32 km (estimating from the Forum Boarium, where the Tiber was traditionally crossed). Rome and Palestrina are 35 km apart (Figure 6.9). This theory of Rome as the "missing link" will remain just that until material is found, but the main point is that in the FBA we can make a case for interactions between the Tolfa cluster in Etruria and Latium Vetus, with the latter occupying a somewhat marginal position. Indeed, the absence of ties between the three sites in Latium itself mitigates against a network in its own right.

Does the local material culture provide any supporting evidence for a network in south Etruria in the FBA? Decorations on cinerary urns in the region have been used to identify a cultural facies labeled Tolfa-Allumiere, joining together two successive phases: the Tolfa phase and Allumiere phase. The major Tolfa-Allumiere sites, such as San Giovenale and Luni sul Mignone, are nodes in the Tolfa cluster I described in this chapter. The Tolfa-Allumiere facies is characterized by incised and impressed urns and distinctive lids that are thought to imitate huts (much as is argued for Villanovan urns). Bietti Sestieri considers the symbolic replication of the hut form in the urn as a distinctive feature of the ideology of the Tolfa-Allumiere facies, one that distinguishes it from Chiusi-Cetona.[90] Thus, in one aspect of the local material culture, the Tolfa sites stand apart from the Chiusi-Cetona sites.

Discussion

To conclude, the sites of the FBA Etruria network are in what later becomes known as south Etruria, the area demonstrating the earliest settlement hierarchies and later the fulcrum of wealth and power in the second quarter of the first millennium BC. The network data show that

---

[89] Cornell 1995: 48.
[90] Bietti Sestieri 2010: 238.

178 Social Networks and Regional Identity in Bronze Age Italy

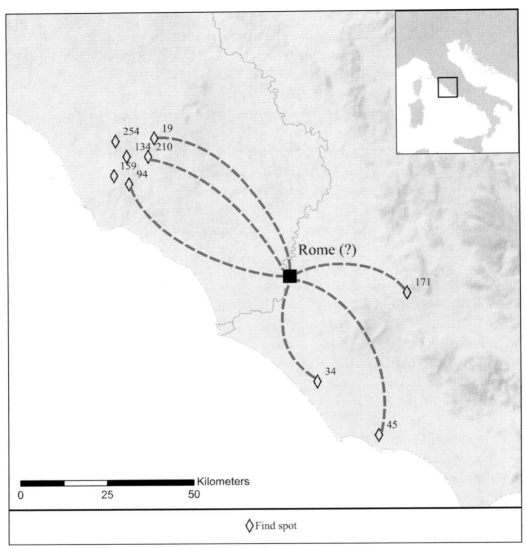

6.9. Map showing sites in FBA Latium and Etruria, with Rome as a hypothetical node (Drawn by R. Biggs)

in the RBA there is no sign of a coherent group in the region, but in the FBA there is evidence of a network composed of two clusters that seem to be in the process of fusing together. This network demonstrates ties to the east (Apennines) and to the south (Latium). Whereas the sites of the Fiora cluster are linked enough to the Apennine sites to be said to be connected to them, the Tolfa cluster remains somewhat distinct and Latium appears as a peripheral zone with no internally driven networks of its own. The network data demonstrate that the first steps toward cultural unity in Etruria begin in the FBA and that the Tolfa and Fiora clusters reveal two short-lived micro-regional groupings that would later fuse with each other to form the core of Etruscan identity. The ties of the Fiora cluster to the Chiusi-Cetona facies may reflect the transhumant economy that several scholars have argued must have prevailed through much of the Bronze Age. Barker posited ties between permanent lowland coastal settlements and seasonal upland sites based on these movements of flocks.[91] Malone and Stoddart describe "stylistic networks" based on shared design elements in local pottery and metals, the mechanisms for which being seasonal and possibly ritualized exchanges occurring in the temporary upland aggregation sites.[92] The network data suggest that the Fiora sites participated in both a transhumant economy across the Apennines and in some shorter distance exchanges with their Tolfa neighbors, and it was the latter relations that ultimately formed the basis for a strong common identity.

As the Bronze Age sites do not survive the FBA-EIA transition, this network is not useful as a predictor of the political territories and social hierarchies to come: none of the sites in the network, with the exception of Luni sul Mignone, carry on into Etruscan times. Rather, the network is simply indicative of a presence on this soil of peoples who interacted with each other closely enough that they came to share a common regional history. We must avoid thinking in terms of fixed polities when delineating the territories of these networks: the boundaries were mutable for quite some time. Indeed, in the case of Latium, Pliny the Elder's list of the names of thirty peoples who participated in festivals at Monte Albano and were thus residents of Latium, many of whom had long since disappeared by the time he was writing, highlights how fragmented the demographic reality was on the ground. The list, in fact, goes some way to explaining why we see no network in early Latium: these groups felt no great affinities with each other.[93] The Roman foundation myths involving miscegenation such as the Rape of the Sabines, and that of Romulus' asylum wherein Rome's founder welcomed other ethnic groups, suggest that the formation of this city involved

---

[91] Barker *et al.* 1991.
[92] Malone and Stoddart 1994b: 130–6.
[93] Cornell 1995: 73, Pallottino 1993: 124.

a polyglot mixture of Latins, Sabines, and others from surrounding groups.[94]

The ceramic and metal industries of the FBA may reflect an incipient regionalism in west-central Italy, but the evidence from local material culture alone is not sufficient, when, as discussed in Chapter 3, there is no reliable connection between identity and its material expression. The Tolfa-Allumiere and Chiusi-Cetona facies, are distinct from each other, and the latter facies extends east of the later boundaries of Etruria. These facies give way in the Iron Age to a far more widespread set of material practices grouped under the Villanovan label. In short, the evidence of early regionalism of local industries is confusing.

The network data tell a different story. The FBA Etruria network is in an area conceived as the Etruscan heartland, occupying a small portion of the larger, later ethnic territory. This suggests that the ensuing ethnicization of Etruria was an aggregative process, rather than an ossification of extant relations. We cannot detect any traces of interactions in the RBA or FBA between the northern part of Etruria and the south: it seems likely that those populations were later incorporated into the larger Etruscan grouping. Nor did this ethnic formation process involve breaking off from a larger, more loosely defined group to forge a tighter but smaller identity: this is the theory Bietti Sestieri proposes to explain the transition from the Villanovan Iron Age to Archaic Etruria. Instead, the network evidence suggests that ethnicity formation in Etruria entailed building out from those Bronze Age ties to incorporate adjacent, previously marginal communities. Jonathan Hall proposes a similar aggregative process for Archaic Greece, when, through myths of common descent, formerly separate groups came to emphasize affinities that allowed them to share in a Hellenic identity. Although Hall's primary focus was the replacement of smaller regional identities with a pan-Hellenic one, he observed that regional identity formation could have followed a similar process earlier.

> If Hellenic identity in the Archaic period was constructed cumulatively from pre-existing Dorian, Ionian or Aiolian identities, we should not assume that the latter constituted the primary and irreducible

---

[94] Cornell 1995: 75–7; Dench 2005.

building blocks in the process. There remains the possibility that even these groups were themselves the product of aggregation or ethnic assimilation. Indeed, this may explain the seemingly puzzling phenomenon of eponymous heroes who appear as leaders rather than ancestors.[95]

In the central Italian case, the argument that the process was aggregative is supported by the linguistic evidence, in which Etruscan stands apart from all her neighbors. These early close ties between sites in south Etruria strengthen and persist for hundreds of years in the process of path dependence, resulting in a strong collective identity in the region.

---

[95] Hall 1997: 50.

CHAPTER SEVEN

MARCHE, UMBRIA, AND THE APENNINE MOUNTAIN MUDDLE

Background: Marche and the North-Central Apennines in the Bronze Age

As Chapter 4 demonstrated, the Terramare culture in the RBA had a reach that extended beyond its territory, with a network that stretched along the northern Adriatic coast and into the Apennines.[1] Following the collapse of that network and the demise of the Terramare culture, a new network emerged in the Apennines and Adriatic coast. This chapter begins by looking closely at these regions in the Bronze Age and after, as a prelude to examining the networks identified in the study.

Along the northern Adriatic, the modern administrative region known as Marche is bordered on the west by the Apennines and on the east by the sea.[2] This mountainous zone lacked mineral resources and fertile farmland, and the peoples of the Bronze Age there are poorly known. The territory is mostly mountainous virtually up to the water's edge, but benefits from east-west running river valleys connecting the coast with the interior, some of which served in earlier times as passes across the Apennines. Urban sites do not emerge until the Roman period. Instead, the so-called pagus-vicus settlement system is frequently cited in scholarly literature on Apennine peoples, with *pagi* being Latin for the local territorial divisions and *vici* were the small villages dotting the *pagi*.

---

[1] The specific area is called in Italian the *appennino umbro-marchigiano*.
[2] Riva 2007: 83.

Bradley notes that from this circumscribed definition, the terms have come to be applied loosely to all Italic groups in a "pre-urban stage of development," often without sufficient confirmation.[3] Indeed, and perhaps unsurprisingly, as far as I know, no *pagi* have ever been identified archaeologically. In the Bronze Age, what we do have are clusters of small settlements that may speak to some localized communities, but that is all one can say. Bronze Age settlements are found in a range of topographical zones, but along the coast or along rivers seem to have been favorite choices.[4] One excavated settlement, Cortine di S. Maria in Campo, was constructed on wooden piles with both oval and rectangular huts, recalling the Terramare settlements to the northwest. The settlements are modest in size, dispersed, and there is no clear settlement hierarchy, but scholars have suggested from the distribution that there may have been territorial groupings of settlements in naturally delimited areas such as river valleys.[5] The MBA and RBA appear to have been remarkably stable periods in the region. Seventy-three sites were occupied from the late MBA through the RBA, while only ten are recorded as falling out of use after the MBA and thirteen began only in the RBA.[6]

In northern Marche, there is a decline in settlement numbers at the end of the RBA that may be tied to the Terramare collapse somehow, whereas in the southern part of Marche, the transition to the FBA is not marked by a similar decline.[7] The implication is that the northern zone, being closer to the Terramare region, was more influenced by it and its fortunes were more tied with it, unlike the south. We can see if this pattern is evident in the networks constructed here. The FBA-EIA transition also showed some upheaval, although Peroni interprets it in terms other than a decline. Whereas Bronze Age sites in Marche do not exceed 4 ha in area, Peroni notes that most of those settlements that span the FBA and EIA become bigger than that in the second phase, reaching 30, 40, even 100 ha in the case of Fermo.[8] Sites that are occupied for

---

[3] Bradley 2000: 56.
[4] Baldelli *et al*. 2005: 570.
[5] Baldelli *et al*. 2005: 570.
[6] Baldelli *et al*. 2005: 566–7.
[7] Damiani 2010: 435.
[8] Peroni 2005.

the first time in the EIA do not grow as big. It seems, therefore, that the most successful Iron Age settlements were those that selected a good spot in the Bronze Age and were thus primed for success in the Iron Age. The picture is not one of straightforward continuity, however. Some settlements show periods of apparent abandonment in the latter part of the FBA, and then reoccupation in the EIA. Peroni nevertheless argues that the discontinuity is only partial in that the mindset and social framework bridged the two periods. As he puts it: "Questo singolare fenomeno è a mio avviso il sintomo rivelatore di un importante processo socio-culturale e socio-politico, nel cui ambito il nascere e l'evolversi di una qualche forma di gerarchia insediamentale ci appaiono in un certo qual modo predeterminati dalle scelte ubicative iniziali, e al tempo stesso inscindibili dal fattore della continuità demografica."[9] Peroni thus sees the events of the Bronze Age conditioning the developments of the Iron Age, whereas previous scholars had seen nothing but discontinuity in the region. He also suggests that these large settlements in Marche were protourban, although the term is misleading as, unlike in Etruria, they are not followed by an urban phase until, arguably, the Roman conquest itself.[10] The main indigenous town, Asculum, may have constituted a city-state in the late first millennium BC, but this is not certain.[11]

Despite the occasional weapons finds at the settlements, Marche is yet another region of Italy where "warriors" as a discrete social category cannot be attested in the Bronze Age. Burials in the Middle, Recent, and Final Bronze Ages in the region are not well known, but those that have been found do not point to anything but modest social hierarchies.[12] There are inhumations primarily in the MBA and RBA, with cremations becoming more popular (but not replacing inhumations altogether) in the FBA. The inhumations generally contain no grave goods at all (hence the difficulty in finding them) and the cremations contain modest

---

[9] Peroni 2005: 735. "This singular phenomenon is, in my opinion, symptomatic of an important socio-cultural and socio-political process, in which the birth and evolution of a settlement hierarchy were predetermined by the initial choice of settlement locations, and at the same time are characterized by demographic continuity" (my translation).
[10] Naso 2000: 93–4.
[11] David 1997: 23.
[12] Bergonzi 2005: 698.

assemblages of toiletries, fibulae, and razors.[13] Some weapons – daggers and a few swords – are known from the region, so presumably some proportion of the population engaged in warfare on occasion, but there is nothing to suggest that the social role of "warrior" had crystallized here as it would in the Iron Age.

In light of this picture of a small-scale Bronze Age society with few, if any, status distinctions and modest settlements, it is unexpected that four Bronze Age sites in the region have yielded Aegean-style ceramics.[14] Although one sherd from the site of Treazzano is securely of Aegean manufacture, and there are probable ones from Montagnolo di Ancona as well,[15] the results of an archeometric study suggest that many of the other sherds, from Cisterna di Tolentino, Montagnolo, and Jesi, were manufactured in the Marche region. As the authors of the study themselves noted, this surprising conclusion obliges us to look more closely at a region that has traditionally been perceived as a backwater in the Bronze Age.[16] Damiani examined the settlement types where Aegean pottery had been found in the region and noticed a coastal-interior distinction. Coastal sites such as Montagnolo di Ancona and Treazzano had the imported LH IIIB materials while interior sites yielded the local versions that were less easily datable, in some cases spanning LH IIIB and LH IIIC: Montagnolo again, Cisterna di Tolentino, and Jesi.[17] Indeed, Jesi had to be excluded from my study because of the imprecise dating of its sherds. The site numbers are too small to extrapolate much from this pattern, and Montagnolo has, as noted, both the local and imported sherds so we cannot overstate the coastal-interior distinction, but this pattern as it stands is very different from that in the southern part of the peninsula where, as we shall see in Chapter 8, the local production of Aegean-style pottery seems to always occur at the same coastal sites with extensive Aegean ceramic imports.

One settlement with no Aegean-style pots as yet – but nonetheless a pivotal site in the region – is Moscosi di Cingoli. This inland settlement

---

[13] Bergonzi 2005: 696–7.
[14] Cisterna di Tolentino, Jesi, Montagnolo di Ancona, Treazzano di Monsampolo. Vagnetti *et al.* 2006.
[15] Vagnetti *et al.* 2006: 1168.
[16] Vagnetti *et al.* 2006: 1169.
[17] Damiani 2010: 454–5.

that spanned the RBA and FBA has yielded a wide array of metal objects including weapons, ornaments, and tools and it is thought that metallurgy was practiced in the settlement. Bronze finds include a number of dagger types and violin-bow fibulae. Some of the bronzes were apparent tools for bone and antler working, which was a craft that was practiced at this site.[18] The antler objects at Moscosi find many matches in the Terramare area and the lowland Veneto, but show no ties to the south.[19] Some amber beads and three glass beads were found at the site, the latter recalling both Aegean and Terramare examples, but they seem to have been manufactured differently from the beads from those places and may be of a local production.[20] Also from the site are limestone weights with matches at numerous Terramare sites. Finally, some of the incised pottery from the site includes typical Terramare motifs.[21] Clearly the residents of Moscosi were closely tied to the Terramare culture.[22]

Cisterna di Tolentino, an inland site along the Chienti River, shows similar craft industries and ties to the north, indicating that Moscosi was not unique. It has yielded some fifty Aegean-style sherds, dating to LH IIIB and LH IIIC, as well as other distinctive finds.[23] Similar to Moscosi, metalworking equipment points to an onsite metallurgical industry, while finished bronze pieces include Glisente B and Torre Castelluccia daggers and a twisted violin-bow fibula. As at Moscosi, there were also bronze tools for bone and antler working, glass beads of similar local production, and the same kind of limestone weight.[24] Despite very limited knowledge about the settlement of Cisterna, these features bear such resemblances to Moscosi that the two sites have been compared carefully. The bronzes from both sites seem largely standardized, with similar copper-tin ratios averaging 85–90 percent and 9–11 percent respectively, and with closely matching technologies.[25] Given the similarities between the two sites and their proximity – approximately 20 km apart – it is all the more surprising that no Aegean-style pottery has been

---

[18] Sabbatini and Silvestrini 2005: 650–2.
[19] Pasquini 2005.
[20] Sabbatini and Silvestrini 2005: 652–3.
[21] Damiani 2010: 454–5.
[22] Sabbatini and Silvestrini 2005: 654.
[23] Baldelli *et al.* 2005: 568; Percossi *et al.* 2005: 671–3.
[24] De Marinis *et al.* 2005: 687; Percossi *et al.* 2005: 674–5.
[25] De Marinis *et al.* 2005: 680–3.

Marche, Umbria, and the Apennine Mountain Muddle

found at Moscosi. From the evidence of these two sites, the picture that emerges is of a highly regionalized exchange of objects and technologies, in which the Terramare featured prominently while the Aegean played only a small part.

In later times the residents of this region were known to the Romans variously as Picenes, Picentes, and Picentini. According to a legend recounted by Strabo, the Picenes had been a group of Sabines who migrated to fulfill a *ver sacrum*, led by a woodpecker (picus), which became their totemic animal and gave its name to the group. The northern border of Picene territory, the Esino River, is fairly well established. North of that river the numbers of traditionally Picene materials decline, and the settlement of Novilara and its environs seem to be their own entity.[26] In contrast, the southern border of this group's territory is much debated.[27] Using the limits of the Augustan Region V is no help here as it extends further south than the conventional limits of Picene territory, as far as the Pescara (Aternus) River, thus incorporating the Praetuttii and Marrucini territories as well. One reasonable boundary line is the Tronto River, at which point the territory of the Praetuttii is thought to have begun. This is the boundary that Naso favors in his study of the Picenes, although he acknowledges that, in part, the choice reflects modern circumstances.[28] He does note that in the eighth and seventh centuries BC, the distinctive Picene burial practice of trench graves with the deceased on a bed of gravel disappears south of the Tronto, as do the decorated bronze defensive discs, so there are valid archaeological grounds for selecting the Tronto as the boundary as well.[29] I will adopt it tentatively here.

There are two known languages in the region: north Picene and south Picene. The north Picene language has not been successfully translated and may be a non–Indo-European language. It is known from four stelae from the site of Novilara, north of the Esino River. These stelae are thought to date to the sixth century BC and are written in a northern

---

[26] Naso 2000: 18–19.

[27] Cf. Naso 2000: 18–26 for a useful discussion of the debate.

[28] Naso 2000: 23. The Tronto River is the contemporary boundary between the regions of Marche and Abruzzo; there is a separate book in the same series as Naso's – Biblioteca di Archeologia (Longanesi and Co.) – planned for the groups occupying Abruzzo, so he limited his study accordingly.

[29] Naso 2000: 23; 140; fig. 13.

Etruscan writing system akin to that from Verucchio just to the north.[30] In sum, there is nothing "Picene" about the north Picene language except its name, and it does not warrant further discussion here. The south Picene language, however, belongs to the Sabellic subfamily of Italic languages and is most akin to Umbrian. A couple dozen inscriptions, dating primarily to the fifth century BC, are known from the area south of the Esino River, with a particular preponderance along the Tronto River. That the inscriptions are found south of the Tronto as well as north of it problematizes the river's identification as the southern boundary of Picenum. Moreover, further south still, in Abruzzo, traditionally Picene objects are found in Archaic-period burials. But as Riva notes, the mobility of the mountain populations may be behind these blurred boundaries, a point to be explored later in this chapter.[31]

The south Picene alphabet falls out of use in the fourth century BC, and by the third century, no further documents in the Picene language are known, reflecting the impact of the Roman conquest.[32] The Picenes made an alliance with Rome in 299 BC but later rebelled. In 269 BC, many Picenes were relocated forcibly by the Romans to an area along the south-Tyrrhenian coast in punishment for rebelling.[33] In 264 BC, the establishment of the Latin colony at Firmum Picenum secured Roman control of Picene territory. With their own language, ethnonym, and origin myths, but without cities or common object types, the Picenes present an interesting case. A distinctive Picene material culture is challenging to identify as they were affected by Etruscan and Greek cultural productions while operating within Apennine traditions as well. In Picene funerary contexts from the Orientalizing period on, material culture is more easily read as a status marker than as a regional marker. There is some doubt whether they constituted a cohesive cultural group at all. Thus, Riva writes, "[u]ltimately, we must ask ourselves whether we can truly speak of a Picene material culture and distinguish it in regional terms."[34] Alternatively, Naso works from the premise that there was indeed an ethnic group in Italy known as the Picenes, perhaps

---

[30] Riva 2007: 84.
[31] Riva 2007: 87–9.
[32] Naso 2000: 35; 232.
[33] Strabo 5.4.13
[34] Riva 2007: 108.

finding the textual evidence and use of the ethnonym (some of the south Picene inscriptions use the term *pupun-*, which may be a self-label) to be sufficient proof of a Picene identity around which one may identify some archaeological correlates, such as the aforementioned bronze discs.[35]

The other area covered in this chapter is the north-central Apennines, southwest of Marche. This was the traditional territory of the Umbrians who were thought to occupy the land east of the Tiber in the stretch of Apennines north of Sabine territory in addition to, for a time, a swath of Adriatic coastline between the Conero peninsula and the Po Delta.[36] Augustan Region VI conforms generally to that traditional territory, although by the time of Roman rule, the Po Delta had been settled by Celtic groups and that appendage of the region was no longer Umbrian in character. Bradley's sustained work on the Umbrians has gone a long way to illuminate this group,[37] but as he himself notes, "archaeological evidence in reality provides no precise means of defining an 'Umbrian region.'"[38] Herodotus, writing in the fifth century, mentions the Umbrians having territory extending as far as the Alps, which simply cannot be true.[39] Otherwise, though, the first millennium BC Greek authors were fairly uniform in insisting that Umbrian territory covered the southeast Po Valley and the central Adriatic coast, although this almost certainly derives from the reports of Greeks traveling up that coast, hence the absence of information on the westward extent of the group.[40] To the west lay the Etruscans; the Umbrians were influenced, but not absorbed, by Etruscan culture – even if some of their territory, such as Perugia, did fall under Etruscan control. Pliny notes that the territory between the Marecchia and Esino Rivers was Umbrian until it was taken over in the fourth century BC by a Celtic group, the Senones. This migration is attested from Celtic-style burials in that area, as well as textually.[41] Little is certain concerning the nature of that migration or its scale, however,

---

[35] Naso 2000.
[36] Riva 2007: 89.
[37] Bradley 1997; 2000.
[38] Bradley 1997: 55.
[39] Herodotus 4.49
[40] Bradley 1997: 56.
[41] Pliny, *Natural History* 3.19.112.

with some Celtic finds turning up farther south in presumably Picene territory. Further, the archaeological evidence, demonstrating apparent intermixing between Picenes and Celts, suggests a more peaceful arrival than the ancient sources claimed.[42] The Augustan Region VI's coastal strip was known as the Ager Gallicus in acknowledgment of its Celtic inhabitants. Whereas Naso has taken Pliny's account to mean that the Umbrians were themselves late arrivals to the coast (probably only in the sixth century BC), Riva notes that there is no archaeological evidence for that movement in that period.[43] I will return to this debate when analyzing the networks in the area.

Not only is Umbrian territory imprecisely defined, but the people themselves are also difficult to detect. The earliest-known use of the term Umbrian is graffiti with names meaning "Umbrian" on two sixth century BC Greek vases from Etruria.[44] Likewise, a fifth century BC bronze bracelet – found not in Umbria, but in modern Abruzzo – displays an early incised text in south Picene that includes the ethnic designation "Umbrian."[45] From the fourth century, the Etruscan alphabet takes hold there. In the fourth and third centuries BC, the epigraphic evidence from Umbria refers to smaller communities and towns, not Umbria as a whole, and Bradley notes that the overall impression "is one of particularism."[46] Bradley argues that smaller named tribal groups within the territory that would become Umbria prevailed, although he suggests this localism may be attributable to the context of the evidence so that within Umbria the larger ethnic designation would have been taken as a given and did not need to be expressed.[47] However, without strong counterevidence of a unified group identity, an Umbrian ethnicity is a matter of debate. Bradley himself notes it may have been only with military service under Rome after the Social War that an Umbrian ethnicity was forged; during the third century they urbanized. Bradley argues for a very late ethnic formation in the region, in which the boundaries become more defined only at the end of the first millennium BC, "for the period before the conquest we should treat the region as an almost random geographical

---

[42] Riva 2007: 107.
[43] Naso 2000: 23; 214–15; Riva 2007: 87.
[44] Bradley 1997: 56.
[45] Bradley 2000: 24.
[46] Bradley 1997: 56.
[47] Bradley 1997: 57.

segment of Italy."[48] Although this pushes the ethnicity formation rather late, it is true that in Umbria at least the processes of *state* formation cannot be traced before the middle of the first millennium BC, and the settlement of the sites that would later become the major Umbrian towns does not occur until the first centuries of the Iron Age.[49] Even though Bradley's skepticism is well taken, the external recognition by Umbria's neighbors in the sixth to fifth centuries BC does suggest a coherent group by the Archaic period. A key question, then, is to what extent can the Bronze Age networks shed light on the origins of the Umbrians and Picenes?

The RBA Network

As observed in Chapter 4, several sites in the RBA in the territory of Marche and the north-central Apennines are nodes in the Terramare network, constituting an apparent tail or extension of the core cluster of Terramare sites. In order to get a closer look at this portion of the network, we can disconnect it from the northern sites. In other words, the fifteen sites from this region that were formerly part of the Terramare network can be looked at independently. There are other sites in the area as well, so in this chapter I will be working with a total of twenty-one RBA sites: thirteen settlements, three cemeteries, and five sites of unknown function. At least two from this last group are caves, which seem to have served as both burial places and ritual sites in the RBA. The finds from the sites of unknown function are primarily weapons – in particular, daggers – so these are likely ritual deposits or grave goods from unidentified cemeteries.[50] There are no known hoards in this period.

There are seventeen object types circulating in the region in the RBA, the most widespread turning up at eleven sites (awl handles) and many found at just one site (Table 7.1). Among the bronze objects, the prevalence of daggers has led Bergonzi to suggest that this was the primary weapon of combat in the area rather than the sword.[51] The objects are in

---

[48] Bradley 2000: 28.
[49] Bradley 2000: 44.
[50] Bergonzi 2005: 696–8. Bergonzi suggests that Montegiorgio, for example, may have been a cemetery.
[51] Bergonzi 2005: 703.

Table 7.1. *Object types circulating in Marche and Umbria in the RBA*

Object types present in Marche and Umbria in the RBA	Number of find spots
Awl handle	11
Miniature spoked wheel	5
Small hoe	5
Torre Castelluccia dagger	4
Glisente B dagger	3
LH IIIB pottery	3
Pertosa dagger	3
Boccatura del Mincio dress pin	2
Montegiorgio sword	2
Twisted violin-bow fibula	2
Bacino Marina dress pin	1
Barrel bead with wavy lines	1
Bertarina dagger	1
Cataragna dress pin	1
Fornovo S. Giovanni dagger	1
Merlara dagger	1
Montegiorgio knife	1

many cases northern forms, but not exclusively, and local industries are attested. As noted earlier, Moscosi di Cingoli and Cisterna di Tolentino had an antler-working industry. Exact matches of an hourglass-shaped handle thought to have been made at Moscosi are known from the nearby sites of Santa Paolina da Filottrano and Conelle di Arcevia, but not from the Terramare region,[52] suggesting a hyper-localized circulation contemporary with the longer distance circuits. Local manufacture of bronze objects is also known at Moscosi and Cisterna di Tolentino.[53] Though many of the bronze forms are traced to the Po region, the subtype of Pertosa dagger found in Marche (Type A) finds closer matches in the Tyrrhenian area and in the south than in the north.[54] Finally, the Aegean pottery speaks to alternative contacts as well. Thus, a closer examination of the particular object types in Marche belies the seeming dependence of the region on the Terramare economy, or at least mitigates it.

[52] Pasquini 2005: 987–9.
[53] Bergonzi 2005: 703.
[54] Bianco Peroni 1994: 152.

Marche, Umbria, and the Apennine Mountain Muddle

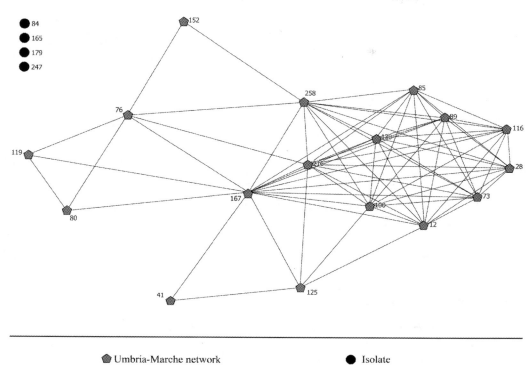

7.1. Graph of RBA network in Umbria and Marche

Given that the focus here is on a circumscribed geographic area, I can proceed as I have in the earlier chapters and relax the criteria for ties to get an overview of how goods may have been circulating here. Thus, I remove the 50 km cut off and build a new network in which ties between sites are based on the co-presence of object types solely. Within this reconfigured network there emerges a cluster of seventeen connected sites and four isolates, with a density of 33.8 percent (Figure 7.1). The large cluster almost matches the one identified in Chapter 4, with the addition of two sites that were formerly a separate dyad, Laferola and Treazzano, because they were more than 50 km away from the nearest site in the cluster. The two cemeteries are isolates, so it may be that the absence of similar object types at those sites reflects patterns of deposition that differed between cemeteries and other types of sites rather than an exclusion from the network. Placed on a map, the network displays no preference for the coast, with only five of the seventeen sites in the cluster coastal or sub-coastal in character (Figure 7.2).

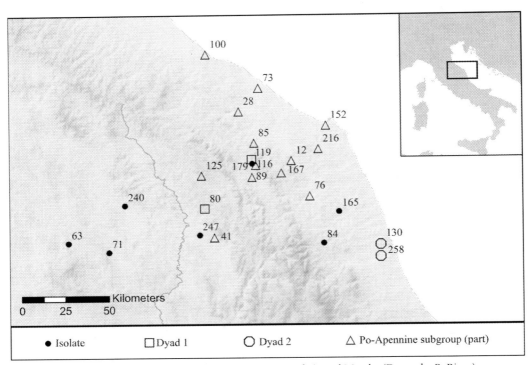

7.2. Map showing RBA find spots in Umbria and Marche (Drawn by R. Biggs)

However, rivers do seem to have played a role in the movement of goods in this period, as suggested by the tight grouping of sites along the Esino River. As the region is very mountainous with the exception of a narrow stretch of coastline, this inland network may be reframed as a mountainous network. This contradicts what one might expect about the isolation of mountain regions and echoes the pattern observed by Riva in her description of Picenum.[55]

Within the cluster, there is a core of eleven sites that are fully connected to each other (density=100%) along with six outlying sites that have fewer ties. The eleven sites are united by the co-presence of the awl handles. As noted earlier, these useful objects were made locally and can hardly be considered exotica. They are therefore convincing evidence of the homegrown character of the network. These do not turn up as the end of the line of long-distance movements, but instead were a product of local circulations. Even if, as is thought, the catalyst for this

[55] Riva 2007: 79.

network's formation was the economic powerhouse of the Terramare to the north, once established, local goods could follow these same paths. The handles' distribution does not extend far to the west. While there is no clear geographic inflection to this core-margin pattern within the cluster, it is worth noting that three of the four westernmost sites in the region are among the least connected in the cluster[56] and the fourth site, Torre d'Andrea, is an isolate. As noted already, no sites further west than these are joined to the network, so at this stage it would seem that the interactions in the mountains were limited to the eastern slopes of this portion of the Apennines. Thus, when examined independently of the Terramare network, we can see that although the RBA Apennine network may have been driven by Terramare pressures, it has a certain internal coherence. The FBA network that follows reveals what happens once the driving force of the north is no longer an influence.

The FBA Network

The peninsular study in Chapter 4 identified a relatively cohesive network of nine sites spanning the modern territories of Marche and Umbria in the FBA, covering much of the same territory as the earlier RBA tail of the Terramare network. Although this FBA network mapped closely onto the local material-culture facies known as the Chiusi-Cetona facies, it did not apparently honor later boundaries between Umbrian and Picene territories. Here we can look more closely at this network. Overall there are seventeen sites with the relevant object types in this area in the FBA, twenty when some newly connected sites in the future Etruria are included. Whereas the site numbers vary little from the RBA, the proportions of site types differ considerably. Among these twenty sites, just three are securely settlements and two are securely cemeteries. Five of the sites are hoards and ten are of unknown function, consisting of casual finds of metal objects. As noted for the unknown sites of the RBA, the latter were likely either ritual deposits or burials – and now possibly hoards in this period – but without more information, their function is not secure. There were also clearly upheavals between the RBA and FBA at the scale of individual sites. Just four RBA sites continue into

---

[56] Gubbio-Monte Ingino, Coccorano, Capitan Loreto.

Table 7.2. *Object types circulating in Marche and Umbria in the FBA*

Object types present in Marche and Umbria in the FBA	Number of find spots
Pertosa axe	7
Ponte S. Giovanni axe	3
Casalecchio axe	2
Frattesina comb	2
Miniature spoked wheel	2
Pick ingot	2
Torri d'Arcugnano dress pin	2
Twisted asymmetrical violin-bow fibula	2
Allerona sword	1
Blue glass-barrel bead with spirals	1
Fontanella knife	1
Frassineto sword	1
LH IIIC Aegean pot	1
Menaforno axe	1
Tiryns bead	1
TMES socketed shovel	1

the FBA, and three of these now constitute the sole settlements recorded in the FBA network.[57] Moreover, of the four sites, only Gubbio-MI is a connected node in both periods, with the other three sites being isolates in one or another period. Sixteen of the object types in this study were circulating in the region in the FBA, but the number of find spots for individual object types is low. The most common object type, the Pertosa axe, was found at seven sites, and almost all other objects are known from just one or two sites (Table 7.2).

Among the object types present, in addition to the Pertosa axe, there are three other axe types in the area, as well as pick ingots and a socketed shovel: the objects in the region speak to the relatively high numbers of hoards there. The daggers have disappeared and two sword types and a knife are now recorded, suggesting other changes from the RBA as well, but whether these reflect changes in fighting techniques, depositional practices, or site functions, it is difficult to determine. The important role of the axe as a weapon along the mid-Adriatic coast seems to continue for many centuries, as the high numbers of axes in eighth and

---

[57] Cisterna di Tolentino, Gubbio, Montegiorgio, Pianello di Genga.

seventh centuries BC contexts attest.[58] As expected in light of the dissolution of the Terramare culture, the object forms no longer derive from that territory. The sword types, for example, are most common in the central Apennines, and the axes from hoards are common there as well, although their production centers are not known. However, the influence of the north is still evident in many objects, including the Frattesina comb, the glass-barrel bead with spirals, and the Tiryns bead. All of these have parallels at Frattesina or nearby in the Po Delta, and may have been produced there. Likewise, pick ingots also are found at Frattesina, and one scholar has suggested that these followed the same route down the Adriatic coast that amber and the Frattesina combs may have followed.[59] Further, the socketed shovels are thought to originate at Frattesina.[60] In sum, contacts with the north remained significant in this period.

We can proceed as before and construct a new network for the region in which ties between nodes are based on the co-presence of objects alone, independent of distance. The resulting network is quite sparsely connected, with a density of just 14.76 percent (Figure 7.3). This is far lower than the 63.2 percent density recorded for the Apennine network in the peninsular study, but that is because this new network includes isolates (of which there are five) in the density calculations, whereas the earlier network measures were based solely on the connected sites (see Chapter 4 for a description of how these numbers were obtained). Along with a triad, there are five isolates and a cluster of thirteen connected sites that mirror the Apennine network identified in the peninsular study, with only four additional sites (three of which are the newly added hoards). Thus, the distance criterion of Chapter 4's network was not a particularly limiting factor in this case; most of the sites with shared objects in the region were fairly near each other anyway. The connected cluster is structured similarly to its RBA counterpart, composed of a core of fully connected sites (100% density) and strings of weakly connected sites that form a tail. Here the core consists of seven sites joined by the co-presence of Pertosa axes, much as the awl handles linked the

---

[58] Naso 2000: 59–61.
[59] Pellegrini 1989: 594.
[60] Bellintani and Stefan 2008: 15.

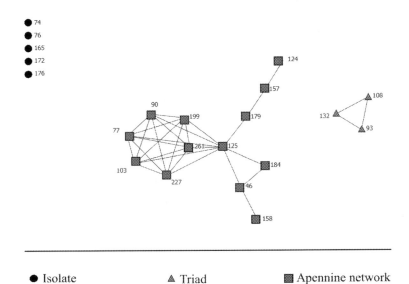

7.3. Graph of FBA network in Umbria and Marche, with ties based on shared objects only

sites of the RBA core earlier. Site function may play a role in the pattern: none of the hoards have yielded Pertosa axes, so none of the core sites in the cluster are hoards, but three of the six outlying sites in the cluster are hoards. The triad is composed of two ritual deposits and an unknown site. This tie between an unknown site and two ritual deposits, together with the absence of shared objects between the known hoards and these unknown site types, would seem to support Bergonzi's suggestion that the latter are unidentified ritual deposits or burials, not hoards.[61]

When the network is mapped, its pronounced inland character becomes evident, with the nearest site to the coast, Ripatransone, some 9 km inland (Figure 7.4). Like its RBA predecessor, the FBA network is most decidedly oriented toward the mountains. The distinction between connected sites and isolates does not immediately appear to be geographically determined; the sites within the connected cluster are spread over the region and the southernmost, northernmost, easternmost, and westernmost sites in the area are each part of that cluster. Likewise, the isolates are scattered among the connected sites, although they display a slight

---

[61] Bergonzi 2005. Presumably settlements would leave enough remains that they would not be overlooked.

Marche, Umbria, and the Apennine Mountain Muddle

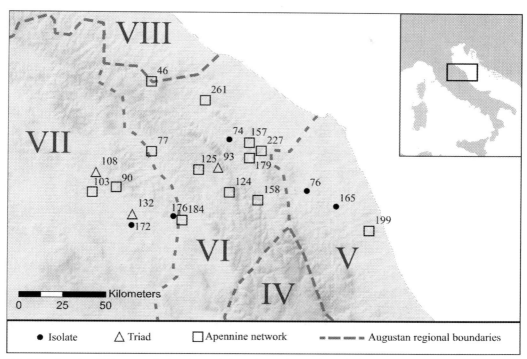

7.4. Map showing FBA network sites in Umbria and Marche, with probable boundary between Augustan regions IV, V, and VI (Drawn by R. Biggs)

tendency to be south of the bulk of them. Therefore, at first glance, geography would seem to have very little role in connectedness. Looking more closely, however, one observes that nine of the thirteen connected sites are located somewhere along the Esino River or further west of it along the same west-southwest–east-northeast axis, continuing even into the future Etruria, just northwest of Lake Trasimeno. Five of the seven core sites within the cluster are found along that axis, suggesting that this was a trans-Apennine route along which the Pertosa daggers were distributed.

Interestingly, the sites that carried on from the RBA seem to have declined in importance by the FBA, with the exception of Gubbio-MI which, as noted earlier, was a node in both periods and in the FBA occupied a pivotal position as a cutpoint whose would detach six sites from the network. As we saw in Chapter 6 on west-central Italy, Gubbio plays an important role in the long-distance networks there as well. Otherwise, however, Cisterna di Tolentino is now an isolate and Moscosi di Cingoli, although still occupied in the FBA, has not yielded examples of any of the objects studied here so is not visible in this particular network.

The hypothesized network of the FBA finds some independent confirmation in the local material culture. In this same region in the FBA, the ceramic facies known as the Chiusi-Cetona facies has been identified, as described in Chapter 6.[62] This facies covers some of the territory of the Apennine network of that period while extending farther into later Etruscan territory. Major Chiusi-Cetona sites include Val di Chiana, Cetona, Perugia, Spoleto, Gubbio-MI, Monte Ansciano, Monte Croce Guardia, Monte Primo, Colle dei Cappuccini, Capannori, and Scarceta.[63] Many of these are in the network identified earlier. Thus, the preferential circulations of goods and the affinities in ceramic production converge quite well. Moreover, just as the FBA Apennine network may be understood as the vestigial tail of the RBA Terramare network, Bietti Sestieri observes that the Chiusi-Cetona facies ceramics also contain decorative elements such as applied features that are apparent vestiges of earlier ties between the center and the north.[64] Thus, the local ceramics of the FBA mirror to a certain extent the circulations of bronzes and other objects in my study and reflect the same history, although Etruria appears more marginal in the network than in the facies itself. Bietti Sestieri has described how, in the EIA, the Chiusi-Cetona group gives way to two regional divisions: one Picene and the other proto-Etruscan.[65] This facies was examined closely from the perspective of Etruria in the network analysis of that region in Chapter 6; here we see it from the other side.

To conclude, despite the impermanence of individual sites, the networks show continuity in the area covered. In the FBA there is a shift west further into Etruria and away from the Adriatic coast, but the core still covers roughly the same geographic area. It therefore seems reasonable to

---

[62] Zanini 1996.
[63] Bietti Sestieri 2010: 227.
[64] Bietti Sestieri 2010: 226–7. "Questi elementi [in the ceramic decoration] mostrano in modo abbastanza chiaro un collegamento con la ceramica delle terramare e degli abitati arginati dell'area padana a sud e a nord del Po, e costituiscono probabilmente la traccia di rapporti intensi che nell'età del bronzo media e recente collegavano le regioni centrali della penisola alla pianura padana."
[65] Bietti Sestieri 2010: 231.

deduce some carryover from the earlier RBA network to the subsequent FBA one. I would argue that the pattern we see is the survival of this extension of the larger Terramare network, perhaps shored up by ties now with Frattesina and neighboring sites in the Veneto, and expanding southwest into Etruria. However, the low numbers of examples of the standard objects occurring at Frattesina such as amber (one site in the central Apennines with a Tiryns bead), glass beads (one site), and combs (two sites) should make us hesitate to overstate those ties in the FBA. The FBA network here fits nicely with the Chiusi-Cetona network described earlier, but it does not map so neatly onto the later regional groups. Indeed, the network in both the RBA and FBA spans later Umbrian and Picene territories and, as noted earlier, is firmly established in the future northern Etruria as well by the FBA. As we know that Picenes and Umbrians were among the better-defined of the regional groups of the first millennium BC, the apparent lack of sustained territorial integrity would seem to contradict this book's hypothesis that some of the regional groups of the Iron Age and after had their origins in the Bronze Age networks. What is going on? To make sense of this we need to take into account the particular circumstances of the Apennines.

Discussion: The Apennine Networks and the Question of Mountain Mobility

The Apennine area demonstrates a cultural and linguistic unity, or at least commonality, despite the political fragmentation derived from tribalism and challenging topography. As Crawford notes, our modern notions of mountains as boundaries almost certainly did not apply in the past and the Marsic, Volscian, Sabine, and other boundaries are impossible to determine now from applying "commonsense" notions of natural divisions.[66] Crawford contends that the Apennine peoples' group identities (whether we use the labels "tribal," "ethnic," or something else) were oriented toward high-mountain pastures rather than lakes or rivers. From this he infers that these identities cannot be simply a response to Roman conquest, but must instead predate that period, going back to the sixth or fifth century BC when sanctuaries and some

---

[66] Crawford 2003: 58–60.

settlements are evidently positioned near to the pastures.[67] The evidence here suggests some identities may extend even farther back in time.

The regional groups that the Greeks first identified do not stay unchanged, and we can imagine similar movements, fusions, and diffusions occurring in earlier times as well. This may give us some insight into why the boundaries and labels are often inconsistent. Thus, one explanation for the blurred boundaries observed in the networks analyzed in this chapter may be that people simply did not stay in the same areas over time. This may have been particularly true of the peoples of the Apennine region. Indeed, some scholars have emphasized a condition of mobility among the populations of the Apennines in ancient times. As Williamson put it, "continual movement seems to have characterized the lives of the majority of Italians, whether urban or tribal, as changing patterns of resource variability led one group or another to move from place to place, some for short periods of time, others for good."[68]

As short-term movements and permanent relocations are quite different phenomena, we can look at each in turn, focusing on the latter first. The theory of large-scale permanent resettling of peoples draws primarily on the well-attested fifth and fourth century evidence of population movements including the Samnites into Campania, the Sabines into Latium, and the Lucanians into south Italy. Cornell notes, "[t]he sources report a succession of tribal migrations at this time which resulted in the spread of the Sabellian peoples and the diffusion of the Osco-Umbrian dialects throughout the central and southern regions of the peninsula."[69] These migrations were distilled in the ancient sources into accounts of the *ver sacrum*, in which a group asking a deity to be saved from a crisis such as a famine would promise to sacrifice everything produced the following spring to the deity. Rather than killing the newborn children the following spring, those children upon adulthood would be sent away from the territory. This practice may explain some population movements in the peninsula. *Ver sacra* were features of the origin myths of some groups, such as the Picenes and the Hirpini. As Cornell notes, "[t]he

---

[67] Crawford 2003: 61.
[68] Williamson 2005: 145.
[69] Cornell 1995: 304–5.

myth is based on an assumption that is real enough, namely that the pressure of overpopulation in a region of poor natural resources was the primary cause of emigration."[70] Population pressures may have caused the movements of Lucanians and Bruttians into coastal southern Italy, and the Samnite takeover of Campania. By the late 490s, the mountain-dwelling Volscians moved into Latium, probably because of these same internal pressures. These periodic movements of peoples demonstrate clearly why we cannot expect to be able to use DNA or any other biological markers to plot the ethnicity of the groups in question.

Were these mid-millennium movements the norm, or were they part of a widespread but punctuated phase of demographic pressures that led to the shifts and movements, including the Celts into northern Italy? There is little reason to think that population movements around Italy were common before those demographic increases. Just as Rome's conquest was an utterly novel event in the history of Italy, so, too, were these other movements of the same period. The Romans used relocation as a tactic for undermining group unity, and this suggests that locality was important in self-definition, or at least the Romans thought so: Broadhead argues that the Romans conceived of geographic fixity as the norm and structured their military recruitment system accordingly, overlooking the realities of demographic shifts.[71] There is some suggestion that movements occurred earlier as well, including the resettling to the south of some of the Terramare people with the collapse of those settlements at the end of the RBA, and the residents of Frattesina's dispersal, perhaps to Bologna and Verucchio, at the end of the FBA.[72] Even more securely we may point to earlier Celtic migrations into northern Italy, as attested by the intrusive materials of the Canegrate culture. Nonetheless, these punctuated incidents do not permit generalizing.

Although large-scale, long-term mobility needs to be examined on a case-by-case basis, scholars also debate the extent of shorter term movements in the Apennine Mountains starting in the second millennium BC in the context of an economy structured around transhumant pastoralism. Transhumance would have facilitated interactions between

---

[70] Cornell 1995: 305.
[71] Broadhead 2008.
[72] Bietti Sestieri 2010: 210–12.

groups on either side of the mountains, meeting in the high meadows in the summer months, negotiating for access to pasturage.[73] This would explain the similarities in material culture across the Apennines from the MBA on. As far back as the MBA, trans-Apennine affinities – that is, similarities in pottery – along an east-west axis were stronger than north-south ones and the role of the Apennines as a meeting place and zone of cultural mixing has long been emphasized. This would certainly be a viable explanation for the distribution of Pertosa axes in the FBA described earlier, for example. However, some scholars are skeptical about just how early the practice of long-distance transhumance actually began. Whittaker, among others, has insisted that specialized pastoralism involving long-distance seasonal transhumance is not possible without the guarantees, by a state-level authority, of safe passage. If he is right, this would mean that in Italy, long-distance transhumance cannot predate the second century BC.[74] Not everyone accepts this, however. Gabba argues that there was long-distance movement of herds well before the Roman period. He insists that agreements could exist between groups without an overarching political authority so that flocks could be moved safely between regions in non-state societies. What changes in the Roman period is not the practice of transhumance itself, but the scale of the undertaking and the shift from small owner-herders to vast flocks managed by herders for absentee owners.[75] Garnsey allows for some pre-Roman transhumance, but suggests it was only small-scale, localized movements between lowland areas and hills. He notes that "caution is advisable in estimating the scale of pastoralism in the context of what was probably an underpopulated society practicing a relatively primitive mixed farming economy."[76] This debate is not easily resolved, but in any case, we could argue that even small movements may have been sufficient to engender the exchanges posited here.[77] But what of the blurred boundaries between Umbrian and Picene territories?

The network of Apennine sites spanning later territories may be understood in several ways. One possibility is that the network belies regional

[73] Bradley 2000: 50.
[74] Whittaker 1988: 2–3.
[75] Gabba 1988: 138. See also Pasquinucci 1979: 93–4.
[76] Garnsey 1988: 200.
[77] See Bradley (2000) on the impact of transhumance on the Umbrians.

differences that are not yet visible materially in the Bronze Age, but which are already in place; in other words, goods were circulating outside of regional territories. This would make particular sense if long-distance transhumance was indeed occurring, as some scholars have posited for this period, leading to interactions between groups to an extent not observed in the other networks of the peninsula. Another possibility is that the network really does reflect the state of things at the time in that as a survivor of the RBA, this large grouping lingered on but ultimately fragmented into the later named groups we know of in the historical period. A third possibility is that subsequent permanent population movements transformed the demographic makeup of that area, breaking the earlier patterns. There is a historical tradition for this, although such stories need to be taken with caution. The network evidence does suggest sustained intermixing of peoples and materials in the RBA and FBA, with the emergence of distinctive Umbrian and Picene peoples a later phenomenon. One feature of the pattern is worth noting, however: the networks identified may cross some later regional boundaries, but not all. In particular, there are no nodes of the network in what is later considered Sabine territory to the south. In fact, both the RBA and FBA networks bypass that area altogether. When we compare the boundary posited for the later Augustan regions, separating region IV (Samnium) from regions V (Picenum) and VI (Umbria et Ager Gallicus) with the network maps, it is striking how closely the boundary holds (see Figure 7.4). This would suggest that already in the Bronze Age there was a distinction between those other Apennine groups and the Umbrian-Picene groups in terms of exchange preferences. It would seem, then, that the intermixing was not without its own structure and that the network can be defined as much by where it is not as where it is. If we accept that the networks of both the RBA and FBA reflect an earlier unity that later fragments into Picene and Umbrian groups respectively, the fact that both networks extend north of the Esino River may suggest that the Umbrian presence in that zone had Bronze Age antecedents. Recall, however, that literary tradition traces Picene origins to the Sabines to the south, not to the Umbrians. This would seem to contradict the network pattern of exclusion of the Sabine peoples, but it is dangerous indeed to look for historical truths in origin myths. The *ver sacrum* myths in particular may say more about the later relations between groups than about their origins.[78] In this respect, they operate much as the Greek origin myths did. Regardless of the historical truth of the *ver sacrum* myth, the myth itself may have encouraged cultural blending as it claimed a common origin for the peoples in this territory.[79] Linguistically, the south Picene language is close to Umbrian, which is compelling support for close ties.[80]

Conclusions

The Bronze Age networks of the Apennines offer particular challenges to the theory of path dependence taken in this book. The RBA and FBA networks along the Adriatic coast and in the north-central Apennines suggest that the mountains did indeed facilitate interactions and intermixing, and that mobility was not solely a phenomenon of the fourth century BC. We also see the evolving influence of the north on the region, first with the Terramare culture and then with the proto-Veneto communities, in particular Frattesina. In these periods we catch a glimpse of a network spanning territories that will later be defined in more circumscribed units, and we cannot at this point detect traces of those smaller units. The fact that Umbrian and south Picene are such similar languages speaks to a long history of interconnections. Later the Etruscan portion of the FBA network breaks away to be incorporated into the southern Etruscan sphere, but the close interactions between Umbrians and Etruscans continue, with border cities such as Perugia changing hands in the process. Thus, while it may be true, as Bradley maintains, that ethnogenesis in the rigorous sense is a late phenomenon in Umbria,[81] clearly there is a broader regional distinctiveness already in place from an early time.

---

[78] Dench 1995: 206.
[79] Bispham 2007: 181.
[80] David 1997: 23.
[81] Bradley 2000: 125.

CHAPTER EIGHT

SOUTHERN ITALY: NETWORKS BY LAND AND BY SEA

"Since the terms Peucetii and Daunii are not at all used by the native inhabitants except in early times, and since the country as a whole is now called Apulia, necessarily the boundaries of these ethnics cannot be told to a nicety either and for this reason neither should I myself make positive assertions about them." (Strabo *Geography* 6.3.8)

"In contrast to the relatively homogeneous cultural patterns of north and central Italy, where a dominant culture can generally be recognized in each geographical area, the picture presented by southern Italy is a much more confused one. Not only is the number of distinct cultural groups greater, and their history and development difficult to follow, but it is often hard to be certain whether we are dealing with genuinely different cultures or merely branches of a single group." (Reich 1979: 98)

Introduction: Setting the Scene

Southern Italy, covering present day Campania, Calabria, Basilicata, and Apulia, is not easily summarized as it includes diverse coastlines and is transected by the Apennines. I will focus primarily on those regions for which a network analysis is informative: the heel (the Salento peninsula and north of it up to the Gargano peninsula of Apulia) and arch (the Gulf of Taranto, covering coastal Basilicata and the northern stretch of

Calabria) of the boot. In Chapter 4 we observed a network in the RBA that covered the Gulf of Taranto and sites of the Salento peninsula. All the nodes in that network were along the coast or in the "subcoastal" zone, just inland, and the network bore the hallmarks of a maritime network. In the FBA, two networks were observable in southern Italy: one along the coast of Basilicata and northern Calabria, and one covering Apulia. This chapter examines the historical contexts of these networks and looks more closely at the networks themselves, refashioning them in various ways. Before focusing on the regions of particular interest here, it is worth noting that the entirety of southern Italy shares several historical features: one is a distinction between coast and interior, and the other is direct contact, albeit rare in some areas, with the Aegean. Both of these characteristics of Bronze Age southern Italy will feature prominently in the discussion that follows.

Given this evidence of foreign contacts in southern Italy in the RBA and FBA, studies of the regional histories of that period have hinged on those outside influences. As noted in Chapter 2, Aegean objects reach the shores of Italy by the MBA and grow in number in the subsequent periods, continuing even into the early part of the FBA (LH IIIC), in Apulia at least. Other than the pots themselves, some technological innovations arrived as well, such as the potter's wheel, and possibly purple dye-making and olive cultivation.[1] In addition to the Aegean contacts, trans-Adriatic relations were almost certainly important. Although there is no evidence that large numbers of Aegean peoples settled in southern Italy, migrations from across the Adriatic and from further north may have been large enough to have had a demographic impact.[2] Historically, the Adriatic has long been recognized as a thoroughfare linking continental Europe to the eastern Mediterranean and Aegean.[3] Contacts across the sea with the eastern coast of the Adriatic are probably under-represented archaeologically, but as early as the Copper Age and EBA, Dalmatian pottery turns up in Apulia.[4] Further, trans-Adriatic contacts at the end of the Bronze Age are suggested by certain Balkan features in

---

[1] Bettelli and Levi 2003; Vagnetti 1999b: 149; Cazzella 1996: 1545–8.
[2] Pallottino 1991: 47.
[3] Cazzella and Recchia 2009; Lenzi 2003.
[4] Bietti Sestieri 2003: 51.

local pottery forms in Apulia and as far north as Marche.[5] This evidence does not prove that people crossed the Adriatic to settle permanently in Apulia, however. Herring for one argues against the popular theory of an Illyrian origin for the native peoples of Apulia known as the Messapians. He notes that although there would certainly have been contacts across the Adriatic Sea, the linguistic similarities that have underpinned theories of a full-fledged migration are "largely illusory." Instead, indigenous origins are more likely.[6]

In any case, it has been the Myceanaean material and its impact that have dominated scholarly discussions and been the subject of extensive research.[7] Along the southern stretch of the Adriatic, coastal Apulia marks the closest point of the Italian peninsula to Greece. Therefore, it is somewhat surprising to discover that Apulia was barely visited during the early Mycenaean forays west. There are very few Aegean imports dating to LH I through LH IIIA periods there.[8] In this early phase of contacts between Greece and Italy, the distribution of Mycenaean sherds suggests visits to multiple points along the Adriatic coast of Apulia, as there are similarly small amounts of pots at most of the known coastal sites. This pattern may be interpreted as evidence of relatively high coastal connectivity, if the goods were moving between these coastal towns.[9] In the next phase, which constitutes the apex of Mycenaean activity in Italy, LH IIIA2 and LH IIIB, northern and southern Apulia appear to bifurcate: fewer sites in the north yield imports while there is an intensification of imports in the south. In other words, the distribution of imported Aegean pots is now skewed southward, and those southern sites also start making local imitations of the Mycenaean imports.[10] Radina and Recchia propose two explanations for the low quantities of Mycenaean goods in the northern part of Adriatic Apulia. One possibility is that the traders were still coming to the north, but that they were bringing goods such as beads and ivory instead of pottery. Alternatively, if the dearth of ceramics really is proof of the cessation of Mycenaean visits by

---

[5] Bietti Sestieri 2003: 52.
[6] Herring 2000: 50.
[7] E.g., Bettelli 2002; Benzi and Graziadio 1996; Affuso and Loruso 2006.
[8] Franco 1996: 1566.
[9] Radina and Recchia 2006: 1558.
[10] Radina and Recchia 2006: 1560.

boat to those northern Apulian sites, then the continued distribution of imported beads there points to internal overland circuits.[11] The latter theory becomes interesting in light of Bronze Age patterns discussed later in this chapter, and will be revisited. I would add a third possibility: that the beads could potentially be coming by boat from the northern Adriatic. In any case, the imports to Apulia, even those in the south, are still less common than in the arch of the boot, the Gulf of Taranto.[12] Finally, Apulia seems to experience a late efflorescence in contacts, in LH IIIC.[13]

To what extent does southern Italy experience the changes outlined in Peroni's list in Chapter 1? In the south in the RBA, the demographic data are patchy and not easy to sum up. In the Sibaritide and Apulia, the population increases,[14] in contrast with southern Calabria, where few settlements are known from this period. Although it may have been the case that the toe of Italy was fairly underpopulated, this picture could be attributable to a problem of poorer archaeological visibility than the preceding and successive periods.[15] The FBA shows more consistent evidence of demographic growth in the south, mirroring trends elsewhere in the peninsula.[16] As for changes to subsistence, in southern Italy in the FBA there is not a lot of botanical data to go on, but what there is shows, according to Malone and colleagues, "no clear evidence of agricultural intensification during the course of the Bronze Age," with presumably a subsistence economy structured around mixed farming, as it had been throughout the Bronze Age.[17] This differs markedly from the picture of agricultural intensification in the RBA and FBA in Etruria. Vagnetti, however, interprets the introduction of large storage jars in Apulia and Basilicata as evidence of expanded agricultural production.[18] In the FBA, Apulia sees an expansion in the consumption and production of metals, and an improvement in their quality, that echoes a trend evident elsewhere in the peninsula.[19]

---

[11] Radina and Recchia 2006: 1563.
[12] Bietti Sestieri 2003: 51.
[13] Benzi and Graziadio 1996.
[14] Damiani 2010: 423; 437; 438.
[15] Sabbione 2003: 184. I learned of the site of Punta di Zambrone, with considerable quantities of Mycenaean ceramics, too late to include in my study.
[16] Malone *et al*. 1994: 171–2.
[17] Malone *et al*. 1994: 179.
[18] Vagnetti 1999b: 149.
[19] Bietti Sestieri 1988: 35.

The degree of social complexity in Apulia in the MBA–FBA is somewhat debated, depending on the evidence one selects. In southeast Italy, many major coastal or subcoastal sites, such as Coppa Nevigata, had been founded by the MBA and continued in the RBA. As in the Veneto, these southern sites often show evidence of craft industries, notably Aegean-style wheel-made ceramics. In southern Italy more generally in the RBA, a preference for defensible sites, both inland and along the coast, attests to new concerns with external threats, real or perceived. In the Plain of Sybaris, for example, minor undefended sites were progressively abandoned and larger well-defended sites selected in the RBA.[20] However, an evident distinction between larger coastal settlements and modest inland ones need not entail the former's control of the latter.[21] Indeed, the lack of penetration of goods from coast to interior suggests exactly an absence of the interaction that would be a precondition for settlement hierarchies and territorial control. Therefore, we must concur with Malone et alia that there are "no true settlement hierarchies until the first millennium BCE" in the south.[22] Despite an absence of settlement hierarchies, an archaeologically visible elite class is suggested by the burial evidence of the Adriatic coast of Apulia. There, the graves are generally collective, in rock-cut tombs, natural caves, or under tumuli, and suggest a broad class of elite families with the means for such burials.[23] Scholars have used the Mycenaean pots in the graves as an index of wealth, which is a tenuous assumption, but there are other objects in the graves as well that signal prosperity.[24] Overall, status differences in the RBA and FBA in southeast Italy seem probable.

Elsewhere in southern Italy, the evidence for a fairly complex social organization comes from the settlement data and is even more convincing. Settlements along the Ionian coast and sub-coast of Basilicata are often fortified. They are placed on terraces overlooking river valleys, the agricultural yield of which they are thought to have controlled.[25] Some sites, such as Broglio di Trebisacce, cover 10 ha or more, which is half

---

[20] Malone et al. 1994: 171–2. Bietti Sestieri 2010: 143.
[21] Malone et al. 1994: 188.
[22] Malone et al. 1994: 188.
[23] Bietti Sestieri 2003: 53, Bietti Sestieri 2010: 154.
[24] Malone et al. 1994: 190; see Blake 2008: 12–15 for a critique of the assumption that Myceanaean pots were luxury objects in Italy.
[25] Affuso and Lorusso 2006: 1403.

the size of the largest contemporaneous settlements in Etruria at the same time, but nonetheless big. A large building found at several of the bigger settlements has been interpreted as the residence of a ruler or perhaps a ritual space.[26] The fortifications of these sites are impressive, and fairly unprecedented in Italy. Those at Coppa Nevigata and Roca Vecchia provide only generic parallels with Aegean examples, and the excavators of Coppa Nevigata do not see a direct Mycenean inspiration.[27] Wherever the idea for their construction came from, these fortified settlements certainly suggest power. Whether they controlled the inland settlements in any direct way or not, wealth was concentrated at those big coastal sites in the south.[28] Cazzella and Recchia lament the tendency to consider inland sites marginal, noting for inland Molise and Apulia that although populations must have been low, the middle altitude levels were economically sustainable zones whose inhabitants were engaged in stock rearing and, importantly, some terrestrial exchange, as amber and glass beads attest.[29] Nonetheless, scholarly interest continues to center on the coast.

The southeast absorbs some of the innovations of the Aegean visitors, such as the local adoption of the potter's wheel, but the technology of the potter's wheel itself did not spread – just the products themselves. It is not until the Iron Age that this technology takes hold widely.[30] Before then, in the Bronze Age, a limited number of sites – Broglio di Trebisacce, Coppa Nevigata, and Roca Vecchia among them – seem to have produced wheel-made pots, including the Italo-Mycenaean painted wares as well as the gray pseudo-Minyan wares and the large storage vessels that were partially wheel-made. These sites all also contained imported Mycenaean pottery.[31] The Aegean techniques and styles never replace the local traditions, and it is unclear if native potters were even making them. In an important study of these Italo-Mycenaean wares, Buxeda i Garrigós

---

[26] Examples are known from Termitito, Scoglio del Tonno, Torre Castelluccia, and Torre S. Sabina (Affuso and Lorusso 2006: 1404).
[27] Cazzella 1996: 1545. The closest match in the Aegean is the Mycenaean site of Gla, but that site postdates the Apulian examples. Guglielmino 2003: 98.
[28] Affuso and Lorusso 2006: 1403–4; sites include Termitito, Scoglio del Tonno, and Torre Castelluccia.
[29] Cazzella and Recchia 2008.
[30] Bettelli and Levi 2003.
[31] Bietti Sestieri 1988: 35.

et alia noted that the choice of calcareous clays, the potters' wheel, and kilns evident in the Italo-Mycenaean products bear no resemblance to the local south Italian ceramic traditions. They concluded that the spread of these ceramic technologies must have been attributable to Mycenaean potters resettling in southern Italy, probably at discrete locations such as the settlements of Broglio di Trebisacce and Termitito, while the local traditions continued as before.[32] The Aegean-style graywares and local impasto vessels do share some of the same forms, which Damiani suggests is a sign of the exchange of ideas between the two groups of potters, but that is the extent of it.[33]

The Aegean-style pots' limited consumption beyond their production areas further suggests that the technology never lost its "foreignness." A new tradition in the twelfth century BC of painted pots in local forms, the South Italian Protogeometric (SIPG), may owe something to the Italo-Mycenaean technology, but the legacy is not clear. Most of the SIPG pots were handmade, and although the dark-paint-on-light-surface technique is almost certainly drawn from the Aegean-style pots, the selection of decorative motifs is rather circumscribed, and seems to be drawn from the local incised impasto pottery repertoire. Further, the SIPG vessel forms replicate contemporary native Protovillanovan impasto vessel forms.[34] Yntema concludes, therefore, that the SIPG, while being the successor stylistically to the Italo-Mycenaean wares, was "mainly rooted in the local pottery traditions of southern Italy."[35] The Iron Age sees the evolution of the matt-painted wares into the South Italian Early Geometric (SIEG). From the ninth century BC, regional distinctiveness in the repertoire becomes visible, and from then on local geometric wares prevail, the most famous subset of which is the Daunian Middle Geometric (DMG).

There has been some debate over whether these painted vessels were made by hand or on a wheel.[36] A radiographic analysis of sherds from Coppa Nevigata generated some interesting results.[37] At that site, two

---

[32] Buxeda i Garrigós *et al.* 2003.
[33] Damiani 1991: 22.
[34] Yntema 1985: 35–7.
[35] Yntema 1985: 37.
[36] Boccuccia *et al.* 1998: 250.
[37] Boccuccia *et al.* 1998.

fragments of Aegean, four of SIPG, three of SIEG, and ten of DMG were analyzed to determine the production technique. The Aegean sherds were made on a fast wheel; half the SIPGs were wheel made, the other half hand built; of the SIEGs, one was wheel made, one was not, and the third was indeterminate. Of the seven DMGs whose production methods could be determined, five were wheel turned, or rather, portions of the vessels were wheel turned, others hand built, and then they were joined together before firing. The authors of the study concluded tentatively (given the small sample size) that from being the favored technique for the Aegean wares of the RBA, there was a progressive decline in the use of the wheel through the ninth century BC, at which point it prevails again in the DMG production. The authors suggest that the changes in technique are related to changes in the organization of production, with potter's wheels pointing to specialist workshops. With the DMG, once again there must have been ceramic specialists, and it is also notable that they were producing on a large enough scale for these wares to increase in relation to the traditional impasto production.[38]

In the RBA and FBA, while the Italo-Mycenaean pots spread to other parts of Italy, their presence did not trigger the intensified trading one might expect in the surrounding area. Levi et alia describe "una molteplicità di centri produttivi e scarsa circolazione a livello regionale. Direttrici di circolazione a lunga distanza sono invece attestate verso il centro-nord della penisola, sia in ambito tirrenico che adriatico, fino alla valle del Po."[39] One type of Aegean inspired pottery that does seem to have circulated is the dolium or large storage vessel. One study showed that 30 percent of RBA dolia moved more than 20 km from their place of production, and 20 percent did so in the FBA.[40] Nonetheless, this regional-scale circulation was not the norm in this period, and the limited regional-level movement of goods, at least the archaeologically visible ones, will be explored further later on in this chapter.

Other goods and innovations are similarly frozen along the coast. For example, the earliest evidence of domesticated donkey in Italy, in the

---

[38] Boccuccia *et al.* 1998: 253.
[39] Levi, Sonnino and Jones 2006: 1095–7: "[A] multiplicity of production centers and scarce circulation at the regional level. Instead, long distance exchange routes towards the north-central part of the peninsula are attested, in both the Tyrrhenian and Adriatic zones, extending as far as the Po Valley" (my translation).
[40] Levi, Sonnino and Jones 2006: 1097.

RBA, comes from the coastal site of Coppa Nevigata, in Apulia.[41] The donkey remains came from the late-Subapennine levels on the site.[42] Because of its usefulness and adaptability in diverse climates, it comes as a surprise that no other donkeys are known for another couple centuries in Italy. It is not until the FBA that the donkey reappears in southern Italy, at Madonna del Petto and Broglio del Trebisacce (although the latter identification is not secure; see Chapter 2), along with several sites in central and northern Italy.[43] Thus, following its early introduction at Coppa Nevigata, the donkey apparently did not take hold. It would seem that the conditions for the dispersion of knowledge and experimentation were lacking in southern Italy in this period, so that innovations such as the donkey never went much beyond their landing point. This introduction contrasts with that of the horse, which, following its arrival into the north of Italy, spread progressively southward from the MBA.[44] Yet another innovation that stalled before it had a chance to take hold may have been olive cultivation. Olive pits from an RBA context at the northern Calabrian site of Broglio di Trebisacce are possible signs of olive tree cultivation, and Coppa Nevigata has yielded some evidence of olive oil use.[45] If so, the practice did not spread beyond those sites, and the sites themselves are so far apart that they may have received the technology independently. While more supporting evidence is needed to demonstrate that the olive stones were neither imported from the Aegean nor the products of wild trees, the pattern is nonetheless one to watch. Finally, ivory working in southern Italy is only known exclusively from Torre Mordillo in the Sibaritide region of the Gulf of Taranto, where a piece of partially worked ivory has been found.[46]

The aforementioned coastal settlement of Coppa Nevigata, in northern Apulia, offers some of the best evidence of foreign contacts and highlights the complexities inherent in linking outside influences to social developments. Mycenaean material does not appear at the site until it was already well established, as a native settlement in the MBA. Coppa Nevigata's first set of defenses, constructed in the Protoapennine

---

[41] De Grossi Mazzorin 1998: 173.
[42] Cazzella 1996: 1547.
[43] De Grossi Mazzorin 1998: 174; Muntoni 1998; Tagliacozzo 1994: 620–1.
[44] D'Ercole 2002: 327.
[45] Vagnetti 1999b: 149; Evans and Recchia 2005: 200.
[46] Arancio et al. 1995: 230.

B phase of the MBA, predates any known Aegean contact. Aegean imports at the site date to the later part of the Apennine period and early Subapennine phases, reaching a peak late in the Subapennine period, and Italo-Mycenaean pottery was apparently produced at the site as well. In the Subapennine phase there is some evidence of a shift in the settlement slightly to the south.[47] Further, a gesture toward city planning may be detected in this phase, with the construction of a straight central road around which the residences were located. There is also one rectilinear building with multiple rooms, unlike the standard one-roomed circular huts, and the defenses are rebuilt in a more elaborate manner. Local wheel-made painted ceramics are prevalent in this period. Particularly noteworthy are the murex shells in large numbers at the site, pointing to purple dye extraction as an industry there. The shells are from late Apennine–early Subapennine levels, making this the earliest evidence of this industry in Apulia. Cazzella suggests it was a technology introduced by the Aegean rather than independently invented at Coppa Nevigata, and this certainly seems likely.[48] If so, it is quite extraordinary. All in all, Cazzella sees the late Subapennine phase as constituting the peak in contacts with the Aegean, what he calls "the moment of most dependence." The author suggests Coppa Nevigata might have been tied into the same circulatory path that Frattesina participated in, with a Tiryns bead from Coppa Nevigata as indication of these ties with the northern Adriatic, where, as we have seen, many such beads have been found.[49] However, there is some evidence mitigating against the picture of an Aegean-dominated emporium and craft center. In particular, the percentages of Aegean sherds are surprisingly low, just 8–9 percent of the diagnostic sherds from excavated contexts. Coppa Nevigata's location by the fertile Tavoliere plain suggests that its residents were not focused solely on the sea. Indeed, many cereal grindstones and remains of wheat and barley at the site point to agricultural surpluses.[50] A local inflection to life at Coppa Nevigata is thus evident beside the site's cosmopolitan flavor.

---

[47] Cazzella and Moscoloni 1998; Cazzella and Recchia 2014.
[48] Cazzella 1996: 1545–8.
[49] Cazzella 1996: 1549.
[50] D'Ercole 2002: 312.

Further south in Apulia, Orlando has done an interesting study of the FBA settlements in the Salento region – the narrow heel of Italy that spans both the Adriatic and Ionian coasts. Salento is the easternmost point of Italy, and a short distance from the eastern shore of the Adriatic, which is visible from it. Orlando organized the settlements of Salento into three types. The most numerous group, numbering ten, are the long-lived settlements occupied since the MBA; these settlements are also the largest, on average, exceeding 4 ha in the FBA. Notable examples include Scoglio del Tonno, Roca Vecchia, and Porto Perone-Satyrion. All but one of the settlements of this type is on the coast, and usually perched on a small promontory or peninsula. They tend to have a defensive wall on the landward side, in use through the RBA, but in at least two cases the wall falls into disuse in the FBA.[51] Between the RBA and FBA, further signs of complexity are evident at Scoglio del Tonno and Torre Castelluccia, where large rectangular structures were built.

The second settlement group in Orlando's study consists of just two settlements. These are sites that are reoccupied late in the FBA after a period of abandonment through the RBA. The third group, of six settlements, consists of those short-lived settlements that were apparently founded and abandoned during the FBA. The sites in the third group favor inland locations (only one is on the coast), usually on high points overlooking the plain.[52] The settlements of the first group are not only the biggest and longest lived of the three types, but they also show the most foreign contacts. It is at the first group of settlements that most of the Aegean-type sherds of the FBA are found, with just a few from the third group of settlements. It is also at the sites of the first group that the majority of local painted wares that began in the FBA, the SIPG wares, are to be found.[53] At the same time, large dolia are found at six sites in Salento, five of which belong to the first group of sites, long-lived and coastal. The dolia resemble those from Broglio di Trebisacce. Orlando concludes that the FBA was a flourishing period for the Salento region. A crisis ensues at the end of the FBA, in the tenth century BC, with the sites of the third group being abandoned and some of the larger long-lived

---

[51] Santa Maria di Leuca and Porto Perone-Satyrion. Orlando 1998: 275.
[52] Orlando 1998: 273–5.
[53] Orlando 1998: 277.

settlements shrinking in size, but Orlando doubts this downturn can be attributed in any way to the decline of the Mycenaeans two centuries earlier. This microscale history highlights the regional variability in the south while underlining once again the coastal-interior divide.

Marino's work in east-central Calabria parallels some of Orlando's results from Salento, demonstrating both a coastal-inland distinction and variations in settlement stability over time. In the RBA, eleven sites are recorded in the region, six of which are new. The sites fall into two size groupings: those up to 5 ha in area (constituting 60%) and those from 10–40 ha in size (40%). In this period there was a fairly even distribution of coastal and inland sites: six coastal and five inland. The only two sites in the region to have yielded Mycenaean sherds in this period, Crotone and Motta di Cirò, are both coastal. Those two are also the only ones to reveal evidence of metalworking. Put another way, one-third of the coastal sites have yielded Mycenaean materials whereas none of the inland sites have yielded any.[54] In the FBA, the settlements of the RBA continue, but there are no Aegean materials. It is not until the EIA that a massive increase in sites and a total restructuring of the region occurs, with only two sites surviving from the FBA. Marino observes a three-tiered settlement hierarchy in the EIA, and a virtual "Calabro-Siculan" koinè linking northeast Sicily and southwest Italy.[55] It is worth noting in passing that social complexity (in the form of this site hierarchy) comes to this region in the absence of Aegean contacts, and so cannot be tied to them.

Returning to the Salento peninsula, among the sites in Orlando's first group, Roca Vecchia stands out as quite remarkable for its overseas contacts. The site was occupied in the MBA and then suffered violent destruction around the mid-fifteenth century BC, with scarce occupation in the RBA and then extensive reuse and restructuring in the FBA, only to end with another violent, fiery destruction. Roca Vecchia has the highest number of Aegean sherds of any site in the western Mediterranean, with several thousand sherds spanning LH II–LH IIIC found on the site.[56] The finds await full publication, so it is not possible to comment on

---

[54] Marino 1998: 287.
[55] Marino 1998: 290–1.
[56] Guglielmino 2007: 93.

Southern Italy: Networks by Land and by Sea

the specific makeup of the assemblage, but it is clearly very important for understanding the Aegean activities in the area. Other elements of possible Aegean influence at the site include earthen altars that may recall those from the Aegean and Near East; a clay figurine that may be a crude copy of a Mycenaean psi type; a double axe; a clay tripod table; sickle-shaped knives; and even the settlement's layout, with paved streets and two rectangular buildings. Dolia are also thought to be influenced by Aegean examples. The metalworking occurring on the site may have been inspired by the Mycenaeans also, with bronze molds of knives and axes that are thought to show links to the Aegean.[57] This is very exciting stuff, but the site nonetheless remains a unicum.

Thus, there is a preponderance of both imported objects and imported ideas in the coastal settlements. Scholars have argued that the significance of this pattern is twofold: first, that this is evidence of site hierarchies, with coastal sites prevailing, thus signalling an emerging social complexity in the region.[58] Second, they argue that this pattern demonstrates the emergence of craft specialization, focused on these coastal sites, and take this as another sign of social complexity.[59] I would suggest that what is being overlooked is an intriguing pattern of the absence of cooperation, and a truly dysfunctional dynamic. The lack of interactions around southern Italy is, in part, geographic, in that the region is bisected by the Apennine Mountains. However, even in the subcoastal plains of Italy's heel, objects and ideas do not seem to be shared, so blaming the pattern on environmental preconditions is perhaps overly simplistic. Whatever the reason, the peoples of southern Italy seem to have maintained only limited contacts with each other, and only occasionally interacted with the rest of the peninsula. Some of the innovations and objects in question are hardly luxuries. Technology such as donkeys for transport would have been useful for the settlements of the interior to supply goods to the coastal towns. Whereas metallurgical production may be worth controlling, and Mycenaean imports worth hoarding, there is no reason why the potter's wheel should have been kept back. Likewise, and most significantly, the Italo-Mycenaean wares made in the

---

[57] Guglielmino 2003: 102–3.
[58] Malone *et al.* 1994.
[59] Cazzella and Moscoloni 1999.

coastal towns would seem likely to find a ready market in the interior, and yet they barely penetrate there. Framing this pattern in terms of a coastal monopoly on information, including the cultural resource of foreign contacts, may be accurate up to a point, but it does not go far enough. The fact is, the coastal settlements themselves share little: think of the purple dye-making technique (restricted to Coppa Nevigata); olive cultivation (Broglio di Trebisacce and Coppa Nevigata); the donkey, both in the RBA and FBA (Coppa Nevigata, and later Broglio di Trebisacce and Madonna del Petto); even the potter's wheel (Coppa Nevigata, Broglio di Trebisacce, Termitito, and a few others). These technologies were all restricted to no more than a few of the numerous settlements that studded the southern coast. Moreover, the coastal sites that were production centers of Italo-Mycenaean pottery were not much in contact with each other, as far as we can tell. Guglielmino et alia's recent archaeometric study of the locally made Aegean-style ware from Roca Vecchia distinguished it from the local products from Scoglio del Tonno and Coppa Nevigata, with no sherds from these other sites turning up at the former site. Further, the authors observed that the technology of decoration from Roca "seems to have little or no relation to other southern Italian productions."[60] These sites were isolated from each other as much as from the interior.

After the Bronze Age, as noted earlier, it is not until the later ninth century BC that regional variations in material culture become apparent in southern Italy, particularly with the matt-painted pottery.[61] There are seven regional pottery styles, which scholars suggest correspond to group identities.[62] Who were these groups of the first millennium BC? Their identification is a vexing project. In the areas examined here, the Daunians, Peucetians, and Messapians (sometimes grouped together as the Iapygians) were thought to occupy Apulia; and in the southwest were the Oenotrians, until the arrival of the Lucanians and Bruttians from the Apennines. As the quote at the start of this chapter makes clear, distinguishing between these groups is far from easy. In the case of Apulia, the ancient sources themselves disagree over whether the Iapygians

---

[60] Guglielmino *et al.* 2010: 277.
[61] Herring 2000.
[62] Herring 2000: 55.

stood on their own or were the broader label for the populations that included Messapians, Peucetians, and Daunians.[63] Whoever the groups were, the Greek settlers and Roman conquerors did not aid in their self-definition, except for those new arrivals: the Lucanians, Bruttians and on the Tyrrhenian coast, the Oscans.

Much of the discussion hinges on whether we can describe the societies of southeast Italy as state-level or not. The evidence for states in southern Italy is tenuous, with anecdotes serving to extrapolate bigger patterns. Thus, the Messapian ruler Artas, mentioned by Thucydides, contributed 150 javelin throwers to the Athenians in 413 BC. The power to mobilize troops is a key feature of state-level governance. So was Artas the ruler of a state? He was at the very least a chief of considerable importance, but that does not make him a king. Herring's take is that there were no state-level societies in southeast Italy, although some may have been moving toward that condition by the time the process was interrupted by the Roman conquest.[64]

To sum up, despite southern Italy's long exposure to the technological developments of the Aegean, the area as a whole never achieved the complexity of the north under the Terramare in the MBA and RBA, or Etruria's ascension in the FBA. Although the fault may lie in part with a particularly brutal colonial experience (by ancient standards) and subsequently a harsh Roman conquest, the groundwork for ethnicity formation is not evident even in the Bronze Age. The network data can reveal in more detail the structure of interactions around the region, and offers some interesting new information.

The RBA Network

In the peninsular network study, southern Italy in the RBA displayed a strong delineation between coastal sites and interior ones. The network is composed of coastal sites along the arch and heel of the boot connected largely through the common presence of Aegean pottery. Aegean-type pots are found at fifteen sites, and although there are eleven other object types circulating in the area, those are found at far fewer sites: no single

---

[63] Herring 2000: 49–50; note 13.
[64] Herring 2000: 51–3.

Table 8.1. *Object types circulating in southern Italy in the RBA*

Object types present in southern Italy in the RBA	Number of find spots
LH IIIB Aegean-style pottery	15
Torre Castelluccia dagger	5
Twisted violin-bow fibula	5
Scoglio del Tonno knife	4
Awl handle	3
Pertosa dagger	3
Violin-bow fibula with two knobs	3
Garda dress pin	2
Donkey	1
Miniature spoked wheel	1
Montegiorgio sword	1
Scoglio del Tonno razor	1

object type turns up at more than five sites (Table 8.1). There are twenty-one sites with RBA objects included in this study (Figure 8.1). Of these, fourteen are settlements, three are cemeteries, one is a ritual site (Pertosa), and one is a find spot of unknown function.[65] Two sites, Toppo Daguzzo and Torre Castelluccia, contain both a settlement and a cemetery. As noted already, Aegean pottery is what ties all these sites to each other. The cluster revealed in Chapter 4, consisting of thirteen connected sites, strongly suggested a maritime network. The other objects circulating in this period seem to barely play a role. For example, the next most common object types, the Torre Castelluccia dagger and twisted violin-bow fibulae (from five sites each) are rarely found at the same sites as the pottery: only two of the twenty-one find spots in southern Italy contain both pots and twisted violin-bow fibulae, and two more have Aegean pots and the Torre Castelluccia daggers. As noted in Chapter 4, the wide distribution of one object type means that the factor structuring the network is the distance cutoff. Therefore, if we proceeded as we did in the previous chapters and reconfigured the network so that ties were based on shared objects alone regardless of distance, the resulting network would be highly connected indeed. In that form the network has a core of fifteen sites with 100 percent connectivity and five outlying sites connected through other objects (Figure 8.2). Only one site, Manaccora,

---

[65] Pertosa was excluded from the peninsular study but will be included here.

Southern Italy: Networks by Land and by Sea

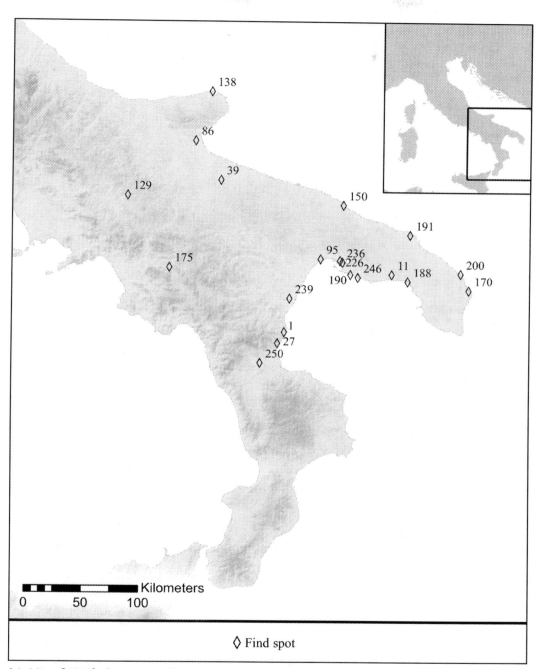

8.1. Map of RBA find spots in southern Italy. N=20 (Drawn by R. Biggs)

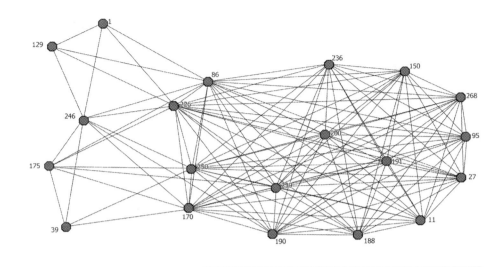

● South Italian network　　　　　　　● Isolate

8.2. Graph of RBA find spots in southern Italy, hoards and ritual deposits included, ties based on shared objects. N=20

is an isolate, as its Montegiorgio sword and Fontanella knife find no matches in the region. As the northernmost site included in this regional study, out on the Gargano peninsula, it may be the case that Manaccora belongs to circuits further north, at least in this period. In any event, this newly configured network, in removing distance as a factor, obscures more than it reveals. First, this sea-based network need not share the localism of terrestrial networks, and so may tell more about the foreign merchants' choices than about local ones. Second, the geography of this network is not insignificant: to group the string of coastal sites into a ball takes away valuable information about the routes these objects may have taken.

Because of the particular circumstances here, another network may be more informative. So, returning to this dichotomy between the sites with the fibulae and daggers and those with the Aegean pots, I propose reconfiguring the network criteria, this time by removing the Aegean pots as objects, and establishing ties based on the other eleven object types. The results, in Figure 8.3, show a fairly densely connected network in its own

Southern Italy: Networks by Land and by Sea

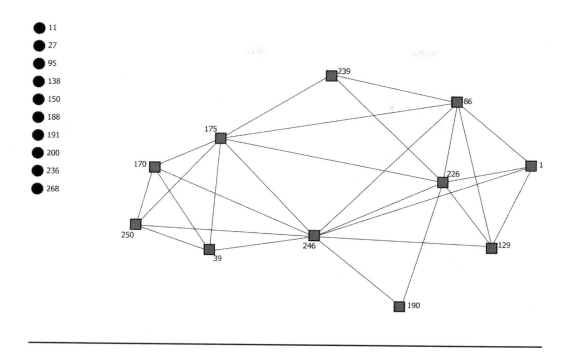

■ Non-ceramic network ● Isolate

8.3. Graph of RBA south-Italian sites, ties based on shared objects, Aegean pottery excluded. N=20

right, although with a large proportion of isolates (10). Network density overall is 12.86 percent, while the density of the cluster itself is 49 percent. When the new network is placed on a map, a startling picture is revealed in which interior sites feature prominently while virtually all the isolates are coastal sites, many of them along the Adriatic coast of Apulia (Figure 8.4).[66] The network covers much of southern Italy but bypasses Campania, southern Calabria, and much of the Adriatic coast. What do we make of this? Given the objects circulating here – Italian-made goods, metals primarily, but also worked bone and horn objects – this network recalls the local networks of central and northern Italy. These objects seem to have moved in at least some cases along terrestrial routes and therefore were likely native-driven. Furthermore, the objects that reveal

---

[66] Toppo Daguzzo is a notable exception, an inland site with Aegean pottery (Cipolloni Sampò 1986).

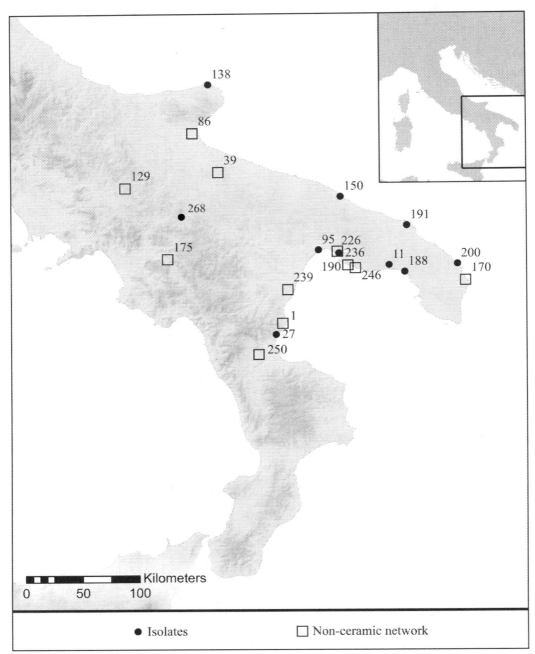

8.4. Map showing RBA find spots in southern Italy, with nodes in the non-ceramic network indicated. N=20 (Drawn by R. Biggs)

this route are of a personal nature – fibulae and dress pins, weapons, and items that would have been carried on the person – so we can imagine that these goods' circulation carried very different meanings from those associated with the exchange of pots.[67] In the same period, there is the maritime network of Aegean pots, and the two networks operated largely independently, with only four sites participating as nodes in both networks. If the same people were participating in both networks, then in all likelihood all goods would follow similar paths. Even if the pots were brought by Aegean merchants or made by Aegean potters at the coastal sites, one would expect the pots to subsequently move along the same channels as the other goods. As I have argued elsewhere in this book, regardless of where the objects originate, local trade should kick in. Instead, it is difficult not to arrive at the conclusion that the maritime network observed here was not simply supplied, but run by an outside group, some of whom may have been residing in these Adriatic coastal sites, at least for a time. This theory takes me a long way from the minimalist position argued for in an earlier paper.[68] Full-fledged Aegean colonies seem out of the question in Italy because the material culture does not support that. The dominance of coastal sites has been interpreted by some as evidence of a site hierarchy, but that coastal dominance evaporates in the hypothetically native-driven network. In fact, the alternative network's span makes the limited movement of the Aegean goods toward the interior all the more surprising. In any case, what can be established is that although there seems to be a western boundary to these networks (both the native and Aegean ones), with the Tyrrhenian area excluded, their geographic coverage in the RBA offers no hint at all of the regional groups to come. Neither the terrestrial nor the maritime network of the RBA predicts later regional groupings.

The FBA network

In the FBA there are forty-one find spots in the region (Figure 8.5). Of these, twenty sites are settlements, five are cemeteries, ten are of unknown

---

[67] I thank Mark Lawall (pers. comm.) for this observation.
[68] Blake 2008.

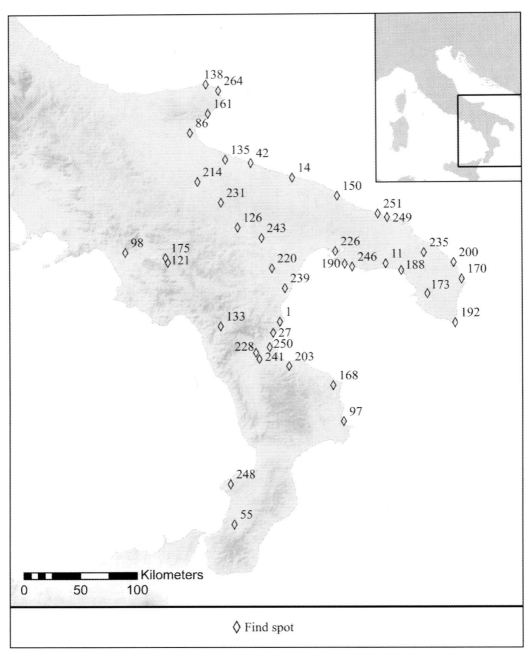

8.5. Map showing FBA find spots in southern Italy. N=41 (Drawn by R. Biggs)

Table 8.2. *Object types circulating in southern Italy in the FBA*

Object types present in southern Italy in the FBA	Number of find spots
LH IIIC Aegean pottery	26
Castellace arch fibula	7
Gargano fibula	4
Timmari fibula	4
Asymmetrical VB fibula with two knobs	3
Donkey	2
Fontanella knife	2
Leaf-shaped violin-bow fibula with two knobs	2
Pertosa axe	2
Frattesina comb	1
Menaforno axe	1
Miniature spoked wheel	1
Tiryns bead	1

function, four are both settlements and cemeteries, one is a hoard, and one is a ritual deposit.[69] The expansion in the number of sites from the RBA is not matched by much of an increase in the range of object types circulating there: thirteen of the object types in the study are found in southern Italy in this period (Table 8.2). What is different however is the objects' distribution: in the FBA, the Aegean-style pottery dominates the network even more, turning up at twenty-six sites, whereas the next most-common object type, the Castellace-type arch fibula, is found at just seven sites. Indeed, among the other object types, fibulae are very well represented, but this may be largely attributable to the thorough catalog recently published by Lo Schiavo for the *Prähistorische Bronzefunde* series.[70] Nonetheless, the limited numbers of bronze weapons in southern Italy, particularly in Apulia, in the Bronze Age seems to be a real phenomenon and not just an accident of publication history.[71] This pattern may be related to the scant hoards and ritual deposits in the south, but even that pattern itself is significant, perhaps reflecting different ideologies. An absence of a pervasive "warrior aristocracy" has been posited to explain the distinct archaeological record of the south.

---

[69] The hoard (Surbo) and ritual deposit (Pertosa) were not included in the peninsular study, but are added in all the networks constructed in this chapter.

[70] Lo Schiavo 2010.

[71] Bianco Peroni's (1970) catalog of swords covers the entire peninsula, for example, and records very few from southern Italy.

Social Networks and Regional Identity in Bronze Age Italy

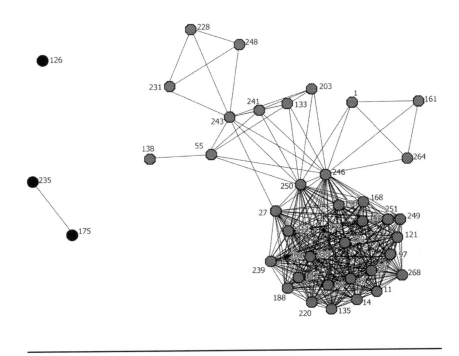

● South Italian network   ● Isolate and Dyad

8.6. Graph of FBA southern Italy cluster, hoards included, ties based on shared objects. N=41

The peninsular study in Chapter 4 revealed two networks in southern Italy in the FBA, one spanning coastal Apulia and the other coastal Basilicata and northern Calabria. Because of the dominance of Aegean-style pottery among the object types, the structure of these networks, as with the RBA network, largely rests on the limits placed on distance between sites. When I refashion the network by removing the distance limit and adding in the ritual deposit at Pertosa and the Surbo hoard, there is a dense cluster of the twenty-six find spots of Aegean pottery, with extensions of less connected sites, one dyad (Pertosa and Surbo), and one isolate (Irsina) (Figure 8.6). But this new network is untrustworthy for the same reasons the RBA version of it was. In accentuating the importance of the Aegean pottery, this new network, like its RBA counterpart, oversimplifies a complex situation and obscures other movements of goods.

Southern Italy: Networks by Land and by Sea 231

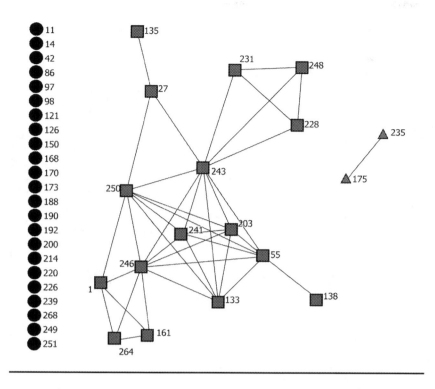

8.7. Graph of FBA southern Italy network, Aegean pots excluded, ties based on shared objects. N=41

To overcome the dominance of the Aegean-type pottery, I again construct an alternative network by removing the Aegean pottery from the recorded object types. This reveals how other goods may be moving around the region. The dominance of the Aegean pottery is made even clearer when it is noted that of the twenty-six FBA sites with Aegean pottery in the south, fully twenty-one of those contain no other recorded object types. The resulting pottery-free network, therefore, is extremely sparse, with a density score of less than 5 percent and twenty-three isolates (other than the sites with just pots, a couple of sites have objects with no matches in the area) (Figure 8.7). Nonetheless, there is a core group of sixteen connected sites. When this network is grounded spatially, another surprising picture emerges (Figure 8.8). This alternate network spreads across southern Italy on a northeast/southwest axis

232 Social Networks and Regional Identity in Bronze Age Italy

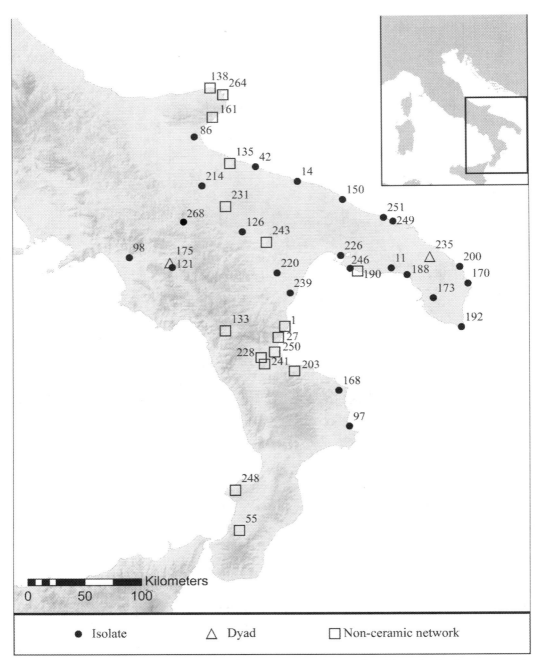

8.8. Map showing FBA find spots in southern Italy, with nodes in the non-ceramic network indicated. N=40 (Drawn by R. Biggs)

Southern Italy: Networks by Land and by Sea

that appears to follow the least-cost path along the geologic subsidence known as the Bradanic Trough, linking the Gargano peninsula to the southwestern portion of the Gulf of Taranto.[72] It is the shortest terrestrial route skirting the edges of the southern Apennine Mountains to the west and the Murge plateau to the east, and in early modern times was a droveway (*trattura*).[73] Further south, at the Gulf of Taranto, there is a cluster that replicates almost perfectly the Basilicata network identified in the peninsular study in Chapter 4. This makes sense as that network was never dependent on the co-presence of Aegean pots for its configuration anyway.[74] Further south and west still, the new network extends as far as Tyrrhenian Calabria, with the Castellace and Torre Galli sites. The heel of the boot is virtually excluded from the alternative network: only two of the original FBA peninsular Apulia network sites, Madonna del Petto and Torre Castelluccia, are nodes in it. Four of the sites in the pottery-free network do also have Aegean pots, and a fifth, Timmari, has yielded Aegean potsherds that were excluded from the study as they could not be dated more precisely than "LH IIIB-C." Overall, however, this alternative network does not parallel the movements of Aegean pots at all, and like its RBA counterpart, seems to represent a very different set of practices and relationships. Even more in this FBA network, the predominance of fibulae suggests personal identity markers, although apparently not inalienable ones. I again posit that we are observing the traces of two distinct exchange networks, one likely foreign driven and one likely native. But does native mean local? Not necessarily, or only in part. This alternative network covers a lot of ground. The distinction between the two networks is not solely coastal versus interior: thirteen of the sixteen sites in the alternative network are coastal or sub-coastal. Further, some Aegean pots did make their way into the interior and, it would seem from their distribution, down the Bradanic Trough; there

---

[72] A notable isolate in this alternative network is again Toppo Daguzzo, which has Aegean pots but none of the other objects I recorded in this study. Several Pertosa swords were found there, but this is understood as an MBA type almost exclusively, although it may continue into the RBA, so I have excluded it from the study. The few Aegean sherds were found in mixed-surface strata and were not connected to the burials and swords (Cipolloni Sampò 1986).

[73] Small *et al.* 1998: 337.

[74] Only Termitito is no longer included here.

may also have been forays west along the Ofanto River Valley – a pass across the southern Apennines – to Campania, from the looks of it.[75] However, these are not the same sites as those in the alternative network: it seems different traders and connections were in place. Further, while the original network seems like a textbook example of the remnants of a maritime network with a few forays inland, the same cannot be argued here, as the coastal sites are grouped in such tight clusters (in the Gargano peninsula and in the Basilicata cluster) that only very short-distance boat trips would have been warranted. This again suggests local travel, so it may be that at either end of this terrestrial network, a truly local set of interactions is visible.

Conclusions

To sum up, by teasing out the movements of distinct categories of object types in southern Italy, we have seen that in both the RBA and FBA, Aegean pots were circulating along very different routes from other objects, with the former moving within a largely maritime network and the latter circulating both along the coast and in the interior, rarely at the same sites. I argued that the distinction can be framed in terms of the drivers of these networks, with foreign influences structuring the movement of Aegean pots while locally made objects were moving through native hands. Given the lack of shared technologies between the coastal sites, the maritime network may, in fact, be the edge of a type of "star" network whose center lay in the Aegean and whose "arms" – the Italian sites – had little to no contact between themselves. Because a premise of this study is that the movement of goods reflects the real interactions of people, one may anticipate that the "alternative" networks would be particularly useful in understanding local affiliations in this early period. In fact, the alternative networks do not map onto later population groups any more than the maritime networks do. The RBA networks, both the Aegean pottery one and the alternative one, span the

---

[75] Among the isolates in the southern interior on the map of the alternative network, the following have LH IIIC pots: S. Maria di Ripalta (214), S. Vito di Pisticci (220), Termitito (239), and Toppo Daguzzo (268). In Campania, Eboli (98) has LH IIIC material.

Southern Italy: Networks by Land and by Sea

later territories of the Oenotrians and various Apulian groups, and the FBA networks are equally independent of later population groupings.

The FBA cluster in Basilicata and Calabria, what later becomes Augustan Region III, is the only grouping in which there is some overlap in the presence of Aegean pots and local goods at some sites, but is not the exclusive territory of any distinctive group in the first millennium BC. The ancient sources described this area as a portion of Oenotrian territory, which extended across Calabria to the Tyrrhenian coast. In fact, the purported Oenotrian territory is too vast to have ever been home to a single group in antiquity, and we may assume smaller groupings operated within it.[76] A subset of the Oenotrians, the Chônes, ostensibly occupied this area of the Ionian coast and sub-coastal zone where the modern-day Basilicata-Calabria border lies. These populations would have contended with the foundation of the Ionian Greek colony of Siris and the Achaean colonies of Metaponto and Sybaris in their midst in the late eighth to seventh centuries BC. Whoever the indigenous people living in the area in the early centuries of the first millennium BC were, the territory in the fifth and fourth centuries BC was apparently overrun by the Lucanians, a people from the Apennine Mountains. The Lucanians were one of several migrations of Oscan-speaking peoples recorded in this period (others being the Bruttians and Samnites). The Lucanian settlement of the area is detectable archaeologically in sometimes delayed transformations to the local material culture, particularly in the proliferation of sanctuaries and settlements with imposing defensive walls in the mid-fourth century.[77] Poltrandolfo contends that a Lucanian "ethnos" emerged only following the insertion of these peoples within the Greek colonial milieu of the coastal zone. The transformation, she argues, was articulated through a highly structured military apparatus.[78] Her argument echoes the recent wave of scholarship tying ethnicity to social complexity and exposure to outside groups. Before the Lucanians, the indigenous populations of the area had not cohered ethnically. As Pallottino notes of the ancient peoples of Basilicata and

---

[76] *pace* Kleibrink 2000: ix.
[77] Barra Bagnasco and Russo Tagliente 1996: 183.
[78] Pontrandolfo 1996: 171–2.

Calabria, "Mancò, in sostanza, a quelli genti, la possibilità di costituirsi in entità unitarie autonome e durevoli, definite storicamente nei loro caratteri linguistici e culturali e nei loro limiti geografici."[79] It would seem that the rather loosely structured far-flung terrestrial networks did not evolve into coherent and enduring regional entities. One could argue that if not for the Lucanian settlement of the area, a "Chônic" (for want of a better label) ethnicization process may have occurred eventually. But the Lucanians were latecomers, and by the fifth century, ethnic categories, if not yet full-fledged ethnic communities, should have been visible in the southwestern Gulf of Taranto if they were ever going to arise. Yet another southern people, the Bruttians, do not appear in the ancient texts until the fourth century BC. Like the Lucanians, the Bruttians were culturally and linguistically close to the Samnites. They are primarily remembered as a bellicose group who fought the Lucanians and Samnites and Greeks. They were conquered by the Romans in 270 BC and were forcibly dispersed, leading to their historical disappearance.[80]

What of Apulia? The territory, what later became the Augustan Region II, covers the heel of Italy up to the Gargano peninsula and west to the Bradano River. Ancient accounts of the early groups of the region are contradictory, with the territory occupied by one, three, or four peoples. The Greeks called the people living in Apulia the Iapygian peoples, who were subdivided into three groups: the Daunians, Peucetians, and Messapians – each named for an eponymous founder. Daunians, Peucetians, and Messapians are linguistically all similar to each other, speaking an IE language that is distinct from the Italic languages.[81] This linguistic distinction has been used as evidence of a Balkan (sometimes referred to as Illyrian) element in the population of the region. The Daunians (Dauni) were traditionally located in northern Apulia, around the modern city of Foggia. Along with the aforementioned pottery, they also were known for their painted and engraved stone slabs. The Peucetians (Peucetii) purportedly occupied central Apulia, around Bari. The

---

[79] Pallottino 1981: 53–4: "These groups essentially lacked the potential to make themselves into autonomous and enduring unitary entities, defined historically by their linguistic and cultural characters and by their geographic territories" (my translation).
[80] Guasco 2006: 77.
[81] Lomas 2000: 81.

site of Gravina is identified as a Peucetian settlement. The Messapians (Messapii) occupied southern Apulia and two excavated Messapian towns are Ugento and Cavallino. If things seem clear so far in Region II, now for the complicated parts: the Messapians were sometimes called the Iapygians or Iapyges, despite Iapygian being used at times for all the peoples of the region, as were the names Sallentini and Apuli (although Sallentini also referred to the group at the southern tip of the heel of the boot, sometimes distinguished from the Messapii). The Calabri was a term also used to describe the residents of the southern half of the peninsula, covering either the combined territory of the Messapians and Sallentini, or just the Messapians. As Reich sums it up, "At any rate all these peoples, whatever their names, shared a basically similar culture and language which show connections with those of the Italic peoples to the west, but also individual peculiarities."[82] Lomas frames the confusion in terms of a Greek interest in ethnos that contrasted with native self-identity structured around kin groups and civic identities, and by the fourth century, state identities.[83] While this disparity in etic and emic perspectives is fascinating for many reasons, here it underscores the weakness of regional-scale collectivities in Apulia.

The picture is no clearer in the Bronze Age. As we have seen, native activities in Apulia are virtually invisible in the RBA and FBA. Even in the FBA, when the peninsular study revealed a network of sites in the territory that would later be Apulia, it is apparent that we cannot tie this in any secure way to native groups at all. Instead, it seems to be the result of extra-peninsular interventions, with Apulia either forming one portion of an Aegean-driven maritime network, or perhaps a trans-Adriatic one. Participation in regional-level exchanges of objects is not detectable. A trans-Adriatic network makes sense as there is a long history of ties between these regions, but more fieldwork in coastal Albania is needed to prove its existence. Either way, in light of the Bronze Age network evidence, it is no surprise that, as the quotes at the start of this chapter make clear, the groups in Apulia never benefited from either a strong internal coherence or external recognition, with chronic confusion over labels and territories evident in the textual sources. This demographic

[82] Reich 1979: 110.
[83] Lomas 2000: 84–8.

disunity is evident in the Bronze Age and through path dependence, becomes too ingrained to overcome.

Nonetheless, while there may have been no internal coherence in Basilicata and Apulia, a rigid geographic separation between those two regions is evident already in the Bronze Age. The area of Apulia covered by the vast flat plateau known as the Murge, together with the coastal territory from the Ofanto River south to the start of the Salento peninsula, is entirely bypassed by the alternative "native" networks proposed in this chapter, and also by the FBA networks described in Chapter 4. The boundary observed seems to follow the geological subsidence known as the Bradanic Trough, separating the Apennines from the Murge. Small et alia note that east-west travel in this area has always been more difficult than north-south travel because of the Apennines to the west and the Murge to the east. By the time of the Roman conquest, the Basentello River running through the Bradanic Trough was the territorial boundary separating the Apulian tribes from the Oscan groups, and would later be formalized as the border between Augustan Regions II and III.[84] Thus, as both an overland passage and a boundary, the Bradanic Trough came to play a key role in regional organization. It is true that among all the inconsistent accounts of Apulian tribal and ethnic groupings in antiquity, the western boundary was never in question. Likewise, the matt-painted geometric pottery groupings from the late ninth century BC on, which Herring argues are a manifestation of group identities, cleave along the Trough: notably the Salento style east of it and so-called West Lucanian style to the west.[85] This geomorphological border seems to have already become a cultural one by the Bronze Age.

To what extent can the weak regionalism in the south be attributed to the foreign presence there, first with probable Mycenaean traders and potters and later, and securely, with the Greek colonies? One could argue that these foreign groups disrupted local dynamics. Certainly this theory makes sense in parts of Magna Graecia in the first millennium BC, but cannot explain the Bronze Age situation. Calabria and Basilicata have yielded far less Aegean material in the RBA and FBA than Apulia and yet they manifest no real tendencies toward ethnicity formation either.

---

[84] Small *et al.* 1998: 337.
[85] Herring 2000: 55.

Southern Italy: Networks by Land and by Sea

Whatever its cause, this lack of regional coherence was an enduring feature of southern Italy in antiquity. The phenomenon is evident in the Bronze Age just as it is evident in the first millennium BC. This weakness may have facilitated both the Greek colonization and the Oscan invasions of the territory.

If these structured relations were so dysfunctional, why would they continue, especially when the sites themselves changed, opening up the possibility for new types of relationships? Suboptimal behaviors are often perpetuated because of historical factors: this is the path dependence idea discussed in Chapter 3. The coastal focus made sense in the Bronze Age when overseas trade was the best game in town, and perhaps it was difficult to overcome mistrust between competing coastal sites. The terrestrial networks were perhaps the result of ambitious individuals covering long distances but could not bind the populations together either. The networks of southern Italy in the Bronze Age thus served as barriers to the formation of successful regional population units later, in a process of path dependence. Such groupings became necessary in the Archaic period if the Greek colonists and others were to be withstood.

CHAPTER NINE

CONCLUSIONS AND AFTERMATH

Scholars no longer pursue the will-o'-the-wisp of a "point of departure," conceived in deterministic fashion as containing in embryo all future developments, located in the distant past, and identified either with immigrations or with the indigenous cultures.... Nor is it now thought reasonable to trace the existence, for example, of a Latin or Etruscan nation or civilisation back beyond this "point of arrival," seeking them (as they were once sought) in far-off times and places – any more than it would be thought reasonable for a historian of the modern period to ingenuously posit a French nation or civilisation *avant la lettre* and to identify it with the Celts, the peoples of Roman Gaul, the Franks, the Visigoths, the Burgundians or the Normans. (Pallottino 1991: 31)

In Italy in the Recent and Final Bronze Ages, metals and other valuable objects moved within circumscribed areas. Although these objects may have been made at a distant location, once they reached an area, local exchange mechanisms took over and the goods circulated most intensively locally. These zones of intensified circulation of goods between neighboring sites, by whatever means they were moving, have been the topic of this book. By reframing the standard object distributions in terms of ties between nearby sites based on the co-presence of common objects, it became possible to identify groupings of connected sites that formed networks. The networks did not cover the entire peninsula, but were instead (for the most part) geographically limited in scope. These networks were the subject of analysis, in what amounted to a type of community detection.

Italy's exchange networks changed considerably from the RBA to the FBA. I pick up the story in the RBA because that is the moment in which there were sufficient exotica circulating to be able to construct these sorts of networks. It may have been the case that the networks were already in place back in the MBA, but the movements of goods were less archaeologically visible. In the RBA, three networks are evident: two in northern Italy and one in the south. Of these three, the network covering the Po Valley and extending southeast into Marche and the Apennines dwarfs the other two in numbers of sites (nodes) and area. It covered the territory of the so-called Terramare culture and is a reflection of the circulation paths operating within that group, and of the Terramare group's economic reach to the south. Of the other two networks of the RBA – one in Lombardy and the other spanning Apulia and Basilicata – only the Lombardy network could be linked to a known archaeological culture: the Canegrate culture. The southern network, in contrast, was made up of coastal sites and showed weak internal structure. I argued that this network reflected long-distance ties to the Aegean rather than any locally driven circuits of exchange. The RBA networks together served to confirm the validity of the approach taken here, namely that social groups will circulate goods more intensively among themselves than with others outside of their group. Therefore, we can, with circumspection, treat robust networks as traces of past groups. This is particularly important when a group's material production may not be distinctive enough to reveal it.

In the FBA, the peninsular picture changed radically with the dissolution of the Terramare and Canegrate networks and the emergence of many more networks of similar size around the peninsula. In the north there were two networks: one around Lake Garda and one in the Veneto. In central Italy there was a network in modern Lazio (ancient Etruria) and another to the east in Marche and Umbria. In the south there were two networks: one in Apulia and one in Basilicata. That in each case these networks are paired latitudinally suggests that neighboring populations may have stimulated network formation in a process akin to peer polity interaction. The structure and degree of cohesion of the networks varied widely, with the Veneto network exhibiting the most cohesion by several measures, and the Basilicata network displaying the least. Aside from these cases however, large swathes of the peninsula contained few of the object types included in the study: this was true of Molise, Liguria, Campania, and Calabria. As a result, no networks were detected there. There may have been groups there, but they were not revealed using the network methodology employed here.

After the initial detection of the networks on a peninsular-wide scale, area studies followed in which the individual networks were reconfigured to illuminate further details about their composition and cohesiveness, and were informed by regional histories. Hoards and ritual deposits, formerly excluded in the peninsular study, were added in, and the distance parameters were removed. In all cases the reconfigured networks did not contradict the earlier patterns of the peninsula study, but instead provided new insights into these areas. Thus, in the south, a closer look showed that two networks could be distinguished: one that was based on the circulation of metals and was terrestrial and native driven, and one that was based on Aegean-type pottery and was maritime and externally driven. In west-central Italy in the FBA, a distinction between south Etruria, north Etruria, and Latium Vetus was evident, with south Etruria involved in interactions across the Apennines, while the other zones were not. Further, in west-central Italy and the Veneto, the Bronze Age networks occupied the same territories as the named regional groups of the Archaic period and beyond, hundreds of years later. Thus, in the Veneto and in the future Etruria, I argue that the FBA networks are the earliest traces of the regional groups – the Veneti and the Etruscans – that will endure through a process of path-dependent behavior and crystallize finally several centuries later. In the far south, by contrast, the regional groups of the first millennium BC are poorly defined, and the Bronze Age networks reveal structural fragility, suggesting that already by the Bronze Age a pattern of weak connections was in place that would continue through the Roman conquest. In the Apennines, a cohesive FBA network spans several later regional groups – the Etruscans, Umbrians, and Picenes – so the case for territorial continuity over time is a weak one. Instead, given the particular circumstances of the mobility of these groups, the network evidence points to some instances of population displacement in later prehistory.

Networks are abstractions, indirect approximations of past patterns of interactions, and not the actual circuits of interactions themselves. Many interactions must have occurred that left no trace in the archaeological record. Further, the circuits that the networks are meant to reveal are themselves proxies for the actual groups. Thus, we are working with proxies of proxies, unavoidable when using the archaeological record alone to construct networks. Moreover, the groups we are trying to reveal are themselves hypothetical in the Bronze Age. In other words, in this study it is uncertain if the networks I identify reflect the preferences for intragroup exchange of groups that have already formed, or if the networks preceded the formation of the groups: that is, did interacting encourage group formation, or did the groups form and then begin to interact? The fact that for most of the networks identified we can find correlates to localized material-culture facies would seem to suggest that the groups were already in place, at least in some form or other, when the networks were operating. Although pottery facies do not necessarily prove the existence of a self-defining group, the combination of material culture similarities and preferential exchange patterns – or put another way, expressions of both categorical and relational identities – suggests a certain level of collective self-awareness among these Bronze Age groups.

The RBA networks are distinct from the groupings of the first millennium BC, and therefore, what we can say is, whether these groups were new or not, it is in the first part of the FBA that the process of regional identity formation is under way. Thus, the continuities between the Bronze Age and Iron Age are greater than previously thought and even if one takes a strongly instrumentalist position on collective identity formation in early Italy – seeing regional identities as tactical constructions – the roots of those later identities ran deep, back to habits of interaction that had been in place for centuries. Why was the Final Bronze Age so important? In historical terms, one of the takeaways from this study is just how fundamental the dissolution of the Terramare culture was in the propulsion toward regionalism. It made possible the rise of a network in the Veneto that would eventually become the Veneti. Likewise, the network in Etruria does not come into its own until after the Terramare collapse, when it demonstrates loose ties with the vestigial Apennine tail of the Terramare network for the first time. The FBA Apennine network's boundaries do not correspond to later groups, revealing a key premise of this study: regional path dependence only works when there is demographic continuity. In the Apennines, populations seem to have moved around. However, there was one hard and fast line: the boundary with the groups to the south, including the Sabines and others. In fact, several other fixed-boundary lines were observed in this study: most famously the Tiber River, but also the Mincio River as the western edge of the FBA Veneto network and the Bradanic Trough in Apulia. With regards to identity formation, it may be the case that rather than needing territorial boundaries that enclosed a group in order to define it, one significant boundary may have been all that was necessary to create an "us" and a "them," the prerequisites for self-definition. Another important point to take from the study concerns the role of outside influences on identity formation. Thus, the greatest impact of the Mycenaean visits to southern Italy may not have been cultural or technological, but social: those foreign visits cemented a coastal bias that prevented stable identity formation at the regional level. The extensive natural coastline may have encouraged this bifurcation anyway, but we can see it most clearly in these Bronze Age trade networks. The largely terrestrial network revealed in Chapter 8 offered an alternative, but the avoidance of coastal sites did not do anything to overcome the bifurcation. The long-term outcome was a weakly defined population in the region all the way up to the Roman conquest.

Tota Italia: Roman Perspectives on Italy's Populations

> "[M]uch of Italy was still palpably 'foreign' in the Augustan period, and the allegiance of some Italians to Augustan Rome downright questionable. The visibility of Italy in the ideology of the Augustan age is a reflection of dramatic change rather than the final stage of an inevitable process."[1]

If the Bronze Age regional networks presage the population groups that follow hundreds of years later, how can the very differently framed groups of the Roman textual sources be parsed in light of that thread of continuity? In other words, what can the Bronze Age networks inform us about the Greek and Roman lens toward the groups that followed? This section examines the Augustan regions, one of the major sources for information on Roman perspectives on the indigenous populations, with the Bronze Age networks in mind.

---

[1] Dench 2005: 103.

Conclusions and Aftermath

Romans modified and rejected the Greek origin myths but "stayed within the Greek system of heroic genealogy."[2] By the fourth century BC, the Romans transformed their own origin myth to exclude Odysseus and emphasize Aeneas, in a reaction against the Etruscans (Odysseus being perceived as too associated with Etruscans because the latter had adopted him into their canon with alacrity).[3] Torelli has described "the fundamental ideological role of the Trojan legend in the Roman and Latin colonizations of the fourth century and what great refinement was used in the propaganda employed to conquer and colonize."[4] By the period of the Roman conquest, ethnic identities had a class component in some circumstances. Rome itself, with an aristocracy of Latin and Sabine stock almost exclusively, is the clearest example of this.[5] This class component is visible in other regions where groups had commingled such as Apulia, with a Daunian (whatever that meant in the Roman period) elite and Samnite subordinate group.[6]

What of the Romans themselves? Dench is the first scholar to treat Roman ethnicity.[7] She notes that Roman ethnic identity has received little attention from scholars, who have instead focused on either the political and legal labels of Romanness, or on Roman cultural practices as translated to the provinces.[8] Rome's own foundation myths are complex and contradictory: "Rome (or the site of Rome) is successively inhabited, founded and/or improved by indigenous Aborigines, indigenous and/or Lacedaemonian Sabines, Latins descended from Saturn, Trojan exiles, twins fathered by Mars and nursed by a she-wolf, Arcadian exiles, Herakles, Trojan exiles and Etruscan kings."[9] Amid these colorful alternatives, there is a consistent recognition of the blend of Latin, Etruscan, and Sabine peoples comprising at least part of Roman origins. If the plurality of Roman identity was proclaimed in the Republic, the Romans themselves likewise recognized ethnic distinctions; that is, they knew who was *not* Roman. In these foundation myths and in their actions it is clear that the Romans were ambivalent toward their neighbors. Romans

---

[2] Farrell 2004: 255.
[3] Malkin 1998: 203.
[4] Torelli 1995: 150.
[5] Farney 2007.
[6] Torelli 1995: 143.
[7] Dench 2005.
[8] Dench 2005: 26.
[9] Dench 2005: 63.

9.1. Map of Italy indicating the Augustan regions (Drawn by R. Biggs)

felt particular affiliation with the Latins, on whose territory the city was, after all, located, but they differentiated themselves from that group by their mythical Trojan forebears.[10] Cornell (1995: 158) sees the historic emphasis on ethnicity in central Italy as anachronistic, arguing that at least in the Archaic period, Romans and others were concerned with familial wealth and status, which trumped ethnic origins. Farney's book would seem to argue against this position, however, as in it he identifies the tactical use of ethnic identities by Roman aristocrats for the purposes of status positioning.[11] In any case, as a component of ancient identity, ethnicity warrants study, disputes over its relative importance aside.

Pliny and the Augustan Regions

Under Augustus "the peninsula was divided into eleven regions that roughly corresponded to the great ethnic groupings,"[12] a clear act of imperialist social engineering (Figure 9.1). Before this, Roman Italy had

---

[10] Dench 2005: 24, although other Latin cities such as Lavinium claimed Trojan origins as well (Cornell 1995: 68).
[11] Farney 2007.
[12] David 1997: 176. Pliny, *Natural History* 3.46.

Conclusions and Aftermath

been a mishmash of municipalities with varying statuses, and this systematization must have aided the smooth running of the state. Pliny the Elder is the main source for the regions, and reconstructing their territory is far from straightforward. Pliny was writing in the 70s AD, sixty or so years after the regions' establishment. The frontiers of each region are only given along the coast, drawing on a periplus, possibly of Varro, as the source. The interior of each region is recorded in the form of alphabetical lists of its towns there, with no borders delineated. To make matters even more difficult, Pliny appears to have compiled his town lists not from Augustus's regional divisions, but from earlier Augustan lists of towns organized according to population group, possibly as part of a census, and then sought to make those town lists fit the regions. Further, no attempt is made to distinguish between kinds of groups. The large groupings and their subsets – the hyper-localized communities that were associated with individualized towns – are not labeled differently, and one must simply follow from the context of the text that some groups were subsets of others. In the regions with multiple population groups, Pliny sometimes has combined multiple lists into one, and other times kept each list intact. Working from these different sources inevitably led to errors, such as towns appearing on the list for one region when the frontier line from the coast puts them in another.[13] Nevertheless, these inaccuracies do not in the end preclude the use of the regions in reconstructing the earlier territories of Italy's population groups.

More problematic, instead, is the larger question of whether or not these regions really do have any bearing on earlier groups, or were instead a concerted attempt at erasure of regional identities by the Romans. If the latter were true, then the Augustan regions would not be helpful after all. The boundaries of the regions do, in part, take into account the Roman road network that permitted long-distance land transport, and in some instances the roads appear to trump ethnic boundaries in determining the layout of the region, as Laurence has observed.[14] Likewise, the treatment of rivers as boundaries may have partially been a Roman innovation.[15] Further, the intention cannot ever have been

---

[13] Thomsen 1947: 18–31.
[14] Laurence 1998: 106.
[15] Thomsen 1947: 144.

a faithful replication of every group's territories: eleven regions would never have been considered enough for such accurate coverage, and the fact that the regions were initially designated only by ordinal numbers, not names, confirms a distancing from ethnic realities. But already by the late first century AD, regional names were in place, and may have been in use for some time.[16]

Laurence states categorically, "The eleven regions of Italy and their associated names (ethnonyms and others) were not a natural division of territory,"[17] arguing that the regions glossed over a far more fragmented demographic reality. He suggests, for example, that the name "Transpadana" for the eleventh region (which, in fact, is the only one to be explicitly mentioned by name by Pliny),[18] "reflects maybe a suppression or loss of the ethnonyms attributed to the peoples of the region."[19] I would counter that the strictly geographic moniker for that region, when so many others were (later) given ethnonyms (accurate or otherwise), tells us something important about that area: there were no well-defined supra-local (that is, beyond the scale of a single township) groups there. Thus, I am arguing that the degree of external recognition that a region's population enjoyed was a factor in determining the division or naming of that region. The naming of the regions, in particular – which seems to have arisen in some cases simply through common usage – would have been a useful heuristic device, so any nontraditional label for a region would have never caught on. Laurence suggests that the Augustan regions went some way to solidifying the ethnic divisions and their artificial mapping to territories:

> Once a territory has become associated with a set ethnonym, the ethnonym can remain in use for a considerable period of time. For example, Procopius (writing in about AD 500, BG5.15.20–30) uses the same ethnonyms to describe Italy as Strabo 500 years earlier. Therefore, the naming of Italy by geographers fixed the populations of regions with an ethnicity that would continue to be associated with the individual regions.[20]

[16] Martial (3.4.8) refers to Region VIII as Aemilia.
[17] Laurence 1998: 108.
[18] Thomsen 1947: 151.
[19] Laurence 1998: 107.
[20] Laurence 1998: 108.

Although Laurence is surely correct in remarking on the regions' oversimplification of demographic realities, at least some of the regions may be truer reflections of the earlier groups than he acknowledges. The Augustan administration's motives in configuring the units of the new Roman Italy along old ethnic lines were not disinterested, and one must be extremely cautious in using the regions as any guide to the territories of the peoples of pre-Roman Italy. However, the very fact that the Romans were not disinterested makes the regions useful as possible remnants of pre-Roman populations. Presumably in designing the regions the administration was attempting to ensure the efficient functioning of these units, so why not use existing territorial divisions?[21] Therefore, although the Augustan regions represent the outcome of factors other than the faithful replication of pre-Roman population groups, they may be valuable for understanding earlier groupings nonetheless. The pragmatic flavor of much Roman administrative decision-making suggests that taking the line of least resistance – working with groups already in place – would have been a priority, and when the groups were either bisected or collapsed in these regional divisions, it was because the regional groups were not so powerful. So we can assume that the Augustan regions were the territorial groupings that made the most sense by the turn of the millennium. When the comparisons fall short and the Augustan regions do not map easily onto known pre-Roman groups, I would suggest that the problem is with the disunity of the local groups that obliged the administrators to make more artificial divisions.

Horsfall makes a good case for regional diversity enduring in Italy in the late republic and early empire.[22] Drawing on a wide range of examples, he notes that authors of those periods comment often on variability in foodstuffs, agricultural techniques, craft production, and settlement patterns. As he notes, given the continuing regional diversity within the modern nation-state of Italy, one should hardly expect

---

[21] We do not know the exact impetus for implementing the regional system, but it came about around the time of the *vicesima hereditatum*, the new 5% inheritance tax of 6 AD. Whether this tax was in mind from the beginning or not, later epigraphic evidence indicates the tax was administered through the regions (Thomsen 1947: 150). For the purposes of tax collection on the ground, moving through a unified area would make the process more efficient.

[22] Horsfall 2001.

any less regionalism in the past. However, what are missing from this patchwork-quilt model of Roman Italy are the population groups of before; the regional diversity is geographical rather than demographic. In fact, the inhabitants are subsumed to their space. This shift from peoples to lands is a radical change from the earlier framework in which peoples were privileged over their specific territories, to the extent that it was difficult to locate these groups in space. This new idea of Italy, which Dench traces back to the early third century BC in its Roman proprietary form, may have evolved from fifth century BC Greek notions of southern Italy that were the first to span the demographic diversity of the region and to conceive of space as an entity independent of the peoples occupying it.[23] But the Romans take this a step further and act on this new conceptualization: indeed, that is how we know about it. The result reinforces the Romanness of Italy in all its diversity. In this respect, the Augustan regions do constitute a radical break with the earlier population groups rather than a reification of them; the regions are spatial units whereas the earlier groups were population units. This shift in emphasis has never been reversed.[24] Nicolet makes a similar point to Horsfall about the decline of the tribe as an administrative unit and the appearance of these neutral spaces, the regions.[25] In Pliny's account we catch a glimpse of this change as it is happening, for he records some towns by their proper names and others by the names of the inhabitants (that is, the group names). Thus, Pliny names a town Beregrani, for the inhabitants, rather than listing it by the town name, Beregra. The inconsistency is attributable to the varied sources from which he was drawing. His periplus source for the coastal areas must have used the proper town names while the Augustan town list based on the tribal groups apparently used the group names.[26] Thus, in Pliny's text the dominance of geographic labels over demographic ones had not yet taken hold.

In light of this, knowing the Bronze Age origins of these early groups can help inform about what follows. So in the case of the Greek *nostoi*, the notion that the Greek origin myths stuck best to those peoples who

---

[23] Dench 2005: 158–64.
[24] Horsfall 2001: 46–9.
[25] Nicolet 1991: 202.
[26] Thomsen 1947: 22–3.

lacked a clear self-definition and ethnos seems to resonate, and from this perspective the determining factor was not just "distance" from the Greeks, but the extent of self-definition that the Greeks discovered in the peoples they were describing. As for the Augustan regions, it seems clear that despite the imperialist engineering at work in configuring these communities into structured territories, the stronger groups were respected while the weaker groups were not. Thus, instead of simply conjecturing on the earlier groups, we can detect, in a shadowy way, the impression they must have made to those who encountered them.

Following conquest, the path to assimilation is far from uniform and Dench insists that telling the history of Italy from the end of the third century BC until the Social War in terms of the "progressive Romanization of Italy" is overly simplistic.[27] Just as the threat of Rome had brought regional unities into focus through collective resistance, the enfranchisement of the Italic peoples – and, in particular, their subsequent absorption into Rome's army in the third and second centuries BC – gave them some investment in the notion of Rome. Indeed, military service may have been the only feasible option for survival for Italic groups whose livelihood had been either severely compromised or destroyed altogether by Roman land dispossession and reallocation, blockage of pasturage rights, and the like.[28] Enlistment in the army did not lead directly to an erasure of the regionalisms, however; instead, the auxiliary troops composed of diverse Italic groups experienced "the sense of variegation grouped together in a common cause."[29] During the Social War of 91 BC, when Italic groups fought for citizenship under the lead of the Samnites, some unified identity was achieved briefly, but Rome was able to play up the underlying distinctions and it all fell apart by 88 BC, with only the Samnites still resisting.[30]

Williamson, in describing the assimilation of Roman Italy, emphasizes the movements of the Romans to undermine the subject populations economically by forcing them out of traditional practices of livelihood, such as transhumant pastoralism, and into activities that were more

---

[27] Dench 2005: 166.
[28] Williamson 2005: 160–1.
[29] Dench 2005: 124.
[30] David 1997: 148–56.

closely bound to the Roman economy as a whole, such as polyculture, boat building, and most significantly, military service.[31] This emphasis on the economic aspects of Romanization is not lost on scholars working in other regions of the empire,[32] although in Italy we see that the new choices were hierarchically inflected. These economic choices were forced on the economically disadvantaged; among Italian aristocrats, non-Latin identities were a luxury they could afford. In the provinces, in contrast, the local elites led the way to Romanization. Thus, non-Latin identities lingered throughout the Republican period, and were drawn on strategically when necessary. Even in central Italy, whose peoples were absorbed early and granted citizenship, tactical regionalism afforded the aristocracy some political advantages.[33] But this did not mean these aristocrats were not also Roman. Cicero emphasized dual citizenship: one to one's home town, one to Rome. These regional identities came to have a moral component to them, too, with ruralness taken as a virtue and set in opposition to the perceived corruption of urban Rome.[34]

These non-Latin identities ultimately disappeared following the spread of Roman citizenship; if traces of old regional practices lingered on, they were not of historic importance. What changed? Acculturation is not the way to think about this; as Dench notes, Hellenism was already "the cultural language of the whole of central and southern Italy" before the Roman conquest.[35] Terrenato suggests using the metaphor of *bricolage*: the making of something new from bits and pieces of what is available to understand the cultural changes, "a process in which new cultural items are obtained by means of attributing new functions to previously existing ones."[36] This approach is more nuanced than straightforward acculturation, but I think it lacks sufficient time depth; it may be a reasonable characterization of the initial processes of cultural change, but a few generations on, when the old traditions have come to service Roman needs, who will remember their earlier functions?

The new Roman idea of Italy as a unit whose bumpy regionalisms had been sanded down entailed the construction of roads and the

---

[31] Williamson 2005.
[32] Important studies include Millett 1990; Mattingly 2011; Woolf 1998.
[33] Farney 2007.
[34] Dench 2005: 173.
[35] Dench 2005: 166.
[36] Terrenato 1998: 23.

displacement of populations, as well as the disruption of links between groups through the imposition of colonies.[37] Dench gives the example of the Latin colonies of Beneventum and Aesernia, "decisively driving wedges between the Pentri, Hirpini, and Caudini," three Samnite peoples.[38] One could reframe this in social network terms and suggest that through these actions the Romans sought to break up the regional networks and establish a new centralized network of relations with Rome at its heart. This new idea of Italy is thus also a new network. We can reframe the decline of the regional groups in terms of the replacement of regional social networks with romanocentric ones, rather than in terms of cultural change. Influenced by an infrastructure encouraging stronger extra-regional ties than regional ones, habits of interaction may have changed before regional self-definitions themselves dissolved. Thus, we can see in the Roman conquest the overwriting of the previous social networks in favor of a new centripetal pull toward Rome.

Dench cautions against overstating Rome's centrality, however. Drawing on Cato's *On Agriculture,* written in the mid-second century BC, in which he recommends purchases of farm gear from many regions, Dench suggests, "Roman hegemony in Italy creates not just one, centripetal pattern, but dozens of new economic, social, and cultural rearrangements."[39] Cato himself highlights the nested local and distant networks at play in early Roman Italy; in his advice on buying a farm, he suggests, "[i]t should be near a thriving town or near the sea or a river where ships go up or a good and well-traveled highway."[40] He implies here that one can benefit economically either from a nearby market or a distant market. Those kinds of choices would not have been on offer before the Roman conquest.

Regionalism after Rome

By the early first century AD, Strabo observes that some of the ethnic groups of the past have faded away. Laurence seems to accept this interpretation of the state of things by Strabo, noting "we can see a general

---

[37] Dench 2005: 164–5.
[38] Dench 1995: 16.
[39] Dench 2005: 171–2.
[40] Cato, *On Agriculture* 1.3.

erosion of neat boundaries in Italy and the formation of larger units of territory, alongside the loss of individual cohesion of ethnic groups... evidently, some ethnic boundaries had ceased to have any meaning for those living there and this could be recognised."[41] It is interesting to note that despite diverse attitudes toward Roman rule – the Veneti by all accounts welcoming it while the Etruscans mounted resistance at various stages – the material distinctiveness of these two groups evaporates at roughly the same time. Despite a backdrop of Veneti swiftly accepting Roman control, neither the substitution of Venetic gods for Roman ones nor the replacement of Venetic inscriptions with Latin ones is complete until the first century AD. Meanwhile, in Etruria, those changes proceed at the same rate despite far more resistance toward the Romans, with hard-fought wars between Rome and the Etruscan cities in the fourth and third centuries BC. Thus, in Etruria, too, the last Etruscan inscriptions date to the Augustan period, approximately the same time as the last Venetic inscriptions; indeed, inscriptions of all the ancient languages of Italy cease to be inscribed at this time as Latin takes over.[42] While the other languages may have continued to be spoken if not written, this bilingualism does not apparently prevail past the early empire, with the exception of some pockets of Greek in the south.[43] This suggests that regardless of the will of local populations, the institutional and structural circumstances were the great equalizers, setting the pace for inevitable cultural loss in the long term. Notions of resistance and accommodation to Roman culture may only have relevance in the extreme short term.

Despite this history, Italy's linguistic regionalism in both modern and ancient times is susceptible to claims of continuity. Jonathan Hall, as an aside to an elegantly constructed and nuanced argument about the origins of Greece's dialects, draws on a study of contemporary Italian dialects as a contrasting example.[44] The Italian language is a nineteenth-century product, the result of the imposition of the Florentine language as the national language to promote unity in the fledgling nation-state.

---

[41] Laurence 1998: 101.
[42] Barker and Rasmussen 1998: 293; David 1997: 179.
[43] Clackson and Horrocks 2007: 37.
[44] Hall 1997: 167.

Conclusions and Aftermath

Hall states that "there never was a period when an undifferentiated proto-Italic was spoken throughout the Italian peninsula. The origins of modern Italian dialects are already inscribed within the linguistic diversity of Iron Age Italy, where Latin-speakers existed alongside Ligurians, Etruscans, Gauls, Picen, Iapygi, Greeks, Sicels and Phoenicians."[45] Although it is technically true that there was linguistic diversity in the Iron Age as there is in modern times, this statement implies a specious continuity between these two periods of multilingualism. In truth, there is almost nothing to connect the Iron Age languages to the modern dialects (or rather, languages, as that is what they are in linguistic terms),[46] other than common territory in some cases. The imposition of Latin transformed the linguistic map of Italy over the course of three centuries, from the fourth to the first century BC, supplanting the other languages of the peninsula, which eventually disappeared altogether.[47] The modern dialects emerged from new rounds of political, economic, and social disunities across the peninsula following the collapse of Roman imperial control, triggering the fragmentation of the Latin language.[48] All the current regional dialects of Italy have their origins in Latin.[49] In fact, there was a period of linguistic unity in Italy, for a good 600 years or so, during the period of Roman rule. Although vernacular languages may have existed alongside official Latin around the empire, these disappeared and Latin "won out."[50] Thus, there is no linguistic evidence that the second phase of regionalism was an atavistic return to the first.

Nor is there archaeological evidence for the "reawakening" of regional groups after Rome's collapse, as Gabba would have it.[51] Certainly under Roman rule there would have been a plurality of regional experiences according to development, economic resources, and relations with Rome, but these regionalisms need have no bearing on the earlier demographic groupings of those areas. The later regional fragmentation came about

---

[45] Hall 1997: 167.
[46] Lepschy *et al.* 1996: 70.
[47] Devoto 1978: 104–10; Clackson and Horrocks 2007: 37.
[48] Devoto 1978: 137–42.
[49] Lepschy *et al.* 1996: 70.
[50] Clackson and Horrocks 2007: 234.
[51] Gabba 1994: 11–6.

under very different circumstances, with political fragmentation crystallizing in Christian parochialism. A few pre-Latin terms survived in some regions, notably Sardinia. These substrate terms are frequent in, for example, local plant names, but their presence is so limited as to make clear the generalized extinction of these earlier languages.[52] Moreover, and perhaps most tellingly, the main modern isoglosses of Italy do not map onto the linguistic boundaries of the pre-Latin peoples.[53] In sum, we cannot retroject from modern circumstances to understand regionalism in Italy prior to the Roman conquest. Similarities with earlier groups probably reflect some natural geographically derived fissures, but no social memory of earlier groupings can be claimed; this is not a case of path dependence.

On post-Roman regionalism in Italy, Christopher Wickham in his study of early charters observes, "In our charter material, from 700 [AD] onwards, every zone of Italy has its own local customs and peculiarities, in social hierarchy, legal formulae, weights and measures. This may be the separate development of different localities after 568, or, quite probably, the first clear evidence of deep local differences that the Romans had never eradicated."[54] This sums up the as yet unresolved debate over Italy's post-Roman regionalism: was it new, or just newly visible? Wickham's favoring of the latter theory aside, it would seem that the evidence (so far) is not there to claim continuity in regional groups over that length of time. Rather than seeing regionalism as continuity, it may be better understood in terms of cycles. Thus, the long-term history of the populations of the Italian peninsula can be told in terms of cycles of atomization and aggregation. This book concerns one such cycle.

---

[52] See Varvaro 1997: 216–18 for a discussion of pre-Latin survivals in Italian.
[53] Compare the modern linguistic map of Italy (Levy 1996: xvi) with the ancient one (Pallottino 1981: fig. 4).
[54] Wickham 1989: 70–1.

APPENDIX

Map ID	Name	Province	Latitude	Longitude	Site Type	RBA	FBA	Material 1	Probable Population Group at Roman Conquest	References
1	Agliastroso/ Amendolara	CS	39.950	16.583	cemetery	RBA	FBA	Torre Castelluccia dagger leaf-shaped vb fib Gargano-type arch fib	Lucanians	Bianco Peroni 1994: 123; Lo Schiavo 2010: 91; 103
2	Alba	CN	44.700	8.035	cemetery	RBA		barrel bead with wavy lines	Ligurians	Bellintani and Residori 2003: 488
3	Aldeno	TN	45.982	11.090	unknown	RBA		Matrei A knife	Rhaetians	Bianco Peroni 1976: 17
4	Alpe di Santa Giulia	MO	44.392	10.663	ritual deposit	RBA		Cetona sword	Ligurians	Bettelli 1997: 726
5	Angarano	VI	45.765	11.718	cemetery		FBA	Torri D'Arcugnano dress pin	Veneti	Carancini 1975: 226
6	Appiano Gentile	CO	45.739	8.980	cemetery	RBA		Torre Castelluccia dagger Glisente B dagger	Insubres	Bianco Peroni 1994: 127; 138
7	Aquileia	UD	45.766	13.365	unknown	RBA	FBA	Cetona sword Pertosa axe	Veneti	Bianco Peroni 1970: 64; Bietti Sestieri 1973: 399
8	Arceto	RE	44.621	10.724	settlement	RBA		Torre Castelluccia dagger Redù dagger Toscanella dagger	Boii	Bianco Peroni 1970: 127; 143; 165

(*continued*)

257

Appendix (*continued*)

Map ID	Name	Province	Latitude	Longitude	Site Type	RBA	FBA	Material 1	Probable Population Group at Roman Conquest	References
9	Arco	TN	45.919	10.887	ritual deposit	RBA		Arco sword	Rhaetians	Bianco Peroni 1970: 34
10	Asola	MN	45.223	10.415	unknown	RBA		Bertarina dagger Toscanella dagger	Cenomani	Bianco Peroni 1994: 158; 165
11	Avetrana	TA	40.340	17.728	settlement	RBA	FBA	LH IIIB Aegean pottery LH IIIC Aegean pottery	Messapians	Vianello 2005: 107
12	Bachero	MC	43.415	13.216	settlement	RBA		awl handle zappetta Fornovo S. Giovanni dagger	Picenes	Bianco Peroni 1994: 121; Pasquini 2005: figs. 1a and 1b
13	Banco	TN	46.375	11.069	unknown	RBA		Matrei A knife	Rhaetians	Bianco Peroni 1976: 17
14	Bari	BA	41.133	16.870	settlement	RBA	FBA	LH IIIC Aegean pottery	Peucetians	Vianello 2005: 107
15	Basiago	RA	44.280	11.949	cemetery (?)	RBA		awl handle Pertosa dagger	Lingones	Bianco Peroni 1994: 150; Pasquini 2005: fig. 1b
16	Bellanda	MN	45.201	10.580	settlement	RBA		miniature spoked wheel RBA Torre Castelluccia dagger Voghera dagger	Cenomani	Bianco Peroni 1994: 128; 171; Pasquini 2005: fig. 1b

17	Bertarina di Vecchiazzano	FC	44.209	12.030	settlement	RBA	Bacino Marina dress pin Cataragna dress pin Monza dagger Bertarina dagger awl handle	Lingones	Bianco Peroni 1994: 132; 158; Caranicini 1975: 127; 179; Pasquini 2005: fig. 1b
18	Bismantova	RE	44.422	10.414	cemetery	RBA FBA	Allumiere bead miniature decorated wheel Tiryns bead glass-eye bead blue glass-barrel bead with spirals	Ligurians	Bellintani and Residori 2003: 491; Negroni Catacchio et al. 2006: 1464–5; Raposso and Ruggiero 1995: 247
19	Blera	VT	42.272	12.030	settlement	FBA	Pertosa axe	Etruscans	Bietti Sestieri 1973: 399; di Gennaro 2007a: 264
20	Bologna	BO	44.495	11.347	hoard	RBA	Glisente B dagger	Boii	Bianco Peroni 1994: 139
21	Bor di Pacengo	VR	45.468	10.723	settlement	RBA FBA	twisted VB fib Peschiera dress pin twisted asymmetrical VB fib	Cenomani	Caranicini 1975: 131; von Eles Masi 1986: 2; 6
22	Borgo Panigale	BO	44.519	11.276	settlement	RBA FBA	Tiryns bead awl handle	Boii	Negroni Catacchio et al. 2006: 1464–5; Pasquini 2005: fig. 1b

(*continued*)

Appendix (*continued*)

Map ID	Name	Province	Latitude	Longitude	Site Type	RBA	FBA	Material 1	Probable Population Group at Roman Conquest	References
23	Borgo San Siro	PV	45.262	8.919	unknown	RBA		Guado di Gugnano dress pin	Insubres	Carancini 1975: 173
24	Bovolone	VR	45.258	11.120	settlement	RBA		LH IIIB Aegean pottery	Veneti	Salzani *et al.* 2006: 1149
25	Brabbia	VA	45.787	8.718	ritual deposit	RBA		Guado di Gugnano dress pin	Insubres	Carancini 1975: 172
26	Brentonico	TN	45.820	10.956	unknown	RBA		Montegiorgio sword	Cenomani	Bianco Peroni 1970: 58
27	Broglio di Trebisacce	CS	39.864	16.505	settlement	RBA	FBA	LH IIIC Aegean pottery donkey asymmetrical VB fib with 2 knobs LH IIIB Aegean pottery	Lucanians	Bettelli 2002: 30–1; de Grossi Mazzorin 1998: 174; Lo Schiavo 2010: 89; Vianello 2005: 109
28	Ca' Balzano	PU	43.690	12.858	settlement	RBA		awl handle	Umbrians	Pasquini 2005: fig. 1b
29	Ca' de' Cessi	MN	45.036	10.534	settlement	RBA		awl handle miniature spoked wheel RBA	Boii/Cenomani	Pasquini 2005: fig. 1b
30	Ca' Morta	CO	45.809	9.086	cemetery	RBA	FBA	twisted VB fib Torri D'Arcugnano dress pin	Insubres	Carancini 1975: 226; von Eles Masi 1986: 3

31	Calavino	TN	46.045	10.983	unknown	RBA	Torre Castelluccia dagger	Rhaetians	Bianco Peroni 1994: 124
32	Caldaro	BZ	46.421	11.242	unknown	RBA	Baierdorf knife	Rhaetians	Bianco Peroni 1976: 13
33	Campegine	RE	44.785	10.533	settlement	RBA	miniature spoked wheel RBA Scoglio del Tonno razor Torre Castelluccia dagger Redu dagger Bertarina dagger Toscanella dagger	Boii	Bianco Peroni 1979: 10; Bianco Peroni 1994: 125; 144; 158; 165; Pasquini 2005: fig. 1b
34	Campo del Fico	LT	41.606	12.561	cemetery	FBA	Allumiere bead	Latins	Negroni Catacchio et al. 2006: 1464-5
35	Campodenno	TN	46.259	11.034	sporadic find	FBA	Allerona sword	Rhaetians	Bianco Peroni 1970: 69
36	Campore (Bargone)	PR	44.826	10.003	settlement	RBA	Torre Castelluccia dagger zappetta	Cenomani	Bianco Peroni 1994: 125
37	Canar	RO	45.060	11.327	settlement	RBA		Veneti	Pasquini 2005: fig. 1a
38	Canegrate	MI	45.570	8.929	cemetery	RBA	Capocchia a Papavero dress pin Guado di Gugnano dress pin Terontola sword Torre Castelluccia dagger	Insubres	Bianco Peroni 1970: 37; Bianco Peroni 1994: 125; 170; Carancini 1975: 172; 236
39	Canosa di Puglia	BT	41.223	16.066	cemetery	RBA	Voghera dagger twisted VB fib	Peucetians	Lo Schiavo 2010: 86

(*continued*)

Appendix (*continued*)

Map ID	Name	Province	Latitude	Longitude	Site Type	RBA	FBA	Material 1	Probable Population Group at Roman Conquest	References
40	Capannori	LU	43.843	10.569	settlement	RBA		twisted VB fib	Ligurians	Cocchi Genick and Zanini 1997: 452
41	Capitan Loreto	PG	43.022	12.647	unknown	RBA		Pertosa dagger	Umbrians	Bianco Peroni 1994: 150
42	Capo Colonna	BT	41.270	16.441	settlement		FBA	LH IIIC Aegean pottery	Peucetians	Bettelli 2002: 22; Vianello 2005: 114
43	Capocolle	FC	44.165	12.176	settlement	RBA		awl handle miniature spoked wheel RBA Toscanella dagger	Lingones	Bianco Peroni 1994: 166; Pasquini 2005: fig. 1b
44	Carbonara al Ticino	PV	45.167	9.063	sporadic find	RBA		Voghera dagger	Insubres	Bianco Peroni 1994: 171
45	Casale Nuovo	LT	41.457	12.764	settlement		FBA	LH IIIC Aegean pottery	Latins	Vagnetti 1999b: 157
46	Casalecchio	RN	43.834	12.255	hoard		FBA	Ponte S. Giovanni axe Casalecchio axe	Umbrians	Bietti Sestieri 1973: 399
47	Casalmoro	MN	45.290	10.415	settlement	RBA	FBA	Matrei A knife Frattesina asymmetrical VB fib Twisted asymmetrical VB fib Capocchia a Papavero dress pin Torri d'Arcugnano dress pin	Cenomani	De Marinis 1999: 516–19

48	Casaroldo	PR	44.982	10.043	settlement	RBA		awl handle miniature spoked wheel RBA Torre Castelluccia dagger Bertarina dagger Redu dagger	Cenomani	Bianco Peroni 1994: 125; 143; 159; Pasquini 2005: fig. 1a
49	Casier	TV	45.644	12.296	ritual deposit	RBA		Cetona sword Tenno dagger Toscanella dagger	Veneti	Bianco Peroni 1970: 63; Bianco Peroni 1994: 156; 164
50	Casinalbo	MO	44.593	10.859	settlement	RBA		Toscanella dagger barrel bead with wavy lines	Boii	Bellintani and Residori 2003: 489; Bianco Peroni 1994: 165
51	Cassano d'Adda	MI	45.527	9.517	ritual deposit	RBA		Monza sword	Insubres	Bianco Peroni 1970: 30
52	Casteggio	PV	45.014	9.124	unknown	RBA		Bertarina dagger	Insubres	Bianco Peroni 1994: 159
53	Castel Beseno	TN	45.932	11.111	unknown		FBA	Fontanella knife	Rhaetians	Bianco Peroni 1976: 19
54	Castelbonafisso	MN	45.215	10.894	unknown	RBA		Bertarina dagger	Cenomani	Bianco Peroni 1994: 160
55	Castellace	RC	38.318	15.941	cemetery		FBA	Castellace-type arch fib Fontanella knife	Bruttians	Bianco Peroni 1976: 20; Lo Schiavo 2010: 99–100
56	Castellaro del Vho	CR	45.128	10.382	settlement	RBA		Redu dagger Toscanella dagger	Cenomani	Bianco Peroni 1976: 145; 165

(*continued*)

Appendix (*continued*)

Map ID	Name	Province	Latitude	Longitude	Site Type	RBA	FBA	Material 1	Probable Population Group at Roman Conquest	References
57	Castellaro di Gottolengo	BS	45.285	10.273	settlement	RBA		Guado di Gugnano dress pin Baierdorf knife Torre Castelluccia dagger Monza dagger Redu dagger Bertarina dagger Toscanella dagger Scoglio del Tonno razor	Cenomani	Bianco Peroni 1976: 13; Bianco Peroni 1979: 9; Bianco Peroni 1994: 125; 132; 144; 159; 165; Carancini 1975: 172
58	Castellaro Lagusello	MN	45.376	10.638	settlement	RBA		Pertosa dagger	Cenomani	Bianco Peroni 1994: 151
59	Castellazzo di Fontanellato	PR	44.883	10.173	settlement	RBA		Pertosa dagger miniature spoked wheel RBA Guado di Gugnano dress pin Redu dagger	Cenomani	Bianco Peroni 1994: 143; 151; Carancini 1975: 172; Pasquini 2005: fig. 1b
60	Castello del Tartaro	VR	45.115	11.236	settlement	RBA		Toscanella dagger Torre Castelluccia dagger Merlara dagger	Veneti	Bianco Peroni 1994: 125; 155; 165
61	Castelnuovo di Sotto	RE	44.814	10.560	settlement	RBA		Bertarina dagger	Boii	Bianco Peroni 1994: 158

62	Castenaso	BO	44.508	11.469	settlement	FBA	donkey	Lingones	de Grossi Mazzorin 1998: 174
63	Castiglioncello d'Orcia	SI	43.017	11.617	unknown	RBA	Pertosa dagger	Etruscans	Bianco Peroni 1994: 150
64	Castione dei Marchesi	PR	44.877	10.063	settlement	RBA	Bacino Marina dress pin Guado di Gugnano dress pin Santa Caterina dress pin Scoglio del Tonno razor Toscanella dagger Bertarina dagger Fornovo S. Giovanni dagger Torre Castelluccia dagger	Cenomani	Bianco Peroni 1979: 10; Bianco Peroni 1994: 121; 125; 144; 158; 165; Carancini 1975: 124; 127; 173
65	Castions di Strada – Evade Viere	UD	45.908	13.186	cemetery	FBA	Redu dagger Frattesina comb	Veneti	Bettelli et al. 2006: 909
66	Cataragna	BS	45.390	10.550	ritual deposit	RBA	Cataragna dress pin	Cenomani	Carancini 1975: 179
67	Cavallo Morto	LT	41.504	12.677	cemetery	RBA	VB fib with 2 knobs	Latins	Angle et al. 2004
68	Cavedine	TN	46.001	10.976	unknown	FBA	Torri D'Arcugnano dress pin	Rhaetians	Carancini 1975: 226
69	Cazzago	VA	45.797	8.735	settlement	RBA	Redu dagger	Insubres	Bianco Peroni 1994: 144
70	Celano	AQ	42.087	13.541	unknown	RBA	Matrei A knife	Aequi/Marsi	Bianco Peroni 1976: 17

(*continued*)

Appendix (*continued*)

Map ID	Name	Province	Latitude	Longitude	Site Type	RBA	FBA	Material 1	Probable Population Group at Roman Conquest	References
71	Cetona	SI	42.963	11.901	settlement	RBA		Cetona sword awl handle	Etruscans	Bianco Peroni 1970: 64; Pasquini 2005: fig. 1b
72	Cevola	PR	44.637	10.372	settlement	RBA		Torre Castelluccia dagger Merlara dagger Scoglio del Tonno razor	Boii/ Ligurians	Bianco Peroni 1979: 9; Bianco Peroni 1994: 127; 154
73	Chiaruccia	PU	43.808	13.007	settlement	RBA		awl handle miniature spoked wheel RBA Montegiorgio sword	Senones	Bergonzi 2005: 704; Pasquini 2005: fig. 1a
74	Chiuse del Frontone	PU	43.513	12.799	hoard		FBA	pick ingot	Umbrians	Pellegrini 1989: 590
75	Cisano	VR	45.531	10.727	settlement	RBA		twisted VB fib Santa Caterina dress pin Torre Castelluccia dagger Gorzano dagger Merlara dagger	Cenomani	Bianco Peroni 1994: 126; 153; 155; Carancini 1975: 123; von Eles Masi 1986: 3
76	Cisterna di Tolentino	MC	43.222	13.334	settlement	RBA	FBA	LH IIIB Aegean pottery LH IIIC Aegean pottery Twisted VB fibula Torre Castelluccia dagger Glisente B dagger	Picenes	Percossi *et al.* 2005: 671–4

77	Citta di Castello	PG	43.460	12.244	unknown	FBA	Pertosa axe	Umbrians	Bietti Sestieri 1973: 399
78	Cividale del Friuli	UD	46.090	13.433	unknown	FBA	Ponte S. Giovanni axe	Veneti	Bietti Sestieri 1973: 399
79	Cles	TN	46.370	11.033	unknown	FBA	Matrei B knife	Rhaetians	Bianco Peroni 1976: 17
80	Coccorano	PG	43.179	12.589	unknown	RBA	Torre Castelluccia dagger	Umbrians	Bianco Peroni 1994: 123
81	Colle della Mola	RM	41.775	12.779	settlement	RBA	Torre Castelluccia Dagger	Latins	Bianco Peroni 1994: 123
82	Collelongo	AQ	41.886	13.584	settlement	FBA	donkey	Aequi/Marsi	de Grossi Mazzorin 1998: 174
83	Colombare di Bersano	PC	44.987	9.955	settlement	RBA	miniature spoked wheel RBA Pertosa dagger	Cenomani	Bianco Peroni 1994: 150; Pasquini 2005: fig. 1b
84	Comunanza	AP	42.968	13.416	cemetery	RBA	Bacino Marina dress pin	Picenes	Carancini 1975: 128
85	Conelle	AN	43.518	12.957	settlement	RBA	awl handle	Umbrians	Pasquini 2005: fig. 1b
86	Coppa Nevigata	FG	41.558	15.834	settlement	RBA	Torre Castelluccia dagger Tiryns bead donkey awl handle Scoglio del Tonno knife LH IIIB Aegean pottery LH IIIC Aegean pottery	Daunians	Bettelli 2002: 20–1; Bianco Peroni 1976: 14; Bokonyi and Siracusa 1987; Negroni Catacchio et al. 2006: 1464–5; Pasquini 2005: fig. 1b

(*continued*)

Appendix (*continued*)

Map ID	Name	Province	Latitude	Longitude	Site Type	RBA	FBA	Material 1	Probable Population Group at Roman Conquest	References
87	Cornocchio	PR	44.815	10.315	settlement	RBA		Capocchia a Papavero dress pin Torre Castelluccia dagger	Boii	Bianco Peroni 1994: 125; Carancini 1975: 236
88	Corte Lazise	VR	45.129	11.314	ritual deposit	RBA		Terontola sword Baierdorf knife	Veneti	Salzani 1994
89	Cortine	AN	43.336	12.933	settlement	RBA		awl handle Boccatura del Mincio dress pin	Picenes	Lollini 1979: 187; Pasquini 2005: fig. 1b
90	Cortona	AR	43.275	11.985	unknown		FBA	Pertosa axe	Etruscans	Bietti Sestieri 1973: 399
91	Cossila	VC	45.565	8.059	unknown	RBA		Monza sword	Insubres	Bianco Peroni 1970: 30
92	Costa Cavallina	BG	45.765	9.604	cemetery		FBA	Tiryns bead	Insubres	Negroni Catacchio et al. 2006: 1464–5
93	Costacciaro	PG	43.364	12.713	unknown		FBA	Frassineto sword	Umbrians	Bianco Peroni 1970: 65
94	Coste del Marano	RM	42.152	11.937	hoard		FBA	Leaf-shaped vb fib	Etruscans	Peroni et al. 1980: 48–9
95	Cozzo Marziotta	TA	40.520	17.021	unknown	RBA		LH IIIB Aegean pottery	Messapians	Bettelli 2002: 28; Vianello 2005: 118
96	Croara	BO	44.445	11.387	sporadic find	RBA		Bertarina dagger	Lingones	Bianco Peroni 1994: 159
97	Crotone	KR	39.082	17.129	settlement		FBA	LH IIIC Aegean pottery	Bruttians	Bettelli 2002: 32

98	Eboli	SA	40.617	15.056	settlement	FBA	LH IIIC Aegean pottery	Lucanians	Schnapp Gourbeillon 1986
99	Este	PD	45.229	11.657	cemetery	RBA	Arco sword Redu dagger	Veneti	Bianco Peroni 1970: 34; Bianco Peroni 1994: 145
100	Ex Podere Conti Spina	RN	44.000	12.641	settlement	RBA	awl handle miniature spoked wheel RBA zappetta	Senones	Pasquini 2005: figs. 1a and 1b
101	Fabbrica dei Soci/ Franzine Nuovo	VR	45.086	11.336	settlement	RBA FBA	LH IIIC Aegean pottery miniature spoked wheel FBA lenticular bead with radial incisions	Veneti	Bianchin Citton 2003: 120
102	Felonica	MN	44.981	11.354	unknown	RBA	Merlara dagger	Boii/Veneti	Bianco Peroni 1994: 154
103	Foiano	AR	43.253	11.815	unknown	FBA	Pertosa axe	Etruscans	Bietti Sestieri 1973: 399
104	Fondo Paviani	VR	45.121	11.291	settlement	FBA	LH IIIC Aegean pottery Tiryns bead Fondo Paviani socketed shovel glass-eye bead blue glass-barrel bead with spirals	Veneti	Bellintani and Residori 2003: 491; Bellintani and Stefan 2008: 13; Bianchin Citton 2003: 120; Negroni Catacchio *et al.* 2006: 1464–5

(*continued*)

269

Appendix (*continued*)

Map ID	Name	Province	Latitude	Longitude	Site Type	RBA	FBA	Material 1	Probable Population Group at Roman Conquest	References
105	Fontanella Grazioli	MN	45.195	10.328	cemetery	RBA	FBA	Cataragna dress pin Torri D'Arcugnano dress pin Fontanella knife	Cenomani	Bianco Peroni 1976: 19; Carancini 1975: 180; 226
106	Forli	FO	44.224	12.044	ritual deposit	RBA		Terontola sword	Lingones	Bianco Peroni 1970: 36
107	Fornovo S. Giovanni	BG	45.499	9.680	cemetery	RBA		Fornovo S. Giovanni dagger	Insubres	Bianco Peroni 1994: 121
108	Frassineto	AR	43.357	11.842	ritual deposit		FBA	Frassineto sword	Etruscans	Bianco Peroni 1970: 64
109	Frattesina	RO	45.023	11.653	settlement and cemetery	RBA	FBA	LH IIIC Aegean pottery Allumiere bead miniature decorated wheel pick ingot miniature spoked wheel FBA Ponte S. Giovanni axe Frattesina comb Frattesina asymmetrical VB fib twisted asymmetrical VB fib	Veneti	Bellintani and Residori 2003: 487; 489; 491; Bellintani and Stefan 2008; Bettelli *et al.* 2006: 909; Bianchin Citton 2003: 120; De Marinis 1999: 532; Negroni Catacchio *et al.* 2006: 1464–5; Pasquini 2005: fig. 1b; Pellegrini 1989:

270

							twisted asymmetrical VB fib	Veneti	590; Raposso and Ruggiero 1995: 247; von Eles Masi 1986: 5–7; Zanini 1999: 321; 326
							Matrei B knife		
							Tiryns bead		
							Fondo Paviani socketed shovel		
							TMES socketed shovel		
							barrel bead with wavy lines		
							lenticular bead with radial incisions		
							Fontanella knife		
							Allerona sword		
							Torri d'Arcugnano dress pin		
							glass-eye bead		
							blue glass-barrel bead with spirals		
110	Fucino	AQ	42.000	13.500	cemetery	RBA	FBA	Allerona sword Cetona Sword Menaforno axe	Aequi/Marsi	Bianco Peroni 1970: 62–3; 68; Carancini 1984: 199
111	Gallizia di Turbigo	MI	45.531	8.740	cemetery	RBA		Montegiorgio knife	Insubres	Bianco Peroni 1976: 12
112	Gallo	BO	44.419	11.550	unknown	RBA		awl handle	Lingones	Pasquini 2005: fig. 1b
113	Garlasco	PV	45.201	8.924	cemetery	RBA		Toscanella dagger	Insubres	Bianco Peroni 1994: 165
114	Gazzade (San Lorenzo)	MO	44.582	10.966	settlement	RBA		Bacino Marina dress pin	Boii	Carancini 1975: 127

(*continued*)

Appendix (*continued*)

Map ID	Name	Province	Latitude	Longitude	Site Type	RBA	FBA	Material 1	Probable Population Group at Roman Conquest	References
115	Gazzo Veronese	VR	45.143	11.077	cemetery	RBA	FBA	Bertarina dagger TMES socketed shovel	Veneti	Bellintani and Stefan 2008: 15; Bianco Peroni 1994: 159
116	Gola di Frasassi	AN	43.398	12.962	settlement	RBA		awl handle	Picenes	Pasquini 2005: fig. 1b
117	Golasecca	VA	45.701	8.659	cemetery		FBA	twisted asymmetrical VB fib	Insubres	Bianco Peroni 1976: 18; von Eles Masi 1986: 6
118	Gorzano	MO	44.516	10.879	settlement	RBA		Matrei B knife awl handle Gorzano dagger miniature spoked wheel RBA zappetta Santa Caterina dress pin Scoglio del Tonno razor Redu dagger	Boii/Ligurians	Bianco Peroni 1979: 10; Bianco Peroni 1994: 145; 152; Carancini 1975: 122; Pasquini 2005: figs. 1a and 1b
119	Grotta dei Baffoni	AN	43.431	12.936	cave	RBA		Torre Castelluccia dagger	Picenes	Bianco Peroni 1994: 123
120	Grotta dell'Orso	GR	43.058	11.162	cave	RBA		Peschiera dress pin	Etruscans	Carancini 1975: 133
121	Grotta di Polla	SA	40.510	15.489	cave		FBA	LH IIIC Aegean pottery	Lucanians	Vagnetti 1974: 666
122	Grotte S. Stefano	VT	42.516	12.178	hoard		FBA	Casalecchio axe	Etruscans	Bietti Sestieri 1973: 399; D'Erme 2007: 331

123	Guado di Gugnano	LO	45.289	9.342	cemetery	RBA	Guado di Gugnano dress pin	Insubres	Carancini 1975: 172
124	Gualdo Tadino	PG	43.230	12.786	hoard	FBA	twisted asymmetrical VB fib	Umbrians	Bettelli 1997: 734
125	Gubbio	PG	43.355	12.573	settlement	RBA	Pertosa dagger zappetta Frattesina comb Torri d'Arcugnano dress pin TMES socketed shovel blue glass-barrel bead with spirals Pertosa axe Ponte S. Giovanni axe	Umbrians	Bellintani and Residori 2003: fig. 4; Bellintani and Stefan 2008: 15; Bettelli *et al.* 2006: 909; Bianco Peroni 1994: 150; Pasquini 2005: fig. 1a; Zanini 1999: 321; 326
126	Irsina	MT	40.752	16.240	unknown	FBA	Menaforno axe	Lucanians	Carancini 1984: 200
127	Isolino di Varese	VA	45.812	8.718	settlement (?)	FBA	Allumiere bead Voghera dagger	Insubres	Bianco Peroni 1994: 170; Negroni Catacchio *et al.* 2006: 1464–5
128	Isolone del Mincio	MN	45.317	10.717	settlement	RBA	Guado di Gugnano dress pin Peschiera dress pin Torre Castelluccia dagger Bertarina dagger	Cenomani	Bianco Peroni 1994: 125; 160; Carancini 1975: 132; 172

(*continued*)

Appendix (*continued*)

Map ID	Name	Province	Latitude	Longitude	Site Type	RBA	FBA	Material 1	Probable Population Group at Roman Conquest	References
129	La Starza	AV	41.154	15.087	settlement	RBA		Torre Castelluccia dagger	Hirpini	Bianco Peroni 1994: 127
130	Laferola	AP	42.945	13.812	unknown	RBA		awl handle	Picenes	Pasquini 2005: fig. 1b
131	Lago di Garda	BS	45.581	10.621	settlement	RBA	FBA	twisted VB fib Boccatura del Mincio dress pin Cataragna dress pin Garda dress pin Peschiera dress pin Santa Caterina dress pin asymmetrical VB fib with 2 knobs	Cenomani	Carancini 1975: 125; 129; 132; 178; 180; von Eles Masi 1986: 2; 11
132	Lago Trasimeno	PG	43.130	12.095	ritual deposit	RBA	FBA	Montegiorgio sword Frassineto sword Cetona sword	Etruscans	Bianco Peroni 1970: 59; 63; 64
133	Laino Borgo	CS	39.955	15.974	sporadic find		FBA	Castellace-type arch fib	Lucanians	Lo Schiavo 2010: 100
134	Luni sul Mignone	VT	42.226	11.933	settlement		FBA	Torri D'Arcugnano dress pin donkey LH IIIC Aegean pottery	Etruscans	Carancini 1975: 226; De Gennaro 2007b: 266; de Grossi Mazzorin 1998: 174; Vagnetti 1999b: 157

135	Madonna del Petto	BT	41.316	16.179	settlement	FBA	LH IIIC Aegean pottery donkey	Daunians	Muntoni 1998; Wilkens 1998: 224
136	Madriolo	UD	46.095	13.477	hoard	FBA	pick ingot	Veneti	Pellegrini 1989: 597
272	Magliano de' Marsi	AQ	42.093	13.365	hoard	FBA	Menaforno axe	Aequi/Marsi	Carancini 1984: 199
137	Malcantone	PC	45.080	9.746	ritual deposit	RBA	Arco sword	Cenomani	Calvani Marini 1975
138	Manaccora	FG	41.947	16.044	cave (burials)	RBA	Montegiorgio sword Fontanella knife	Daunians	Bianco Peroni 1970: 59; Bianco Peroni 1976: 20; Tunzi Sisto 1999
139	Manciano Samprugnano	GR	42.663	11.519	hoard	FBA	TMES socketed shovel pick ingot	Etruscans	Bellintani and Stefan 2008: 15; Pellegrini 1989: 597
140	Marendole	PD	45.229	11.725	settlement	RBA	Bertarina dagger	Veneti	Bianco Peroni 1994: 160
141	Mariconda	RO	45.064	11.198	settlement	FBA	Frattesina asymmetrical VB fib miniature spoked wheel FBA	Veneti	Pasquini 2005: fig. 1b; von Eles Masi 1986: 5
142	Marola	RO	45.027	11.286	unknown	RBA	awl handle miniature spoked wheel RBA	Veneti	Pasquini 2005: fig. 1b
269	Marsia	AP	42.861	13.477	hoard	FBA	pick ingot	Picenes	Pellegrini 1989: 602
270	Menaforno	AQ	41.956	13.685	hoard(?)	FBA	Menaforno axe	Aequi/Marsi	Carancini 1984: 199

(continued)

Appendix (*continued*)

Map ID	Name	Province	Latitude	Longitude	Site Type	RBA	FBA	Material 1	Probable Population Group at Roman Conquest	References
143	Mensa	RA	44.222	12.242	settlement	RBA		awl handle	Lingones	Pasquini 2005: fig. 1b
144	Merlara	PD	45.168	11.443	hoard	RBA		Merlara dagger	Veneti	Bianco Peroni 1994: 154
145	Mezzano	VT	42.613	11.770	settlement	RBA	FBA	Pertosa axe Arco sword	Etruscans	Pellegrini 1993: 79; 80
146	Mezzocorona	TN	46.215	11.120	hoard	RBA		Torre Castelluccia dagger	Rhaetians	Bianco Peroni 1994: 126
147	Mezzolombardo	TN	46.210	11.098	ritual deposit	RBA		Montegiorgio sword	Rhaetians	Bianco Peroni 1970: 59
148	Mirandola	MO	44.888	11.067	settlement	RBA		awl handle	Boii	Pasquini 2005: fig. 1b
149	Missiano	BZ	46.485	11.254	unknown		FBA	Matrei B knife	Rhaetians	Bianco Peroni 1976: 17
150	Monopoli	BA	40.935	17.306	settlement	RBA	FBA	LH IIIC Aegean pottery LH IIIB Aegean pottery	Messapians	Cinquepalmi and Carrieri 1998
151	Montagnana	PD	45.230	11.475	settlement		FBA	LH IIIC Aegean pottery TMES socketed shovel pick ingot	Veneti	Bellintani and Stefan 2008: 15; Bianchin Citton 2003: 120; Pellegrini 1989: 602
152	Montagnolo	AN	43.595	13.476	settlement	RBA		LH IIIB Aegean pottery	Picenes	Vagnetti *et al.* 2006: 1168

153	Montale	MO	44.571	10.906	settlement	RBA	miniature spoked wheel RBA Torre Castelluccia dagger Merlara dagger zappetta Peschiera dress pin	Boii	Bianco Peroni 1994: 123; 154; Carancini 1975: 133; Pasquini 2005: fig. 1a
154	Montata	PC	44.846	9.977	settlement	RBA	Torre Castelluccia dagger Redu dagger lenticular bead with radial incisions	Cenomani	Bellintani and Residori 2003: 481; Bianco Peroni 1994: 125; 144
155	Monte Battaglia	RA	44.218	11.580	hoard	FBA	Tiryns bead	Lingones/ Umbrians	Negroni Catacchio et al. 2006: 1464-5
156	Monte Castellaccio	BO	44.342	11.717	settlement	RBA	zappetta	Lingones	Pasquini 2005: fig. 1a
157	Monte Croce Guardia	AN	43.491	12.940	settlement		miniature spoked wheel FBA twisted asymmetrical VB fib	Umbrians	Pasquini 2005: fig. 1a; von Eles Masi 1986: 6
158	Monte Primo	MC	43.183	12.987	hoard	FBA	Fontanella knife Casalecchio axe	Picenes	Bianco Peroni 1976: 20; Bietti Sestieri 1973: 399
159	Monte Rovello/ Poggio la Pozza	RM	42.175	11.886	settlement and cemetery	RBA FBA	LH IIIC Aegean pottery Allumiere bead Torri d'Arcugnano dress pin leaf-shaped vb fib	Etruscans	Carancini 1975: 227; Lo Schiavo 2010: 91; Negroni Catacchio et al. 2006: 1464; Vagnetti 1999b: 157

(*continued*)

Appendix (*continued*)

Map ID	Name	Province	Latitude	Longitude	Site Type	RBA	FBA	Material 1	Probable Population Group at Roman Conquest	References
160	Monte Sant' Antonio	RM	41.889	13.169	sporadic find	RBA		Montegiorgio sword	Aequi/ Hernici	Belardelli 2007: 127; Bianco Peroni 1970: 58
161	Monte Saraceno	FG	41.704	16.041	cemetery		FBA	Gargano-type arch fib	Daunians	Lo Schiavo 2010: 102
162	Monte Tesoro	VR	45.599	10.959	sporadic find	RBA		Matrei A knife	Veneti	Bianco Peroni 1976: 16
163	Monte Venera	MB	44.512	10.503	settlement	RBA		Peschiera dress pin Scoglio del Tonno razor awl handle	Ligurians	Bianco Peroni 1979: 9; Carancini 1975: 132
164	Montecchio Emilia	RE	44.699	10.449	unknown	RBA		awl handle Torre Castelluccia dagger	Boii	Bianco Peroni 1994: 127; Pasquini 2005: fig. 1b
165	Montegiorgio	FM	43.133	13.536	unknown	RBA	FBA	Montegiorgio sword Allerona sword Montegiorgio knife	Picenes	Bianco Peroni 1970: 58, 69; Bianco Peroni 1976: 12
166	Monza	MB	45.585	9.275	cemetery	RBA		Guado di Gugnano dress pin Monza sword Monza dagger Voghera dagger	Insubres	Bianco Peroni 1970: 30; Bianco Peroni 1994: 132; 170; Carancini 1975: 172

167	Moscosi	MC	43.352	13.142	settlement	RBA	awl handle Pertosa dagger miniature spoked wheel RBA Cataragna dress pin zappetta Bertarina dagger Torre Castelluccia dagger Glisente B dagger Boccatura del Mincio dress pin twisted VB fibula barrel bead with wavy lines	Picenes	Pasquini 2005: figs. 1a and 1b; Sabbatini and Silvestrini 2005: 650–3
168	Motta di Ciro	KR	39.384	17.060	settlement	FBA	LH IIIC Aegean pottery	Bruttians	Vianello 2005: 139
169	Ortucchio	AQ	41.955	13.645	cemetery	FBA	Torri D'Arcugnano dress pin Pertosa axe Matrei A knife	Aequi/Marsi	Bianco Peroni 1976: 17; Bietti Sestieri 1973: 399; Carancini 1975: 227
170	Otranto	LE	40.145	18.489	settlement	FBA	LH IIIC Aegean pottery twisted VB fib LH IIIB Aegean pottery	Messapians	Bettelli 2002: 26; Lo Schiavo 2010: 86; Vianello 2005: 141
171	Palestrina	RM	41.834	12.883	sporadic find	FBA	Pertosa axe	Latins	Belardelli 2007: 140–1; Bietti Sestieri 1973: 399

(*continued*)

Appendix (*continued*)

Map ID	Name	Province	Latitude	Longitude	Site Type	RBA	FBA	Material 1	Probable Population Group at Roman Conquest	References
172	Panicarola	PG	43.071	12.087	cemetery		FBA	Tiryns bead	Etruscans	Negroni Catacchio 1999: 251; Negroni Catacchio *et al.* 2006: 1464-5
173	Parabita	LE	40.058	18.119	settlement		FBA	LH IIIC Aegean pottery	Messapians	Bettelli 2002: 26
174	Pastrengo	VR	45.495	10.801	ritual deposit		FBA	Matrei B knife	Cenomani	Bianco Peroni 1976: 17
175	Pertosa	SA	40.550	15.467	ritual deposit	RBA	FBA	twisted VB fib Pertosa dagger Pertosa axe Scoglio del Tonno knife	Lucanians	Bianco Peroni 1976: 14; Bianco Peroni 1994: 150; Bietti Sestieri 1973: 399; Lo Schiavo 2010: 85
176	Perugia	PG	43.112	12.385	unknown		FBA	Menaforno axe	Etruscans	Carancini 1984: 200
177	Peschiera del Garda	VR	45.440	10.689	settlement	RBA	FBA	Pertosa dagger twisted VB fib Bacino Marina dress pin Boccatura del Mincio dress pin Capocchia a Papavero dress pin	Cenomani	Bianco Peroni 1976: 12; 13; Bianco Peroni 1979: 9; Bianco Peroni 1994: 121; 124; 143; 151; 152; 156; 159; 166;

| 178 | Piadena | CR | 45.133 | 10.370 | unknown | RBA | Cataragna dress pin
Garda dress pin
Guado di Gugnano dress pin
Peschiera dress pin
Santa Caterina dress pin
twisted asymmetrical VB fib
asymmetrical VB with 2 knobs
Baierdorf knife
Montegiorgio knife
Fornovo S. Giovanni dagger
Torre Castelluccia dagger
Redu dagger
Gorzano dagger
Tenno dagger
Bertarina dagger
Toscanella dagger
Scoglio del Tonno razor
Bertarina dagger | Carancini 1975: 122; 127; 129; 130; 172; 173; 179; 236; von Eles Masi 1986: 2; 6; 11

Cenomani

Bianco Peroni 1994: 158 |

(*continued*)

Appendix (*continued*)

Map ID	Name	Province	Latitude	Longitude	Site Type	RBA	FBA	Material 1	Probable Population Group at Roman Conquest	References
179	Pianello di Genga	AN	43.409	12.938	cemetery	RBA	FBA	miniature spoked wheel FBA Torri D'Arcugnano dress pin Frattesina comb miniature decorated wheel	Picenes	Bettelli *et al.* 2006: 910; Bianco Peroni *et al.* 2010; Carancini 1975: 226; Pasquini 2005: fig. 1b; Raposso and Ruggiero 1995: 247
180	Pianizza	VT	42.504	11.821	hoard		FBA	Casalecchio axe	Etruscans	Bietti Sestieri 1973: 399; Petitti 2007a: 300
181	Piano di Tallone	GR	42.590	11.518	hoard	RBA	FBA	Matrei A knife Pertosa axe Casalecchio axe	Etruscans	Bianco Peroni 1976: 16; Bietti Sestieri 1973: 399
182	Pieve San Giacomo	CR	45.134	10.187	settlement	RBA		Bacino Marina dress pin Santa Caterina dress pin Terontola sword Torre Castelluccia dagger Redu dagger Gorzano dagger Merlara dagger Bertarina dagger Toscanella dagger Glisente B dagger	Cenomani	Bianco Peroni 1970: 36; Bianco Peroni 1994: 128; 139; 143; 152; 155; 158; 165; Carancini 1975: 124; 127

183	Poggio Berni	RN	44.042	12.410	hoard	FBA	pick ingot TMES socketed shovel Ponte S. Giovanni axe	Senones	Bellintani and Stefan 2008: 15; Bietti Sestieri 1973: 393–4; Pellegrini 1989: 590
184	Ponte S. Giovanni	PG	43.090	12.446	unknown	FBA	Ponte S. Giovanni axe	Etruscans	Bietti Sestieri 1973: 399
185	Ponte S. Marco	BS	45.478	10.413	settlement	FBA	Frattesina asymmetrical VB fib Fondo Paviani socketed shovel Tiryns bead	Cenomani	Bellintani and Stefan 2008: 11; Lo Schiavo 2010: 86; Negroni Catacchio et al. 2006: 1464–5
186	Ponte S. Pietro	VT	42.523	11.606	cemetery	FBA	Tiryns bead	Etruscans	Negroni Catacchio et al. 2006: 1464–5; Petitti 2007: 300–1
187	Porpetto	UD	45.859	13.218	settlement	FBA	TMES socketed shovel	Veneti	Bellintani and Stefan 2008: 18
188	Porto Cesareo	LE	40.271	17.881	settlement	RBA	LH IIIC Aegean pottery LH IIIB Aegean pottery	Messapians	Bettelli 2002: 26–7
189	Porto di Pacengo	VR	45.468	10.712	settlement	RBA	Bacino Marina dress pin Cataragna dress pin Garda dress pin	Cenomani	Carancini 1975: 128; 129; 179

(*continued*)

283

Appendix (*continued*)

Map ID	Name	Province	Latitude	Longitude	Site Type	RBA	FBA	Material 1	Probable Population Group at Roman Conquest	References
190	Porto Perone/ Satyrion	TA	40.372	17.308	settlement	RBA	FBA	LH IIIC Aegean pottery LH IIIB Aegean pottery VB fib with 2 knobs	Messapians	Bettelli 2002: 27; Lo Schiavo 2010: 87
191	Punta Le Terrare	BR	40.645	17.958	settlement	RBA		LH IIIB Aegean pottery	Messapians	Bettelli 2002: 25; Lo Porto 1998
192	Punta Meliso	LE	39.795	18.368	settlement		FBA	LH IIIC Aegean pottery	Messapians	Bettelli 2002: 26
193	Quingento	PR	44.779	10.399	settlement	RBA		miniature spoked wheel RBA Torre Castelluccia dagger Toscanella dagger	Boii	Bianco Peroni 1994: 124; 165; Pasquini 2005: fig. 1b
194	Rastellino	MO	44.635	11.099	settlement	RBA		zappetta	Boii	Pasquini 2005: fig. 1a
195	Rebbio	CO	45.790	9.076	cemetery		FBA	Torri D'Arcugnano dress pin	Insubres	Carancini 1975: 226
196	Redu	MO	44.656	11.071	settlement	RBA		awl handle miniature spoked wheel RBA Cetona sword Santa Caterina dress pin Redu dagger Gorzano dagger Merlara dagger Bertarina dagger Toscanella dagger	Boii	Bianco Peroni 1970: 63–4; Bianco Peroni 1994: 143; 152; 154; 159; 164; Carancini 1975: 124; Pasquini 2005: fig. 1b

197	Regnano	RE	44.561	10.576	settlement	RBA	Bertarina dagger	Ligurians	Bianco Peroni 1994: 160
198	Riparo dell'Ambra	LU	43.933	10.300	ritual deposit		Tiryns bead	Ligurians	Negroni Catacchio 1999: 251; Negroni Catacchio et al. 2006: 1464-5
199	Ripatransone	AP	42.996	13.761	unknown	FBA	Pertosa axe	Picenes	Bietti Sestieri 1973: 399
200	Roca Vecchia	LE	40.287	18.427	settlement	RBA	LH IIIC Aegean pottery LH IIIB Aegean pottery	Messapians	Bettelli 2002: 25
201	Roddi	CN	44.690	7.977	ritual deposit	FBA	Frassineto sword	Ligurians	Bianco Peroni 1970: 65
202	Rogorea di Rogoredo	LC	45.680	9.333	cemetery	RBA	Voghera dagger	Insubres	Bianco Peroni 1994: 171
203	Rossano	CS	39.577	16.634	cemetery	FBA	Castellace-type arch fib	Bruttians	Lo Schiavo 2010: 100
204	Roteglia	RE	44.483	10.680	settlement	RBA	Torre Castelluccia dagger	Ligurians	Bianco Peroni 1994: 125
205	Rovereto	TN	45.891	11.040	ritual deposit	FBA	Allerona sword	Rhaetians	Bianco Peroni 1970: 69
206	S. Agata Bolognese	BO	44.665	11.135	settlement	RBA	zappetta Bacino Marina dress pin Torre Castelluccia dagger Redu dagger Merlara dagger Toscanella dagger	Boii	Bianco Peroni 1994: 126; 144; 155; 164; Carancini 1975: 127; Pasquini 2005: fig. 1a

(*continued*)

Appendix (*continued*)

Map ID	Name	Province	Latitude	Longitude	Site Type	RBA	FBA	Material 1	Probable Population Group at Roman Conquest	References
207	S. Ambrogio	MO	44.624	11.000	settlement	RBA		miniature spoked wheel RBA Santa Caterina dress pin Monza dagger Fornovo S. Giovanni dagger	Boii	Bianco Peroni 1994: 121; 132; Carancini 1975: 122; Pasquini 2005: fig. 1b
208	S. Antonino	TV	45.646	12.270	ritual deposit	RBA		Arco sword Bertarina dagger	Veneti	Bianco Peroni 1970: 34; Bianco Peroni 1994: 159
209	S. Caterina di Tredossi	CR	45.187	9.994	settlement	RBA		Torre Castelluccia dagger Bacino Marina dress pin Santa Caterina dress pin Redu dagger Merlara dagger Tenno dagger Bertarina dagger Toscanella dagger Scoglio del Tonno razor	Cenomani	Bianco Peroni 1979: 9; Bianco Peroni 1994: 125; 144; 154; 157; 158; 165; Carancini 1975: 124; 127
210	S. Giovenale	VT	42.224	12.007	settlement	RBA	FBA	miniature decorated wheel LH IIIC Aegean pottery	Etruscans	Di Gennaro 2007c: 269; Raposso and Ruggiero 1995: 247; Vagnetti 1999b: 157

211	S. Giuliano di Toscanella	BO	44.383	11.646	settlement	RBA	Redu dagger	Lingones	Bianco Peroni 1994: 145
212	S. Ilario d'Enza	RE	44.764	10.449	settlement	RBA	Torre Castelluccia dagger	Boii	Bianco Peroni 1994: 125
213	S. Marco di Belvedere	UD	45.733	13.367	unknown	RBA	Montegiorgio sword	Veneti	Bianco Peroni 1970: 58
214	S. Maria di Ripalta	FG	41.153	15.867	settlement	FBA	LH IIIC Aegean pottery	Daunians	Bettelli 2002: 22
271	S. Marino Seconda Torre	San Marino	43.933	12.452	hoard	FBA	TMES socketed shovel	Senones/Umbrians	Bellintani and Stefan 2008: 15
215	S. Michele di Valestra	RE	44.456	10.566	settlement	FBA	awl handle blue glass-barrel bead with spirals glass-eye bead	Ligurians	Bellintani and Residori 2003: 491; Pasquini 2005: fig. 1a
216	S. Paolina	AN	43.471	13.412	settlement	RBA	awl handle miniature spoked wheel RBA Glisente B dagger zappetta	Picenes	Bianco Peroni 1994: 139; Pasquini 2005: fig. 1a and 1b
217	S. Pietro (Legnago)	VR	45.186	11.280	unknown	RBA	twisted VB fib	Veneti	von Eles Masi 1986: 3
218	S. Polo d'Enza	RE	44.628	10.425	settlement	RBA	awl handle miniature spoked wheel RBA Torre Castelluccia dagger Boccatura del Mincio dress pin Capocchia a Papavero dress pin Montegiorgio knife Merlara dagger Pertosa dagger	Boii/Ligurians	Bianco Peroni 1976: 12; Bianco Peroni 1994: 124; 151; 155; Carancini 1975: 176; 236; Pasquini 2005: fig. 1b

(*continued*)

Appendix (*continued*)

Map ID	Name	Province	Latitude	Longitude	Site Type	RBA	FBA	Material 1	Probable Population Group at Roman Conquest	References
219	S. Rosa di Poviglio	RE	44.858	10.565	settlement	RBA		awl handle miniature spoked wheel RBA Peschiera dress pin barrel bead with wavy lines lenticular bead with radial incisions Torre Castelluccia dagger Cataragna dress pin	Boii	Bellintani and Residori 2003: 487; Bernabo Brea *et al.* 1997: 348–50; Pasquini 2005: fig. 1b
220	S. Vito di Pisticci	MT	40.393	16.556	unknown		FBA	LH IIIC Aegean pottery	Lucanians	Bettelli 2002: 29
221	Sabbionara di Veronella	VR	45.333	11.277	settlement	RBA	FBA	barrel bead with wavy lines twisted VB fib Fondo Paviani socketed shovel blue glass-barrel bead with spirals	Veneti	Bellintani and Residori 2003: 487; Bellintani and Stefan 2008: 14; Lo Schiavo 2010: 86
222	Sassa	AQ	42.353	13.303	unknown		FBA	Torri D'Arcugnano dress pin	Sabines	Carancini 1975: 227
223	Sassuolo	MO	44.549	10.786	unknown	RBA		Merlara dagger Toscanella dagger	Boii/Ligurians	Bianco Peroni 1994: 154; 164

224	Savana di Cibeno	MO	44.801	10.870	settlement	RBA	awl handle Pertosa dagger Torre Castelluccia dagger	Boii	Bianco Peroni 1994: 127; 150; Pasquini 2005: fig. 1b
225	Scarceta	GR	42.589	11.519	settlement	RBA	miniature decorated wheel donkey Pertosa axe leaf-shaped vb fib Frattesina asymmetrical VB fib	Etruscans	de Grossi Mazzorin 1998: 174; Lo Schiavo 2010: 91; Pellegrini 1993: 80; Raposso and Ruggiero 1995: 247
226	Scoglio del Tonno	TA	40.483	17.225	settlement	RBA	LH IIIC Aegean pottery LH IIIB Aegean pottery awl handle Pertosa dagger Scoglio del Tonno knife Torre Castelluccia dagger Garda dress pin Scoglio del Tonno razor VB fib with 2 knobs	Messapians	Bettelli 2002: 28; Bianco Peroni 1976: 14; Bianco Peroni 1979: 9; Bianco Peroni 1994: 123; 150; Carancini 1975: 129; Lo Schiavo 2010: 87; Pasquini 2005: fig. 1b
227	Serra San Quirico	AN	43.445	13.022	unknown	FBA	Pertosa axe	Picenes	Bietti Sestieri 1973: 399
228	Sibari	CS	39.749	16.454	unknown	FBA	Timmari-type arch fib	Lucanians	Lo Schiavo 2010: 101
229	Siena	SI	43.320	11.330	unknown	FBA	Ponte S. Giovanni axe	Etruscans	Bietti Sestieri 1973: 399

(continued)

289

Appendix (*continued*)

Map ID	Name	Province	Latitude	Longitude	Site Type	RBA	FBA	Material 1	Probable Population Group at Roman Conquest	References
230	Sorgenti della Nova	VT	42.550	11.728	settlement		FBA	donkey	Etruscans	Arancio 2007: 288–9
231	Spinazzola	BT	40.968	16.092	sporadic find		FBA	Timmari-type arch fib	Peucetians	Lo Schiavo 2010: 101
232	St. Martin de Corleans	AO	45.738	7.306	unknown	RBA		Terontola sword	Taurini	Bianco Peroni 1970: 37
233	Stenico	TN	46.051	10.855	unknown	RBA		Terontola sword	Rhaetians	Bianco Peroni 1970: 36
234	Sulmona	AQ	42.047	13.926	unknown	RBA		Cetona sword	Paeligni	Bianco Peroni 1970: 62–3
235	Surbo	LE	40.395	18.133	hoard		FBA	Pertosa axe	Messapians	Bietti Sestieri 1973: 399
236	Taranto (S. Domenico)	TA	40.477	17.227	settlement	RBA		LH IIIB Aegean pottery	Messapians	Bettelli 2002: 28; Vianello 2005: 161
237	Tenno	TN	45.920	10.833	unknown	RBA		Tenno dagger	Rhaetians	Bianco Peroni 1994: 156
238	Teor	UD	45.856	13.055	ritual deposit	RBA		Torre Castelluccia dagger	Veneti	Bianco Peroni 1994: 124
239	Termitito	MT	40.220	16.668	settlement	RBA	FBA	LH IIIC Aegean pottery awl handle Pertosa dagger miniature spoked wheel RBA LH IIIB Aegean pottery	Lucanians	Bettelli 2002: 29; Bianco Peroni 1994: 150; Pasquini 2005: fig. 1b
240	Terontola	AR	43.211	12.024	unknown	RBA		Terontola sword	Etruscans	Bianco Peroni 1970: 36

290

241	Terranova da Sibari	CS	39.658	16.340	sporadic find	FBA	Castellace type arch fib	Lucanians	Lo Schiavo 2010: 100
242	Tierno	TN	45.849	10.982	unknown	FBA	asymmetrical VB with 2 knobs	Rhaetians	Laviosa Zambotti 1938: 172
243	Timmari	MT	40.649	16.479	settlement and cemetery	FBA	Timmari-type arch fib miniature spoked wheel FBA asymmetrical VB with 2 knobs Castellace-type arch fib	Lucanians	Bettelli 2002: 29; Bianco and Orlando 1995; Lo Schiavo 2010: 89; 100; 101; Pasquini 2005: fig. 1b
268	Toppo Daguzzo	PZ	40.976	15.675	settlement and cemetery	RBA	LH IIIB Aegean pottery LH IIIC Aegean pottery	Hirpini	Cipolloni Sampò 1986; Vianello 2005: 166-8
244	Torbole	TN	45.870	10.877	unknown	RBA	Matrei A knife	Rhaetians	Bianco Peroni 1976: 17
245	Torino	TO	45.072	7.695	ritual deposit	RBA	Monza sword	Taurini	Bianco Peroni 1970: 31
246	Torre Castelluccia	TA	40.343	17.382	settlement and cemetery	RBA	LH IIIC Aegean pottery twisted VB fib Gargano-type arch fib Scoglio del Tonno knife Torre Castelluccia dagger Garda dress pin VB fib with 2 knobs Castellace-type arch fib	Messapians	Bettelli 2002: 27; Bianco Peroni 1976: 14; Bianco Peroni 1994: 123; Carancini 1975: 129; Lo Schiavo 2010: 85; 87; 100; 103

(*continued*)

Appendix (*continued*)

Map ID	Name	Province	Latitude	Longitude	Site Type	RBA	FBA	Material 1	Probable Population Group at Roman Conquest	References
247	Torre d'Andrea	PG	43.039	12.546	cemetery	RBA		Merlara dagger	Umbrians	Bianco Peroni 1994: 155
248	Torre Galli	VV	38.645	15.936	unknown		FBA	Timmari-type arch fib	Bruttians	Lo Schiavo 2010: 101
249	Torre Guaceto	BR	40.716	17.799	unknown		FBA	LH IIIC Aegean pottery	Messapians	Bettelli 2002: 24–5; Vianello 2005: 169
250	Torre Mordillo	CS	39.713	16.312	settlement	RBA	FBA	LH IIIB Aegean Pottery Frattesina comb twisted VB fib leaf-shaped vb fib asymmetrical VB with 2 knobs LH IIIC Aegean pottery Castellace-type arch fib	Lucanians	Bettelli *et al.* 2006: 909; Lo Schiavo 2010: 85; 89; 91; 100; Trucco and Vagnetti 2001
251	Torre Santa Sabina	BR	40.755	17.706	settlement and cemetery		FBA	LH IIIC Aegean pottery	Messapians	Bettelli 2002: 24; Coppola 1998
252	Torretta di Cella	RE	44.730	10.546	settlement	RBA		Torre Castelluccia dagger	Boii	Bianco Peroni 1994: 126
253	Torri D'Arcugnano	VI	45.497	11.552	settlement (probable)		FBA	Torri D'Arcugnano dress pin	Veneti	Carancini 1975: 226

254	Torrionaccio	VT	42.268	11.895	settlement	FBA	donkey Torri D'Arcugnano dress pin	Etruscans	de Grossi Mazzorin 1998: 174; Trucco 2007: 308; Zanini 1999: 321
255	Toscanella Imolese	BO	44.383	11.643	settlement	RBA	awl handle miniature spoked wheel RBA zappetta Merlara dagger Tenno dagger Bertarina dagger Toscanella dagger	Lingones	Bianco Peroni 1994: 155; 157; 158; 164; Pasquini 2005: figs. 1a and 1b
256	Tragno	TN	45.821	10.956	hoard	FBA	Matrei B knife Fontanella knife	Rhaetians	Bianco Peroni 1976: 17; 19
257	Trasacco	AQ	41.958	13.536	settlement	FBA	asymmetrical VB with 2 knobs	Aequi/Marsi	Lo Schiavo 2010: 90
258	Treazzano	AP	42.880	13.808	settlement	RBA	LH IIIB Aegean pottery awl handle miniature spoked wheel RBA	Picenes	Pasquini 2005: fig. 1b; Vagnetti et al. 2006: 1168; Vianello 2005: 171
259	Trebbo Sei Vie	BO	44.502	11.509	settlement	RBA	miniature spoked wheel RBA Fornovo S. Giovanni dagger Torre Castelluccia dagger Merlara dagger Bertarina dagger Toscanella dagger Scoglio del Tonno razor	Lingones	Bianco Peroni 1979: 9; Bianco Peroni 1994: 121; 127; 154; 158; 166; Pasquini 2005: fig. 1b

(*continued*)

Appendix (*continued*)

Map ID	Name	Province	Latitude	Longitude	Site Type	RBA	FBA	Material 1	Probable Population Group at Roman Conquest	References
260	Tromello	PV	45.212	8.870	unknown	RBA		Voghera dagger	Insubres	Bianco Peroni 1994: 171
261	Urbino	PU	43.725	12.636	unknown		FBA	Pertosa axe	Umbrians	Bietti Sestieri 1973: 399
262	Venezia (Laguna Nord)	VE	45.490	12.413	unknown	RBA		LH IIIB Aegean pottery	Veneti	Bianchin Citton 2003: 122
263	Vicopo	PR	44.814	10.367	settlement	RBA		Torre Castelluccia dagger	Boii	Bianco Peroni 1994: 127
264	Vieste	FG	41.882	16.173	sporadic find		FBA	Gargano-type arch fib	Daunians	Lo Schiavo 2010: 102
265	Villamarzana	RO	45.015	11.699	settlement		FBA	TMES socketed shovel	Veneti	Bellintani and Stefan 2008: 15
266	Viverone	BI	45.404	8.028	ritual deposit	RBA		Monza sword	Insubres	Bianco Peroni 1970: 30
267	Voghera	PV	44.994	9.010	sporadic find	RBA		Voghera dagger	Insubres	Bianco Peroni 1994: 171

BIBLIOGRAPHY

Affuso, A. & Lorusso, P. 2006, "Produzione materiale e circolazione dei beni nella Basilicata ionica tra Bronzo tardo e prima età del Ferro" in *Atti della XXXIX Riunione Scientifica. Materie prime e scambi nella preistoria italiana*, ed. D. Cocchi Genick, Istituto Italiano di Preistoria e Protostoria, Florence, pp. 1403-14.

Angelini, I., Artioli, G., Bellintani, P., Diella, V., Gemmi, M., Polla, A. and Rossi, A. 2004, "Chemical analyses of Bronze Age glasses from Frattesina di Rovigo, Northern Italy," *Journal of Archaeological Science*, vol. 31, no. 8, pp. 1175-84.

Angle, M. 2003, "'Gifts offered in Reciprocation should be proportionate to those received' at the dawn of myth: The Mycenaeans in Latium" in *Sea Routes... From Sidon to Huelva. Interconnections in the Mediterranean 16th-6th c. BC*, ed. N. Stampolidis, Museum of Cycladic Art, Athens, pp. 116-19.

Angle, M., di Gennaro, F., Guidi, A. & Tusa, S. 2004, "La Necropoli ad Incinerazione di Cavallo Morto (Anzio, Roma)" in *L'età del bronzo recente in Italia*, ed. D. Cocchi Genick, Mauro Baroni edn, Lucca, pp. 125-40.

Antonaccio, C. 2004, "Siculo-Geometric and the Sikels: Ceramics and Identity in Eastern Sicily," in *Greek Identity in the Western Mediterranean: Papers in Honour of Brian Shefton*, ed. K. Lomas, Brill Academic Publishers, Leiden, Belgium, pp. 55-82.

Arancio, M. 2007, "Castellaccio delle Sorgenti della Nova" in *Repertorio dei siti protostorici del Lazio. Province di Roma, Viterbo e Frosinone*, eds. C. Belardelli, M. Angle, F. di Gennaro & F. Trucco, All'Insegna del Giglio, Florence, pp. 288-9.

Arancio, M. L., Buffa, V., Damiani, I., Tagliacozzo, A., Trucco, F. & Vagnetti, L. 1995, "L'Abitato di Torre Mordillo nel Quadro dello Sviluppo dell'Insediamento Protostorico nell'Alto Ionio (Sibaritide)" in *Settlement and Economy in Italy 1500 BC- AD 1500. Papers of the Fifth Conference of Italian Archaeology*, ed. N. Christie, Oxbow Monograph 41, Oxford, pp. 227-39.

Arenoso Callipo, C. M. S. & Bellintani, P. 1994, "Dati archeologici e paleoambientali del territorio di Frattesina di Fratta Polesine (RO) tra la tarda età del bronzo e la prima età del ferro," *Padusa*, vol. 30, pp. 7-65.

Baffetti, A., Carancini, G. L., Conti, A. M., Franco, M. C., Garagnani, G. L., Mancini, B., Mitchell, E., Pellegrini, E., Persiani, C., Petitti, P., Poggiani Keller, R., Sadori, L. & Spinedi, P. 1993, *Vulcano a Mezzano. Insediamento e Produzioni Artigianali nella media Valled del Fiora nell'età del Bronzo*, Museo Civico di Valentano, Viterbo.

Baldelli, G., Bergonzi, G., Cardarelli, A., Damiani, I. & Lucentini, N. 2005, "Le Marche dall'antica alla recente età del bronzo" in *Atti della XXXVIII Riunione Scientifica. Preistoria e Protostoria delle Marche. Vol. 2.*, ed. D. C. Genick, Istituto Italiano di Preistoria e Protostoria, Florence, pp. 539-79.

Bankoff, H. 1996, "Handmade Burnished Ware and the Late Bronze Age of the Balkans," *Journal of Mediterranean Archaeology*, vol. 9, no. 2, pp. 193-209.

Barbaro, B., Bettelli, M., Damiani, I., DeAngelis, D., Minniti, C., & Trucco, F. 2012, "Etruria meridionale e Mediterraneo nella tarda eta del bronzo" in *Le Origini degli Etruschi. Storia Archeologia Antropologia*, ed. V. Bellelli, L'Erma di Bretschneider, Rome, pp. 195-247.

Barbieri, M. E. & Manzelli, V. 2006, *Emilia-Romagna*, Libreria dello Stato, Rome.

Barfield, L. 1994, "The Bronze Age of Northern Italy: Recent Work and Social Interpretation" in *Development and Decline in the Mediterranean Bronze Age*, eds. C. Mathers & S. Stoddart, J. R. Collis, Sheffield, pp. 129-44.

Barker, G. 1995, *A Mediterranean Valley: Landscape Archaeology and Annales History in the Biferno Valley*, Leicester University Press, London and New York.

Barker, G., Grant, A., Beavitt, P., Christie, N., Giorgi, J., Hoare, P., Leggio, T. & Migliavacca, M. 1991, "Ancient and Modern Pastoralism in Central Italy: An Interdisciplinary Study in the Cicolano Mountains," *Papers of the British School at Rome*, vol. 59, pp. 15-88.

Barker, G. & Rasmussen, T. 1998, *The Etruscans*, Blackwell, Oxford/Malden.

Barker, G. & Stoddart, S. 1994, "The Bronze Age of Central Italy: c. 2000-900 BC" in *Development and Decline in the Mediterranean Bronze Age*, eds. C. Mathers & S. Stoddart, J. R. Collis, Sheffield, pp. 145-65.

Barra Bagnasco, M. & Russo Tagliente, A. 1996, "I Culti" in *Greci, Enotri e Lucani nella Basilicata meridionale*, eds. S. Bianco, A. Bottini, A. Pontrandolfo, A. Russo Tagliente & E. Setari, Electa, Naples, pp. 183-93.

Barth, F. (ed.) 1969, *Ethnic groups and boundaries: The social organization of culture difference*, Universitetsforlaget, Bergen.

Bartoloni, G. 2009, "Periodo protostorico, periodo etrusco: una sequenza ambigua" in *Etruria e italia Preromana. Studi in onore di giovannangelo Camporeale*, ed. S. Bruni, Fabrizio Serra, Pisa and Rome, pp. 61-72.

Belardelli, C. 2007, "Monte Sant'Antonio" in *Repertorio dei siti protostorici del Lazio. Province di Roma, Viterbo e Frosinone*, eds. C. Belardelli, M. Angle, F. di Gennaro & F. Trucco, All'Insegna del Giglio, Florence, p. 127.

Belardelli, C. & Bettelli, M. 2007, "Different technological levels of pottery production: Barbarian and Grey Ware between the Aegean and Europe in the Late Bronze Age" in *Between the Aegean and Baltic Seas. Prehistory Across Borders*, eds. I. Galanaki, H. Tomas, Y. Galanakis & R. Laffineur, Université de Liège, Liège, pp. 481-5.

Bibliography

Bellato, F. & Bellintani, G. F. 1975, "Dati per uno studio della tecnologia e tipologia dei manufatti in corno e osso nell'abitato protostorico di Frattesina di Fratta Polesine," *Padusa*, vol. 11, pp. 15–52.

Bellintani, P. 1992, "Frattesina di Fratta Polesine: Il materiale ceramico conservato presso il museo civico di Rovigo," *Padusa*, vol. 28, pp. 245-97.

Bellintani, P., Angelini, I., Artioli, G. & Polla, A. 2006, "Origini dei materiali vetrosi italiani: esotismi e localismi" in *Atti dell XXXIX Riunione Scientifica. Materie Prime e Scambi nella Preistoria Italiana Vol. III*, ed. D.C. Genick, Istituto Italiano di Preistoria e Protostoria, Florence, pp. 1495–1531.

Bellintani, P. & Residori, G. 2003, "Quali e quante conterie; perele ed altre manufatti vetrosi dell'italia settentrionale nel quadro dell'eta del Bronzo Eur" in *Atti della XXXV riunione scientifica. Le comunità della preistoria italiana: studi e ricerche sul neolitico e le età dei metalli. Castello di Lipari 2–7 giugno 2000, in memoria di Luigi Bernabò Brea*, ed. D. Cocchi Genick, Istituto Italiano di Preistoria e Protostoria, Florence, pp. 483–98.

Bellintani, P. & Stefan, L. 2008, "Sulla tipologia delle palette con immanicatura a cannone dell'eta del Bronzo finale," *Rivista di Scienze Prehistoriche*, vol. 58, pp. 1–19.

Benzi, M. & Graziadio, G. 1996, "The last Mycenaeans in Italy? LHIIIC pottery from Punta Meliso, Leuca," *Studi Micenei ed Egeo-Anatolici* vol. 38, pp. 95–138.

Bérard, C. 1957, *La colonisation grecque de l'Italie méridionale et de la Sicile dans l'antiquité: Histoire et légende*, 2nd ed., A. Colin, Paris.

Bergonzi, G. 2005, "Armi e guerrieri nell'Italia centrale adriatica, dal Bronzo Antico al Bronzo Recente" in *Atti della XXXVIII Riunione Scientifica. Preistoria e Protostoria delle Marche. Vol. 2.*, ed. D. Cocchi Genick, Istituto Italiano di Preistoria e Protostoria, Florence, pp. 695–708.

Bernabò Brea, L., Bronzoni, L., Mutti, A. & Provenzano, N. 1997, "Lo strato sommitale del Villaggio grande di S. Rosa a fodico di Poviglio (RE)" in *Le Terramare: La più antica civiltà padana*, eds. M. Bernabò Brea, A. Cardarelli & M. Cremaschi, Electa, Milan, pp. 348–50.

Bernabò Brea, L., Cardarelli, A., and Cremaschi, M. 1997, "Terramare. Cinque secoli di vita nella Grande pianura," in *Le Terramare: La Più Antica Civiltà Padana*, eds. L. Bernabò Brea, A. Cardarelli, & M. Cremaschi, Electa, Milan, pp. 23–9.

Bernabò Brea, M. & Cremaschi, M. 1997, "Le Terramare: 'Palafitte a secco' o 'villaggi arginati'?" in *Le Terramare: La più antica civiltà padana*, eds. L. Bernabò Brea, A. Cardarelli & M. Cremaschi, Electa, Milan, pp. 187–95.

Bettelli, M. 1994, "La cronologia della prima età del ferro laziale attraverso i dati delle sepulture," *Papers of the British School at Rome*, vol. 62, pp. 1–66.

Bettelli, M. 1997, "Elementi di culto nelle terramare" in *Le Terramare. La più antica civiltà padana*, eds. M. Bernabò Brea, A. Cardarelli & M. Cremaschi, Electa, Milan, pp. 720–41.

Bettelli, M. 2002, *Italia meridionale e mondo miceneo: Ricerche su dinamiche di acculturazione e aspetti archeologici, con particolare riferimento ai versanti adriatico e ionico della penisola italiana*, all'Insegna del Giglio, Florence.

Bettelli, M. & Damiani, I. 2005, "I pettini di materia dura animale nell'età del bronzo italiana: Alcune considerazioni" in *L'Avorio in Italia nell'età del Bronzo*, eds. L. Vagnetti, M. Bettelli & I. Damiani, CNR-ICEVO, Rome, pp. 17-26.

Bettelli, M., Damiani, I. & Vagnetti, L. 2006, "Prime osservazioni sulla circolazione e la lavorazione dell'avorio in Italia durante l'età del bronze" in *Atti dell XXXIX Riunione Scientifica. Materie Prime e Scambi nella Preistoria Italiana. Vol. III.*, ed. D. C. Genick, Istituto Italiano di Preistoria e Protostoria, Florence, pp. 905-16.

Bettelli, M., and Levi, S. 2003, "Lo Sviluppo Delle Produzioni Ceramiche Specializzate in Italia Meridionale Nell'Età Del Bronzo in Rapporto Ai Modelli Egei e Alla Ceramica d'Impasto Indigena," in *Atti Della XXXV Riunione Scientifica. Le Comunità Della Preistoria Italiana: Studi e Ricerche Sul Neolitico e L' età Dei Metalli. Castello Di Lipari 2–7 Giugno 2000, in Memoria Di Luigi Bernabò Brea*, ed. D. Cocchi Genick, Istituto Italiano di Preistoria e Protostoria, Florence, pp. 435-54.

Bianchin Citton, E. 2003, "L'Adriatico Nord-Orientale: Nuove Scoperte e Nuove Interpretazioni. La Tarda Età del Bronzo" in *L'Archeologia dell'Adriatico dalla Preistoria al Medioevo*, ed. F. Lenzi, All'Insegna del Giglio, Florence, pp. 120-30.

Bianco Peroni, V. 1970, *Die Schwerter in Italien/Le Spade nell'Italia Continentale*, Prähistorische Bronzefunde IV.1, C.H. Beck, Munich.

Bianco Peroni, V. 1976, *Die Messer in Italien/I coltelli nell'Italia continentale*, Prähistorische Bronzefunde VII.2, C.H. Beck, Munich.

Bianco Peroni, V. 1979, *I rasoi nell'Italia continentale*. Prähistorische Bronzefunde VIII.2, C.H. Beck, Munich.

Bianco Peroni, V. 1994, *I pugnali nell'Italia Continentale*. Prähistorische Bronzefunde VI.10, Franz Steiner Verlag, Stuttgart and Rome.

Bianco Peroni, V., Peroni, R. & Vanzetti, A. 2010, *La Necropoli del Bronzo Finale di Pianelli di Genga*, ed. All'Insegna del Giglio, Florence.

Bianco, S. & Orlando, M. A. 1995, "A proposito di un dolio del tipo 'Cordonato' di Timmari," *Studi Antichi*, vol. 8, no. 1, pp. 171-82.

Bickerman, E. 1952, "Origines Gentium," *Classical Philology*, vol. 47, pp. 65-81.

Bietti Sestieri, A. M. 1973, "The metal industry of continental Italy, 13th to 11th century BC, and its connections with the Aegean," *Proceedings of the Prehistoric Society*, vol. 39, pp. 383-424.

Bietti Sestieri, A. M. 1988, "The 'Mycenaean Connection' and its impact on the Central Mediterranean Societies," *Dialoghi di Archeologia*, vol. 6.1, pp. 23-51.

Bietti Sestieri, A. M. 1992, *The Iron Age community of Osteria dell'Osa: A study of socio-political development in central Tyrrhenian Italy*, Cambridge University Press, Cambridge.

Bietti Sestieri, A. M. 1997, "Italy in Europe in the Early Iron Age," *Proceedings of the Prehistoric Society*, vol. 63, pp. 371-402.

Bietti Sestieri, A. M. 1998, "L'Italia in Europa nella prima età del ferro: Una proposta di ricostruzione storica," *Archeologia Classica*, vol. 50, pp. 1-67.

Bietti Sestieri, A. M. 2000, "The role of archaeological and historical data in the reconstruction of Italian protohistory" in *Ancient Italy in its Mediterranean Setting*, eds. D. Ridgway, F. R. Ridgway, M. Pearce, E. Herring, R. Whitehouse & J. Wilkins, pp. 13-31.

Bibliography

Bietti Sestieri, A. M. 2003, "L'Adriatico Fra l'età del Bronzo e gli inizi dell' età del Ferro (ca. 2200–900 A.C.)" in *L'Archeologia dell'Adriatico dalla Preistoria al Medioevo*, ed. F. Lenzi, All'Insegna del Giglio, Florence, pp. 49–64.

Bietti Sestieri, A. M. 2005, "A Reconstruction of Historical Processes in Bronze and Early Iron Age Italy Based on Recent Archaeological Research" in *Papers in Italian Archaeology VI. Communities and Settlements from the Neolithic to the Early Medieval Period*, eds. P. Attema, A. Nijboer & A. Zifferero, pp. 9–24.

Bietti Sestieri, A. M., 2010, *L'Italia nell'età del bronzo e del ferro: Dalle palafitte a Romolo*, Carocci, Rome.

Bietti Sestieri, A. M. & De Santis, A. 2004, "Analisi delle decorazioni dei contenitori delle ceneri dale sepulture a cremazione dell'età del bronzo Finale nell'area centrale tirrenica" in *Preistoria e Protostoria in Etruria VI*, ed. N. Negroni Catacchio, Centro Studi, Milan, pp. 165–92.

Bignozzi, G. 1988, "I pettini di Castione di Marchesi nel quadro della produzione terramaricola" in *La terramara di Castione dei Marchesi*, eds. A. Mutti, N. Provenzano, & M. G. Rossi, Nuova Alfa, Bologna, pp. 439–56.

Bispham, E. 2007, "The Samnites" in *Ancient Italy: Regions without Boundaries*, eds. G. Bradley, E. Isayev & C. Riva, University of Exeter Press, Exeter, pp. 179–223.

Blake, E. 2008, "The Mycenaeans in Italy: A minimalist position," Papers of the British School at Rome, vol. 76, pp. 1–34.

Boccuccia, P., Desogus, P. & Levi, S. T. 1998, "Il Problema dell'uso del tornio tra la fine dell' età del bronzo e la prima età del ferro: Ceramica figulina da Coppa Nevigata (FG)" in *Protovillanoviani e/o Protoetruschi. Ricerche e Scavi*, ed. N. Negroni Catacchio, Octavo, Florence, pp. 249–59.

Bokonyi, S. & Siracusano, G. 1987, "Reperti faunistici dell'età del Bronzo del sito di Coppa Nevigata: Un commento preliminare" in *Coppa Nevigata e il suo territorio. Testimonianze archeologiche dal VII al II millennio a.C.*, eds. S. M. Cassano, A. Cazzella, A. Manfredini & M. Moscoloni, Quasar, Rome, pp. 205–10.

Bonetto, J. 2009, *Veneto*, Libreria dello Stato, Rome.

Borgna, E. 1992, *Il Ripostiglio Di Madriolo Presso Cividale e I Pani a Piccone Del Friuli-Venezia Giulia*. Quasar, Rome.

Bourdin, S. 2012, *Les peuples de l'Italie préromaine: Identités, territoires et relations inter-ethniques en Italie centrale et septentrionale*, École Française de Rome, Rome.

Bradley, G. 1997, "Iguvines, Umbrians and Romans: Ethnic identity in central Italy" in *Gender and Ethnicity in Ancient Italy*, eds. T. Cornell & K. Lomas, Accordia Specialist Studies on Italy, London, pp. 53–67.

Bradley, G. 2000, *Ancient Umbria: State, culture, and identity in central Italy from the Iron Age to the Augustan era*, Oxford University Press, Oxford.

Bradley, G., Isayev, E. & Riva, C. (eds.) 2007, *Ancient Italy: Regions without Boundaries*, University of Exeter Press, Exeter.

Braun, D. P. & Plog, S. 1982, "Evolution of 'Tribal' Social Networks: Theory and Prehistoric North American Evidence," *American Antiquity*, vol. 47, no. 3, pp. 504–25.

Broadhead, W. 2008, "Migration and hegemony: Fixity and mobility in second-century Italy" in *People, Land, and Politics: Demographic Developments and the*

Transformation of Roman Italy, 300 BC-AD 14, eds. L. de Ligt & S. J. Northwood, Brill, Leiden, pp. 451–70.

Brodie, N. 2008, "The Donkey: An Appropriate Technology for Early Bronze Age Land Transport and Traction" in *Horizon: A Colloquium on the Prehistory of the Cyclades*, eds. N. Brodie, J. Doole, G. Gavalas & C. Renfrew, McDonald Institute for Archaeological Research, Cambridge, pp. 299–304.

Broodbank, C. 2000, *An Island Archaeology of the Early Cyclades*, Cambridge University Press, Cambridge.

Brughmans, T. 2012, "Thinking Through Networks: A Review of Formal Network Methods in Archaeology," *Journal of Archaeological Method and Theory*, pp. 1–40.

Burt, R. S. 1987, "Social Contagion and Innovation: Cohesion versus Structural Equivalence," *American Journal of Sociology*, vol. 92, no. 6, pp. 1287–1335.

Buxeda i Garrigos, J., Jones, R. E., Kilikoglou, V., Levi, S. T., Maniatis, Y., Mitchell, J., Vagnetti, L., Wardle, K. A. & Andreou, S. 2003, "Technology transfer at the periphery of the Mycenaean world: The cases of Mycenaean pottery found in Central Macedonia (Greece) and the Plain of Sybaris (Italy)," *Archaeometry*, vol. 45, no. 2, pp. 263-84.

Calvani Marini, M. 1975, "Una spada del bronzo recente rinvenuta nel Po, presso Piacenza," *Emilia Preromana Modena*, vol. 7, pp. 391–5.

Capuis, L., 1993, *I Veneti: Società e cultura di un popolo dell'Italia preromana*, Longanesi, Milan.

Carancini, G. L. 1975, *Die Nadeln in Italien/ Gli spilloni nell'Italia continentale: Prähistorische Bronzefunde XIII.2*, C.H. Beck, Munich.

Carancini, G. L. 1984, *Le asce nell'Italia continentale II: Prähistorische Bronzefunde IX.12*, C.H. Beck, Munich.

Carandini, A. 1997, *La nascita di Roma: Dèi, Lari, eroi e uomini all'alba di una civiltà*, Giulio Einaudi, Turin.

Cardarelli, A. 2009, "Insediamenti dell'Età del Bronzo fra Secchia e Reno. Formazione, affermazione e collasso delle Terramare" in *Atlante dei Beni Archeologici della Provincia di Modena III: Colllina e Alta Pianura*, eds. A. Cardarelli & L. Malnati, All'Insegna del Giglio, Florence, pp. 33–58.

Cary, M. & Scullard, H. H. 1989, *A History of Rome Down to the Reign of Constantine*, 3rd ed., Macmillan, London.

Cassola Guida, P. 1999, "Lineamenti delle culture altoadriatiche tra Bronze finale e prima eta del ferro" in *Protostoria e Storia del 'Venetorum Angulus.' Atti del XX Convegno di Studi Etruschi ed Italici*, ed. O. Paoletti, Istituti Editoriali e Poligrafici Internazionali, Pisa, pp. 47–72.

Castellana, G. 2000, *La cultura del Medio Bronzo nell'agrigentino ed i rapporti con il mondo miceneo*, Assessorato Regionale Beni Culturali Ambientali e della Pubblica Istruzione, Agrigento.

Cazzella, A. 1996, "La Puglia come are periferica del Mondo Miceneo: Il Caso di Coppa Nevigata" in *Atti e Memorie del Secondo Congresso Internazionale di Micenologia. Vol. 3, Archeologia*, eds. E. De Miro, L. Godart & A. Sacconi, Gruppo Editoriale Internazionale, Rome, pp. 1543–9.

Cazzella, A. 1999, "L'Egeo e il Mediterraneo centrale fra III e II millennio: Una riconsiderazione" in *Epi Ponton Plazomenoi. Simposio Italiano di Studi Egei Dedicato*

Bibliography

a Luigi Bernabò Brea e Giovanni Pugliese Carratelli. Roma, 18–20 febbraio 1998, eds. V. La Rosa, D. Palermo & L. Vagnetti, Scuola Archeologica Italiana di Atene, Rome and Athens, pp. 397–404.

Cazzella, A. & Moscoloni, M. 1998, "Il Passaggio Bronzo Recente-Bronzo Finale a Coppa Nevigata e nella Puglia Nord-Orientale" in *Protovillanoviani e/o Protoetruschi. Ricerche e Scavi*, ed. N. Negroni Catacchio, Octavo, Florence, pp. 239–47.

Cazzella, A. & Moscoloni, M. 1999, "The walled Bronze Age settlement of Coppa Nevigata, Manfredonia and the development of craft specialisation in south-eastern Italy" in *Social Dynamics of the Prehistoric Central Mediterranean*, eds. R. H. Tykot, J. Morter & J. E. Robb, Accordia Research Institute, London, pp. 205–16.

Cazzella, A. & Recchia, G. 2008, "A View from the Apennines: The Role of the Inland Sites in Southern Italy During the Bronze Age" in *Mountain Environments in Prehistoric Europe: Settlement and Mobility Strategies from the Palaeolithic to the Early Bronze Age*, eds. S. Grimaldi, T. Perrin & J. Guilaine, Archaeopress, Oxford, pp. 137–43.

Cazzella, A. & Recchia, G. 2009, "The 'Mycenaeans' in the Central Mediterranean: A Comparison between the Adriatic and Tyrrhenian Seaways," *Pasiphae*, vol. 3, pp. 27–40.

Cazzella, A., and Recchia, G. 2014, "Nuovi Dati Sulle Fortificazioni Dell'Eta Del Bronzo Di Coppa Nevigata," *Scienze dell'Antichità*, vol. 19, pp. 117–32.

Cerchiai, L. 2010, *Gli antichi popoli della Campania. Archeologia e storia*, Carocci, Rome.

Chapman, J. 2000, *Fragmentation in archaeology: People, places, and broken objects in the prehistory of south eastern Europe*, Routledge, London; New York.

Cifani, G. 2010, "State Formation and Ethnicities from the 8th to 5th Century BC in the Tiberine Valley (Central Italy)," *Social Evolution and History*, vol. 9, no. 2, pp. 53–69.

Cinquepalmi, A. & Carrieri, M. 1998, "Monopoli centro storico" in *Documenti dell'eta del Bronzo*, eds. A. Cinquepalmi & F. Radina, Schena, Egnazia, pp. 101–5.

Cipolloni Sampò, M. 1986, "La tomba 3 dell'Acropoli di Toppo Daguzzo (Potenza). Elementi per uno studio preliminare," *Annali dell'Istituto Universitario Orientale di Napoli*, vol. 8, pp. 1–39.

Clackson, J. & Horrocks, G. 2007, *The Blackwell history of the Latin language*, Wiley-Blackwell, Oxford.

Clutton-Brock, J. 1992, *Horse Power: A History of the Horse and the Donkey in Human Societies*, Harvard University Press, Cambridge.

Clutton-Brock, J. 1999, *A Natural History of Domesticated Mammals*, 2nd ed., Cambridge University Press, Cambridge.

Cocchi Genick, D. 2006, "La ceramica del Bronzo Medio dell'Italia centrale: Meccanismi di cercolazione e processi di comunicazione con l'ambiente meridionale e l'area padana" in *Atti della XXXIX riunione scientifica* Istituto Italiano di Preistoria e Protostoria, Florence, pp. 1113–27.

Cocchi Genick, D. & Zanini, A. 1997, "L'area toscana nell'età del bronzo media e recente" in *Le Terramare. La più antica civiltà padana*, eds. L. Bernabò Brea, A. Cardarelli & M. Cremaschi, Electa, Milan, pp. 445–51.

Coppola, D. 1998, "Torre Santa Sabina" in *Documenti Dell'Eta Del Bronzo: Ricerche Lungo Il Versante Adriatico Pugliese,* eds. A. Cinquepalmi & F. Radina, Schena, Fasano, BR, pp. 147–51.

Cornell, T. J. 1995, *The Beginnings of Rome: Italy and Rome from the Bronze Age to the Punic Wars (c. 1000–264 BC)*, Routledge, London and New York.

Coward, F. 2010, "Small Worlds, material culture and ancient Near Eastern social networks" in *Social Brain, Distributed Mind*, eds. R. Dunbar, C. Gamble & J. Gowlett, Oxford University Press, Oxford, pp. 449–80.

Crawford, M. 2003, "Land and People in Republican Italy" in *Myth, History and Culture in Republican Rome. Studies in honour of T. P. Wiseman*, eds. D. Braund & C. Gill, University of Exeter Press, Exeter, pp. 56–72.

Creamer, W. 2000, "Regional Interactions and Regional Systems in the Protohistoric Rio Grande" in *The Archaeology of Regional Interaction: Religion, Warfare, and Exchange Across the American Southwest and Beyond*, ed. M. Hegmon, University Press of Colorado, Boulder, CO, pp. 99–118.

Cremaschi, M., Pizzi, C. & Valsecchi, V. 2006, "Water management and land use in the Terramare and a possible climatic co-factor in their collapse: The case study of the Terramara of Poviglio Santa Rosa (Northern Italy)", *Quaternary International*, vol. 151, no. 1, pp. 87–98.

Cristofani, M. 1986, "Economia e società" in *Rasenna. Storia e Civiltà degli Etruschi*, ed. G. Pugliese Carratelli, Libri Scheiwiller, Milan, pp. 77–156.

Cultraro, M. 2006, "I vaghi di ambra del tipo Tirinto nella protostoria italiana: Nuovi dati dall'area egeo-balcanica" in *Atti dell XXXIX Riunione Scientifica. Materie Prime e Scambi nella Preistoria Italiana. Vol. III.*, ed. D. Cocchi Genick, Istituto Italiano di Preistoria e Protostoria, Florence, pp. 1533–53.

Cultraro, M. 2007, "Evidence of amber in Bronze Age Sicily: Local sources and the Balkan-Mycenaean connection" in *Between the Aegean and Baltic Seas. Prehistory Across Borders*, eds. I. Galanaki, H. Thomas, Y. Galanakis & R. Laffineur, University of Liège, Liège, pp. 377–88.

Cuozzo, M. 2007, "Ancient Campania: Cultural Interaction, Political Borders and Geographic Boundaries" in *Ancient Italy: Regions without Borders*, eds. G. Bradley, E. Isayev & C. Riva, University of Exeter Press, Exeter, pp. 224–67.

Cupitò, M. 2011, "Un torques Canegrate dal sito di Fondo Paviani (Verona). Spunti per la lettura dei rapporti tral l'Italia nord-occidentale e il mondo palafitticolo-terramaricolo nel Bronzo recente" in *Tra protostoria e storia. Scritti in onore di Loredana Capuis*, ed. G. Leonardi, Antenor Quaderni 20, University of Padua Press, Padua, pp. 19–33.

Damiani, I. 1991, "Aspetti ceramici dell'età del Bronzo recente in Italia peninsulare e nelle isole Eolie: la facies subappeninica a trent'anni dalla sua definizione," *Dialoghi di Archeologia*, vols. 1–2, pp. 5–33.

Damiani, I. 2010, *L'Eta del Bronzo Recente nell'Italia Centro-Meridionale*, All'Insegna del Giglio, Florence.

David, J. 1997, *The Roman Conquest of Italy*, Blackwell, Malden.

David, P. A. 1985, "Clio and the economics of QWERTY," *American Economic Review*, vol. 75, pp. 332–37.

de Grossi Mazzorin, J. 1998, "Analisi dei resti faunistici da alcune strutture di Sorgenti della Nova" in *Protovillanoviani e/o Protoetruschi. Ricerche e Scavi.*

Bibliography

Preistoria e protostoria in Etruria III, ed. N. Negroni Catacchio, Octavo, Milan, pp. 169–80.

de Grossi Mazzorin, J. & Riedel, A. 1997, "La fauna delle terramare" in *Le Terramare: La più antica civiltà padana*, eds. L. Bernabò Brea, A. Cardarelli & M. Cremaschi, Electa, Milan, pp. 475–86.

De La Genière, J. 1978, "La colonisation Grecque en Italie méridionale et en Sicile et l'acculturation des non-Grecs," *Revue Archéologique*, vol. 2, pp. 257–76.

De Marinis, G., Giumlia-Mair, A., Miccio, M. & Pallecchi, P. 2005, "Tecnologie produttive nei siti dell'Età del Bronzo di Moscosi di Cingoli e Cisterna di Tolentino" in *Atti della XXXVIII Riunione Scientifica. Preistoria e Protostoria delle Marche. Vol. 2*, ed. D. Cocchi Genick, Istituto Italiano di Preistoria e Protostoria, Florence, pp. 679–94.

De Marinis, R. 1999, "Il confine occidentale del mondo proto-veneto/paleoveneto dal bronzo finale alle invasioni galliche del 388 A.C." in *Protostoria e Storia del 'Venetorum Angulus.' Atti del XX Convegno di Studi Etruschi ed Italia*, ed. O. Paoletti, Istituti Editoriali e Poligrafici Internazionali, Pisa, pp. 511–64.

De Marinis, R. 2006, "Circolazione del metallo e dei manufatti nell'eta del Bronzo dell'Italia settentrionale" in *Atti della XXXIX riunione scientifica* Istituto Italiano di Preistoria e Protostoria, Florence, pp. 1289–1317.

De Marinis, R. C. 2000a, "Il Bronzo Finale nel Canton Ticino" in *I Leponti tra mito e realtà*, eds. R. C. De Marinis & S. Biaggio Simona, Dadò, Locarno, pp. 123–55.

De Marinis, R. C. 2000b, "Il Bronzo Recente nel Canton Ticino e la cultura di Canegrate" in *I Leponti tra mito e realtà*, eds. R. C. De Marinis & S. Biaggio Simona, Dadò, Locarno, pp. 93–121.

Dench, E. 1995, *From Barbarians to New Men. Greek, Roman, and Modern Perceptions of Peoples of the Central Apennines*, Clarendon Press, Oxford.

Dench, E. 2005, *Romulus' asylum: Roman identities from the age of Alexander to the age of Hadrian*. Oxford University Press, New York and Oxford.

D'Ercole, M. C. 2002, *Importuoso. Italiae Litora: Paysage et échanges dans l'Adriatique méridionale archaique*, Centre Jean Bérard, Naples.

D'Erme, L. 2007, "Grotte Santo Stefano" in *Repertorio dei siti protostorici del Lazio. Province di Roma, Viterbo e Frosinone*, eds. C. Belardelli, M. Angle, F. di Gennaro & F. Trucco, All'Insegna del Giglio, Florence, p. 331.

De Siena, A. 1986, "Termitito" in *Traffici micenei nel mediterraneo: Problemi storici e documentazione archeologica. Atti del convegno di Palermo*, eds. M. Marazzi, S. Tusa & L. Vagnetti, Istituto per la storia e l'archeologia della Magna Grecia, Taranto, pp. 41–54.

Devoto, G. 1978, *The Languages of Italy*, V. Louise Katainen, transl., University of Chicago Press, Chicago and London.

Dickinson, O. 1994, *The Aegean Bronze Age*, Cambridge University Press, Cambridge and New York.

di Gennaro, F. 1986, *Forme di insediamento tra Tevere e Fiora dal Bronzo Finale al Principio dell'eta del ferro*, Olschki, Florence.

di Gennaro, F. 2007a, "Blera" in *Repertorio dei siti protostorici del Lazio. Province di Roma, Viterbo e Frosinone*, eds. C. Belardelli, M. Angle, F. di Gennaro & F. Trucco, All'Insegna del Giglio, Florence, p. 264.

di Gennaro, F. 2007b, "Luni sul Mignone-Fornicchio" in *Repertorio dei siti protostorici del Lazio. Province di Roma, Viterbo e Frosinone*, eds. C. Belardelli, M. Angle, F. di Gennaro & F. Trucco, All'Insegna del Giglio, Florence, p. 266.

di Gennaro, F. 2007c, "San Giovenale" in *Repertorio dei siti protostorici del Lazio. Province di Roma, Viterbo e Frosinone*, eds. C. Belardelli, M. Angle, F. di Gennaro & F. Trucco, All'Insegna del Giglio, Florence, pp. 269.

Dobson, L. 2005, "Time, Travel and Political Communities. Transportation and Travel Routes in Sixth and Seventh-century Northumbria," *The Heroic Age* [Online], vol. 8, pp. 1-16. Available from: http://www.mun.ca/mst/heroicage/issues/8/dobson.html.

Edensor, T. 2000, "Walking in the British Countryside: Reflexivity, Embodied Practices and Ways to Escape," *Body & Society*, vol. 6, no. 3-4, pp. 81-106.

Eder, B. & Jung, R. 2005, "On the Character of Social Relations between Greece and Italy in the 12th/11th c. B.C." in *Emporia. Aegeans in the Central and Eastern Mediterranean. Proceedings of the 10th International Aegean Conference. Athens, Italian School of Archaeology, 14–18 April 2004*, eds. R. Laffineur & E. Greco, Université de Liège, Liège, pp. 485-95.

Erskine, A. 2005, "Unity and Identity: Shaping the Past in the Greek Mediterranean" in *Cultural Borrowings and Ethnic Appropriations in Antiquity*, ed. E. S. Gruen, Franz Steiner, Stuttgart, pp. 121-36.

Evans, J. & Recchia, G. 2005, "Pottery function: Trapped residues in Bronze Age pottery from Coppa Nevigata (Southern Italy)," *Scienze dell'Antichità*, vol. 11, pp. 187-201.

Evans, T., Knappett, C. & Rivers, R. 2009, "Using statistical physics to understand relational space: A case study from Mediterranean prehistory" in *Complexity perspectives in innovation*, eds. D. Lane, D. Pumain, S. Van Der Leeuw & G. West, Springer, Berlin, pp. 451-79.

Farney, G. D. 2007, *Ethnic identity and aristocratic competition in Republican Rome*, Cambridge University Press, Cambridge and New York.

Farrell, J. 2004, "Roman Homer" in *The Cambridge Companion to Homer*, eds. R. Fowler and R. L. Fowler, Cambridge University Press, Cambridge, pp. 254-71.

Forsythe, G. 2005, *A Critical History of Early Rome from Prehistory to the First Punic War*, University of California Press, Berkeley.

Franco, M. C. 1996, "Salento ed Egeo: Note Preliminari sull'insediamento protostorico di Punta Le Terrare (Brindisi)" in *Atti e Memorie del Secondo Congresso Internazionale di Micenologia. Vol. 3, Archeologia*, eds. E. De Miro, L. Godart & A. Sacconi, Gruppo Editoriale Internazionale, Rome, pp. 1561-70.

Freeman, L. 2004, *The Development of Social Network Analysis: A Study in the Sociology of Science*, Empirical Press, Vancouver.

Fugazzola Delpino, M. A. 1992, "Note di topografia preistorica," *Bullettino di Paletnologia Italiana*, vol. 83, pp. 279-322.

Fulminante, F. 2012, "Social Network Analysis and the Emergence of Central Places: A case study from Central Italy (Latium Vetus)," *BABESCH*, vol. 87, pp. 1-27.

Gabba, E. 1988, "La pastorizia nell'età tardo-imperiale in Italia" in *Pastoral Economies in Classical Antiquity. Proceedings of the Cambridge Philological Society*

Bibliography

Supp. Vol. 14., ed. C. R. Whittaker, Cambridge Philological Society, Cambridge, pp. 134-42.

Gabba, E. 1994, *Italia Romana*, Edizioni New Press, Como.

Gambari, F. M. 1998, "Elementi Di Organizzazione Sociale ed Economica Delle Comunità Protostoriche Piemontesi" in *Archeologia in Piemonte Vol. I: La Preistoria*, eds. L. Mercando & M. V. Gambari, Umberto Allemandi and Company, Turin, pp. 247-60.

Garnsey, P. 1988, "Mountain Economies in Southern Europe: Thoughts on the early history, continuity and individuality of Mediterranean upland pastoralism" in *Pastoral Economies in Classical Antiquity. Proceedings of the Cambridge Philological Society Supp. Vol. no. 14*, ed. C. R. Whittaker, Cambridge Philological Society, Cambridge, pp. 196-209.

Giardino, C. 1995, *Il Mediterraneo Occidentale fra XIV ed VIII secolo a.C. Cerchie minerarie e metallurgiche*, Tempus Reparatum, Oxford.

Giardino, C. 2000, "Sicilian hoards and protohistoric metal trade in the Central West Mediterranean" in *Metals Make the World Go Round: The Supply and Circulation of Metals in Bronze Age Europe*, ed. C. F. E. Pare, Oxbow, Oxford, pp. 99-107.

Gillis, C. 1995, "Trade in the Late Bronze Age" in *Trade and Production in Premonetary Greece: Aspects of Trade. Proceedings of the Third International Workshop, Athens 1993*, eds. C. Gillis, C. Risberg & B. Sjöberg, P. Åströms Förlag, Jonsered, pp. 61-86.

Girvan, M. & Newman, M. E. J. 2002, "Community structure in social and biological networks," *Proceedings of the National Academy of Sciences*, vol. 99, no. 12, pp. 7821-6.

Gorgoglione, M. A. 1986, "L'insediamento dell'eta del Bronzo di Cozza Marziotta, Palagiano, Taranto. Presenza di ceramica micenea" in *Traffici micenei nel mediterraneo: Problemi storici e documentazione archeologica. Atti del convegno di Palermo*, eds. M. Marazzi, S. Tusa & L. Vagnetti, Istituto per la storia e l'archeologia della Magna Grecia, Taranto, pp. 23-25.

Gosselain, O. 2000, "Materializing Identities: An African Perspective," *Journal of Archaeological Method and Theory*, vol. 7, no. 3, pp. 187-217.

Graham, S. 2006, "Networks, Agent-Based Models and the Antonine Itineraries: Implications for Roman Archaeology," *Journal of Mediterranean Archaeology*, vol. 19, pp. 45-64.

Guasco, D. 2006, *Popoli italici. L'Italia prima di Roma*, Giunti, Florence and Milan.

Guglielmino, R. 2003, "Il sito di Roca Vecchia: testimonianze di contatti con l'Egeo" in *L'Archeologia dell'Adriatico dalla Preistoria al Medioevo*, ed. F. Lenzi, All'Insegna del Giglio, Florence, pp. 91-119.

Guglielmino, R. 2005, "Due manufatti di avorio d'ippopotamo rinvenuti negli scavi di Roca Vecchia (Lecce)" in *L'Avorio in Italia nell'eta del Bronzo*, eds. L. Vagnetti, M. Bettelli & I. Damiani, CNR Istituto di studi sulle civilta dell'egeo e del vicino oriente, Rome, pp. 35-43.

Guglielmino, R. 2007, "Roca Vecchia (Lecce). New evidence for Aegean contacts with Apulia during the Late Bronze Age" in *Accordia Research Papers 10*, eds. E. Herring, R. Whitehouse & J. Wilkins, Accordia Research Institute, London, pp. 87–102.

Guglielmino, R., Levi, S. T. & Jones, R. 2010, "Relations between Apulia and the Aegean in the Late Bronze Age: The evidence from an archaeometric study of the pottery at Roca (Lecce)," *Rivista di Scienze Preistoriche*, vol. 60, pp. 257–82.

Guidi, A. 1980, "Luoghi di culto dell'eta del bronzo finale e della prima eta del ferro nel Lazio meridionale," *Archeologia Laziale*, vol. 3, pp. 148–55.

Guidi, A. 1993, *La necropoli Veiente dei Quattro Fontanili nel quadro della fase recente della prima età del ferro italiana*, Olschki, Florence.

Hall, J. M. 1997, *Ethnic identity in Greek antiquity*, Cambridge University Press, Cambridge.

Hall, J. M. 2005, "Arcades his oris: Greek projections on the Italian ethnoscape?" in *Cultural Borrowings and Ethnic Appropriations in Antiquity*, ed. E. S. Gruen, Franz Steiner, Stuttgart, pp. 259–84.

Hanneman, R. A. & Riddle, M. 2005, *Introduction to Social Network Methods* [Online homepage of University of California Riverside]. Available from: http://faculty.ucr.edu/%3C;hanneman/.

Harding, A. F. 1984, *The Mycenaeans and Europe*, Academic Press, London and Orlando.

Häussler, R. 2007, "At the Margins of Italy: Celts and Ligurians in North-West Italy" in *Ancient Italy: Regions without Boundaries*, eds. G. Bradley, E. Isayev & C. Riva, University of Exeter Press, Exeter, pp. 45–78.

Haynes, S. 2000, *Etruscan Civilization: A cultural history*, Getty Publication, Los Angeles.

Hegmon, M. (ed.) 2000, *The Archaeology of Regional Interaction: Religion, Warfare, and Exchange Across the American Southwest and Beyond*, University Press of Colorado, Boulder, CO.

Herring, E. & Lomas, K. (eds.) 2000, *The emergence of state identities in Italy in the first millennium BC*, Accordia Research Institute, University of London, London.

Herring, E. 2000, "'To See Oursels as Others See Us!'. The Construction of Native Identities in Southern Italy" in *The Emergence of State Identities in Italy in the First Millennium BC*, eds. E. Herring & K. Lomas, Accordia Research Institute, University of London, London, pp. 45–77.

Heusch, L. 2000, "*L'ethnie*: The vicissitudes of a concept," *Social Anthropology*, vol. 8, pp. 99–115.

Hodder, I. 2012, *Entangled: An archaeology of the relationships between humans and things*, Wiley-Blackwell, Malden, MA.

Hodos, T. 2006, *Responses to Colonization in the Iron Age Mediterranean*, Routledge, London and New York.

Holloway, R. R. 1981, *Italy and the Aegean 3000–700 B.C*, Art and Archaeology Publications, Louvain-la-Neuve.

Horsfall, N. 2001, "The unity of Roman Italy: Anomalies in context," *Scripta classica israelica*, no. 20, pp. 39–50.

Isayev, E. 2007, "Why Italy?" in *Ancient Italy: Regions without Boundaries*, eds. G. Bradley, E. Isayev & C. Riva, University of Exeter Press, Exeter, pp. 1–20.

Bibliography

Izzet, V. 2007, "Etruria and the Etruscans: Recent Approaches" in *Ancient Italy: Regions without Boundaries*, eds. G. Bradley, E. Isayev & C. Riva, University of Exeter Press, Exeter, pp. 179-223.

Jenkins, R. 1996, *Social Identity*, Routledge, New York and London.

Jones, R. E., Levi, S. T., Williams, J., Jenkins, D. & de Guido, A. 2002, "Mycenaean Pottery from Northern Italy. Archaeological and Archaeometric Studies," *Studi Micenei ed Egeo-Anatolici*, vol. 44, pp. 221-61.

Jones, S. 1997, *The Archaeology of Ethnicity*, Routledge, London and New York.

Kamp, K. A. & Yoffee, N. 1980, "Ethnicity in Western Asia during the Early Second Millenium B.C.: Archaeological Assessments and Ethnoarchaeological Perspectives," *Bulletin of the American Schools of Oriental Research*, vol. 237, pp. 85-104.

Karageorghis, V. 1995, "Cyprus and the Western Mediterranean: Some new evidence for interrelations" in *The Age of Homer: A Tribute to Emily Townshend Vermeule*, eds. J. B. Carter & S. Morris, University of Texas Press, Austin, pp. 93-7.

Kassianidou, V. 2001, "Cypriot Copper to Sardinia: Yet Another Case of Bringing Coals to Newcastle?" in *Italy and Cyprus in Antiquity: 1500-450 BC*, eds. L. Bonfante & V. Karageorghis, Costakis and Leto Severis Foundation, Nicosia, Cyprus, pp. 97-120.

Kayafa, M. 2006, "From Late Bronze Age to Early Iron Age Copper Metallurgy in Mainland Greece and Offshore Aegean Islands" in *Ancient Greece: From the Mycenaean Palaces to the Age of Homer*, eds. S. Deger-Jalkotzy & I. S. Lemos, Edinburgh University Press, Edinburgh, pp. 213-31.

Kleibrink, M. 2000, *Oenotrians at Lagaria near Sybaris: A native proto-urban centralised settlement*, Accordia Research Institute, London.

Knappett, C. 2011, *An Archaeology of Interaction: Network Perspectives on Material Culture and Society*, Oxford University Press, Oxford.

Knappett, C. 2013, *Network Analysis in Archaeology: New Approaches to Regional Interaction*, Oxford University Press, Oxford.

Knappett, C., Evans, T. & Rivers, R. 2011, "The Theran eruption and Minoan palatial collapse: New interpretations gained from modelling the maritime network" *Antiquity*, vol. 85, no. 329, pp. 1008-23.

Knoke, D. & Yang, S. 2008, *Social Network Analysis*, Sage, Thousand Oaks, CA.

Kristiansen, K. & Larsson, T. 2005, *The rise of Bronze Age society: Travels, transmissions and transformations*, Cambridge University Press, Cambridge and New York.

Kristiansen, K. & Larsson, T. 2007, "The Classical Tradition Strikes Back: Reply to Comments on the Rise of Bronze Age Society from Gullög Nordquist and Helène Whittaker," *Norwegian Archaeological Review*, vol. 40.1, pp. 85-93.

Kuusisto, A. & Tuppi, J. 2009, "Research on the Crustumerium Road Trench," *The Journal of Fasti Online*, [Online], pp. 1-9. Available from: www.fastionline.org/docs/FOLDER-it-2009-143.pdf.

Lattanzi, E., Marino, A., Vagnetti, L. & Jones, R. E. 1987, "Nota preliminare sul sito protostorico di Capo Piccolo presso Crotone," *Klearchos*, pp. 113-16.

Laurence, R. 1998, "Territory, Ethnonyms and Geography: The construction of identity in Roman Italy" in *Cultural Identity in the Roman Empire*, eds. R. Laurence & J. Berry, Routledge, London and New York, pp. 95–110.

Laviosa Zambotti, P. 1938, "Le civiltà preistoriche e protostoriche nell'Alto Adige," *Monumenti Antichi dei Lincei*, vol. 37, p. 172.

Leighton, R. 2005, "Later prehistoric settlement patterns in Sicily: Old paradigms and new surveys," *European Journal of Archaeology*, vol. 8, no. 3, pp. 261–87.

Lenzi, F. (ed.) 2003, *L'Archeologia dell'Adriatico dalla Preistoria al Medioevo*, All'Insegna del Giglio, Florence.

Leonardi, G. 2010, "Premesse sociali e culturali alla formazione dei centri protourbani del Veneto," *Bollettino di Archeologia Online*, [Online], vol. F, pp. 23–35. Available from: www.archeologia.beniculturali.it/pages/pubblicazioni.html.

Lepschy, A., Lepschy, G. & Voghera, M. 1996, "Linguistic Variety in Italy" in *Italian Regionalism: History, Identity and Politics*, ed. C. Levy, Berg Publishers, Oxford, pp. 69–80.

Levi, M. 1997, "A Model, a Method, and a Map: Rational Choice in Comparative and Historical Analysis" in *Comparative Politics: Rationality, Culture, and Structure*, eds. M. I. Lichbach & A. S. Zuckerman, Cambridge University Press, Cambridge, pp. 19–41.

Levi, S. T. 2004, "Produzioni artigianali: La ceramica" in *L'età del bronzo recente in Italia*, ed. D. Cocchi Genick, Mauro Baroni edn, Lucca, pp. 233–42.

Levi, S. T., Sonnino, M. & Jones, R. E. 2006, "Eppur si muove... Problematiche e risultati delle indagini sulla circolazione della ceramica dell'eta del bronzo in Italia" in *Atti della XXXIX riunione scientifica*, Istituto Italiano di Preistoria e Protostoria, Florence, pp. 1093–1111.

Levy, C. 1996, "Introduction: Italian Regionalism in Context" in *Italian Regionalism: History, Identity and Politics*, ed. C. Levy, Berg Publishers, Oxford, pp. 1–30.

Lollini, D. G. 1979, "Il Bronzo Finale nelle Marche," *Rivista di Scienze Preistoriche*, vol. 34, nos. 1–2, pp. 179–215.

Lomas, K. 2000, "Cities, states and ethnic identity in southeast Italy" in *The emergence of state identities in Italy in the first millennium BC*, eds. E. Herring & K. Lomas, Accordia Research Institute, London, pp. 79–90.

Lomas, K. 2007, "The Ancient Veneti: Community and State in Northern Italy" in *Ancient Italy. Regions without Boundaries*, eds. G. Bradley, E. Isayev & C. Riva, University of Exeter Press, Exeter, pp. 21–44.

Lo Porto, F. G. 1998, "L'Insediamento dell'età del Bronzo di Punta Le Terrare" in *Documenti dell'età del Bronzo: Ricerche Lungo Il Versante Adriatico Pugliese*, eds. A. Cinquepalmi & F. Radina, Schena, Fasano BR, pp. 171–3.

Lo Schiavo, F. 2006, "Ipotesi sulla circolazione dei metallic nel Mediterraneo centrale" in *Atti della XXXIX Riunione Scientifica. Materie Prime e Scambi nella Preistoria Italiana, Vol. III*, ed. D. Cocchi Genick, Istituto Italiano di Preistoria e Protostoria, Florence, pp. 1319–37.

Lo Schiavo, F. 2010, *Le Fibule dell'Italia meridionale e della Sicilia dall età del bronzo recente al VI secolo a.C.* Franz Steiner Verlag, Stuttgart.

Lyttelton, A. 1996, "Shifting Identities: Nation, Region and City" in *Italian Regionalism: History, Identity and Politics*, ed. C. Levy, Berg Publishers, Oxford, pp. 33–52.

Bibliography

Macchiarola, I. 1995, "La Facies Appenninica" in *Aspetti culturali della media eta del bronzo nell'Italia centro-meridionale*, ed. D. Cocchi Genick, Franco Cantini, Florence, pp. 441–63.

Magness, J. 2001, "A Near Eastern Ethnic Element among the Etruscan Elite?" *Etruscan Studies*, vol. 8, pp. 79–117.

Mahoney, J. 2000, "Path Dependence in Historical Sociology," *Theory and Society*, vol. 29, no. 4, pp. 507–48.

Malkin, I. 1998, *The Returns of Odysseus: Colonization and Ethnicity*, University of California Press, Berkeley.

Malkin, I. 2011, *A Small Greek World: Networks in the Ancient Mediterranean*, Oxford University Press, Oxford.

Malkin, I., Constantakopoulou, C. & Panagopoulou, K. 2009, "Introduction" in *Greek and Roman Networks in the Mediterranean*, eds. I. Malkin, C. Constantakopoulou & K. Panagopoulo, Routledge, London and New York, pp. 1–11.

Mallory, J. P. 1989, *Search of the Indo-Europeans: Language, Archaeology, and Myth*, Thames and Hudson, London.

Malnati, L., Ruta Serafini, A., Bianchin Citton, E., Salzani, L. & Bonomi Munarini, S. 1999, "Nuovi rinvenimenti relativi alla civiltà veneta nel quadro dell'Italia settentrionale" in *Protostoria e Storia del 'Venetorum Angulus.' Atti del XX Convegno di Studi Etruschi ed Italia*, ed. O. Paoletti, Istituti Editoriali e Poligrafici Internazionali, Pisa, pp. 347–75.

Malone, C. & Stoddart, S. 1994a, "The Settlement System of Gubbio in the Late Bronze Age and Early Iron Age" in *Territory, Time and State:. The Archaeological Development of the Gubbio Basin*, eds. C. Malone & S. Stoddart, Cambridge University Press, Cambridge, pp. 106–27.

Malone, C. & Stoddart, S. 1994b, "The Regional Setting of Gubbio in the Later Bronze Age and Early Iron Age" in *Territory, Time and State. The Archaeological Development of the Gubbio Basin*, eds. C. Malone & S. Stoddart, Cambridge University Press, Cambridge, pp. 127–41.

Malone, C., Stoddart, S. & Whitehouse, R. 1994, "The Bronze Age of Southern Italy, Sicily and Malta c. 2000–800 BC" in *Development and Decline in the Mediterranean Bronze Age*, eds. C. Mathers & S. Stoddart, J. R. Colliss, Sheffield, pp. 167–94.

Manning, S. W. & Weninger, B. 1992, "A Light in the Dark: Archaeological Wiggle-matching and the Absolute Chronology of the Close of the Aegean Late Bronze Age," *Antiquity*, vol. 66, pp. 636–63.

Marazzi, M. 2003, "The Mycenaeans in the Western Mediterranean (17th-13th c. BC)" in *Sea Routes... From Sidon to Huelva: Interconnections in the Mediterranean 16th-6th c. BC*, ed. N. C. Stampolidis, Museum of Cycladic Art, Athens, pp. 108–15.

Marazzi, M. & Mocchegiani Carpano, C. 1998, *Vivara: Un'isola al centro della storia*, Altrastampa, Naples.

Marino, D. A. 1998, "Aspetti dell'insediamento nella Calabria Centro-Orientale tra età del bronzo recente e prima età del ferro" in *Protovillanoviani e/o Protoetruschi. Ricerche e Scavi*, ed. N. Negroni Catacchio, Octavo, Florence, pp. 287–300.

Martin, R. & Sunley, P. 2006, "Path dependence and regional economic evolution," *Journal of Economic Geography*, vol. 6, pp. 395–437.

Mastrocinque, A. 1987, *Santuari e divinità dei Paleoveneti*, La Linea, Padua.

Mastrocinque, A. 1999, "Le Ambre Di Frattesina" in *Protostoria e Storia Del 'Venetorum Angulus.' Atti Del XX Convegno Di Studi Etruschi Ed Italici*, ed. O. Paoletti, Istituti Editoriali e Poligrafici Internazionali, Pisa, pp. 227–34.

Mattingly, D. 2011, *Imperialism, Power and Identity: Experiencing the Roman Empire*, Princeton University Press, Princeton, NJ.

Mederos Martín, A. 1999, "Ex Occidente Lux. El Comercio Micénico en el Mediterráneo Central y Occidental (1625–1100 AC)," *Complutum*, vol. 10, pp. 229–66.

Millett, M. 1990, *The Romanization of Britain*, Cambridge University Press, Cambridge and New York.

Mills, B., Roberts, J., Clark, J., Haas, W., Huntley, D., Peeples, M., Borck, L., Ryan, S., Trowbridge, M. & Breiger, R. 2013, "The Dynamics of Social Networks in the Late Prehispanic US Southwest" in *Network Analysis in Archaeology*, ed. C. Knappett, Oxford University Press, Oxford, pp. 181–202.

Mizoguchi, K. 2009, "Nodes and edges: A network approach to hierarchisation and state formation in Japan," *Journal of Anthropological Archaeology*, vol. 28, pp. 14–26.

Morgan, C. 2009, "Ethnic expression on the Early Iron Age and Early Archaic Greek mainland: Where should we be looking?" in *Ethnic Constructs in Antiquity: The role of power and tradition*, eds. T. Derks & N. Roymans, Amsterdam University Press, Amsterdam, pp. 11–36.

Morgan, C. 2001, "Ethne, ethnicity, and early Greek states, ca. 1200–480 B.C. An archaeological perspective" in *Ancient perceptions of Greek ethnicity*, ed. I. Malkin, Harvard University Press, Cambridge, pp. 75–112.

Morris, I. 2000, *Archaeology as Cultural History*, Blackwell, Malden and Oxford.

Muntoni, I. 1998, "Madonna del Petto" in *Documenti dell' eta del Bronzo*, eds. A. Cinquepalmi & F. Radina, Schena, Egnazia, pp. 57–60.

Naso, A. 2000, *I Piceni*, Longanesi and Co., Milan.

Negroni Catacchio, N. 1981, *Sorgenti della Nova. Una comunità protostorica e il suo territorio nell'Etruria meridionale*, Consiglio Nazionale delle Ricerche, Rome.

Negroni Catacchio, N. 1999, "Produzione e commercio dei vaghi d'ambra tipo Tirinto e tipo Allumiere alla luce delle recente scoperte" in *Protostoria e Storia del 'Venetorum Angulus.' Atti del XX Convegno di Studi Etruschi ed Italia*, ed. O. Paoletti, Istituti Editoriali e Poligrafici Internazionali, Pisa, pp. 241–65.

Negroni Catacchio, N., Massari, A. & Raposso, B. 2006, "L'ambra come indicatore di scambi nell'Italia pre e protostorica" in *Atti dell XXXIX Riunione Scientifica. Materie Prime e Scambi nella Preistoria Italiana. Vol. III*, ed. D. Cocchi Genick, Istituto Italiano di Preistoria e Protostoria, Florence, pp. 1439–75.

Nelson, R. E. 1989, "The Strength of Strong Ties: Social Networks and Intergroup Conflict in Organizations," *Academy of Management Journal*, vol. 32, no. 2, pp. 377–401.

Nicolet, C. 1991, *Space, Geography and Politics in the Early Roman Empire*, University of Michigan Press, Ann Arbor.

Nijboer, A. 2004, "Characteristics of Emerging Towns in Central Italy, 900/800 to 400 BC" in *Centralization, Early Urbanization and Colonization in First Millenium BC Italy and Greece*, ed. P. Attema, Peeters, Leuven, Belgium, pp. 137–56.

Bibliography

Noble, J. V. 1969, "The Technique of Egyptian Faience," *American Journal of Archaeology*, vol. 73, no. 4, pp. 435-9.

Nordquist, G. & Whittaker, H. 2007, "Comments on Kristian Kristiansen and Thomas B. Larsson (2005): The Rise of Bronze Age Society: Travels, Transmissions and Transformations," *Norwegian Archaeological Review*, vol. 40.1, pp. 75-84.

North, D. C. 1990, *Institutions, Institutional Change and Economic Performance*, Cambridge University Press, Cambridge.

Orlando, M. A. 1998, "Il Bronzo Finale nel Salento. Evidenze e Problemi" in *Protovillanoviani e/o Protoetruschi. Ricerche e Scavi*, ed. N. Negroni Catacchio, Octavo, Florence, pp. 273-85.

Pacciarelli, M. 1994, "Sviluppi verso l'urbanizzazione nell'Italia tirrenica e protostorica" in *La presenza etrusca in Campania meridionale*, eds. P. Gastaldi & G. Maetzke, L. S. Olschki, Florence, pp. 227-53.

Pacciarelli, M. 2000, *Dal Villaggio alla Città. La svolta protourbana del 1000 a.C. nell'Italia tirrenica*, All'Insegna del Giglio, Florence.

Page, S. 2006, "Path Dependence," *Quarterly Journal of Political Science*, vol.1, no. 1, pp. 87-115.

Pallottino, M. 1981, *Genti e culture dell'Italia preromana*, Jouvence, Rome.

Pallottino, M. 1991, *A History of Earliest Italy*, University of Michigan Press, Ann Arbor.

Pallottino, M. 1993, *Origini e storia primitiva di Roma*, Rusconi, Milan.

Pålsson Hallager, B. 1985, "Crete and Italy in the Late Bronze Age III Period," *American Journal of Archaeology*, vol. 89, pp. 293-305.

Pandolfini, M. & Prosdocimi, A. 1990, *Alfabetari e insegnamento della scrittura in Etruria e nell' Italia antica*, L. S. Olschki, Florence.

Pare, C. 2000, "Bronze and the Bronze Age" in *Metals Make the World Go Round: The Supple and Circulation of Metals in Bronze Age Europe*, ed. C. F. E. Pare, Oxbow books, Oxford, pp. 23-38.

Pasquini, M. 2005, "L'industria su corno di Moscosi di Cingoli: forme principali e loro diffusione" in *Atti della XXXVIII Riunione Scientifica. Preistoria e Protostoria delle Marche. Vol. 2.*, ed. D. Cocchi Genick, Istituto Italiano di Preistoria e Protostoria, Florence, pp. 985-91.

Pasquinucci, M. 1979, "La transumanza nell'Italia romana" in *Strutture agrarie e allevamento transumante nell'Italia romana*, eds. E. Gabba & M. Pasquinucci, Biblioteca di Studi Antichi, Pisa, pp. 79-182.

Patterson, O. 1975, "Context and choice in ethnic allegiance: A theoretical framework and Caribbean case study" in *Ethnicity: Theory and Experience*, eds. N. Glazer & D. Moynihan, Harvard University Press, Cambridge, pp. 305-49.

Pearce, M. 1998, "New research on the terramare of northern Italy," *Antiquity*, vol. 72.278, pp. 743-6.

Pearce, M. 2000, "Metals make the world go round: The copper supply for Frattesina" in *Metals Make the World Go Round: The Supply and Circulation of Metals in Bronze Age Europe*, ed. C. F. E. Pare, Oxbow Books, Oxford, pp. 108-15.

Peeples, M. A. 2011, *Identity and Social Transformation in the Prehispanic Cibola World: AD 1150–1325*, PhD ed., Arizona State University, Tempe.

Pellegrini, E. 1989, "Aspetti regionale e relazioni interregionale nella produzione metallurgica del Bronzo Finale nell'Italia continentale: I ripostigli con pane e piccone," *Archeometallurgia ricerche e prospettive: atti del Colloquio internazionale di archeomettalurgia*, Bologna, Dozza Imoless, October 18-21, 1988, ed. E. Antonacci-Sanpaolo, Edizioni CLUEB, Bologna, pp. 589-603.

Pellegrini, E. 1992, "Nuovi Dati Su due Ripostigli Dell' Età Del Bronzo Finale Del Grossetano: Piano Di Tallone e 'Tra Manciano e Samprugnano'," *Bullettino di Paletnologia Italiana*, vol. 83, pp. 341-60.

Pellegrini, E. 1993, "Aspetti della Metallurgia nel Comprensorio del Lago di Mezzano e nella Media Valle del Fiora dal Bronzo Antico all'XI sec. A.C." in *Vulcano a Mezzano. Insediamento e Produzioni Artigianali nella media valle del Fiora nell'eta del Bronzo*, eds. A. Baffetti, G. L. Carancini, A. M. Conti, Museo Civico di Valentino, Viterbo.

Pellegrini, E. 1995, "Aspetti della Metallurgia nell'Italia Continentale tra XVI e XI secolo a.C.: Produzione e Relazione Interregionali tra Area Centrale Tirrenica e Area Settentrionale" in *Settlement and Economy in Italy 1500 BC- AD 1500. Papers of the Fifth Conference of Italian Archaeology*, ed. N. Christie, Oxbow Monograph 41, Oxford, pp. 511-19.

Pellegrini, E. 1998, "Aspetti della metallurgia protovillanoviana in Etruria" in *Protovillanoviani e/o Protoetruschi. Ricerche e Scavi*, ed. N. Negroni Catacchio, Octavo, Florence, pp. 23-34.

Pellegrini, E. (ed.) 1985, *L'insediamento protostorico di Pitigliano. Campagne di Scavo 1982–83*, ATLA, Pitigliano.

Percossi, E., Pignocchi, G. & Sabbatini, T. 2005, "Un sito dell'età del bronzo a Cisterno di Tolentino" in *Atti della XXXVIII Riunione Scientifica. Preistoria e Protostoria delle Marche. Vol. 2*, ed. D. Cocchi Genick, Istituto Italiano di Preistoria e Protostoria, Florence, pp. 659-78.

Peroni, R. 1969, "Per uno studio dell'economia di scambio in Italia nel quadro dell'ambiente culturale dei secoli intorno al Mille a.C.," *La Parola del Passato*, vol. 24, pp. 134-60.

Peroni, R. 1979, "From Bronze Age to Iron Age: Economic, Historical and Social considerations" in *Italy Before the Romans: The Iron Age, Orientalizing and Etruscan periods*, eds. D. Ridgway & F. R. Ridgway, Academic Press, London and New York, pp. 7-30.

Peroni, R. 1989, *Protostoria dell'Italia continentale. La penisola italiana nelle eta del Bronzo e del Ferro*, Popoli e civilta dell'Italia Antica 9, Biblioteca di Storia Patria, Rome.

Peroni, R. 1999, "La cronologia e il contesto storico-culturale" in *Ipogei della Daunia. Preistoria di un territorio*, ed. A. M. Tunzi Sisto, Claudio Grenzi Editore, Foggia, pp. 217-19.

Peroni, R. 2005, "Il Bronzo finale e la prima età del ferro nelle Marche" in *Atti della XXXVIII Riunione Scientifica. Preistoria e Protostoria delle Marche. Vol. 2*, ed. D. Cocchi Genick, Istituto Italiano di Preistoria e Protostoria, Florence, pp. 721-38.

Peroni, R., Carancini, G. L., Bergonzi, G., Lo Schiavo, F. & Von Eles, P. 1980, "Per una definizione critica di facies locali: nuovi strumenti metodologici" in

Bibliography

Il bronzo finale in Italia: Studi a cura di Renato Peroni con gli Atti del Centro Studi di Protostoria 1978–1979, ed. R. Peroni, De Donato, Rome, pp. 9–85.

Peroni, R. & Vanzetti, A. 1998, *Broglio di Trebisacce 1990–1994. Elementi e problemi nuovi dalle recenti campagne di scavo*, Rubbettino, Soveria Mannelli (Catanzaro).

Petitti, P. 2007a, "Pianizza" in *Repertorio dei siti protostorici del Lazio. Province di Roma, Viterbo e Frosinone*, eds. C. Belardelli, M. Angle, F. di Gennaro & F. Trucco, All'Insegna del Giglio, Florence, pp. 300.

Petitti, P. 2007b, "Ponte San Pietro Valle" in *Repertorio dei siti protostorici del Lazio. Province di Roma, Viterbo e Frosinone*, eds. C. Belardelli, M. Angle, F. di Gennaro & F. Trucco, All'Insegna del Giglio, Florence, pp. 300–01.

Pierson, P. 2000, "Increasing Returns, Path Dependence, and the Study of Politics," *The American Political Science Review*, vol. 94.2, pp. 251–67.

Plog, S., 1976, "Measurement of Prehistoric Interaction between Communities" in *The Early Mesoamerican Village*, ed. K. V. Flannery, Academic Press, New York, pp. 255–82.

Poggiani Keller, R. 1993, "Anticipazioni sul complesso dei manufatti di bronzo e sull'attività metallurgica in situ nelle fasi della tarda età del bronzo dell'insediamento di Scarceta" in *Vulcano a Mezzano. Insediamento e Produzioni Artigianali nella media Valled del Fiora nell'età del Bronzo*, eds. A. Baffetti, G. L. Carancini, A. M. Conti, Museo Civico di Valentano, Viterbo, pp. 105–24.

Pontrandolfo, A. 1996, "Per un'archeologia dei Lucani" in *Greci, Enotri e Lucani nella Basilicata meridionale*, eds. S. Bianco, A. Bottini, A. Pontrandolfo, A. Russo Tagliente & E. Setari, Electa, Naples, pp. 171–82.

Prosdocimi, A. 1987, "Celti in Italia prima e dopo il V secolo a.C." in *Celti ed etruschi nell'Italia centro-settentrionale dal V secolo a.C. alla romanizzazione : Atti del Colloquio Internazionale, Bologna, 12–14 aprile 1985*, ed. D. Vitali, University of Bologna Press, Bologna, pp. 561–81.

Provenzano, N. 1997, "Produzione in osso e corno delle terramare emiliane" in *Le Terramare. La più antica civiltà padana*, eds. L. Bernabò Brea, A. Cardarelli & M. Cremaschi,Electa, Milan, pp. 524–44.

Putnam, R. 1993, *Making Democracy Work: Civic Tradtions in Modern Italy*, Princeton University Press, Princeton, NJ.

Radina, F. 1998, "Bari Centro Storico" in *Documenti dell'età del Bronzo: ricerche lungo il versanted adriatico pugliese*, eds. A. Cinquepalmi & F. Radina, Schena, Fasano di Brindisi, pp. 83–93.

Radina, F. & Recchia, G. 2006, "Scambi senza ceramica: Ambra, avorio e pasta vitrea nei rapporti tra Italia sud-orientale e mondo egeo" in *Atti dell XXXIX Riunione Scientifica. Materie Prime e Scambi nella Preistoria Italiana. Vol. III*, ed. D. Cocchi Genick, Istituto Italiano di Preistoria e Protostoria, Florence, pp. 1555–65.

Rahmstorf, L. 2005, " Terramare and Faience: Mycenaean Influence in Northern Italy during the Late Bronze Age" in *Emporia. Aegeans in the Central and Eastern Mediterranean. Proceedings of the 10th International Aegean Conference. Athens, Italian School of Archaeology, 14–18 April 2004*, eds. R. Laffineur & E. Greco, Université de Liège, Liège, pp. 663–72.

Raposso, B. & Ruggiero, M. 1995, "Ambra, osso e pasta vitrea nell'Etruria Protovillanoviana" in *Preistoria e protostoria in Etruria: Atti del secondo incontro di studi*, ed. N. Negroni Catacchio, Centro studi di preistoria e archeologia, Milan, pp. 247-51.

Rasmussen, T. 1997, " The Tarquins and 'Etruscan Rome'" in *Gender and Ethnicity in Ancient Italy*, Accordia Specialist Studies on Italy Vol. 6, eds. T. Cornell & K. Lomas, Accordia, London, pp. 23-30.

Rautman, A. 1993, "Resource variability, risk, and the structure of social networks: An example from the prehistoric Southwest," *American Antiquity*, vol. 58, no. 3, pp. 403-24.

Reich, J. 1979, *Italy before Rome*, Elsevier-Phaidon, Oxford.

Renfrew, C. 1975, "Trade as Action at a Distance: Questions of Integration and Communication" in *Ancient Civilization and Trade*, eds. J. A. Sabloff & C. C. Lamberg-Karlovsky, University of New Mexico Press, Albuquerque, pp. 1-59.

Renfrew, C. 1978, "The Anatomy of Innovation" in *Social Organisation and Settlement: Contributions from Anthropology, Archaeology and Geography*, eds. D. Green, C. Haselgrove, & M. Spriggs, British Archaeological Reports vol. 47, Oxford, pp. 89-117.

Renfrew, C. 1993, "Trade Beyond the Material" in *Trade and Exchange in Prehistoric Europe*, eds. C. S. Scarre & F. Healy, Oxbow, Oxford, pp. 5-16.

Riva, C. 2007, "The Archaeology of Picenum: The Last Decade" in *Ancient Italy: Regions without Boundaries*, eds. G. Bradley, E. Isayev & C. Riva, University of Exeter Press, Exeter, pp. 79-113.

Riva, C., 2010, *The Urbanisation of Etruria: Funerary Practices and Social Change, 700–600 BC*, Cambridge University Press, Cambridge.

Rossenberg, E. V. 2012, *Cultural landscapes, social networks and historical trajectories: A data-rich synthesis of Early Bronze Age networks (c. 2200–1700 BC) in Abruzzo and Lazio (Central Italy)*, PhD ed., University of Leiden, Leiden.

Ruane, J. & Todd, J. 2004, "The Roots of Intense Ethnic Conflict May not in Fact be Ethnic: Categories, Communities and Path Dependence," *European Journal of Sociology*, vol. XLV.2, pp. 209-32.

Ruffini, G. 2008, *Social Networks in Byzantine Egypt*, Cambridge University Press, Cambridge.

Rutherford, I. 2009, "Network Theory and Theoric Networks" in *Greek and Roman Networks in the Mediterranean*, eds. I. Malkin, C. Constantakopoulou & K. Panagopoulo, Routledge, London and New York, pp. 24-38.

Sabbatini, T. & Silvestrini, M. 2005, "Piano di Fonte Marcosa, Moscosi di Cingoli: Un sito pluristratificato dell'Appennino marchigiano. Le fasi del Bronzo Recente" in *Atti della XXXVIII Riunione Scientifica. Preistoria e Protostoria delle Marche. Vol. 2*, ed. D. Cocchi Genick, Istituto Italiano di Preistoria e Protostoria, Florence, pp. 639-57.

Sabbione, C. 2003, "South Calabria: The Aegean and Eastern Mediterranean Contribution and Influence" in *Sea Routes... From Sidon to Huelva. Interconnections in the Mediterranean 16th-6th c. BC*, ed. N. C. Stampolidis, Museum of Cycladic Art, Athens, pp. 184-6.

Bibliography

Salmon, E. 1967, *Samnium and the Samnites*, Cambridge University Press, Cambridge.

Salzani, L. 1994, "Il deposito votivo dell'eta del bronzo da corte lazise di villabartolomea (vr)" in *Studi di Archeologia della X Regio in Recordo di Michele Tombolani*, ed. B. M. Scanfi, L'Erma di Bretschneider, Rome, pp. 57-64.

Salzani, L., Vagnetti, L., Jones, R. E. & Levi, S. T. 2006, "Nuovi ritrovamenti di ceramiche di tipo egeo dall'area veronese: Lovara, Bovolone e Terranegra" in *Atti dell XXXIX Riunione Scientifica. Materie Prime e Scambi nella Preistoria Italiana. Vol. II.*, ed. D. Cocchi Genick, Istituto Italiano di Preistoria e Protostoria, Florence, pp. 1145-57.

Schnapp Gourbeillon, A. 1986, "Ceramica di tipo miceneo a Montedore di Eboli" in *Traffici micenei nel Mediterraneo. Problemi storici e documentazione archeologica*, eds. M. Marazzi, S. Tusa & L. Vagnetti, Istituto per la storia e l'archeologia della Magna Grecia, Taranto, pp. 175-82.

Setterfield, M. 1993, "A Model of Institutional Hysteresis," *Journal of Economic Issues*, vol. 27, no. 3, pp. 755-74.

Sewell, W. H. 1996, "Three Temporalities: Toward an Eventful Sociology" in *The Historic Turn in the Human Sciences*, ed. T. J. McDonald, University of Michigan Press, Ann Arbor, pp. 245-80.

Sherratt, A. 1983, "The Secondary Exploitation of Animals in the Old World," *World Archaeology*, vol. 15, no. 1, pp. 90-104.

Sherratt, S. 2000, "Circulation of metals and the end of the Bronze Age in the Eastern Mediterranean" in *Metals Make the World Go Round: The Supply and Circulation of Metals in Bronze Age Europe*, ed. C. F. E. Pare, Oxbow Books, Oxford, pp. 82-98.

Sherratt, S. 2001, "Potemkin Palaces and Route-Based Economies" in *Economy and Politics in the Mycenaean Palace States: Proceedings of a Conference held on 1-3 July 1999 in the Faculty of Classics, Cambridge*, eds. S. Voutsaki & J. Killen, Cambridge Philological Society, Cambridge, pp. 214-38.

Small, A., Small, C., Campbell, I., MacKinnon, M., Prowse, T. & Sipe, C. 1998, "Field Survey in the Basentello Valley on the Basilicata-Puglia Border," *Classical Views*, vol. 42, pp. 337-71.

Smith, A. 1999, *Myths and Memories of the Nation*, Oxford University Press, Oxford.

Smith, A. D. 1986, *The ethnic origins of nations*, Oxford University Press, Oxford.

Smith, C. 2006, *The Roman Clan: The gens from ancient ideology to modern anthropology*, Cambridge University Press, Cambridge.

Smith, C. 2007, "Latium and the Latins: The Hinterland of Rome" in *Ancient Italy: Regions without Boundaries*, eds. G. Bradley, E. Isayev & C. Riva, University of Exeter Press, Exeter, pp. 161-78.

Snodgrass, A. M. 1980, "Iron and Early Metallurgy in the Mediterranean" in *The Coming of the Age of Iron*, eds. T. Wertime & J. Muhly, Yale University Press, New Haven, CT, pp. 335-74.

Tagliacozzo, A. 1994, "I dati archeozoologici: Economia di allevamento e caccia a Broglio di Trebisacce" in *Enotri e Micenei nella Sibaritide*, eds. R. Peroni & F. Trucco, Istituto per la Storia e l'Archeologia della Magna Grecia, Taranto, pp. 587-652.

Taylour, W. 1958, *Mycenaean Pottery in Italy and Adjacent Areas*, Cambridge University Press, Cambridge.

Terrenato, N. 1998, "The Romanization of Italy: Global acculturation or cultural bricolage?" in *TRAC 97: Proceedings of the Seventh Annual Theoretical Roman Archaeology Conference*, eds. C. Forcey, J. Hawthorne & R. Wicher, Oxbow, Oxford, pp. 20-7.

Thomsen, R. 1947, *The Italic Regions from Augustus to the Lombard Invasion*, Gyldendals Forlagstrykkeri, Copenhagen.

Torelli, M. 1995, *Studies in the Romanization of Italy*, University of Alberta Press, Edmonton.

Toti, O. 1987, *La Civiltà Protovillanoviana dei Monti della Tolfa. Società ed economia tra XI e IX secolo a.C.*, Amministrazione Provinciale di Roma Assessorato alla Publica Istruzione e Cultura, Civitavecchia.

Trucco, F. 2007, "Torrionaccio-Le Grotte" in *Repertorio dei siti protostorici del Lazio. Province di Roma, Viterbo e Frosinone*, eds. C. Belardelli, M. Angle, F. di Gennaro & F. Trucco, All'Insegna del Giglio, Florence, p. 308.

Trucco, F. & Vagnetti, L., 2001, *Torre Mordillo 1987-1990: Le relazioni egee di una comunità protostorica della Sibaritide*, Consiglio Nazionale delle Ricerche, Istituto per gli studi micenei ed egeo-anatolici, Rome.

Tunzi Sisto, A. M. 1999, "Il Grottone di Manaccora" in *Ipogei della Daunia. Preistoria di un territorio*, ed. A. M. Tunzi Sisto, Claudio Grenzo, Foggia, pp. 46-7.

Tunzi Sisto, A. M. 2005, "Gli avori di Trinitapoli" in *L'Avorio in Italia nell'eta del Bronzo*, eds. L. Vagnetti, M. Bettelli & I. Damiani, Consiglio Nazionale delle Ricerche Istituto di studi sulle civilta dell'egeo e del vicino oriente, Rome, pp. 45-57.

Upham, S. 1992, "Interaction and Isolation: The Empty Spaces in Panregional Political and Economic Systems" in *Resources, Power, and Interregional Interaction*, eds. E. M. Schortman & P. A. Urban, Plenum Press, New York and London, pp. 139-56.

Vagnetti, L. 1974, "Appunti sui bronzi egei e ciprioti del ripostiglio di Contigliano (Rieti)," *Mélanges de l'Ecole française de Rome. Antiquité*, vol. 86, no. 2, pp. 657-61.

Vagnetti, L. 1993, "Mycenaean Pottery in Italy: Fifty Years of Study" in *Wace and Blegen: Pottery as Evidence for Trade in the Aegean Bronze Age 1939-1989*, ed. C. Zerner, J. C. Gieben, Amsterdam, pp. 143-54.

Vagnetti, L. 1999a, "Mycenaeans and Cypriots in the Central Mediterranean before and after 1200 BC" in *The Point Iria Wreck: Interconnections in the Mediterranean ca. 1200 BC*, eds. W. Phelps, Y. Lolos & Y. Vichos, Hellenic Institute of Marine Archaeology, Athens, pp. 187-208.

Vagnetti, L. 1999b, "Mycenaean pottery in the central Mediterranean: Imports and local production in their context" in *The Complex Past of Pottery: Production, Circulation and Consumption of Mycenaean and Greek Pottery (sixteenth to early fifth centuries BC)*, eds. J. P. Crielaard, V. Stissi & G. J. van Wijngaarden, J. C. Gieben, Amsterdam, pp. 137-61.

Bibliography

Vagnetti, L. & Lo Schiavo, F. 1989, "Late Bronze Age long distance trade in the Mediterranean: The role of the Cypriots" in *Early Societies in Cyprus*, ed. E. Peltenburg, Edinburgh University Press, Edinburgh, pp. 217–43.

Vagnetti, L., Percossi, E., Silvestrini, M., Sabbatini, T., Jones, R. & Levi, S. 2006, "Ceramiche egeo-micenee dalle Marche: analisi archeometriche e inquadramento preliminare dei risultati" in *Atti della XXXIX riunione scientifica: materie prime e scambi nalle preistoria Italiana* Instituto Italiano di Preistoria e Protostoria, Florence, pp. 1159–72.

Vanzetti, A. 2002, "Some current approaches to protohistoric centralisation and urbanisation in Italy" in *New developments in Italian Landscape Archaeology*, eds. P. Attema, A. Nijboer & A. Zifferero, Cambridge University Press, Cambridge, pp. 36–51.

Varvaro, A. 1997, "Lexical and semantic variation" in *The Dialects of Italy*, eds. M. Maiden & M. Parry, Routledge, London and New York, pp. 214–21.

Vianello, A. 2005, *Late Bronze Age Mycenaean and Italic Products in the West Mediterranean: A social and economic analysis*, British Archaeological Reports, Oxford.

von Eles Masi, P. 1986, *Le fibule dell'Italia settentrionale*, C.H.Beck, Munich.

Wasserman, S. & Faust, K. 1994, *Social Network Analysis: Methods and Applications*, Cambridge University Press, Cambridge and New York.

Webb, N. M. 1982, "Group composition, group interaction, and achievement in cooperative small groups," *Journal of Educational Psychology*, vol. 74, no. 4, pp. 475–84.

Whitehouse, R. D. 1995, "From Secret Society to State Religion: Ritual and Social Organization in Prehistoric and Protohistoric Italy" in *Settlement and Economy in Italy 1500 BC to AD 1500*, ed. N. Christie, Oxbow Books, Oxford, pp. 83–8.

Whittaker, C. R. 1988, "Introduction" in *Pastoral Economies in Classical Antiquity: Proceedings of the Cambridge Philological Society Supp. Vol. 14*, ed. C. R. Whittaker, Cambridge Philological Society, Cambridge, pp. 1–5.

Whittaker, D. 2009, "Ethnic discourses on the frontiers of Roman Africa" in *Ethnic Constructs in Antiquity*, eds. T. Derks & N. Roymans, Amsterdam University Press, Amsterdam, pp. 189–205.

Wickham, C. 1989, *Early Medieval Italy: Central power and local society, 400–1000*, University of Michigan Press, Ann Arbor.

Wilkens, B. 1998, "Le risorse animali" in *Documenti dell' eta del Bronzo*, eds. A. Cinquepalmi & F. Radina, Schena, Egnazia, pp. 223–47.

Williams, J. H. C. 1997, "Celtic ethnicity in northern Italy: Problems ancient and modern" in *Gender and Ethnicity in Ancient Italy*, eds. T. Cornell & K. Lomas, Accordia Research Institute, London, pp. 69–81.

Williamson, C. 2005, *The Laws of the Roman People: Public Law in the Expansion and Decline of the Roman Republic*, University of Michigan Press, Ann Arbor.

Wittke, A., Olshausen, E. & Szydlak, R. 2009, *Historical Atlas of the Ancient World*, Brill, Leiden.

Woolf, G. 1998, *Becoming Roman: The Origins of Provincial Civilization in Gaul*, Cambridge University Press, Cambridge and New York.

Yntema, D. 1985, *The Matt-Painted Pottery of Southern Italy: A General Survey of the Matt-Painted Pottery Styles of Southern Italy during the Final Bronze Age and Early Iron Age*, Drukkerij Elinkwijk, Utrecht.

Zanini, A. 1996, "L'età del Bronzo finale nella Toscana interna alla luce delle più recente acquisizioni," *Rivista di Scienze Preistoriche*, vol. 46, pp. 87–144.

Zanini, A. 1999, "Rapporti fra Veneto ed Area Medio-Tirrenicia nel Bronzo Finale. Nuovi Contributi per la Definizione del problema" in *Protostoria e Storia del 'Venetorum Angulus.' Atti del XX Convegno di Studi Etruschi ed Italia*, ed. O. Paoletti, Istituti Editoriali e Poligraficia Internazional, Pisa, pp. 307–43.

Zifferero, A. 1991, "Miniere e metallurgia estrattiva in Etruria meridionale: per una lettura critica di alcuni dati archeologici e minerari," *Studi Etruschi*, vol. 57, pp. 201–41.

INDEX

Adriatic, 6, 16–17, 27, 29, 37–38, 41, 44, 49, 61, 114, 122, 124, 136–137, 144, 156, 158, 169, 182, 189, 196, 200, 206, 208–209, 211, 214, 216–217, 225, 237
Aegean pottery, 18, 37, 41–45, 52, 54, 85, 98, 101, 105, 131, 165, 176, 186, 192, 209, 211, 216, 218, 221–222, 225, 229–231, 233–234
   in Marche, 185
   Italo-Mycenaean pottery, 42–44, 73, 212–214, 216, 219–220
Aeolian Islands, 8, 20, 26, 43
Agrios, 11
amber, 18, 24, 37–38, 41, 44–47, 51, 118, 131, 159, 165, 186, 197, 201, 212
   Allumiere bead, 45–47, 85, 88, 165, 176
   Tiryns bead, 45–47, 85, 88, 143–144, 165, 197, 201, 216
Antiochus, 7
antler, 41, 47, 48, 131, 186
Apennine culture, 23–24
Apennine period, 22, 24, 26
Appiano Gentile, 128
Apuli, 237
Apulia, 4, 10, 19, 29, 41, 43–44, 47, 51, 62, 93, 101, 104, 111, 207, 208–212, 215, 217, 220, 225, 229–230, 233, 236–238, 241, 244–245
Artas, 221
Asculum, 184
Atestine culture, 132
Augustan regions, 1, 147, 246–249, 251

Region II, 236, 238
Region III, 235, 238
Region IV, 205
Region V, 187, 205
Region VI, 189, 190, 205
Region VIII, 148, 248
Region X, 136
awl handles, 49, 191, 194
axes, bronze, 36, 60, 196
   Casalecchio type, 60
   Menaforno type, 60
   Pertosa type, 60, 164, 166, 176, 196, 198
   Ponte San Giovanni type, 60

Bartoloni, Gilda, 14
Basilicata, 19, 26, 43, 75, 102, 104, 207, 210–211, 230, 233, 235, 238, 241, 295
Belardelli, Clarissa, 37
Bellintani, Paolo, 50, 51
Bettelli, Marco, 12, 24, 37–38, 157
Bianco Peroni, Vera, 55, 57
Bickerman, Elias, 8
Bietti Sestieri, Anna Maria, 5, 12, 20, 23–25, 27, 29–30, 53, 56, 118, 131, 152, 155–156, 159, 177, 180, 200
Biferno Valley, 29
Blera, 170, 176
Boii, 102, 121, 148
Bologna, 203
bone artifacts, 41, 48, 131
Bor di Pacengo, 115, 117
Borgna, Elisabetta, 41

319

Index

Bourdin, Stéphane, 2–3
Bradanic Trough, 233, 238, 244
Bradley, Guy, 189, 190–191
Brodie, Neil, 62
Broglio di Trebisacce, 43, 44, 211–212, 215, 217, 220
bronzes, 51–61
    Coste del Marano hoard, 52
    Gualdo Tadino hoard, 52
    Mottola hoard, 52
    Piano di Tallone hoard, 52
    Surbo group, 52
Broodbank, Cyprian, 82
Brughmans, Tom, 80–81
Bruttians, 203, 220–221, 236

Calabri, 237
Calabria, 30, 40, 43–44, 88, 109, 207, 210, 218, 225, 230, 233, 235, 238, 242
Calcinato, 130
Campania, 26, 30, 39, 75, 152, 156, 158, 202, 207, 225, 234, 242
Campo del Fico, 176, 177
Canegrate, 128
Canegrate culture, 28, 75, 101–102, 108, 114, 119–120, 122, 125, 128, 146, 148, 203, 241
Cape Gelidonya wreck, 38
Capo Piccolo, 43
Carancini, Gian Luigi, 59
Carandini, Andrea, 157
Casale Nuovo, 176
Casalmoro, 130, 139, 140
Case Cocconi, 117
Case del Lago,' 117
Castellace, 233
Cato, 20, 21, 253
Cavallo Morto, 176
Cazzella, Alberto, 64
Celtic language, 15
Celtic people, 28, 75, 102, 108, 119–122, 135–136, 147–149, 189–190, 203
Cenomani, 135
centrality, 32, 101, 107, 123, 140
    betweenness centrality, 140, 167
Cerveteri, 164, 170
Chiusi-Cetona facies, 30, 108, 131, 169–171, 177, 179–180, 195, 200–201
Chônes, 235
Cicero, 252

Circe, 11
Cisano, 117
Cisterna di Tolentino, 185–187, 192, 199
clique, 96, 105
clustering coefficient, 97, 106, 122, 128
cohesive subgroups, properties of, 96–97
Colle della Mola, 176
Colline Metallifere, 5, 118, 151
combs, 47–48. *See* ivory; antler
    Frattesina type, 48, 197
community detection, 32, 71, 87, 122, 126, 241
Conelle di Arcevia, 192
Coppa Nevigata, 62, 211–213, 215–216, 220
Cornell, Tim, 14, 157
Cortine, 183
Costa Cavallina, 142
Crostoletto di Lamone, 165
Crotone, 218
cutpoint, 79, 99, 100, 106, 137
Cypriots, 18, 38–39, 41–42, 131

daggers, bronze, 36, 54–55, 191
    Bertarina type, 54, 88
    Fornovo S. Giovanni type, 54
    Glisente B type, 54, 128, 186
    Gorzano type, 54
    Merlara type, 54
    Monza type, 54
    Pertosa type, 54–55, 192, 199
    Redu type, 55, 128
    Tenno type, 54
    Torre Castelluccia type, 54–55, 128, 176, 186, 222
    Toscanella type, 54
    Voghera type, 55
Damiani, Isabella, 13, 27–28, 102, 185, 213
Daunian Middle Geometric, 213
Daunians, 102, 220–221, 236, 245
Daunii. *See* Daunians
De Grossi Mazzorin, Jacopo, 62
de la Genière, Juliette, 4, 8–10
degree, nodal, 100, 107, 140
Dench, Emma, 3, 14, 20–21, 66, 79, 245, 250–253
density, 32, 91–92, 97–98, 103, 105–106, 122, 137, 193, 197–198, 225
diameter, 32, 98, 106
Diodorus Siculus, 8, 40

Index

Dionysius of Halicarnassus, 3, 7
donkey, 62–63, 73, 85, 164, 166, 214–215, 220
dress pins, bronze, 36, 58–59
   Bacino Marina type, 59
   Boccatura del Mincio type, 59
   Capocchia a Papavero type, 59, 128
   Cataragna type, 59
   Garda type, 59
   Guado di Gugnano type, 59, 128
   Peschiera type, 59
   Santa Caterina type, 59
   Torri d'Arcugnano type, 59, 88, 165

Eboli, 234
Elceto, 162, 165
Elymians, 4
Esino River, 187, 188, 189, 194, 199, 205
ethnicity, 3, 5, 10, 17, 66–70, 75–76, 78, 147, 158, 180, 190, 203, 221, 235, 238, 245, 248
   instrumentalist approach to, 5, 66, 70
   primordialist approach to, 66
ethnicization, 3, 180, 236
ethnie, 10, 69
Etruria, 15, 19, 25–26, 29–30, 105, 110–111, 118, 131, 133–134, 143, 146, 150–154, 156, 158–160, 162, 164, 168, 170–171, 173, 175–177, 180, 184, 190, 195, 199–200, 210, 212, 221, 242–243, 254
Etruscan alphabet, 190
Etruscan language, 17
Etruscans, 1, 3–6, 10–11, 19, 75, 109, 111, 120, 133–134, 147, 150–152, 189, 206, 242, 245, 254–255

Fabbrica dei Soci, 124
faction analysis, 140–144, 166–167
faience, 49–51
   lenticular beads with radial incisions, 51
fibulae, bronze, 36, 57
   asymmetrical violin bow with two knobs, 56
   Castellace type, 56, 229
   Frattesina type, 56
   Gargano type, 56
   leaf-shaped violin bow, 56
   Timmari type, 56, 57
   twisted asymmetrical violin bow, 56
   twisted violin bow, 55–56, 186, 222
   violin bow with two knobs, 56, 176
Firmum Picenum, 188
flow, 99, 100, 106
Fondo Paviani, 117, 132
fossa-grave group, 29
Franzine Nuovo, 51
Frattesina, 34–41, 44, 47–48, 51, 56, 61–62, 94, 107, 124, 130–132, 137, 139, 140, 146, 156, 159, 197, 201, 203, 206, 216

Gabii, 157, 158
geodesic distance, 98, 106
Giardino, Claudio, 39–40
glass, 41, 49–51, 131, 186, 212
   barrel beads with wavy lines, 51
   blue barrel beads with white spirals, 51, 143, 197
   eye beads, 51
glassy faience, 49–51
   lenticular beads with radial incisions, 51
Golasecca culture, 102, 120–122, 132
Graham, Mark, 83
Gravina, 237
Greek colonists, 3–4, 7, 9, 11, 19, 70, 239
Greek colonization, 239. *See* Greek colonists
Greeks. *See* Greek colonists
Gubbio, 107–108, 143, 173, 175, 196, 199

Hall, Jonathan, 9, 10, 17, 67–68, 180, 254–255
Hallstatt, 24, 25
Hallstatt culture, 121
Handmade Burnished Ware, 37
Harding, Anthony, 36, 39, 64
Häussler, Ralph, 121
Herodotus, 7, 189
Hesiod, 8, 11
Hirpini, 202
hoards, 23, 39, 52–53, 60–61, 88, 123, 125–126, 128–129, 137, 139, 141, 145, 159, 160, 164, 167, 171, 191, 195–196, 198, 229
hoes, 49
horse, 23, 25, 62, 215

Iapygians, 4, 220–221, 236–237

identity formation, 19, 20, 243. *See* ethnicization
  interactionist model of, 17, 20, 76
Illyrian people, 16
Indo-European languages, 16
Insubres, 28, 102, 121
Iron Age, 1–18, 26, 32, 45, 52, 102, 118, 120, 132, 137, 147, 150–153, 156–157, 168, 171, 180, 184–185, 191, 201, 212–213, 243, 255
isoide, 31
Isolino di Varese, 142
Isolone del Mincio, 115
Italic languages, 15–17, 188, 236
  disappearance of, 255
ivory, 18, 41, 47–49, 131–132, 209, 215

Jesi, 185

Knappett, Carl, 81
knives, bronze, 36, 53–54
  Baierdorf type, 53, 54
  Fontanella type, 54, 224
  Matrei A type, 53, 54, 89, 126, 162
  Matrei B type, 54
  Montegiorgio type, 53, 54
  Scoglio del Tonno type, 54
Kristiansen, Kristian, 64–65, 75

La Tène culture, 121
Laferola, 193
Laghetto del Monsignore, 155
Lake Trasimeno, 199
Larsson, Tom, 64–65, 75
Latial period, 24, 30, 150, 175
Latino-Faliscan subgroup, 15, 16
Latins, 11, 150, 152, 180, 245
Latinus, 11
Latium, 10, 20, 24, 26, 30, 75, 84, 150, 152, 154–156, 158–159, 175, 177–179, 202–203, 242
Latium Vetus, 26, 84, 152, 176–177, 242
Laurence, Ray, 247–249
Lavinium, 158
Liguria, 20, 137, 242
Lingones, 102
Lipari, 40, 56
Livy, 3, 135
Lombardy, 20, 28, 30–31, 98, 100–101, 108, 113, 115, 119–120, 136, 146

Lucanians, 75, 202–203, 220–221, 235
Luni sul Mignone, 62, 153, 164, 168, 177

Macchiarola, Ida, 26, 27
Madonna del Petto, 220, 233
Malkin, Irad, 7–11, 84
Manaccora, 222
Manciano-Samprugnano hoard, 164, 169
Marche, 19, 29–30, 33, 93, 102, 111, 146, 148, 159–160, 169, 171, 182–185, 189, 191–192, 195, 209, 241
Mariconda, 130, 132
Marrucini, 187
Marsic territory, 201
Matt-Painted Geometric pottery, 30, 238
Messapians, 102, 209, 220–221, 236–237
Messapic language, 16
Mezzano, 162, 164
Mincio River, 56, 127, 133, 135, 143, 192, 244
miniature decorated wheels, 49
mobility of Apennine populations, 201–206
Molise, 20, 212, 242
Montagnana, 130, 132
Montagnolo di Ancona, 185
Montale, 115
Monte Grande, Sicily, 43
Monte Ingino. *See* Gubbio
Monte Rovello, 162, 164, 168, 176
Monte Venere, 88
Morris, Ian, 40
Moscosi di Cingoli, 185–186, 192, 200
Motta di Cirò, 218
Mycenaeans, 18, 39, 42, 46, 75, 219
myth, 3, 9–10, 206, 245
  Greek, 8–11, 245

Negroni Catacchio, Nuccia, 45
nostoi, 8–11, 250
Novilara, 187
Nuraghe Antigori, 44

Odysseus, 8, 11, 245
Oenotrians, 8, 102, 220, 235
Oscan language, 16
Oscans, 221, 239
Osteria dell'Osa, 88
Otranto, 98

Index

pagus-vicus settlement system, 182
palafitte, 52, 115–116
Paleoveneti, 133
Palestrina, 176–177
pane a piccone. See pick ingots, bronze
path dependence, 18, 32, 67, 76–79, 111–112, 121, 181, 206, 239, 243, 256
   QWERTY keyboard example of, 78
Pearce, Mark, 41, 159
Pellegrini, Enrico, 61
peninsular network, Final Bronze Age, 102–108
   Apennine subgroup, 105–108, 111, 195, 198, 241
   Apulia subgroup, 104–107, 208, 241
   Basilicata subgroup, 104, 106–107, 208, 241–242
   Etruria subgroup, 105–108
   Etruscan subgroup, 241
   Garda subgroup, 105–108, 137, 241
   Veneto subgroup, 105–108, 113, 137, 241
peninsular network, Recent Bronze Age, 91–102
   Lombardy subgroup, 93, 99, 101–102, 113, 241
   Po-to-Apennines subgroup, 97, 99–102, 108–109, 113, 241
   Southern subgroup, 93, 98–99, 101–102, 104, 108, 208, 241
Peroni, Renato, 5, 22, 24–26, 31, 52, 155, 183–184, 210, 229, 268
Pertosa, 222, 230
Perugia, 189, 206
Peschiera del Garda, 53, 59, 115, 139–140
Peucetians, 102, 220–221, 236. *See* Peucetii
Peucetii, 5, 207, 236
Philistus of Syracuse, 7
Pianello di Genga, 169
Piano di Tallone, 162, 164, 168
Piano di Tallone hoard, 162
Picene languages, 16, 187–188
   North Picene, 187
   South Picene, 16, 187–190, 205–206
Picenes, 5, 20, 187–191, 200–202, 205, 242
Picenum, 153
pick ingots, bronze, 61, 143, 196, 197
Piedmont, 28, 114, 119–120
pile dwelling culture. *See* palafitte

Pitigliano, 168
Pliny the Elder, 147, 179, 189, 247, 250
Po Valley, 6, 12, 15, 22–23, 28, 33, 37, 55, 93, 102, 108, 111, 137, 148, 150–151, 156, 189, 214, 241
Poggio Berni, 139, 143
Poggio La Pozza-Allumiere, 176
Polada culture, 116
Ponte S. Marco, 144
populi, 3
Populonia, 88
Porto Perone-Satyrion, 217
potter's wheel, 38, 208, 212–214, 219
Praetuttii, 187
Proto-Apennine period, 22
Protovillanovan, 13, 16, 24, 29–30, 53, 108, 130–131, 137, 152, 158, 175, 213
Protovillanoviano padano, 108, 136
Punta Meliso, 37
purple dye industry, 208, 216, 220

Radina, Francesca, 41–42, 209
Rhaetic, 15
razors, bronze, 36, 55
   Scoglio del Tonno, 55
reachability, 96
Recchia, Giulia, 41–42, 209, 212
regional systems, 11–15, 17
regionalism, 1–27, 29, 32, 37–38, 58, 67, 108–109, 180, 238, 243, 250, 252, 254–256
   Middle Bronze Age, 26–27
regression, 110–111
Renfrew, Colin, 62–63, 106
Rhaeti, 134
Rhaetia, 126
Ripatransone, 198
Roca Vecchia, 37, 47, 212, 217–220
Roman conquest, 1, 2, 6, 14–15, 33, 78, 109, 110, 121, 135–136, 148, 184, 188, 201, 221, 236, 238, 242, 244–245, 252–253, 256
Romanization, 1, 33, 121, 251–252
Rome, 1, 20–21, 33, 136, 150, 156–157, 176–177, 179, 188, 190, 203, 244–245, 251–255
   myths of foundation, 179
Ruffini, Giovanni, 83
Rutherford, Ian, 83

Index

Sabellian subgroup, 15–17
Sabine territory, 201, 205
Sabines, 187, 189, 202, 205, 245
Sallentini, 237
Samnites, 3, 14, 66, 79, 202–203, 235–236, 245, 251, 253
Samnium, 153
San Giovenale, 173, 176–177
San Michele di Valestra, 143
San Vito di Pisticci, 234
Santa Maria di Leuca, 217
Santa Maria di Ripalta, 234
Santa Paolina da Filottrano, 192
Santa Rosa di Poviglio, 115
Sardinia, 20, 40, 44–46, 256
Satricum, 156, 158
Scamozzina culture, 119
Scarceta, 164, 165, 167–168, 173, 175
Scoglio del Tonno, 43, 212, 217, 220
Senones, 148, 189
Sherratt, Susan, 37–39, 41
Sicily, 4, 20, 24, 30, 40, 43, 46–47, 51, 218
Smith, Anthony, 3, 9–10, 69–70, 76
Smith, Christopher, 157
Social War, 1, 190, 251
socketed shovels, bronze, 60–61, 196, 197
    Fondo Paviani type, 60
    'Tra Manciano e Samprugnano' type, 60
Sorgenti della Nova, 153, 164, 170
South Italian Early Geometric pottery, 213
South Italian Protogeometric pottery, 213
state formation, 5, 82, 191
Strabo, 7, 187, 207, 248, 253
Subapennine culture, 28
Subapennine period, 13, 24, 27–28, 118–119, 158, 215–216
sulfur, 24
Surbo hoard, 230
swords, bronze, 36, 57–58
    Allerona type, 58, 60
    Arco type, 57–58, 162
    Canegrate type, 162
    Cetona type, 57–58
    Frassineto type, 58
    Montegiorgio type, 57, 89, 224
    Monza type, 57
    Pertosa type, 233
    Terontola type, 57, 58

Tarquinia, 164, 170
Tarquins, 157
Termitito, 43, 212–213, 220, 233–234
Terramare, 6, 20, 22–23, 28, 33, 37, 49, 52, 56, 75, 102, 108, 111, 113–120, 122, 124–125, 127–128, 130–131, 137, 146, 148, 159, 169, 175, 182–183, 186–187, 191–192, 195, 197, 200–201, 203, 206, 221, 241, 243
Terramare network, 122–125, 195
Thucydides, 7–8, 221
Tiber River, 151–152, 176–177, 189, 244
Timaeus of Taormina, 7
Timmari, 94, 233
Tolfa-Allumiere facies, 30, 108, 169, 171, 175, 177, 180
Toppo Daguzzo, 222, 225, 233–234
Torre Castelluccia, 212, 217, 222, 233
Torre d'Andrea, 195
Torre Galli, 233
Torre Mordillo, 47–48, 98, 107, 215
Torre S. Sabina, 212
Torrionaccio, 164
transhumance, 203–205
Treazzano, 185, 193
Trinitapoli, 47
Tuscany, 5, 41, 111, 159, 175
Tyrsenoi, 11

Umbria, 30, 93, 111, 131, 143, 146, 159, 160, 169, 171, 182, 190, 192, 195, 206, 241
Umbrian language, 16, 205–206
Umbrian territory, 26, 122, 189–190
Umbrians, 3, 5, 189–191, 201, 204–206, 242
urbanization, 5, 84, 150–153, 156–157
    of Etruria, 153
    of Rome and Latium, 158

Val d'Adige, 144, 149
Varro, 247

Index

Veneti, 1, 5, 19, 109, 111, 133–137, 143, 147, 242–243, 254
Venetic language, 16, 134, 136
Veneto, 29, 30, 33, 40–41, 44, 50, 52, 57, 93, 105, 111, 113–114, 126, 129–137, 139, 144, 146, 149–150, 159, 160, 169, 171, 186, 201, 206, 211, 242, 243
ver sacrum, 187, 202–203, 205

Verucchio, 203
Villanovan period, 16, 17, 150, 152
Villanovan culture, 29, 150, 156, 171, 180
Vivara, 43
Volscian territory, 201
Volscians, 75, 152, 203

zappette. See hoes

Printed in the United States
by Baker & Taylor Publisher Services